Object Lessons in American Art

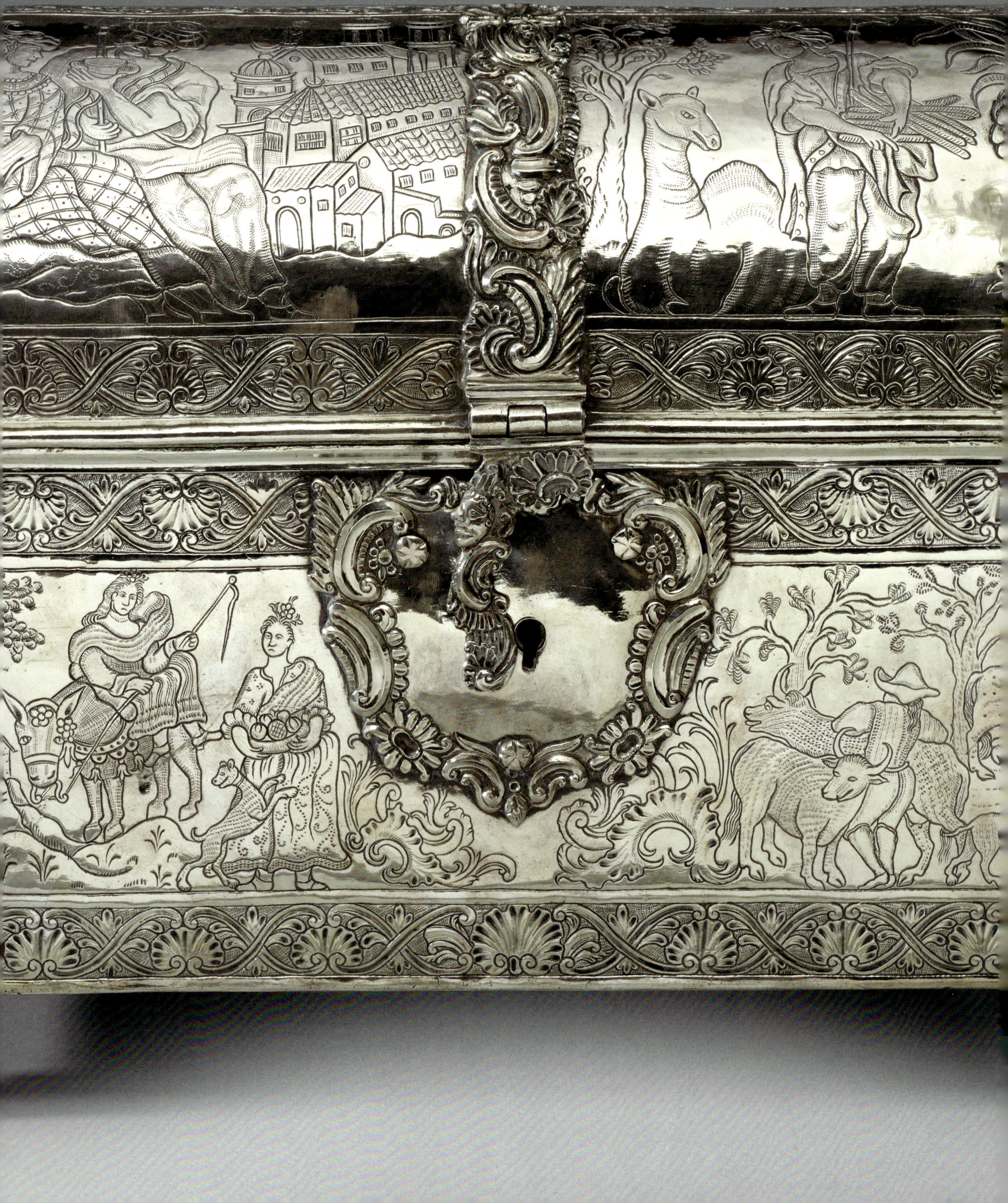

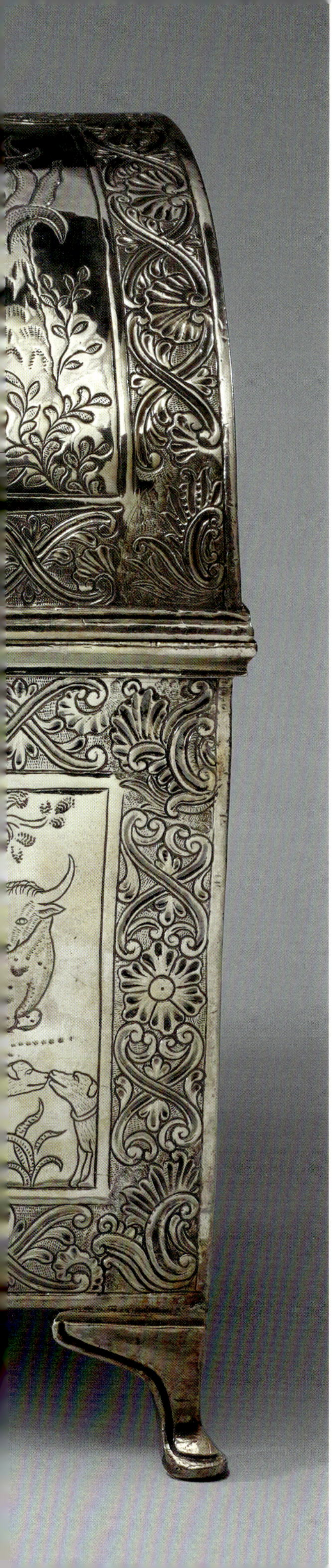

Object Lessons in American Art

EDITED BY
Karl Kusserow

WITH CONTRIBUTIONS BY
Horace D. Ballard
Kirsten Pai Buick
Ellery E. Foutch
Karl Kusserow
Jeffrey Richmond-Moll
Rebecca Zorach

Princeton University Art Museum
Distributed by Princeton University Press,
Princeton and Oxford

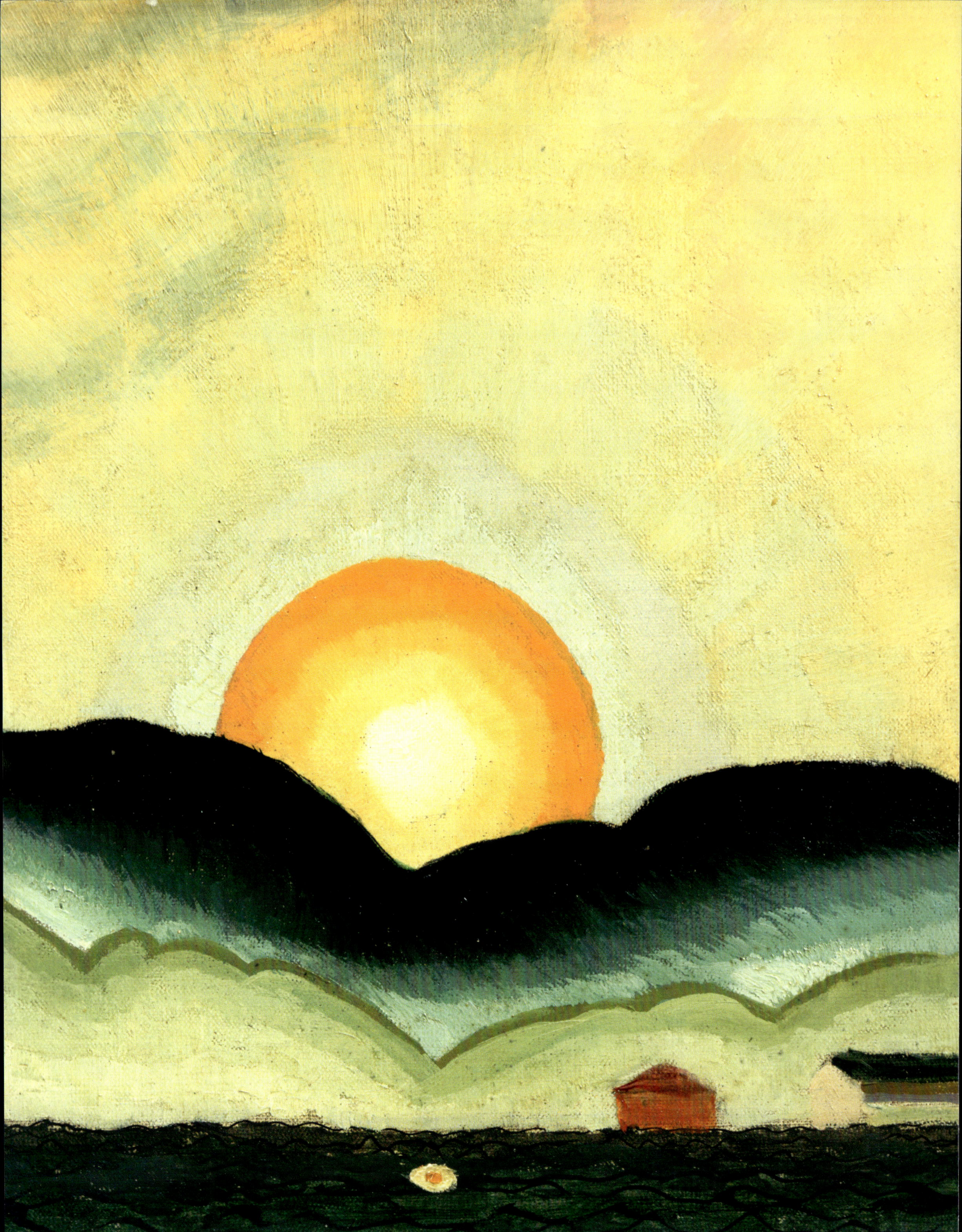

Contents

Foreword

This book and the traveling exhibition that together comprise *Object Lessons in American Art* result from circumstances at once institutionally specific and broadly philosophical. In spring 2020, the Princeton University Art Museum temporarily closed its main facility, first because of the outbreak of the COVID-19 pandemic and then to enable construction of a new museum building, one more expansive both spatially and in the scope of its ambitions and concerns. The new facility is expected to open late in 2024, creating a period of several years in which an opportunity presented itself to share aspects of our collections with other institutions and their audiences. The present traveling exhibition and this book are one such manifestation of our aims both to share the collections we steward and to do so inclusively, approaching objects in a new spirit of inquiry.

When we first conceptualized *Object Lessons*, we saw the occasion of institutional disruption as a chance to interrogate objects in new ways and explore different modes of presenting and interpreting works of art. I'd like to particularly thank and recognize Karl Kusserow, John Wilmerding Curator of American Art, for undertaking this project and seeing in it the possibility of extending his groundbreaking work in ecocritical art history to questions of environmental justice and more. Karl's contributions are amplified and extended by the similarly principled approaches of the volume's five additional authors, who focus on equally essential aspects of race and gender in American art and history. By bringing these voices to the fore in considering works in Princeton's collections, we have learned much—and trust that you will, too.

Coming at a time when our institutional resources are particularly stretched by the project of making a dramatic and much enlarged new facility, the support of external benefactors for *Object Lessons* has been crucial, and it is particularly gratifying that these resources have come broadly from foundation, individual, and institutional funders. Leadership support results from the generosity of the Terra Foundation for American Art, whose president and CEO Sharon Corwin continues to extend the organization's expansive vision for American art. The accompanying publication is enabled by the equally generous support of Annette Merle-Smith, among the Museum's most stalwart advocates and friends, and by the Barr Ferree Foundation Fund for Publications, Department of Art and Archaeology, Princeton University, another major abettor of our scholarly pursuits.

Object Lessons will travel to three distinctive institutions, each with a deep interest in and commitment to the thoughtful presentation and interpretation of American art. For their enthusiastic support of the exhibition, I offer thanks to William Eiland, the longstanding and now retiring director of the Georgia Museum of Art in Athens, Georgia; Raphaela Platow, director of the Speed Art Museum in Lexington, Kentucky; and Rebekah Beaulieu, former director of the Florence Griswold Museum in Old Lyme, Connecticut.

When the objects of *Object Lessons* return to Princeton, they will take their place in a boldly reimagined new museum, in which art and culture are engaged for their capacity to ignite and inspire, educate and elucidate, and offer ways of understanding the human experience that promote its best intentions. These are object lessons to which we can all aspire.

James Christen Steward
NANCY A. NASHER–DAVID J. HAEMISEGGER, CLASS OF 1976, DIRECTOR

Preface and Acknowledgments

Object Lessons in American Art brings contemporary perspectives on race, gender, and the environment to bear on historical American art. It does so primarily through the application by its contributors of current discourse on these crucial concerns, but also by juxtaposing objects, old and new, to help reveal considerations only latently engaged by historical works of art. The objects at hand are drawn from one of the most venerable collections of American art, formed beginning in the eighteenth century by Princeton University—erratically at first; then programmatically, if narrowly, during the nineteenth century; broadly and indiscriminately through much of the twentieth century; and, now, intentionally and inclusively in the twenty-first century. Like most institutional assemblages of American art, the contents and parameters of Princeton's collection evolved initially according to institutional priorities, then largely around aesthetic concerns, and more lately in keeping with the incorporation of sociopolitical considerations to the study of visual culture. Thus the collection, like understandings of it, reflects historical circumstance.

Since this project was conceived, dynamic social movements dedicated to racial, gender, and environmental justice—Black Lives Matter, #MeToo, and the Sunrise Movement—have continued to inflect approaches to and the constitution of American art, beneficially expanding its scope and preoccupations. As an artifact of this wider development, *Object Lessons* aims to inform and enhance the meaning of American art, affording new insights into its past implications, present relevance, and future directions.

This book and the exhibition it accompanies benefitted from the advice and assistance of many colleagues. The project was embraced from the start by Princeton University Art Museum Director James Steward, whose abiding support is abundantly appreciated. Initial conceptualization was insightfully abetted by Jeffrey Richmond-Moll and Lucy Partman, then both graduate students in American art, and later by Museum colleagues Juliana Ochs Dweck and Caroline Harris, along with Princeton curators Mitra Abbaspour, Katherine Bussard, Laura Giles, and Bryan Just. For the exhibition, the sensitive preparation of many of the objects for display was undertaken by conservators Bart Devolder, Elena Torok, and Andrew Haines. Todd Baldwin, Alexia Hughes, Justin Webb, and especially Carol Rossi ably handled registration and installation concerns. The exhibition's three-venue tour was very competently managed by Cassandra DiCarlo, and Chris Newth brought welcome oversight to the project, generally. Sarah Brown, Janna Israel, and Gabrielle Langholtz each contributed meaningfully, and Andrew Rose, Class of 1982, Stephanie Wiener, and Eric White generously facilitated select loans. Erika Holmquist-Wall, Amy Kurtz Lansing, Jennifer Stettler Parsons, and Jeffrey Richmond-Moll enthusiastically encouraged the show's appearance at their respective venues.

The catalogue is constituted by the efforts and insights of contributors Horace D. Ballard, Kirsten Pai Buick, Ellery E. Foutch, Jeffrey Richmond-Moll, and Rebecca Zorach, with each of whom it was a pleasure to work and learn from. Anna Brouwer skillfully supervised the catalogue's production with the assistance of Nora McGreevy, and Julie Dweck and Caroline Harris offered beneficial criticism of the manuscript, along with two anonymous readers. Jeffrey Evans produced compelling photography of the objects, and Katie Hameetman, Class of 2023, facilitated their organization. In Seattle, Marquand Books expertly oversaw the creation of the catalogue, including its design, editing and proofreading, and file preparation, with guidance from Adrian Lucia and a sensitive and responsive design by Ryan Polich. Tanya Heinrich provided expert editing, and Melissa Duffes, Ted Gilley, and Dave Luljak offered additional assistance in preparing the text. The color separations and printing of the book were beautifully executed in Rhode Island at Meridian Printing under the supervision of Daniel Frank.

Essential support from three generous funders enabled the project's realization. Sincere thanks are extended to the Terra Foundation for American Art, a vital force in American art scholarship; to friend and perennial exponent Annette Merle-Smith; and to members of the grant committee of the Barr Ferree Foundation Fund for Publications—Rachael DeLue, Brigid Doherty, Wendy Heller, Anne Jarvis, and Rick Myers—for their special generosity. Thanks as well, and as ever, to Courtney Lacy for expertly facilitating fundraising.

Together, each of the foregoing contributed crucially to an undertaking that could not have succeeded without their greatly appreciated efforts.

Karl Kusserow
JOHN WILMERDING CURATOR OF AMERICAN ART

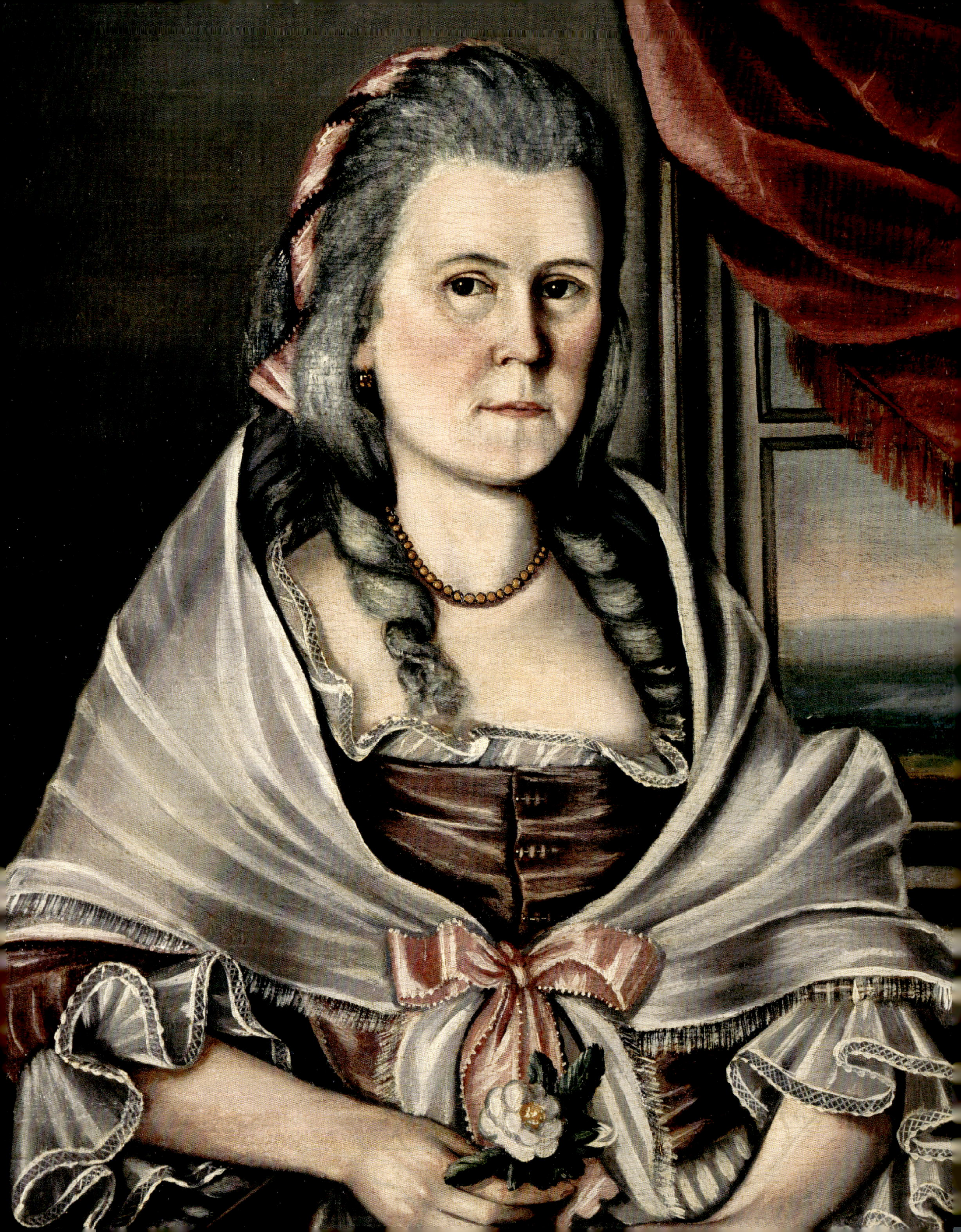

Karl Kusserow

INTRODUCTION
Lenticular*: Subject and Object in American Art

> Although every image embodies a way of seeing, our perception or appreciation of an image depends also upon our own way of seeing. . . . The relation between what we see and what we know is never settled.
>
> —John Berger, *Ways of Seeing*, 1972

> To say it another way, thinking, however abstract, originates in an embodied subjectivity, at once overdetermined and permeable to contingent events.
>
> —Teresa de Lauretis, *Freud's Drive: Psychoanalysis, Literature and Film*, 2008

At the beginning of January 1761, a large box containing an elaborately framed, full-length portrait of England's King George II arrived at the fledgling College of New Jersey, already colloquially known as Princeton. The portrait, by the king's Principal Painter in Ordinary, John Shackleton, was immediately installed in the prayer room of Nassau Hall, the central space in the college's recently completed home, then perhaps the most impressive

*Of or pertaining to a lens; employing a lens or lenses.

Detail, figure 5

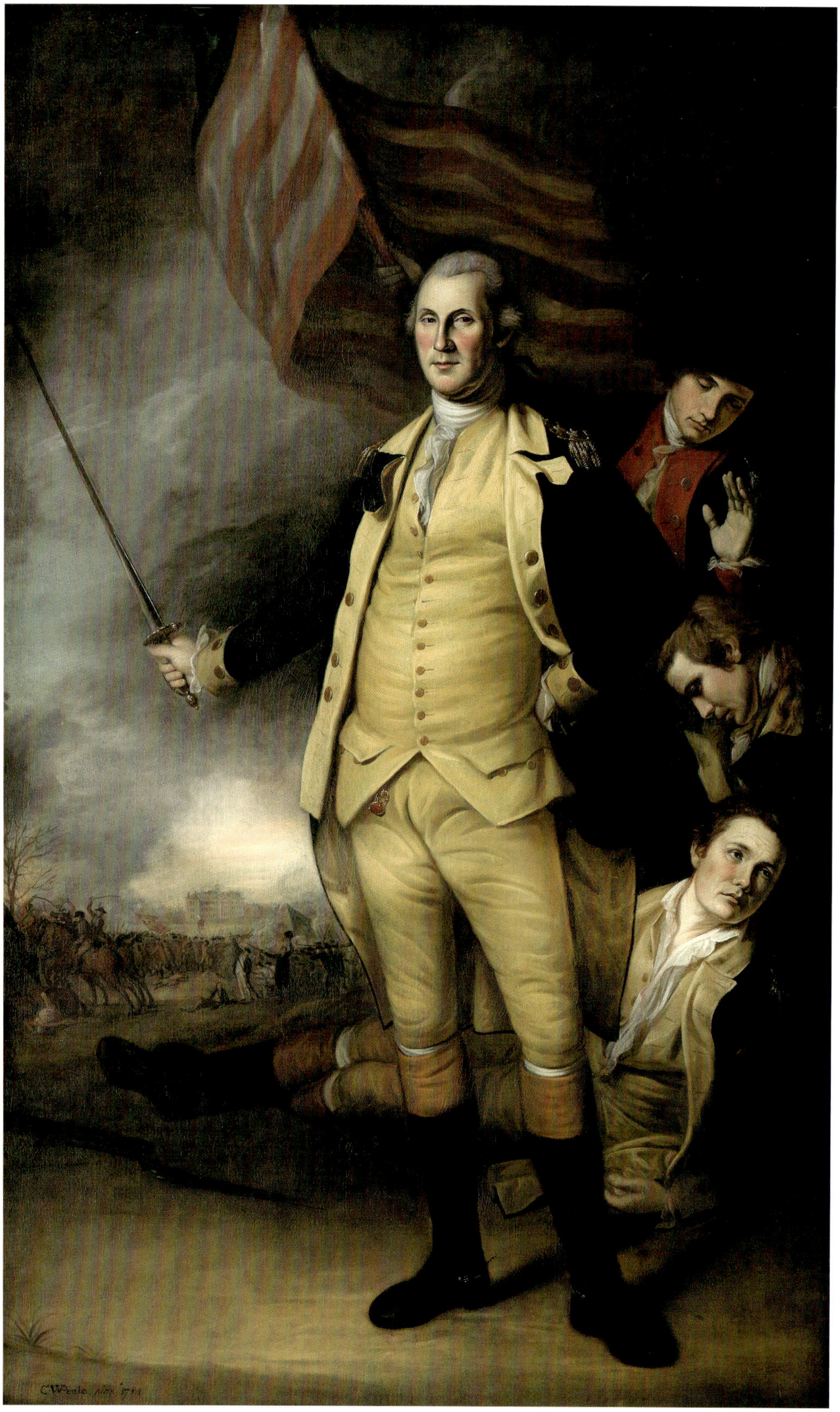

building in the colonies. The painting's sudden appearance seems due to formal exercises in Princeton on January 14 to mark the death of George II, in whose name the school had been granted its charter.[1]

King George was not alone in Nassau Hall. Another portrait, of college patron and former colonial governor Jonathan Belcher, adorned the prayer room, a donation from Belcher along with ten smaller "Heads of the Kings and Queens of England." None survived the Battle of Princeton sixteen years later, when American forces bombarded British troops occupying the building with artillery fire, which ricocheted around the prayer room, destroying, most appropriately, the king's portrait. Its frame, however, was spared and, in a famous act of Revolutionary recycling, repurposed to house an equally grand portrayal of the battle's American hero, General George Washington, painted by Charles Willson Peale, who had also fought in Princeton that day (fig. 1).[2]

These initial images set the tone for the institution's collection over the following half century and more, when portraits of its worthies, valued as much for their role in explicating the college's unfolding narrative as for their inherent aesthetic qualities, constituted the entirety of Princeton's enterprise in collecting art. The divergent sympathies accorded its first few portraits—of an English monarch, a royal governor, and a Revolutionary hero—by the different audiences encountering them, from British and American troops to students at the college of disparate political persuasions, underscore how the meaning of art is in essential ways in the eye of the beholder. Frames are both literal—made of wood and gilt—and metaphorical, referring to broader frames of reference. The portrait of King George surrounded by an ornate frame meant something very different to its various constituencies than the portrait of the other George that eventually replaced it in that same frame. The subject position, or social point of view, of an image's maker and perceivers crucially determines meaning. Perception is lenticular, and both "perceive" and "perspective" share the same Latin root (*perspicere*, to examine, observe, or see through). *Object Lessons in American Art* explores this phenomenon within the context of a single collection of American art, as manifest by shifts in meaning in objects that move through time and are variably understood by various subjects, even at the same time, depending on the lens through which they are viewed.

FIGURE 1 Charles Willson Peale (1741–1827; born Chester, MD; died Philadelphia, PA), *George Washington at the Battle of Princeton*, 1783–84. Oil on canvas, 237 × 145 cm. Princeton University. Commissioned by the Trustees (PP222)

Looking again at the two paintings that shared, one after the other, the same gilded frame, one might ask how different, really, were the two depicted Georges? We know how the destroyed portrait of the king looked, based on a replica completed in 1762 with an almost identical frame (fig. 2). Both images, of the monarch

FIGURE 2 John Shackleton (active 1742, London, United Kingdom; died 1767, London), *King George II*, 1762. Oil on canvas, 231.1 × 147.3 cm. British Museum, London (Painting.12)

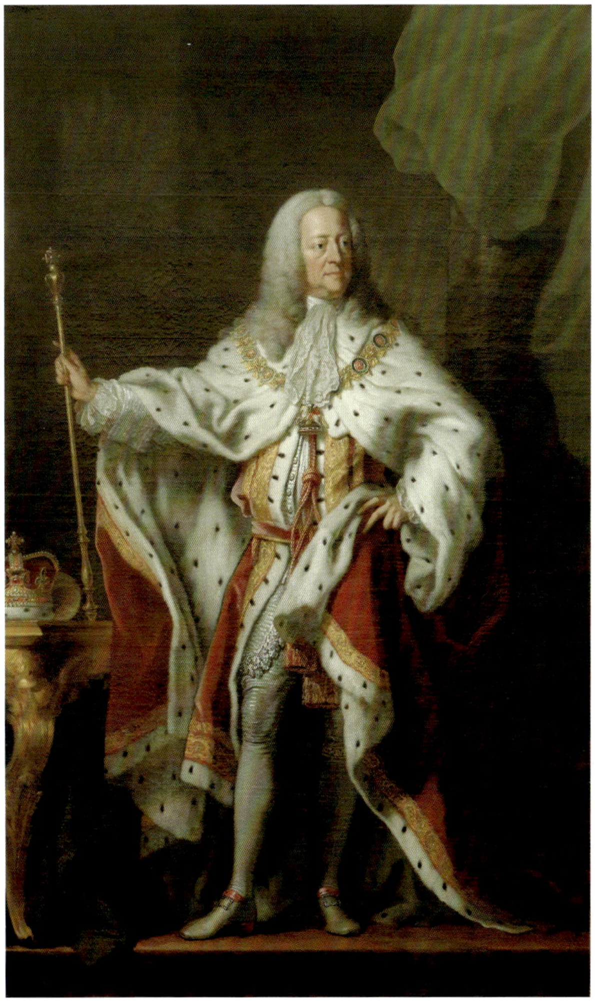

and the future president, represent white men of extraordinary privilege, portrayed by esteemed artists in remarkably similar poses with appropriate accoutrements of power. To some who encountered them successively in Nassau Hall's prayer room, George II and George Washington must have seemed much the same. When the switch took place—between the Battle of Princeton in 1777 and the unveiling of Peale's portrait in 1784—John Witherspoon was president of Princeton College. A Presbyterian minister, he used his platform to speak on behalf of slavery, arguing, and voting, against its abolition. Witherspoon enslaved two people, who lived mostly at Tusculum, his estate outside town. It is unclear how much time they spent in the college's President's House, located adjacent to Nassau Hall, but surely they would have visited the prayer room at some point, and seen the paintings, as would other people in servitude locally at the time. To them, what had seemed to many a world of difference must have looked like little difference at all, not least because Washington was himself an extensive slaveholder.[3]

Two hundred thirty-four years after the completion of Peale's portrait, the Black artist Titus Kaphar shifts the lens to reveal the social and political context of Witherspoon's predecessor, Samuel Finley, in *To Be Sold* (2018; see p. 56, fig. 15; also see p. 55, fig. 14). For Kaphar, the salient point in Finley's biography—literally occluding the rest—is the sale of six people Finley enslaved in a public auction held in the same President's House that Witherspoon later occupied. Instead of replicating Finley's portrait within a frame, Kaphar "reframes" him in his own actions and beliefs, reclothing Finley in strips of auction poster.

The Jamaican American artist Renee Cox stages a similarly compelling transformation using Howard Chandler Christy's *Scene at the Signing of the Constitution* (fig. 3), the vast historical tableau installed outside the Hall of the House of Representatives in the US Capitol Building. With *The Signing* (fig. 4), Cox reimagines Christy's painting as a scene of racial and gender redemption, replacing the roomful of bewigged white men with Black people, many of them women—the very individuals denied voice and agency in both the nation's foundational document and its early history. She thus "flips the script," in her own memorable phrase, to "give people who were considered three-fifths of a person when they wrote the Constitution a presence." The photograph shows the artist herself standing in the same pose and location as Washington, powerfully claiming the place in Christy's composition of the country's "founding father."[4]

Since the classic epigraph by John Berger that begins this essay was written, the scope of art history has steadily broadened to address questions of race and gender—each of crucial significance in America's past and present—and lately to encompass environmental considerations, reflecting current urgent concerns. At the same time, and now with renewed vigor, vital social campaigns regarding racial, gender, economic, and environmental justice have heightened the relevance of bringing such perspectives to bear on the art of the past. With recent attention to reconceptualizing museum practice, the same shift in perspective has similarly inflected the exhibition and display of historical objects—most of them, by the received conventions of collecting and patronage, Eurocentric and by male artists. This book and the exhibition it accompanies examine a gathering of Euro-American, Native American, and African American art from a range of contemporary interpretive positions, illustrating how multifaceted analysis of historical art can inform and enhance its meaning and afford new relevance to artifacts of the American past. The essays within *Object Lessons* excavate and interrogate history and power, collecting, and categories of knowledge and analysis from the various subject positions of their authors, which, although rooted in particular areas of expertise—gender, race, and the environment—are also inherently intersectional in their points of view, formed by the multitude of social, cultural, and political factors that collectively constitute them.[5]

The exhibition takes its title from the nineteenth-century didactic exercise of the object lesson—the study of a material thing to convey an embodied or underlying idea—here enhanced to embrace the added possibilities of groups of objects in juxtaposition. *Object Lessons* is grounded in the understanding that the meaning of art changes over time, in different contexts, and as a consequence of the ways in which it is considered, even as collections evolve to accommodate shifting priorities and perspectives. The works are drawn primarily from

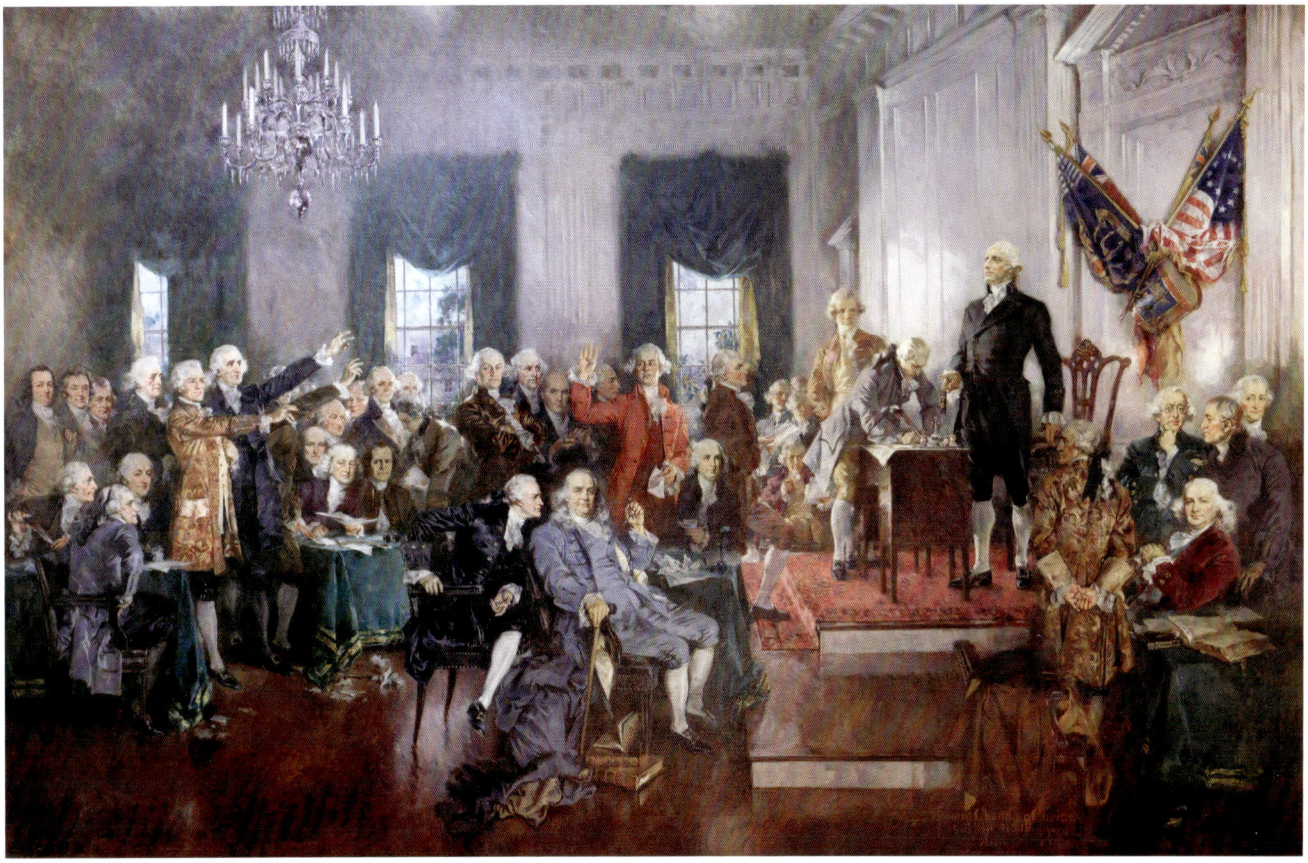

FIGURE 3 Howard Chandler Christy (1873–1952; born Morgan County, OH; died New York, NY), *Scene at the Signing of the Constitution*, 1940. Oil on canvas, 6.1 × 9.1 m. Architect of the Capitol, United States Capitol Building, Washington, DC

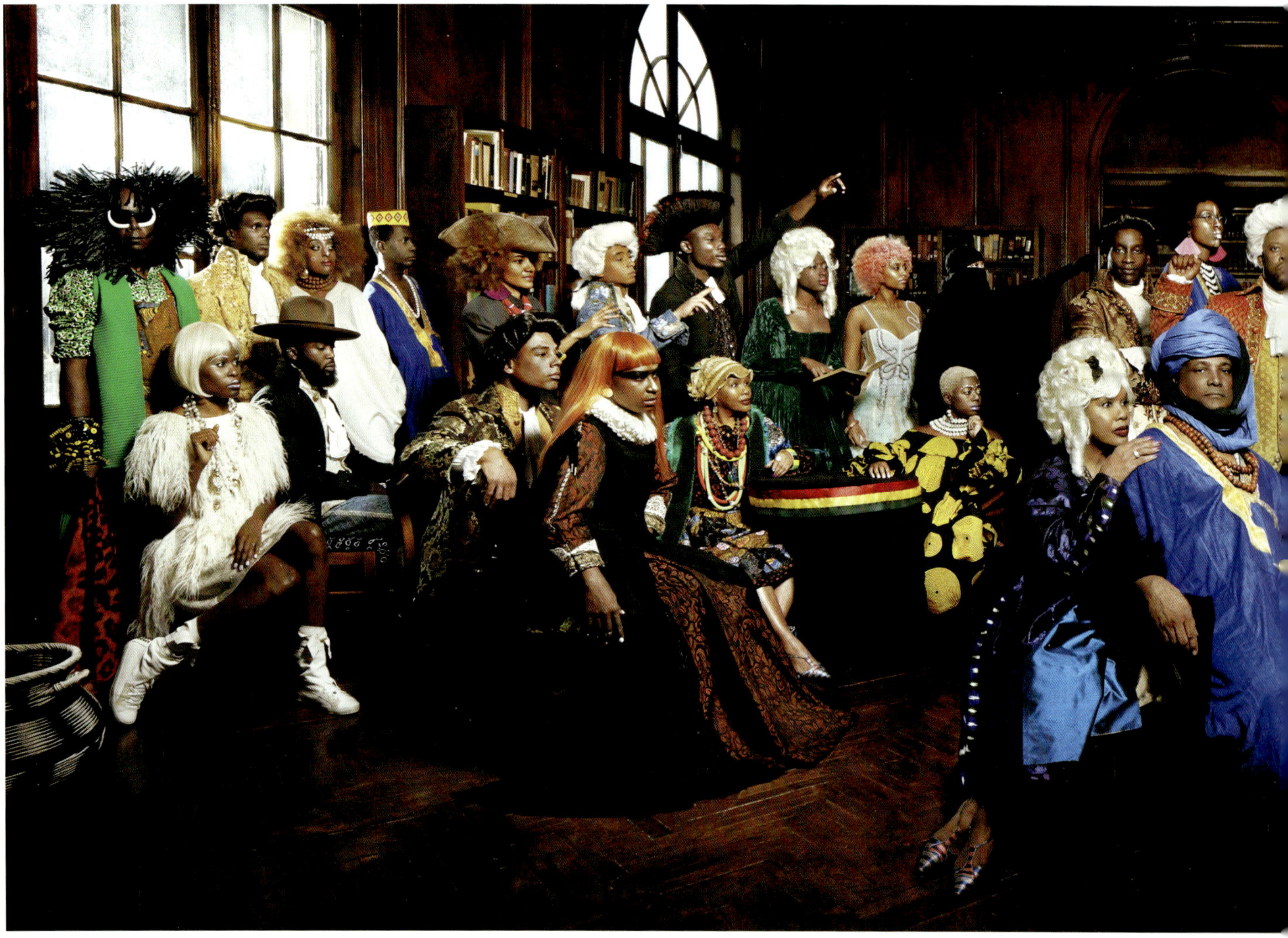

FIGURE 4 Renee Cox (born 1960, Colgate, Jamaica; active New York, NY), *The Signing*, 2018. Inkjet print, 121.9 × 213.4 cm. Princeton University Art Museum. Museum purchase, Kathleen Compton Sherrerd Fund for Acquisitions in American Art (2021-38)

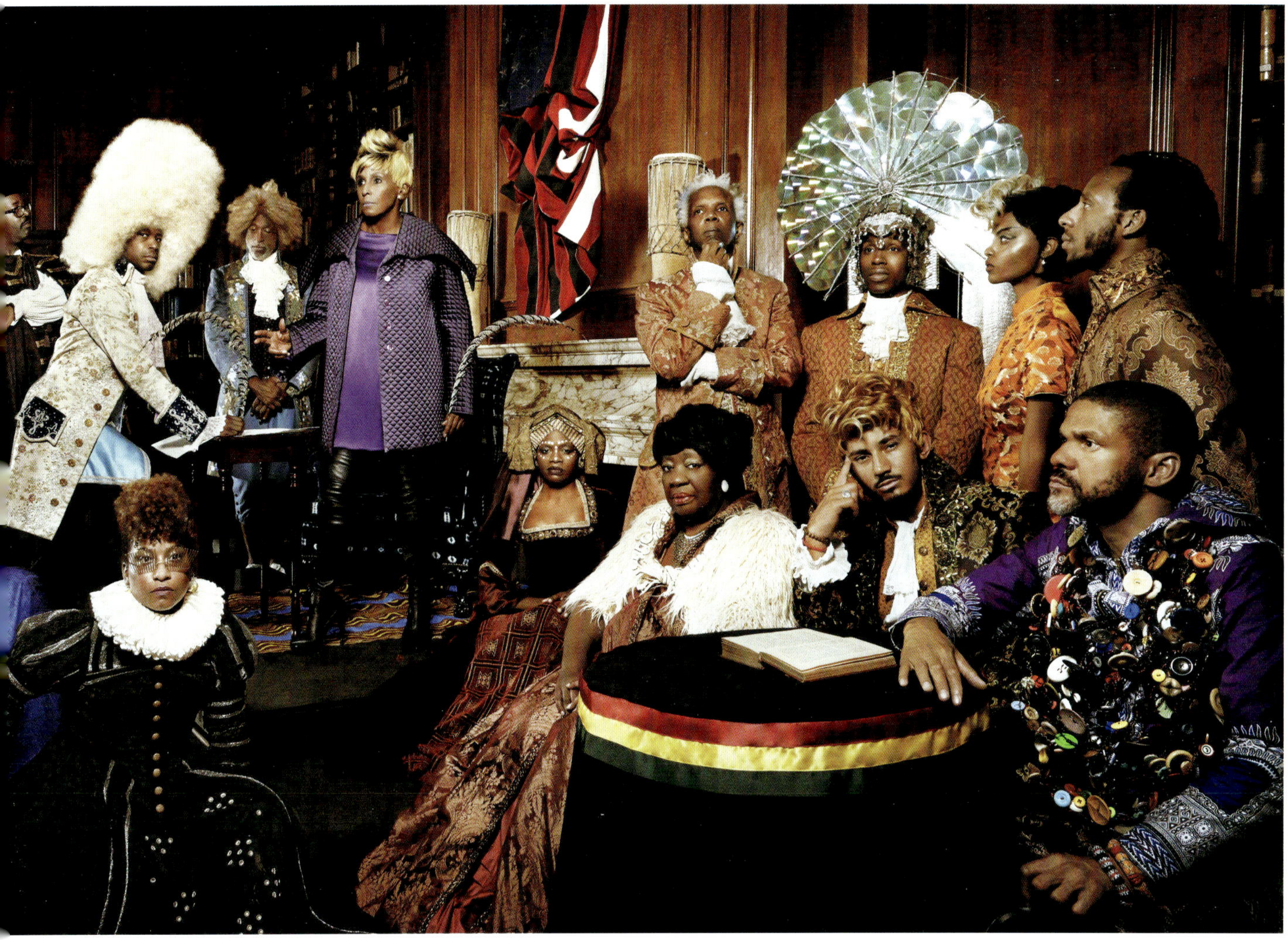

the historical collections of the Princeton University Art Museum, additionally inflected by examples from other campus collections and by contemporary art that imaginatively appropriates and reframes the subjects, style, and content of historical objects.[6]

Of course, Princeton's collections assumed their current size and scope across many decades, though even now their broadened parameters bespeak the enduring absences and imbalances of American history. In the beginning, its collection of portraits staunchly affirmed the overarching anthropocentric orientation of both the times and the institution, and more particularly the pervasive white, patriarchal character of collectors, subjects, and artists. The first American portrait by a woman artist did not enter the collection until 1958 (fig. 5). Princeton acquired its first portrait *of* a woman in 1909, and then it was primarily for her role as the spouse of one of its leaders. Society portraitist John White Alexander painted Isabella Guthrie McCosh some two decades after his portrait of her husband, James McCosh, the school's eleventh president. The pair of portraits make an interesting comparison. Whereas *James McCosh* (fig. 6) exudes a sense of the sitter's deep thought and psychological presence, the same could hardly be said of Alexander's painting of Isabella (fig. 7). Despite the two portraits' similarity in pose and composition—and notwithstanding Isabella McCosh's evident accomplishments and keen intellect—she appears more pained than profound, her expression oddly pinched as she perches on a narrow settee with pillows to bolster her. The focus in *James McCosh* is on the sitter's head and hand, and by extension his intellect and instrumentality—suggested by the papers he

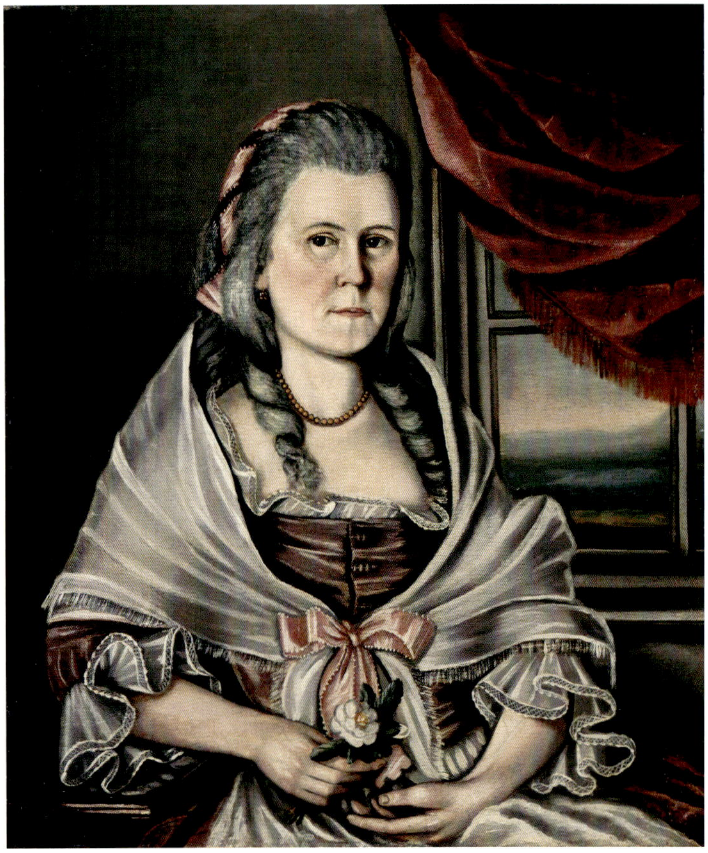

FIGURE 5 Sarah E. Perkins (1771–1831; born Plainfield, CT), *Colonial Dame*, ca. 1790. Oil on canvas, 73.7 × 63.5 cm. Princeton University Art Museum. Gift of Edward Duff Balken, Class of 1897 (y1958-57)

authoritatively grasps—but in *Isabella Guthrie McCosh* attention is dispersed across the picture plane, with almost as much accorded the supporting pillow as the subject's head, with which it visually rhymes, and her hands are half-hidden, diffidently, in her lap. The portrait of James McCosh was installed prominently in the Faculty Room at Nassau Hall, alongside images of other Princeton—and several American—presidents; *Isabella Guthrie McCosh*, by contrast, was placed unobtrusively in the infirmary named after her, for her selfless devotion to the health of students.

Both paintings are included in the first publication to appear on *Princeton Portraits*, as the catalogue by faculty art historian Donald Drew Egbert is titled. By 1947, when the book appeared, the collection featured 236 portraits—227 of them men. The nine women included occupy the end of the book, appended to its last pages much as they were deemed appendages to the institution, despite the noteworthy contributions of Isabella McCosh and others to its sustenance and growth. Princeton did not admit women until 1969, and it is perhaps unfair to remark on the paucity of images of them in an institution so long and so resolutely male (obviously, a problem in itself). In any case, James McCosh was more generous in avowing his wife's agency, affirming "she advised and assisted me in all my work."[7]

Although Alexander's portrait reveals neither Isabella McCosh's "fine intellect" nor her "notable sense of humor," as Egbert described it, she was at least granted a measure of recognition in the patriarchal world Princeton was constructing. Appropriately so, given the many accomplishments her husband, with her help, brought forth at the college, which effectively became a university during his tenure as president, with the gathering of a distinguished faculty, a revised and modernized plan of study, and the institution of graduate

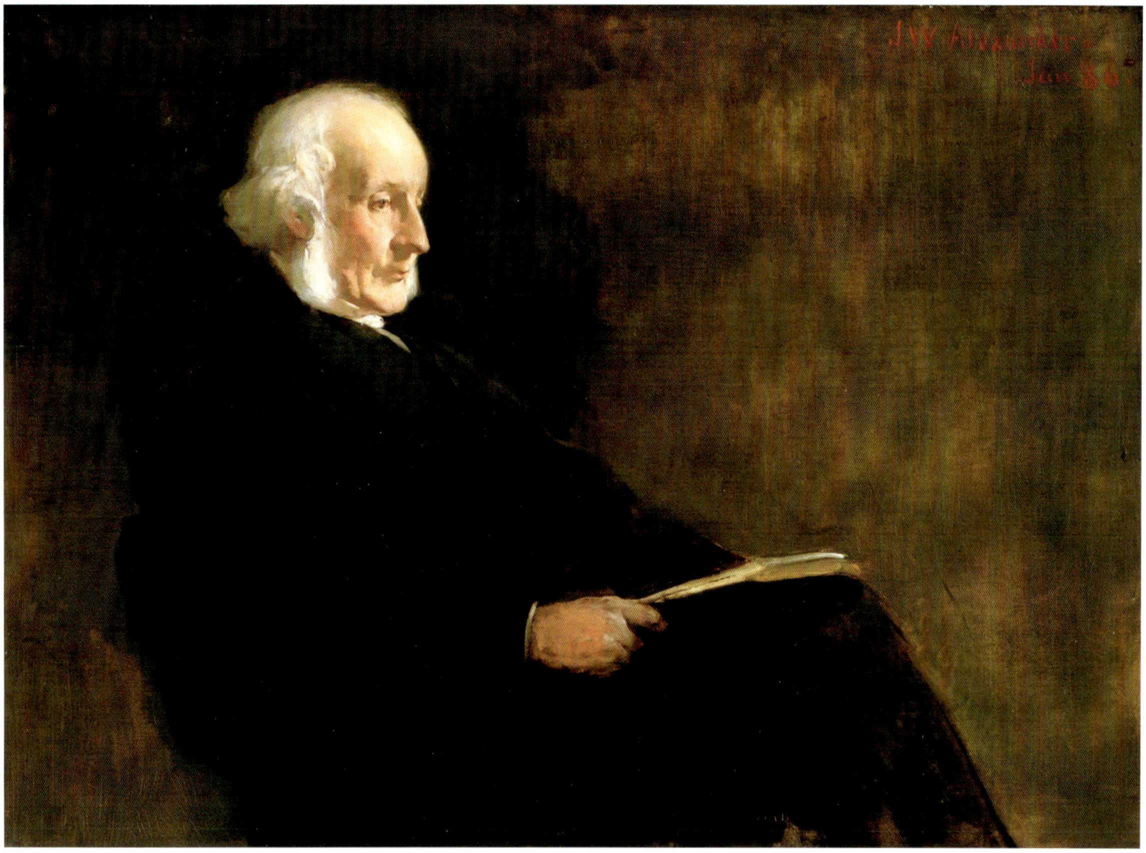

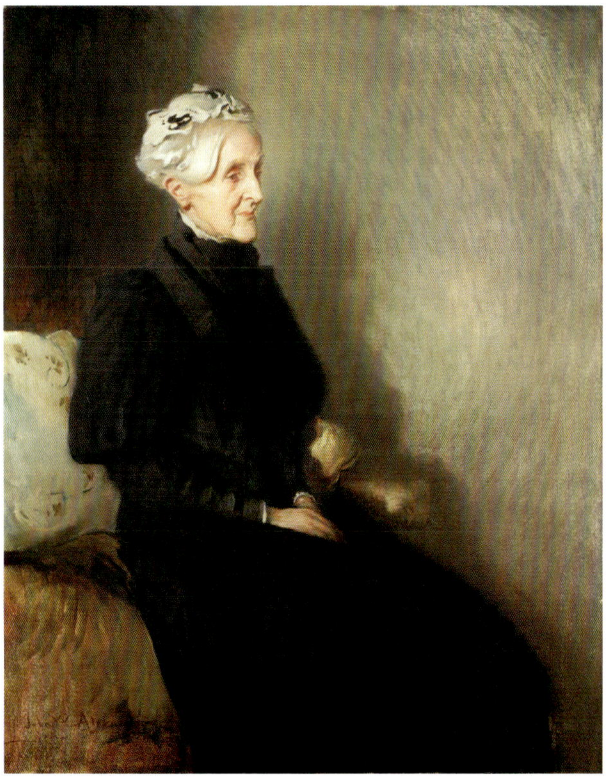

FIGURE 6 John White Alexander (1856–1915; born Allegheny, PA; died New York, NY), *James McCosh*, 1886. Oil on canvas, 89.2 × 123 cm. Princeton University. Gift of alumni (PP37)

FIGURE 7 John White Alexander, *Isabella Guthrie McCosh*, 1908–9. Oil on canvas, 125 × 100 cm. Princeton University. Gift of John White Alexander (PP232)

work. These efforts at modernizing Princeton—which had been founded primarily to train Presbyterian clergy and whose first twelve presidents were all ministers—notably included McCosh's position on the science of evolution. When Darwin's *Origin of Species* (1859) threatened established belief in divine creation and dominion, recapitulating the era's larger discussion about the proper relationship of science and religion, Princeton's intellectuals staked out an unexpectedly wide range of positions. In 1865, the college apparently aimed to tackle the issue head-on with the appointment of Reverend Charles Woodruff Shields to a professorship in the "harmony of religion and revealed science." McCosh himself defended evolutionary doctrine, noting "We do not subject religion to science; but we are equally careful not to subject science to religion. . . . When a scientific theory is brought to us, our first inquiry is not whether it is consistent with religion, but whether it is true," and insisting ultimately that the Darwinian hypothesis, far from denying the existence of God, was a manifestation of God's unfolding plan, serving "to increase the wonder and mystery of the process of creation."[8]

Princeton's first real museum was constituted in the midst of this great debate. The completion in 1873 of the school's new library, Chancellor Green, meant the removal of books from Nassau Hall, where they had occupied the old prayer room, and the refitting of the space as an ambitiously expanded Museum of Geology and Archaeology. The repurposing of the central place once dedicated to religion signaled the growing importance of science at the college. Renowned geographer Arnold Guyot was charged with the design of what by 1875 had officially become the E. M. Museum, named after an anonymous benefactor. Despite its jumbled appearance to contemporary eyes, the E. M. Museum was no haphazard Victorian cabinet of curiosities (see fig. 9). On the contrary, its scientific collections were considered second only to the Smithsonian's, and were similarly intended both to instruct and to advance the frontiers of knowledge. Underscoring the Museum's didactic function, Guyot referred to the gallery as his "Synoptic Room," where "the leading idea in the arrangement . . . is that [the displays] should strike the eye as an open book in which the student can read, at a glance, the history of the creation from the dawn of life to the appearance of man." The room's diverse geological, paleontological, and archaeological contents were all arrayed to this end. So, too, was the remarkable series of paintings arranged around the room: seventeen canvases depicting prehistoric life commissioned by Guyot in 1875 from British scientist and natural history artist Benjamin Waterhouse Hawkins. Set into panels on the exterior of the gallery balustrade, they presented a progressive pictorial account of life itself, from its imagined invertebrate beginnings through the development of mammals (figs. 8, 9). Joining the small and haphazard assemblage of plaster casts of ancient art the college had recently acquired, these were the first paintings commissioned by the college other than portraits—the first, that is, to depict nonhuman life. However, their very purpose was to explain the emergence of mankind, and moreover to help reconcile it, per McCosh's schema, with Christian orthodoxy, which placed humans explicitly above all other kinds of existence.[9]

These three vignettes of Princeton's early art history—as it pertains, with the two Georges in the prayer room, to race; with Isabella McCosh in the infirmary, to gender; and with the Hawkins paintings in the nascent Museum, to anthropocentrism—underscore how the institution's collecting habits reified entrenched ideologies. But we can change the lens. As the examples show, objects that once served to reinscribe racist, patriarchal, human self-centeredness can, when approached and understood differently, serve to dismantle such beliefs. Both the essays in this book and the arrangement of works in the accompanying exhibition shift the meaning of the objects by shifting the subjective lens through which they are viewed.

Princeton did not build a proper museum of art until the end of the nineteenth century, at which point the plaster casts were separated from the E. M. Museum's natural history displays and, reflecting the era's epistemological evolution toward increased specialization and classification of knowledge, reinstalled in its new Museum of Historic Art. There the collection grew in ways that might be expected: Western antiquities and later European art were the focus, as they were of the department of art history that developed in tandem with the Museum. Later, faculty members with interest and expertise in Asian art, and eventually what was known as pre-Columbian art, as well as photography, substantially diversified the Museum's holdings in an era before the institution of a specialized curatorial staff. Native American materials came to Princeton from

FIGURE 8 Benjamin Waterhouse Hawkins (1807–1894; born and died London, United Kingdom), *Cretaceous Life of New Jersey*, 1877. Oil on canvas, 81 × 221.6 cm. Princeton University. Department of Geosciences (PP336)

FIGURE 9 Pach Brothers (active 1867–1947, New York, NY), *E. M. Museum*, 1886. Albumen print, 17.8 × 22.9 cm. Princeton University Library, Department of Special Collections. Princeton University Archives, Historical Photograph Collection

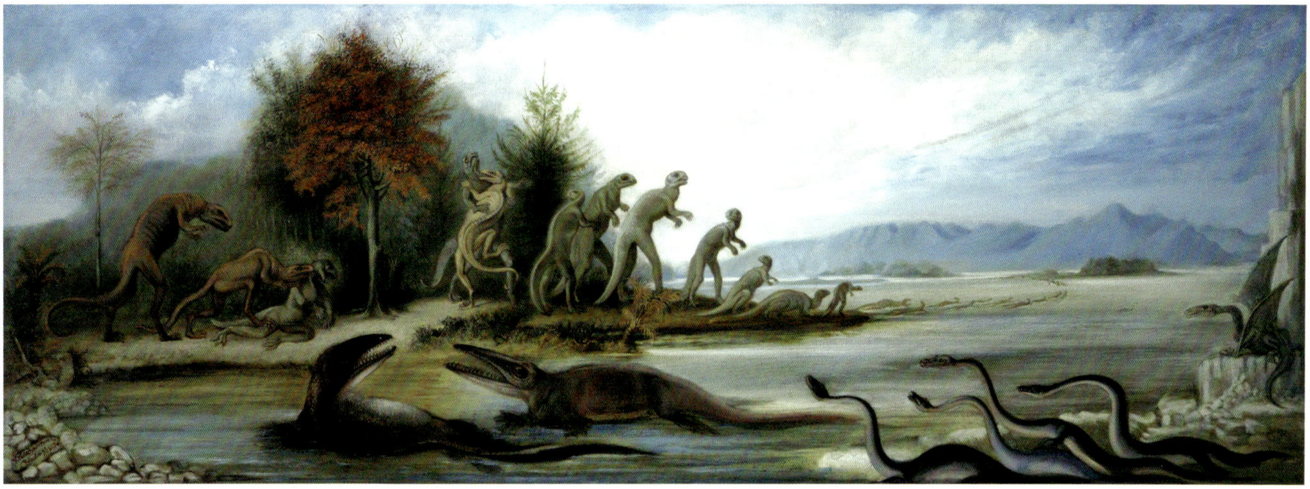

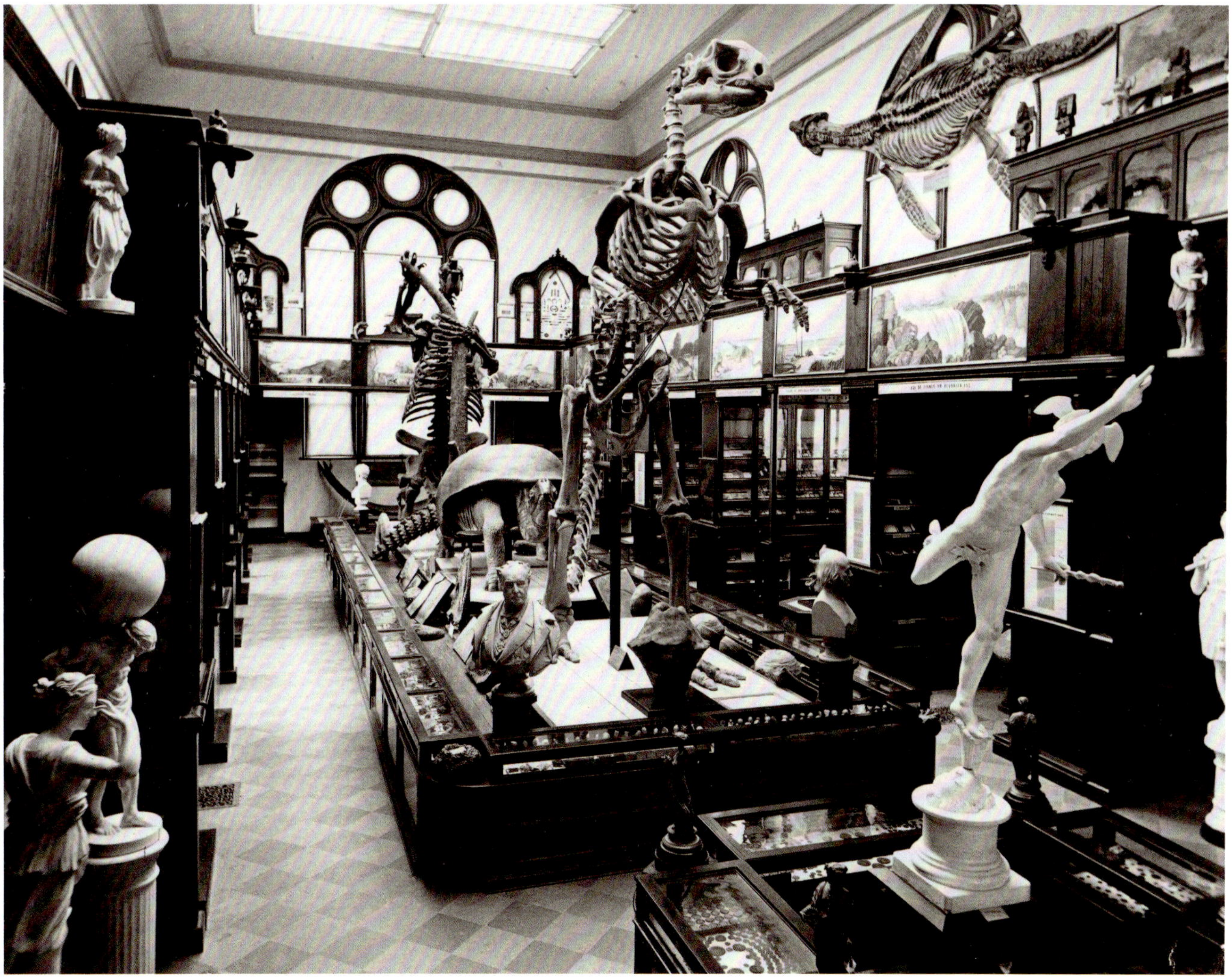

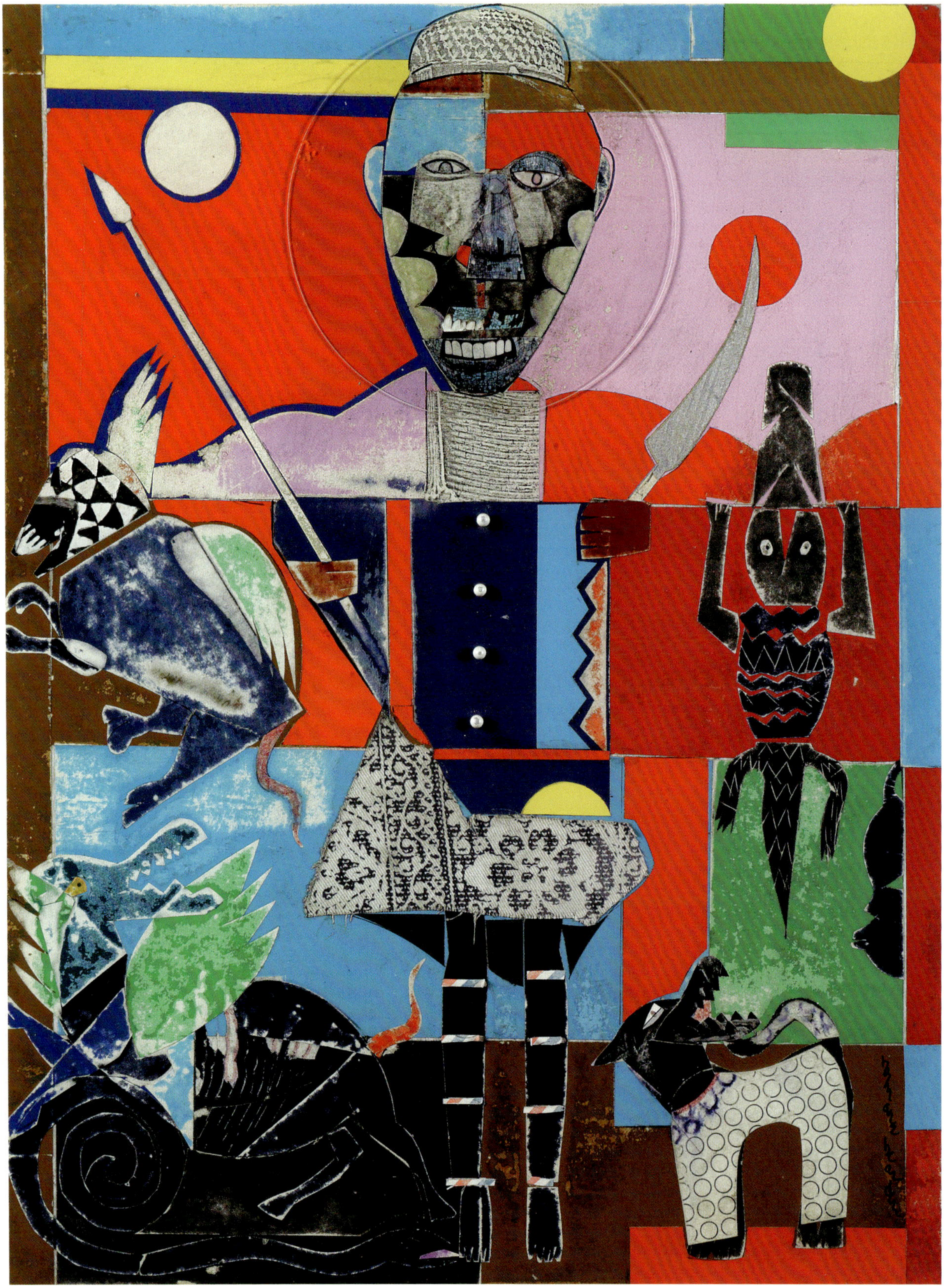

the 1880s through the missionary and exploratory activities of several individuals, often in ways now considered unethical, but these were dismissively deemed the purview of the ethnological sciences and until recently located in the Department of Geosciences. Missionary Sheldon Jackson's promiscuous acquisition of objects from the American Northwest Coast as well as the Southwest forms the basis of these collections, meant to demonstrate "the present condition and needs of Pagan Lands."[10]

Euro-American art had an early champion in the Museum's second director, Frank Jewett Mather, during whose tenure (1922–46) many of the collection's signature works were acquired, often as the gift of Mather himself. Following publication of his *The American Spirit in Art* (1927), one of the field's first surveys, Mather began building the collection in earnest. In the 1940s faculty member Donald Drew Egbert's teaching of American art and his scholarship on Princeton's portrait collection, as well as the University's establishment in 1942 of a Program of Study in American Civilization, created a conducive atmosphere for American art, culminating in 1943 with the Museum's first exhibition in the field.[11]

Even so, it remained, like Princeton more generally, an overwhelmingly white and male affair. The Museum's first acquisition of art by an American woman did not occur until 1938, by which time male American artists represented in the collections already exceeded one hundred. Mather's donation that year of three drawings by artist and illustrator Wanda Gág resulted from her dual role as a writer for *The Nation*, where Mather had served as art critic. African American art was not represented at Princeton until 1972, when the American Academy of Arts and Letters gifted Romare Bearden's vivid collage *Moon and Two Suns* (fig. 10). Four years later, professor John Ralph Willis, a Black scholar of Islam in Africa, organized the first exhibition of African American art at the Museum, nearly a century after it opened.[12]

FIGURE 10 Romare Bearden (1911–1988; born Charlotte, NC; died New York, NY), *Moon and Two Suns*, 1971. Paper, cloth, and plastic on Masonite, 61 × 46 cm. Princeton University Art Museum. Gift of The American Academy and Institute of Arts and Letters, Childe Hassam Fund (y1972-1)

Moving forward a half century from that same period, much has changed. Now there are hundreds of female and Black artists among the approximately 2,300 American artists in Princeton's collections, the result of both broad cultural developments and the institution's own belated reckonings with racial and gender bias. Native American materials have been relocated to the Museum, where they are studied and appreciated on their own terms, as more than ethnographic curiosity or "salvage" anthropology. Perhaps the most profound shift is how objects long in the collections are approached and understood, according to paradigms in which social politics, ethics, and justice factor alongside aesthetic, historical, and cultural concerns. Collections are by nature aggregative entities that grow slowly by accretion. They can be shaped over time, gradually evolving to more fully and fairly characterize the thing they purport to represent, but changes in approach to what is already there may occur more quickly, responding to the issues and attitudes of the era. Even as Princeton moves to bring the balance of representation in its collections more in line with historical realities, it must demonstrate a similar commitment to the reinterpretation and renewed understanding of the preponderance of objects it holds by dominant groups to reveal how hegemonies of gender, race, and species are inscribed in works that take such hierarchies for granted, and naturalize them politically to ensure their continuance.[13]

As definitions of American art become more inclusive, the geopolitical parameters that circumscribed it are also becoming more capacious, with the recognition that notions of the bounded nation-state bear little relation to Indigenous cultures, that adhering to them only reinforces discredited ideas about US exceptionalism, and that the European imperial project that produced the term "America" (after fifteenth-century explorer Amerigo Vespucci) is most productively applied to the hemispheric region originally intended by it. In so doing, the shared essential motivations of colonialism in America, North and South—instilling Christianity and extracting resources—can be holistically engaged and understood. A remarkable group of eighteenth-century casta paintings by Buenaventura José Guiol just acquired by the Museum would not until recently have been considered "American" art. Yet the racial calculus

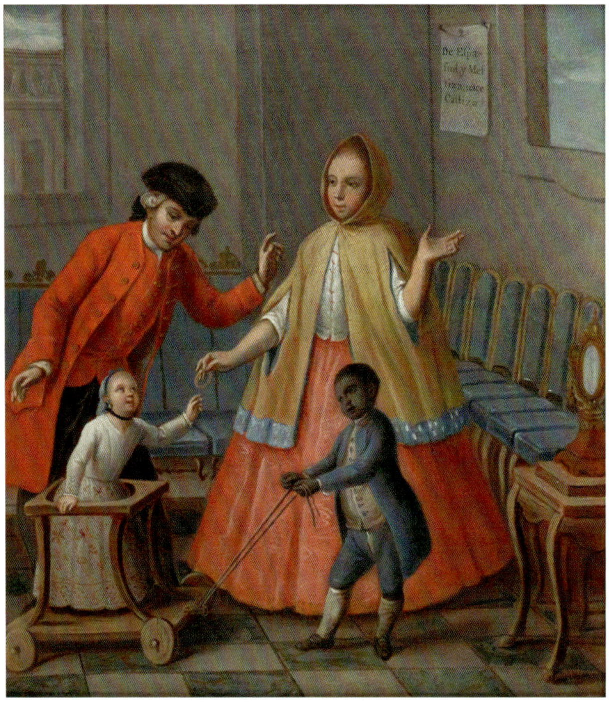

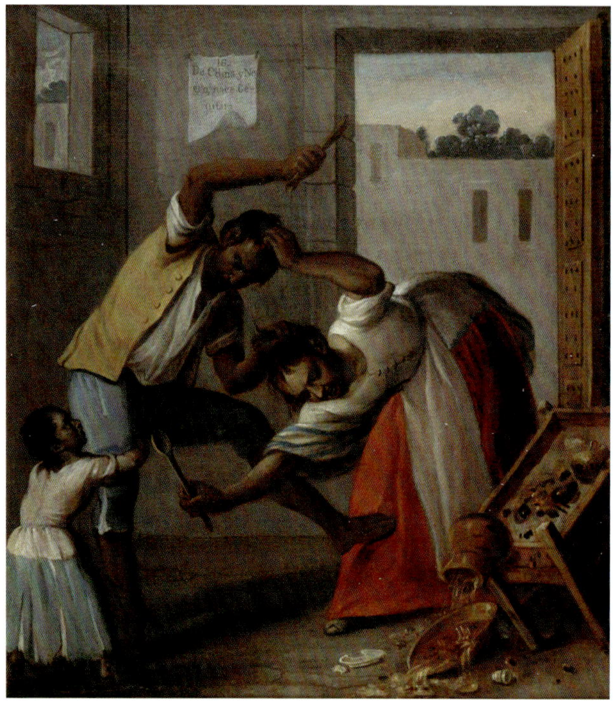

FIGURE 11 Buenaventura José Guiol (active late 18th century, Mexico), *2. From Spaniard and Mestiza, a Castiza Is Born*, 1777. Oil on canvas, 62.3 × 55.2 cm. Princeton University Art Museum. Museum purchase, Fowler McCormick, Class of 1921, Fund (2022-45)

FIGURE 12 Buenaventura José Guiol, *16. From Black and China, a Genisara Is Born*, 1777. Oil on canvas, 62.3 × 55.2 cm. Princeton University Art Museum. Museum purchase, Fowler McCormick, Class of 1921, Fund (2022-49)

they embody and sought to affirm relates to similar racist hierarchies in the United States. A unique genre, Mexican casta paintings were one response to the same collision of Indigenous peoples with European colonizers and enslaved Africans experienced throughout the hemisphere. *Casta*, the Spanish word for "caste," referred to New Spain's mixed-race people and the hegemonic system whereby social, cultural, and economic status was tied to race. A typical series of casta paintings comprised a set of sixteen related works, with each scene illustrating different interracial couples and their offspring. As the scenes progress, they transition from the most "superior" families to the least, with Spanish heritage and purity of blood unsurprisingly elevated above other racial types. In them, art worked not only to reflect and reify but also to actively create and define the complex social realities of the so-called New World. The examples by Guiol show how behavior, ranging from exemplary (fig. 11) to depraved (fig. 12), was explicitly linked to race, gender, and class, thereby justifying as if by natural order the malign social order they impose.[14]

When originally produced, these paintings were construed by their makers and target audiences less as overtly racist instruments of domination than salutary didactic aids, intended to clearly and persuasively explicate the arrangement and precedence of colonial subjects, in which racialized, gendered, and classed identities were mutually constructed to reciprocally affirm one another. Of course now, as what might be considered archetypes of intersectionality for the cumulative ways that multiple forms of discrimination are combined within them, casta paintings signify something entirely different, showing again how meaning is labile and dependent on circumstance, with images once meant to structure racist social relations now deployed to unmask them.

Something similar might be said about *Object Lessons*'s essays, which in their diversity of voice, focus, and approach perform the interpretive subjectivity that is their mutual concern and offer new ways of

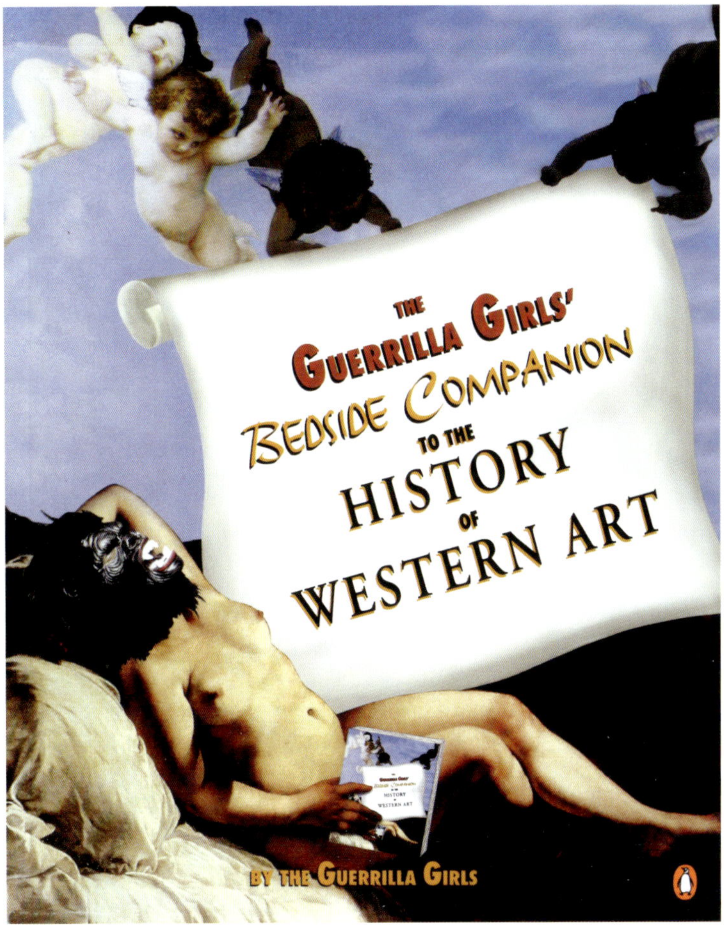

FIGURE 13 Guerrilla Girls (active 1985–), *The Guerrilla Girls' Bedside Companion to the History of Western Art*, 1998. Printed book, 25 × 20 cm. Princeton University Art Museum. Museum purchase, Fowler McCormick, Class of 1921, Fund (2012-143.86)

understanding their often shared subjects. They thus reflect not only the primary transformations of knowledge and perspective that have occurred over time, but also their authors' positionality, a sociological term referring, like intersectionality, to the social contingency of experience and meaning, here with particular regard to identity formation and hence outlook or worldview—the ways social forces produce discerning subjects just as, with intersectionality, they produce perceived ones. The varying perspectives on race, gender, and the environment that each contributor brings to the objects of *Object Lessons*—sometimes the same ones—demonstrate the subjective nature of attention and interpretation. While the indistinct quality of Fitz Henry Lane's atmospheric *Ship in Fog, Gloucester Harbor* (see p. 149, fig. 29) prompts essayist Rebecca Zorach to speculate on the veiled imbrication of slavery with both Gloucester and the depicted vessel, my own consideration of the same attribute focuses on ecology. Even when the broad category of analysis is the same, perception and treatment differ: for Ellery E. Foutch, *From a New Jersey Weekend II* by Georgia O'Keeffe (see p. 92, fig. 23, and p. 108, fig. 1) is framed by the artist's determination to be known as more than Mrs. Alfred Stieglitz. Thus, perhaps the painting's two depicted headstones are "evoking the aged couple who might be buried beneath, the wife's name subsumed to that of her husband." On the other hand, Horace D. Ballard's engagement with gender is "oblique," as his essay is titled; he reads the work queerly as "a landscape that plays on the edges of its genre," or "a still life depicting an interior landscape," insisting that queerness is not inherently about sexual desire. This multiplicity of

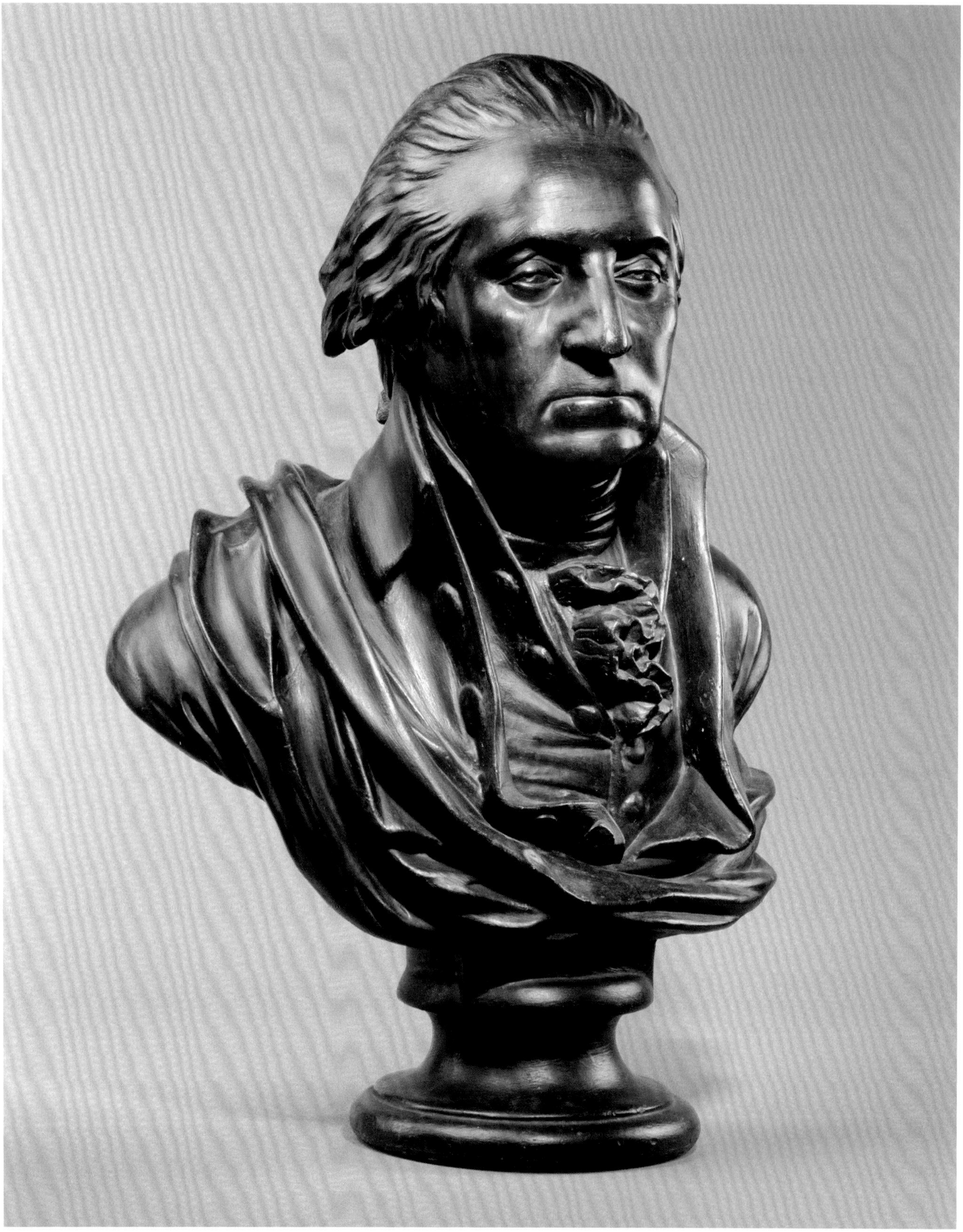

lenses gives new life to the conventional "object lesson." When objects were introduced in US schools during the nineteenth century as pedagogical tools, the assumption was that their lessons had a universality about them that ensured their efficacy and broad applicability. But if postmodernism has taught us anything, it is that disparate subjects learn different lessons from objects, and different objects mean different things at different times (fig. 13).[15]

To return again to the image of George Washington, in 1946 the Museum acquired a plaster bust of the first American president, painted to look like bronze, by Philadelphia sculptor William Rush, who had fought with Washington during the Revolution and knew him firsthand (fig. 14). The bust once belonged to Thomas Jefferson, who kept it at Poplar Forest, his country retreat near Lynchburg, Virginia. Jefferson's enslaved carpenter John Hemings, half-brother of Jefferson's enslaved servant and intimate Sally Hemings, worked extensively there, crafting the house's interior woodwork and furniture, and the carriage that carried Jefferson between Poplar Forest and Monticello. Perhaps Hemings installed the bust of Washington when it arrived. We know Hemings had a close working relationship with Jefferson, but he was not freed until after the third American president's death. Other versions of Rush's bust are in Lexington, Virginia, at the university—Washington and Lee—named after the first presidents of the United States and the Confederate States of America, and in the US Capitol in Washington. In each context and to its various audiences, the bust of America's founding father of freedom carries different associations. To contemplate the many meanings this object has and continues to hold—across time, place, and people—brings us back to the words with which this essay began: "Our perception or appreciation of an image depends also upon our own way of seeing. . . . The relation between what we see and what we know is never settled."

FIGURE 14 William Rush (1756–1833; born and died Philadelphia, PA), *George Washington*, ca. 1817. Painted plaster, 69.8 × 57.1 × 36.5 cm. Princeton University Art Museum. Museum purchase, John Maclean Magie, Class of 1892, and Gertrude Magie Fund (y1946-78)

NOTES

1. The box was transported south from the town of Elizabeth by one Daniel Price, who was paid for his efforts with more than twice the amount received by George Prince, his presumed relative, for making it. The invoice for the transaction, addressed to Samuel Woodruff, mayor of Elizabeth and a trustee of the college, is preserved in the Pyne-Henry Collection of the Princeton University Library and is transcribed in V. Lansing Collins, "The Lost Portrait of George the Second," *Bibla* 5, no. 1 (February 1934): 11.
2. For more on the portraits of King George, George Washington, the frame they share, and early collecting at Princeton, see Karl Kusserow, "Memory and Meaning in the Faculty Room," in *Inner Sanctum: Memory and Meaning in Princeton's Faculty Room at Nassau Hall*, ed. Karl Kusserow (Princeton, NJ: Princeton University Press, 2010), 47–114; also see Elizabeth Baughan and Karl Kusserow, "Framing History in Early Princeton," *Record of the Princeton University Art Museum* 70 (2011): 18–29.
3. On Witherspoon and slavery, see Lesa Redmond, "John Witherspoon," Princeton & Slavery, 2022, https://slavery.princeton.edu/stories/john-witherspoon; and Redmond, "Slavery in the Witherspoon Family," Princeton & Slavery, 2022, https://slavery.princeton.edu/stories/slavery-in-the-witherspoon-family#:~:text=.
4. Cox quoted in Karl Kusserow, "The Case for Reparations, in Pictures," *CNN*, May 3, 2021, https://www.cnn.com/2021/05/03/opinions/slavery-reparations-in-us-in-two-images-hr-40-kusserow/index.html.
5. Several "histories of art history" chart the evolution of the field toward an increased engagement with social politics, including Michael Hatt and Charlotte Klonk, *Art History: A Critical Introduction to Its Methods* (Manchester, UK: Manchester University Press, 2006); and Vernon Hyde Minor, *Art History's History*, 2nd ed. (London: Pearson, 2001); also see Michael W. Cothren and Anne D'Alleva, *Methods and Theories of Art History*, 3rd ed. (London: Laurence King, 2021); Laurie Schneider Adams, *The Methodologies of Art: An Introduction*, 2nd ed. (New York: Routledge, 2009); and Jonathan Harris, *The New Art History: A Critical Introduction* (New York: Routledge, 2001). Art history's reckoning with race transpired relatively recently; see Kymberly N. Pinder, ed., *Race-ing Art History: Critical Readings in Race and Art History* (New York: Routledge, 2002). The discipline's engagement with environmental and ecological themes occurred more recently still; see Alan C. Braddock and Christoph Irmscher, eds., *A Keener Perception: Ecocritical Studies in American Art History* (Tuscaloosa: University of Alabama Press, 2009); Karl Kusserow and Alan C. Braddock, eds., *Nature's Nation: American Art and Environment* (New Haven, CT: Yale University Press, 2018); and Andrew Patrizio, *The Ecological Eye: Assembling an Ecocritical Art History* (Manchester, UK: Manchester University Press, 2018). Numerous texts on the democratization and decolonization

of museums have recently appeared; the most substantial and wide-ranging is Annie E. Coombes and Ruth B. Phillips, eds., *Museum Transformations: Decolonization and Democritization* (Chichester, UK: Wiley Blackwell, 2015). Among broader social justice movements, race is powerfully engaged by the Black Lives Matter movement, gender by #MeToo, economics by Occupy, and environment by Sunrise; for museum culture more specifically, see Museums Are Not Neutral and Decolonize This Place. The concept of intersectionality was initially articulated by Kimberlé Crenshaw in "Demarginalizing the Intersection of Race and Sex: A Black Feminist Critique of Antidiscrimination Doctrine, Feminist Theory and Antiracist Politics," *University of Chicago Legal Forum* 1989, no. 1 (1989): 139–67, https://chicagounbound.uchicago.edu/uclf/vol1989/iss1/8. In its original formulation, intersectionality referred to the ways in which multiple forms of oppression and discrimination combine to confer disadvantage; however, the concept is now more widely understood to explain how various socially constructed categories create unique sets of experience and identity. For the confluence of race, gender, and environment in determining experience and identity, see Kathryn Yusoff, *A Billion Black Anthropocenes or None* (Minneapolis: University of Minnesota Press, 2019).

6. On the object lesson as pedagogical tool, see Sarah Anne Carter, *Object Lessons: How Nineteenth-Century Americans Learned to Make Sense of the Material World* (New York: Oxford University Press, 2018). Anticipating and complementing intersectional approaches to social culture, several theoretical traditions have explored the mutability of meaning among cultural productions as determined by evolving historical periodization and changing individual subject position. The Marxian construct of "use value" supplies an initial critical frame for understanding the highly contextual nature of interpretation and meaning. Marx theorized two fundamental aspects of a commodity: its use value and its exchange value. Whereas exchange value denotes a purely objective and quantitative measure of the proportion in which commodities of one sort are exchanged for another based on the amount of labor power contained in them, use value refers, on the contrary, to the subjectively based desire for a commodity by a given person or group at a certain time. Following Marx, sociologist and philosopher Georg Simmel posited that value and the meaning attached to it are not inherent properties of objects but rather are relationally determined by judgments made about them by subjects. More contemporarily, anthropologist Arjun Appadurai has applied Simmel's insights to his exploration of "regimes of value," examining the conditions under which similar objects circulate differently over space and time. Another anthropologist, Igor Kopytoff, has pursued the concept of "cultural biography" to investigate the changing meaning and valuations of specific things as they move through different contexts, uses, and circumstances. And similarly, James Clifford, also from an anthropological perspective, has discussed the crucial, determinative significance of context for the interpretation of cultural artifacts that remain themselves unchanged. In the realm of literary studies, three related bodies of critical work account for differences and developments in subject position and their effect on interpretation: reader-response, reception, and communications theory. Each posits that meaning is codetermined by both perceiving subject and meaningful object. Interpretation, then, is active, mutual, and shifting, decided by evolving and varied subjects as against set indefinitely and immutably by objects and their makers. Such socially situated criticism is attuned to both the diverse and changing nature of historically embedded subjects and the implications of that diversity for the role and meaning of the cultural products with which they interact. On Marx and use value, see Karl Marx, *Karl Marx: The Essential Writings*, 2nd ed., ed. Frederic L. Bender (Boulder, CO: Westview Press, 1972), 327–28; for the complete original text, see Karl Marx, *Capital* (1867), ed. Frederick Engels, trans. Samuel Moore and Edward Aveling (1906; repr., Chicago: Kerr, 1932), 1:41–48. For Simmel, see Georg Simmel, *The Philosophy of Money* (1907), ed. David Frisby, trans. Tom Bottomore and David Frisby (London: Routledge, 1978). Anthropologically based theses are discussed in Arjun Appadurai, ed., *The Social Life of Things: Commodities in Cultural Perspective* (New York: Cambridge University Press, 1986), especially Appadurai, "Introduction: Commodities and the Politics of Value," 3–63; and Igor Kopytoff, "The Cultural Biography of Things: Commoditization as Process," 64–92; also see James Clifford, "On Collecting Art and Culture," in *The Predicament of Culture: Twentieth-Century Ethnography, Literature, and Art* (Cambridge, MA: Harvard University Press, 1988), 215–51. Two anthologies of reader-response criticism—each with contextualizing introductory essays and featuring a range of reader-based approaches, including reception theory—are Jane P. Tompkins, ed., *Reader-Response Criticism: From Formalism to Post-Structuralism* (Baltimore: Johns Hopkins University Press, 1980); and Susan Rubin Suleiman and Inge Crosman, eds., *The Reader in the Text: Essays on Audience and Interpretation* (Princeton, NJ: Princeton University Press, 1980); also see James L. Machor, "Introduction: Readers/Texts/Contexts," in *Readers in History: Nineteenth-Century American Literature and the Contexts of Response*, ed. James L. Machor (Baltimore: Johns Hopkins University Press, 1993), vii–xxix. For communications theory focusing on the social subject, see John Fiske, "Active Audiences," in *Television Culture* (London: Methuen, 1987), 62–83. For a demonstration of art historical analysis embodying the tenets outlined here, see Karl Kusserow, "Portraiture's Use, and Disuse, at the Chamber of Commerce and Beyond," in *Picturing Power: Portraiture and Its Uses in the New York Chamber of Commerce* (New York: Columbia University Press, 2013), 9–133.

7. Donald Drew Egbert, *Princeton Portraits* (Princeton, NJ: Princeton University Press, 1947), McCosh quoted 340.

8. Egbert, *Princeton Portraits*, 339. James McCosh, *The Life of James McCosh: A Record Chiefly Autobiographical*, ed. William Milligan Sloane (New York: Scribner's, 1896), "We do not subject" at 322; also see J. David Hoeveler Jr., *James McCosh and the Scottish Intellectual Tradition: From Glasgow to Princeton* (Princeton, NJ: Princeton University Press, 1981); and, more generally, George S. Marsden, *The Soul of the American University: From Protestant Establishment to Established Nonbelief* (New York: Oxford University Press, 1996). McCosh, "increase the wonder and mystery," quoted in Deborah Blum, *Ghost Hunters: William James and the Search for Scientific Proof of Life after Death* (New York: Penguin, 2006), 82.

9. Guyot quoted in Kusserow, "Memory and Meaning," 85; for more on Princeton's E. M. Museum, see 73–85, from which this account draws; and Sara E. Turner, "The E. M. Museum: Building and Breaking an Interdisciplinary Collection," *Princeton University Library Chronicle* 65, no. 2 (Winter 2004): 237–64. As was later revealed, the Museum received funding from William Libbey, who named it after his wife, Elizabeth Marsh, and whose son, William Libbey Jr., Class of 1877, eventually oversaw it, following Guyot's retirement. Confusingly, Hawkins's own views were actually anti-Darwinian, and accorded with those of Guyot in supporting the notion of limited evolution under God's plan without accepting the theory of natural selection. For McCosh, by contrast, natural selection was but a facet of an overarching intelligent design. Both points of view were accommodated in the Museum, whose displays, while clearly evolutionary in the sense of showing progression over time, did not specifically advocate "evolution" as Darwin theorized the term. For information on the Hawkins paintings, see Valerie Bramwell and Robert M. Peck, *All in the Bones: A Biography of Benjamin Waterhouse Hawkins* (Philadelphia: Academy of Natural Sciences, 2008), 85–89.

10. On the early history of what is now called the Princeton University Art Museum, see "An Art Museum for Princeton: The Early Years," special issue, *Record of the Princeton University Art Museum* 55, no. 1/2 (1996), especially Betsy Rosasco, "The Teaching of Art and the Museum Tradition: Joseph Henry to Allan Marquand," 7–52; J. Michael Padgett, "The Collections of Ancient Art: The Early Years," 107–24; and Cary Y. Liu, "Asian Art Collection: From Exotica to Art and History," 125–34; also see James Christen Steward, "Introduction: Making the Museum," in *Princeton University Art Museum: Handbook of the Collection* (Princeton, NJ: Princeton University Art Museum, 2013); and, for the art history department in relation to the Museum, Marilyn Aronberg Lavin, *The Eye of the Tiger: The Founding and Development of the Department of Art and Archaeology, 1883–1923, Princeton University* (Princeton, NJ: Art Museum, Princeton University, 1983). For Sheldon Jackson and Princeton, see Douglas Cole, *Captured Heritage: The Scramble for Northwest Coast Artifacts* (1985; repr., Vancouver, BC: UBC Press, 1995), quoted at 75.

11. *An Exhibition of Drawings by American Artists, 18th–20th Centuries* was jointly organized by the art history department and the new program in American civilization; also see Frank Jewett Mather Jr., "American Paintings at Princeton University," *Record of the Princeton University Art Museum* 2, no. 2 (Autumn 1943): 2–15. On Mather at Princeton, see Barbara T. Ross, "The Mather Years, 1922–1946," in "An Art Museum for Princeton," 53–76. Previously in the Museum's history, collecting American art was not encouraged; a 1911 letter from an alumnus to Allan Marquand, the Museum's first director, notes, "I have for many years, or since the Art Museum was built, been anxious to see there a good representative exhibition of works by our early American painters, and I will never cease to regret, that through seeming indifference, I could not arouse sufficient interest. . . ." (James B. Townsend to Allan Marquand, November 24, 1911, Princeton University Art Museum, donor file, acc. no. y1943-120). For the history of the eventual American collection, see John Wilmerding, "American Art at Princeton," in *American Art in the Princeton University Art Museum, Volume I: Drawings and Watercolors*, ed. John Wilmerding (Princeton, NJ: Princeton University Art Museum, 2004), 3–47.

12. See John Ralph Willis, *Fragments of American Life: An Exhibition of Paintings* (Princeton, NJ: Art Museum, Princeton University, 1976).

13. Currently, formal initiatives are underway to increase the Museum's representation of photography by Black Americans and contemporary art by Native Americans. In a related undertaking, the University has commissioned a more inclusive range of portraits of individuals affiliated with its history to broaden campus iconography.

14. The paintings illustrated are two of a group of five (from an original set of sixteen) acquired in 2022; see Ana Zabía de la Mata, *Five Casta Paintings by Buenaventura José Guiol: A New Discovery*, no. 4, *Jaime Eguiguren Studies* (Buenos Aires: Jaime Eguiguren, 2018). On casta paintings, generally, see Ilona Katzew, *Casta Painting: Images of Race in Eighteenth-Century Mexico* (New Haven, CT: Yale University Press, 2004); Magali M. Carrera, *Imagining Identity in New Spain: Race, Lineage, and the Colonial Body in Portraiture and Casta Paintings* (Austin: University of Texas Press, 2003); and Susan Deans-Smith, "Creating the Colonial Subject: Casta Paintings, Collectors, and Critics in Eighteenth-Century Mexico and Spain," *Colonial Latin American Review* 14, no. 2 (2005): 169–204.

15. The concept of positionality returns to some of the theoretical paradigms outlined in note 5 above; see Luis Sánchez, "Positionality," in *Encyclopedia of Geography*, ed. Barney Warf (Thousand Oaks, CA: Sage, 2010), 2258, https://dx.doi.org/10.4135/9781412939591.n913.

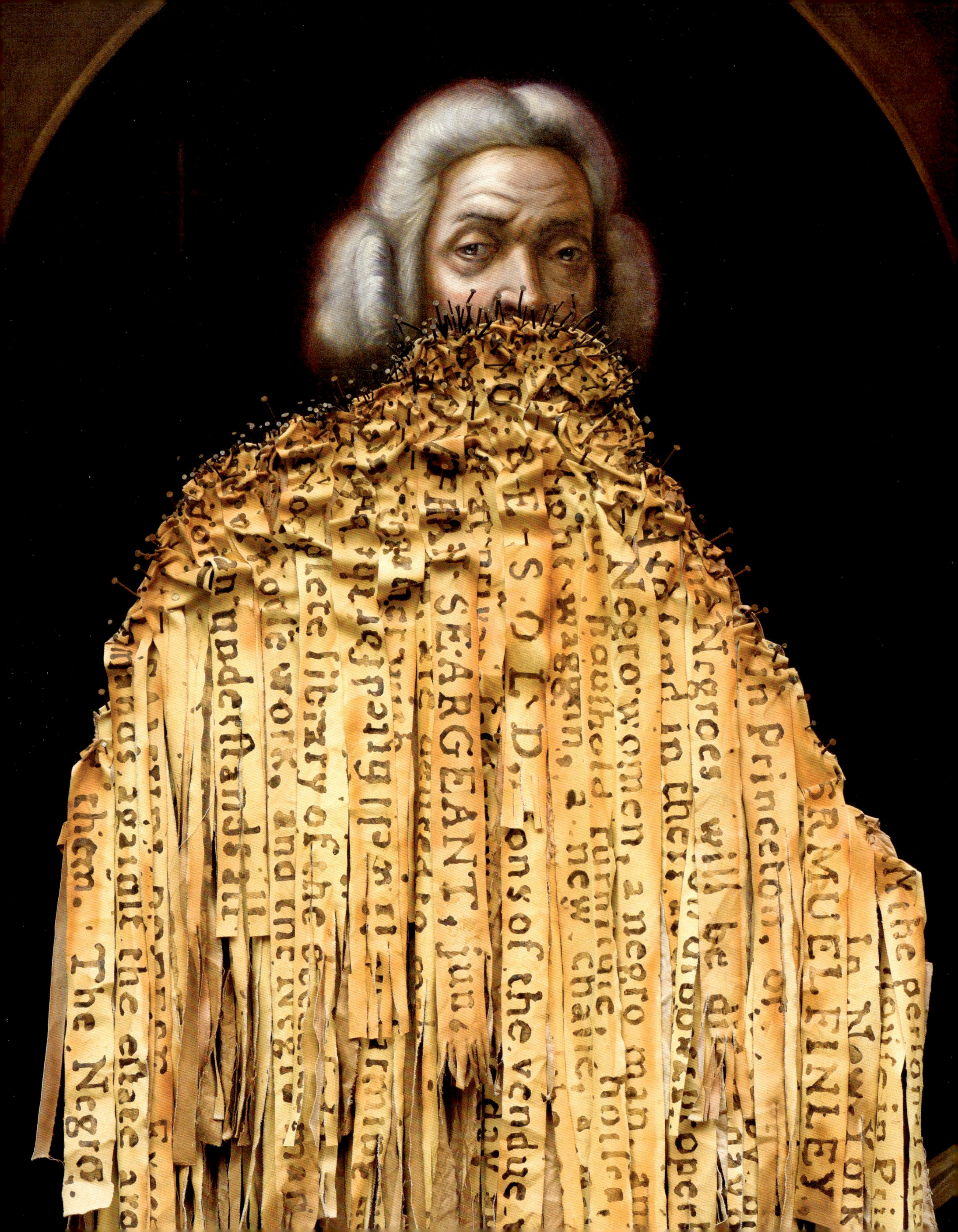
S O L D
SEARGEANT
SAMUEL FINLEY
in Princeton
Negroes will be
negro women, a negro man
household furniture
a new waggon
a new chaise
complete library of the
them. The Negro.

Kirsten Pai Buick

“Race” as Object Lesson: Objects of Rebellion

There was tension in my grandparents’ home in the summer of 1969. It was palpable even to my six-year-old self. All that I knew then was that my grandfather was driving back to Arkansas with my great-uncles, a combination of his and my grandmother’s brothers. And they were taking guns. Despite the pleading of my grandmother and great-aunts to stop them from making the trip from Chicago’s South Side to our property “down South,” they were determined. Later, I learned that a White man had held a gun to my great-uncle Cornge’s head and demanded he sign the deed of the family’s property over for five hundred dollars. It was the exact amount that my great-grandfather had pressed into my grandfather’s hands in 1938 with the entreaty to go north and never return to live in Arkansas. My grandfather was obsessed with property. A descendent of enslaved Africans and sharecroppers, he had land in Arkansas, owned a building and a home in Chicago, and bought vacation property in Michigan. As an iteration of landscape representation, however, “property” is rarely theorized as an issue of ownership for African Americans. We are also limited by the histories of representation, of art, and of collecting, which easily accommodate the visuality of the plantation so that African Americans “have been” property

Detail, figure 15

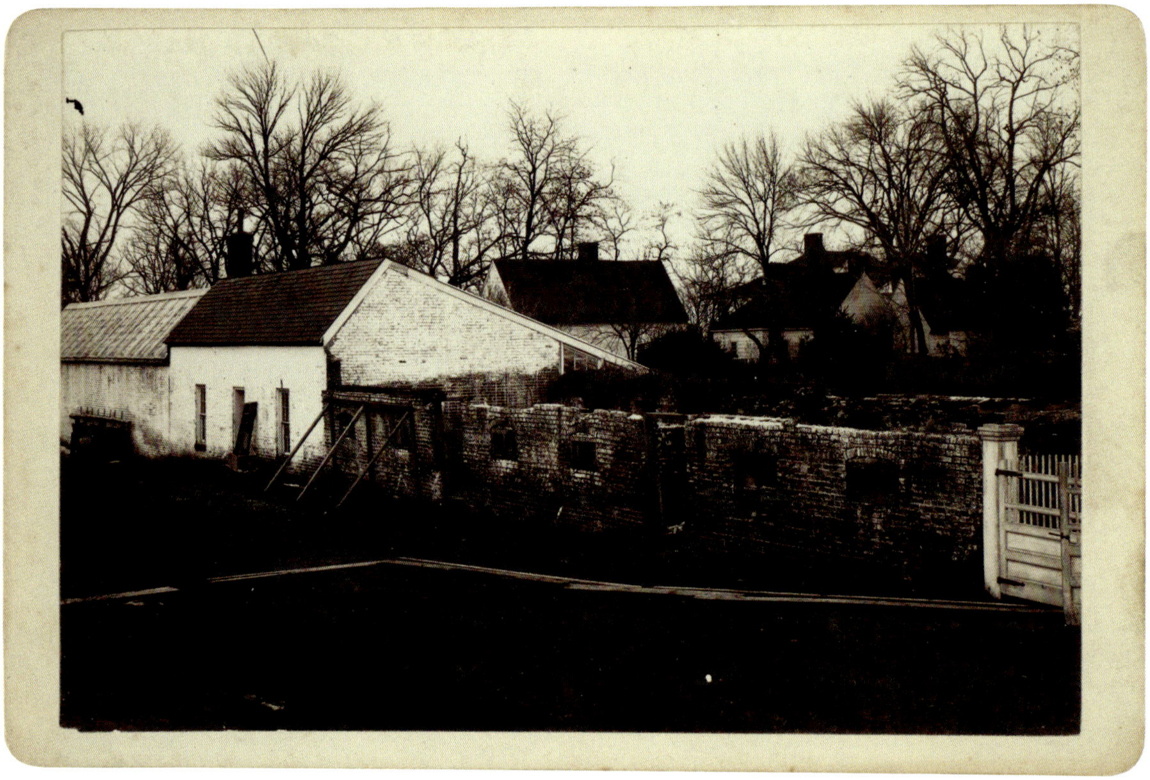

FIGURE 1 Luke C. Dillon (born 1844/45, New York, NY; active ca. 1874–86, Washington, DC), *Ruin of Old Slave Quarters, Mount Vernon*, ca. 1883. Cabinet card, 10 × 14.7 cm. Princeton University Art Museum. Gift of David B. Long in memory of Donald C. Long (2020-399)

and worked the "property" of others. In fact, collectors will pay hundreds of thousands of dollars for those rare photographs of enslaved people on plantations.[1] And in instances where they have not been torn down, collectors will buy images of abandoned slave quarters like the photograph by Luke C. Dillon taken about 1883, *Ruin of Old Slave Quarters, Mount Vernon* (George and Martha Washington's plantation), in Princeton's collection (fig. 1). The specter of the plantation haunts the history and visual memory of Black people and most intimately links them to our founding narratives and "Fathers." Less rare, though not prioritized except in the collections of Historically Black Colleges and Universities (HBCUs), are works that center African Americans as property holders. However, as we comb the archives of established artists, we do find that African Americans were indeed a richer source of inspiration than we previously thought. Recently, a suite of paintings by Andrew Wyeth was rediscovered. Wyeth had chronicled the Black people who lived and owned property in Chadds Ford, Pennsylvania, during the mid-twentieth century. Chadds Ford was a Black community that was centered around a church led by Mother Lydia Archie. Unfortunately, the descendants of the original inhabitants have been driven out by rising land prices, but we do have Wyeth's visual testimony.[2]

I begin with this piece of family lore about racism and property to remind myself of the difficulty of what I have been asked to do here and to remind myself of the complexity of what is owed. Within the history of landscape representation in the United States, property has existed as the underlying rationale for landscape as both symbol and resource.[3] How we are positioned relative to landscape is how we authenticate identity objects. Identity objects serve to classify individuals whose group belonging can be either voluntary or involuntary, who are divided according to gender, ethnicity, race, class, or places of belonging or nonbelonging.[4] They function such that Native Americans "belong" in the wilderness or on reservations; White people "belong" in and to the technologies, towns, and eventually cities that spread civilization westward; and Black people "belong" to plantations and later segregated areas defined by deprivation and violence.[5] With urbanization, immigrant neighborhoods were populated and peopled in tenement spaces. Moreover, immigrant neighborhoods like Chinatowns were formed to both house identity objects and become centers of touristic trade so that identity itself could be housed within objects and sold (whether as souvenirs or as food); and Old Towns are often tourist sites in the Southwest, where Native Americans and Hispanics sell objects associated with their culture and more significantly with the past. Race and racialization, gender, class, time, and nation are all firmly affixed to place, while the history of US art and collecting easily accommodates and reinforces the idea that identity objects are locatable in space or can be reconfirmed in a thing.

There are echoes in the modern university, with its ethnic and gender studies programs and departments siloed across campus. Robyn Wiegman, in *Object Lessons*, writes of the programs and departments as producers of identity objects that are animated by political desires. They center social justice but are largely unsuccessful because, taken singly, identity objects reinstantiate the various fields through a series of distinctions, differentiations, and disidentifications, one from the other, and therefore cannot achieve their ultimate ends, from women's studies to ethnic studies to American studies; instead, she argues, political resolution is to be found in an intersectional approach. Wiegman desires to inhabit the tensions that form and inform the aspirations and priorities of identity objects and the identity knowledges that they produce.[6] While Wiegman gets close to my purpose in exploring "race" as object lesson, Rogers Brubaker, Frederick Cooper, and Adolph Reed get me closer in their proposition that while identity can be an object *of* study and an object *for* study, identity is a category of practice rather than a category of analysis. Categories of practice are the categories we use in everyday life, and as such they remain worthy of examination for how their various ideologies are unleashed on the world. For example, when categories of practice are used and confused for categories of analysis, we presume an abstraction to be a real thing that has an overdetermined impact on the world.[7] "Race" is one such abstraction. Its category of practice is "racism," which normalizes and constitutes the abstraction "race." What follows is an unraveling of sorts. Using a selection of works in the Princeton collection, I hope to demonstrate how interpretation can counter the notion that the objects are the abstractions made concrete. To undo the burden that we place on them to be representative of identity, we must instead understand objects as opportunities and as communicating events. In the words of Henry Glassie, "The artist's creations work in the world, embodying cultural complexities and shaping relations among people, between people and the environment, between people and the forces that rule creation."[8]

"RACE" AS OBJECT LESSON

I begin every class with a vocabulary lesson that is reinforced throughout the semester. I tell my students that it is the ideology that constructs and maintains identity: racism constructs and maintains race; sexism constructs and maintains gender; nationalism constructs and maintains nation. I also tell them that to some degree we are all complicit in the very ideologies that define and delimit our existence. I tell them to keep words active in their minds: when they read "race," translate it to "racism"; "identity" to "identification"; "minority" to "minoritized"; "difference" to "differentiation"; and, finally, "other" should always be read as a verb rather than a noun—"*to* other" rather than "*the* other."[9] In this way, we keep processes of differentiation at the forefront but also become aware of how normalization works on and through us. Why do we accept labels? How do we begin to understand that race, class, gender, ability, et cetera, are performances that rest on the infinitive "to do" rather than "to be"? Instead of inhabiting a state of being or possessing characteristics waiting to be passively realized or discovered, we are works in progress, endlessly complex and contingent. Put simply, difference is the difference that difference makes. Gradually, the students begin to comprehend that our oppressions are relational, performative, and participatory and function to render us legible, "identifiable," and coherent at all registers of society. Ideologies are categories of practice, even as their results (identities) present themselves as real, fixed, true, and eternal rather than as abstractions. Contrarily, objects help to

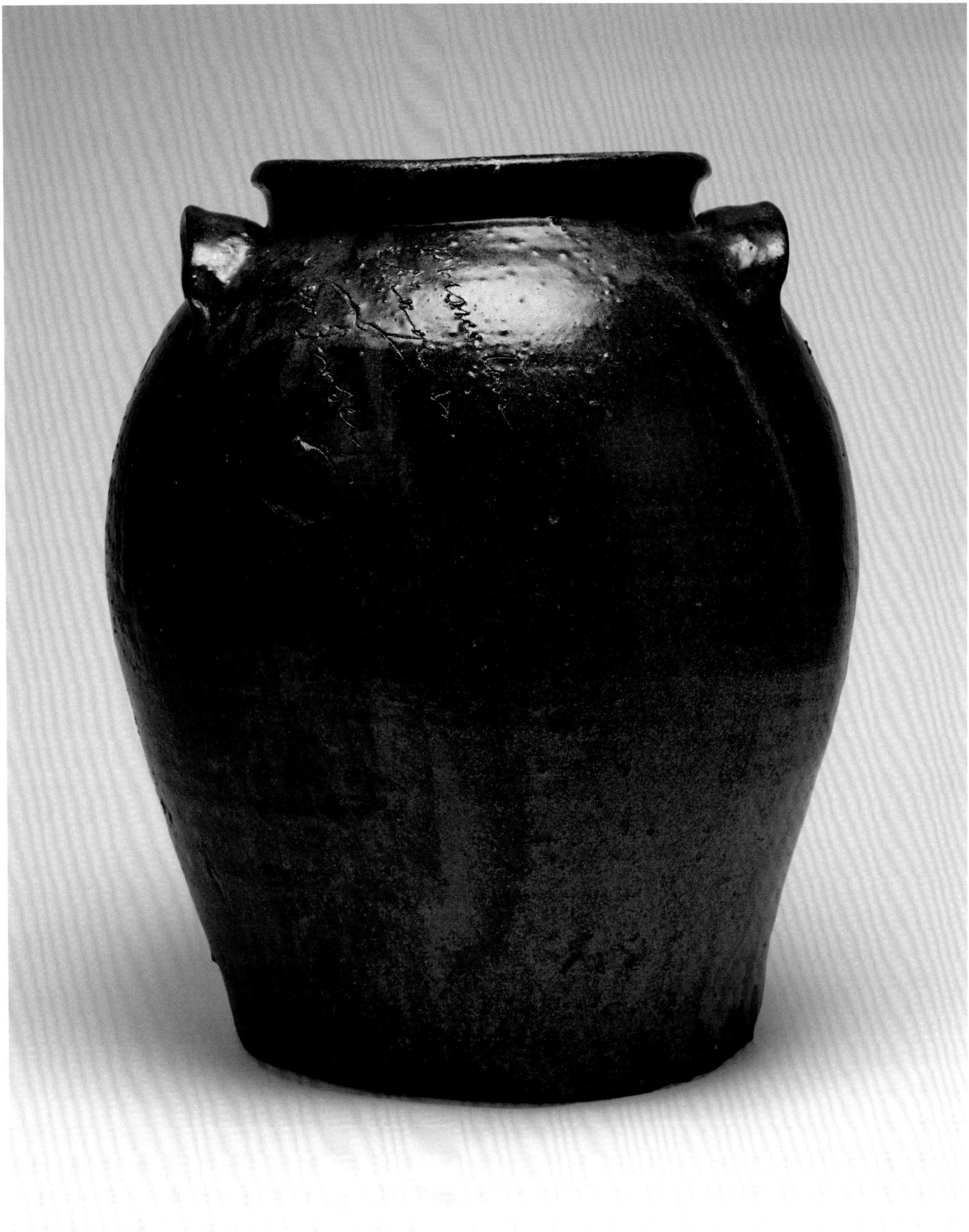

work us into such abstractions, but they can also help us to work our way out. Take, for example, three seemingly disparate objects that act as significant communicating events, which fully engage the cultural complexities invoked by Glassie and which have in common the cataclysmic consequences of rebellion: a storage jar by David Drake (fig. 2), a ceramic figurine made by an unidentified artist from Cochiti Pueblo (fig. 3), and a portrait by John Singleton Copley (fig. 4).

By the time that David Drake was born enslaved about 1800, his status as "slave" was hereditary for people of African descent. The decree was established after the terrifying uprising known as Bacon's Rebellion in Jamestown, Virginia, in 1676. Datable to events around Bacon's Rebellion, "race" thus had a much older history than either Drake or the country. The rebellion was sparked when two powerful Englishmen, Governor Sir William Berkeley and Nathaniel Bacon Jr., who was

FIGURE 2 David Drake (ca. 1800–ca. 1870; born possibly South Carolina; active Edgefield, SC), Storage jar, 1850s. Alkaline glazed stoneware; h. 38.1 cm, diam. 33 cm. Princeton University Art Museum. Museum purchase, Kathleen Compton Sherrerd Fund for Acquisitions in American Art (2019-263)

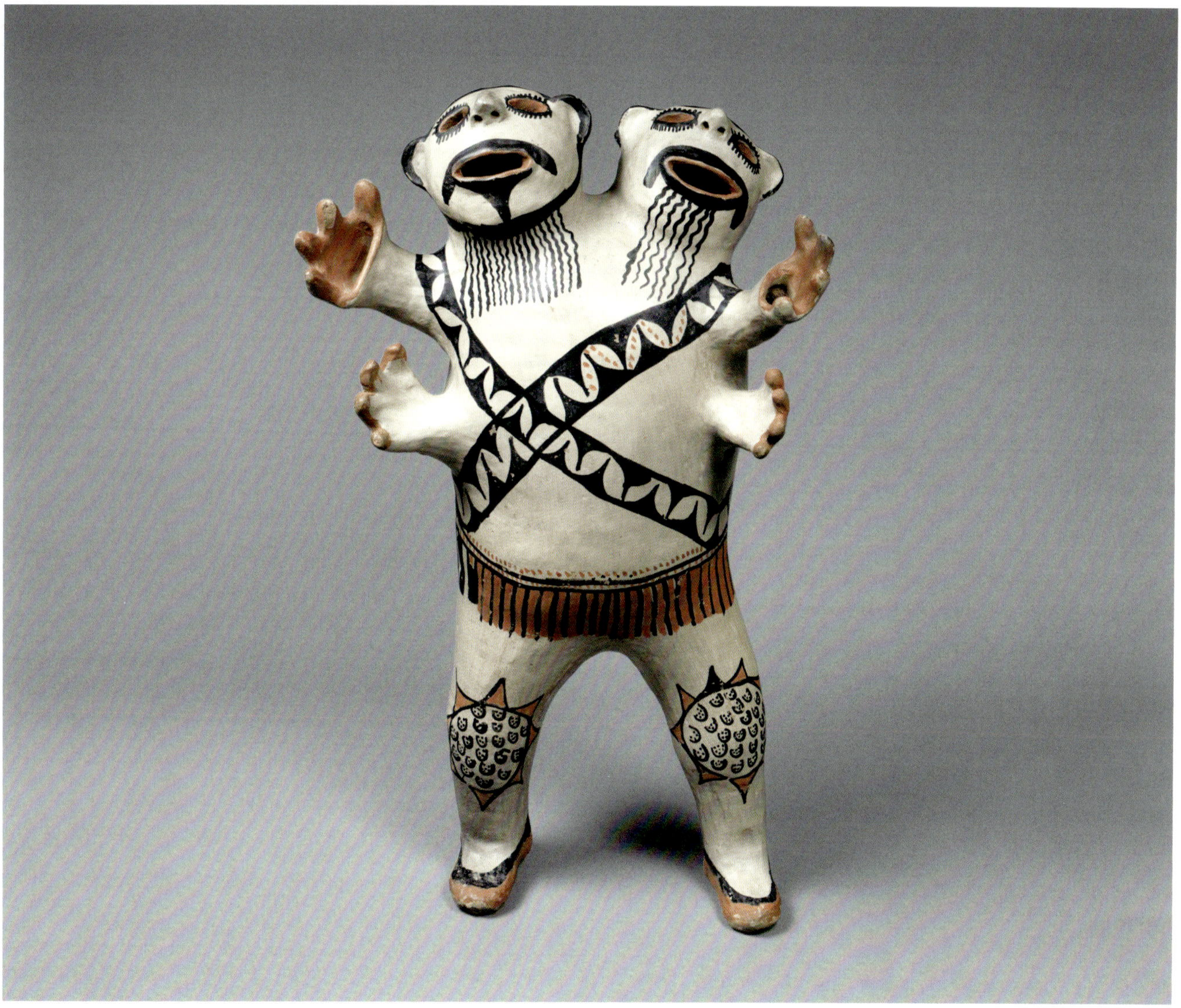

FIGURE 3 Cochiti Pueblo, New Mexico, Large two-headed, four-armed effigy figurine, ca. 1880. Ceramic with black and white slip, 63.5 × 39 × 21 cm. Princeton University. Department of Geosciences (PU 7413)

Berkeley's cousin by marriage, clashed.[10] There is a West African proverb, "When two elephants fight, it is the grass that suffers."[11] In July of 1675, members of the Doeg tribe raided the plantation of Thomas Mathews because of a financial dispute. In retaliation, Bacon raised a militia, illegally, and mistakenly attacked the Susquehanaug instead of the Doeg. Rather than stand down, Bacon used his militia to escalate his attacks, despite the existing treaties between the colony of Virginia and Native American nations. Bacon eventually used the militia to take Pamunkey land as well.[12] What was especially worrying to the ruling colonial elite was the composition of the militia itself: poor men and men who were both African and European serving their periods of indenture. They did the numbers and understood that poor people would always outnumber wealthy ones. In order to permanently divide the individuals who composed the militia, a series of privileges were instituted for men of European descent, while harsher strictures were placed on people of African descent. Until that point, enslavement was not hereditary for African people; however, after the alarming alliance of men who shared common grudges, social class, and material circumstances, a series of laws were put into place to divide them by race. Over the next thirty-five years, these laws allowed freemen to vote, limited the tenure that someone could serve in office, and offered English and Irish people (including bond-laborers) a number of benefits previously denied to them—while not extending those same benefits to African people. African people were no longer allowed to marry European people, and slavery was made hereditary through maternal lineage for people of African descent. Racism as practice was thus instantiated by law, even as "race" became the explanation for why natural rights and freedoms could only be extended to those deemed "White" but not to those who were now racialized as African/Negro/Black.[13] When the colonies broke away from England one hundred years later, "race" was still performing its dirty work of ameliorating class conflict and being deployed as the explanation for why a liberty-loving country would not extend those rights to free its enslaved population. Capitalist exploitation now had a reason and a powerful word that to this day we have yet to abandon.

In this context, the Princeton University Art Museum label for David Drake's storage jar is evocative. The man who was born enslaved, who labored for a White enslaver, and who outlived the condition of his bondage is known variously as David Drake (given name and a surname that implies a patronym passed down to members of a family rather than people who were for sale), Dave the Potter (given name and occupation), and Dave the Slave (given name and both legal and social status with an expectation of forced unpaid labor), but also as "American" (a designation that would never have been his even after his enslavement ended despite the passage of the Fourteenth Amendment that ostensibly granted citizenship to those formerly enslaved). Drake was active in the Edgefield District of west-central South Carolina (known as Pottersville) well into his seventies. He was trained in European forms of pottery by his enslaver, Abner Landrum, who by all accounts was something of a scientist when it came to the manufacture of stoneware, able to make it stronger and cheaper than his contemporaries. Landrum was also the publisher of the *South Carolina Republican*, later known as *The Hive*. He taught Drake to read and made him an apprentice to his newspaper business, where Drake also learned typesetting. Despite the strict slave codes of South Carolina, with its quotas around labor that ensured free White men were employed and the discouragement of teaching enslaved people to read, Drake made a name for himself (literally) with his storage jars that featured his signature, clever rhymes, verses, symbols, and sayings in addition to the markings that informed the purchaser how many gallons a jar could contain.[14] The storage jar in the Princeton collection measures fifteen by thirteen inches and is dated to the 1850s. It carries a horseshoe signature and an inscription down its shoulder, "Princeton / College in / New Jersey," along with markings that indicate it will hold five gallons. Drake's jars generally have slab handles around the rim for transporting and are wide at the shoulder. The bases of Drake's jars conform to the average dimension of twelve inches. Of the potters active in Edgefield at the time, Drake was known for his large-shouldered jars, which required both skill and

FIGURE 4 John Singleton Copley (1738–1815; born Boston, MA; died London, United Kingdom), *Elkanah Watson*, 1782. Oil on canvas, 149 × 121 cm. Princeton University Art Museum. Gift of the estate of Josephine Thomson Swann (y1964-181)

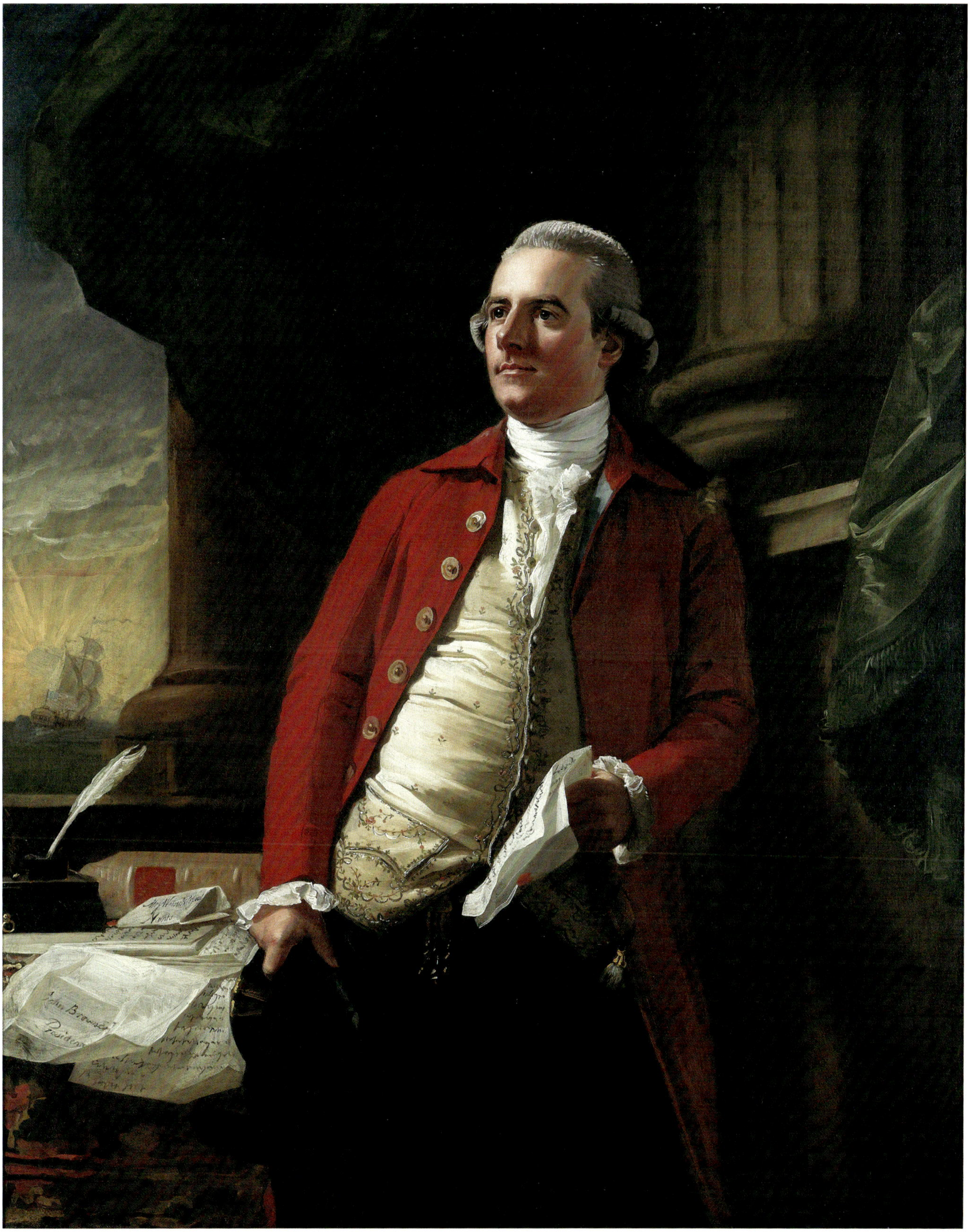

strength to create; his largest known jar holds more that forty gallons and as of 1978 was still the largest piece of nineteenth-century stoneware produced in the South.[15]

Drake's vocabulary was as extensive as his output. One of the first words that Drake is known to have inscribed on a jar is haunting. Resistance began at point of contact, and African people had never rested comfortably in the condition of ongoing and brutal capitalist exploitation. Even as the invention of "race" condoned the practice of "racism," which Bacon's Rebellion certainly facilitated and offered up as a repeated and repeatable solution to class turmoil, enslaved African people and their allies fought back. Therefore, during Drake's time as an enslaved laborer, we must count and credit a series of upheavals even as they worsened the conditions of enslaved people everywhere. Leonard Todd, whose family had enslaved Drake and who much later became Drake's biographer, notes three significant events that frame Drake's first inscribed word: the 1829 publication of David Walker's pamphlet entitled *Appeal to the Colored Citizens of the World*; the 1831 insurrection in Virginia led by Nat Turner; and in 1832, a slave rebellion in the British colony of Jamaica led by a Black Sunday school teacher. In each instance, literacy coupled with biblical imagery was used to support rebellion.[16] Walker, a free man of color, was considered especially dangerous because of his direct petition to "Colored Citizens of the World," since typically, White abolitionists communicated directly with and tended to prioritize the concerns of those who profited from the slave trade. As Todd contends, the slave rebellion in Jamaica "provided the final proof for [slaveholders] that religion plus literacy equaled rebellion. Nullifiers, still powerful, called for a sweeping new law to end slave literacy in South Carolina once and for all." On June 12, 1834, Drake inscribed the date on his jar but also, for the first time that we know of, a word—"Concatination" [*sic*]. Todd reveals, "Though he gave it an 'i' at its center rather than the usual 'e,' it comes from 'catena,' Latin for 'chain,' and means 'a linking together.' The first word that we have from Dave, then, refers at its root to the shackles that held slaves in bondage!"[17] Drake's first word may also be in reference to a "coffle," which signifies a group of prisoners, enslaved people, or animals chained or tied together in a line. Specifically, the slave-coffle was how slave traders and slave owners moved their human merchandise from one place to another (fig. 5). This would have been a common sight and form of transportation for the young man who was born enslaved. Less than two years later, he uses the word again but in a shortened form—"catination"—on the shoulder of another jar (fig. 6). With this word and in the wake of those significant uprisings, Drake signaled his subjectivity and his awareness of a larger human rights movement, and transmitted his demand to be recognized like a cry and an indictment; it is a hostage's note. Drake's object lesson for us? Never question his talent and *know* that "racism" rather than "race" made him a "slave."

Only four years separate Bacon's Rebellion from the Pueblo Revolt of 1680. Leading up to the event, the Spanish Empire deployed missionaries who invaded New Mexico and, with the sanction of corrupt governors, began to abuse and exploit First Nations peoples even as they converted as many as possible to Catholicism. Andrés Reséndez, in *The Other Slavery: The Uncovered Story of Indian Enslavement in America*, sheds new light

FIGURE 5 "A Slave-Coffle passing the Capitol," illustration in William Cullen Bryant, *A Popular History of the United States* (New York: Scribner, Armstrong, 1876–81). Wood engraving. Library of Congress, Washington, DC. Prints and Photographs Division

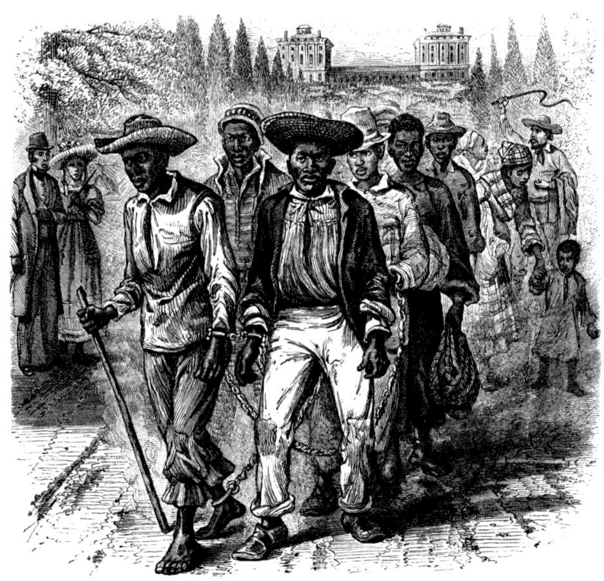

A Slave-Coffle passing the Capitol.

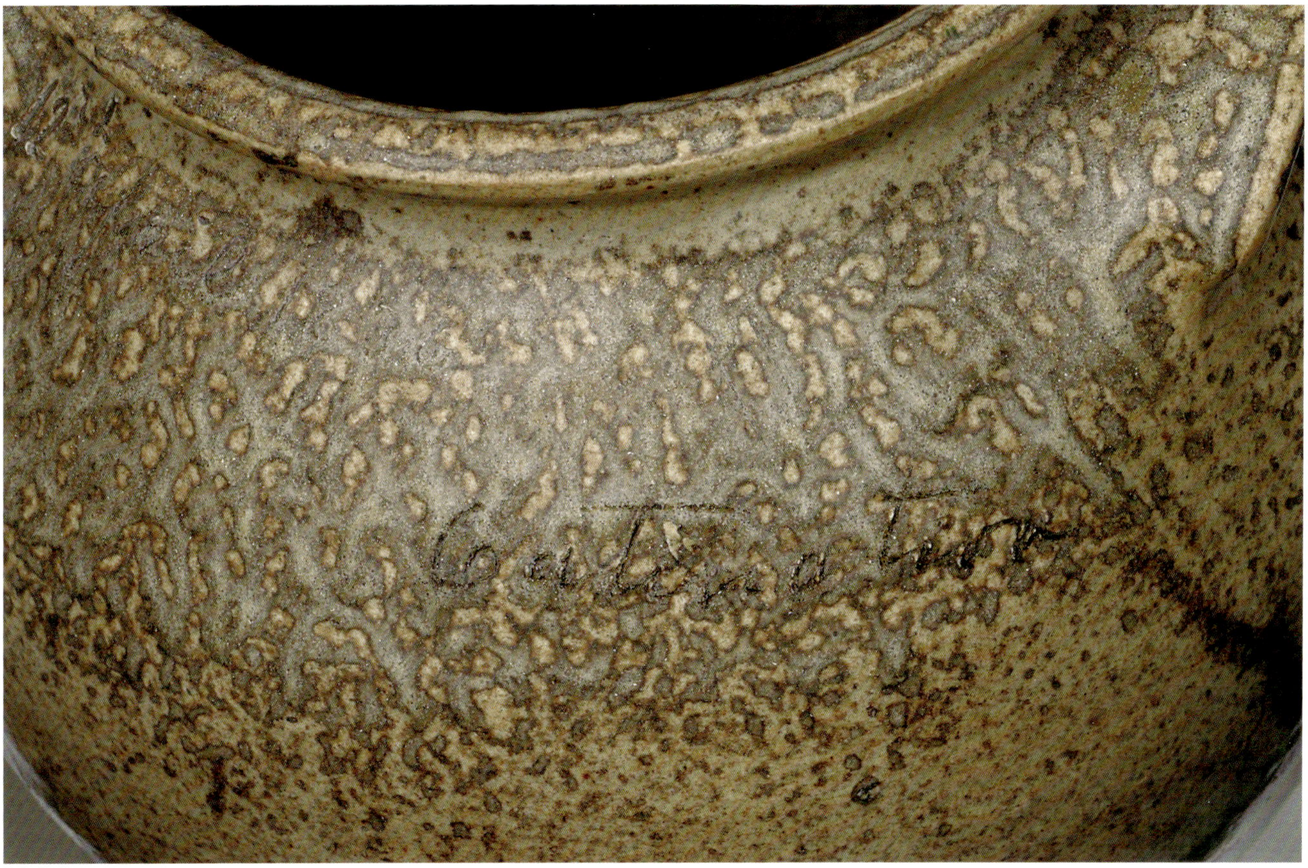

FIGURE 6 David Drake, Pottersville Stoneware Manufactory (1810–1850), "Catination" storage jar (detail), 1836. Glazed stoneware. Fine Arts Museums of San Francisco. Museum purchase, the Calvin L. Malone American Arts and Crafts Fund, the American Art Trust Fund, and the American Decorative Arts Endowment Income Fund (2020.57)

on the conditions that made what some characterize as a revolution rather than a revolt possible. Recent scholarship, he notes, explains the causes of the Pueblo Revolt as a combination of factors, "including short-term disruptions such as famines and epidemics and long-term or structural factors such as religious antagonism. But while all leading explanations are now multicausal, they continue to emphasize the religious character of the revolt."[18] While Reséndez does not minimize religion as a possible impetus for the revolt, he also finds increased exploitation of labor a major contributing factor, as New Mexico was integrated into the silver economy of northern Mexico. During the seventeenth century the silver economy expanded, as did New Mexico's role in the capitalist endeavors of empire. "It did not take the bad behavior of too many Spanish governors, friars, and colonists—compelling Indians to carry salt, robbing their pelts, locking them up in textile sweatshops, and organizing raiding parties to procure Apache slaves—to bring about widespread animosity, resentment, and ultimately rebellion," notes Reséndez.[19] He tests his theory of labor coercion as the main impetus by examining three types of evidence: testimonies of Pueblo rebels; the deepening of commercial ties between New Mexico and the silver mines of northern Mexico; and the ethnic and geographic scope of the insurrection.[20] The ancestral Pueblo were the only Indigenous peoples to successfully send their European invaders away, only to see them return twelve years later and with a vengeance. Nonetheless, because of the revolt, the terms of European occupation were forever changed, whether it was the Spanish, British, or US empires. The Pueblo Revolt helped to ensure the survival of Pueblo cultural traditions, lands, languages, religions, and sovereignty. There was also retention across time of specific pottery traditions among the Pueblos, like the figurine that is our next object lesson. Ironically, the cultural and political retentions that the revolt allowed for made and make the pueblos concentrated sites that invent and connect racialized identity objects to locations.

Two hundred years after the Pueblo Revolt, pueblos and reservations retained (and retain) their status as unceded territories and sovereign nations within the borders of the United States. In this context, an Indigenous artist from Cochiti Pueblo made the two-headed, four-armed figurine in the wake of yet another "invasion"—this time by tourists from the United States as part of the vigorous curio trade sparked by what Jonathan Batkin describes as the "emergence of Euro-American mercantilism in the West, completion of the transcontinental railroad and romantic notions of a vast, untamed wilderness" (see fig. 3).[21] With the signing of the Treaty of Guadalupe Hidalgo in 1848, the United States gained most of the lands ruled by the Spanish Empire and later by Mexico; and in September of 1853 with the Gadsden Purchase, New Mexico became a territory of the United States and was finally admitted to statehood in 1912. Faced with a succession of empires, First Nations peoples continued to fight for sovereignty, even as their linguistic, cultural, and national differences were collapsed and simplified so that they were racialized as "Indian." Depending on the sophistication of souvenir hunters, artifact collectors, and aesthetic shoppers, some travelers to reservations and pueblos, while not always caring about the name of the artist, do make a distinction between the Nations and the artistic treasures for which they are known. Like the Museum's label for Drake's storage jug, the label for the figurine is telling: "Cochiti Pueblo, New Mexico, Large two-headed, four-armed effigy figurine, ca. 1880." We have the name of the pueblo in place of the name of the artist, reflecting the priorities of the collectors who did not require the usual specificity when it comes to museum objects. The lack of specificity is reinforced by the collection in which the object is housed at Princeton. We learn from the label that it is made of ceramic with black and white slip (technically very difficult to do) and that it was lent to the Museum from the University's Department of Geosciences. When collected, the figurine was not categorized as art and was stored among other Native American artifacts. But, as scholars like Ruth B. Phillips argue, souvenirs are how identities are traded. Although her study is localized to the Northeast between 1700 and 1900, her argument is important to consider here. As she demonstrates, souvenirs were a source of economic and cultural survival for Indigenous peoples whose traditions and cultures were undergoing deliberate, concerted, and encompassing tactics labeled "extermination," sanctioned by the federal government and enacted through murder, reservationalization, boarding schools, literature, judicial processes, art, et cetera.[22] Noting that mythic or historical Indian figures were routinely associated with tourist sites through the recounting of historical vignettes and legends in guidebooks, postcards, and other media, sites of souveniring are as important as the identities that get traded.[23] Since the figurine's creation, scholarship has done much to animate the possibilities around meaning and how the object helped to shape relations between people and environment and between the maker and the market(place) of touristic desire and expectation of an "authentic" encounter.

The Southwest is different, nevertheless. While the Northeast must rely on ephemera to evoke the mythic or historical Indian figures, the Southwest "as site" is replete with the presence of Indigenous cultural production and authentic opportunities for acquisition. Photographs of inventories of collections replicate the sales tables for such figurines; for example, George Benjamin Wittick's photograph of pottery figures from the pueblos of New Mexico has behind it a background that simulates the Palace of the Governors, while the figurines rest on an artistically arranged piece of fabric (fig. 7). At the upper left of the photograph is a large ceramic that may very well be the Princeton figurine. Each of its twin heads has an elaborate mustache, a straggly beard, an open mouth, and eyes that are actual voids in the sculpture. The single body is crossed with bandoliers and has four arms that open wide and four hands with fingers that spread greedily.[24] Characterized in Museum materials as a "humorous, two-headed likeness of a white newcomer to the Southwest," sculptures like this one were sold to unknowing Anglo collectors "seeking 'Indian' curios." The juxtaposition of Anglo and Indian is here key to understanding the long process of racialization and the contingencies on which it relies ("Anglo" or "White" can only be meaningful in relation to "Indian") and how makers of souvenirs comprehend what is needed from them and what is expected of them. As Barbara Babcock writes, "Despite the diversity of whatever it is that we call Southwest, it is also apparent that there are key symbols, dominant tropes, and paradigmatic designs and colors that everyone recognizes, and that these are presently very marketable."[25] These symbols, dominant tropes, and paradigmatic designs are how "race" is fixed and reconfirmed within "things." The incredible feat of the Cochiti Pueblo figurine is that it multiplies and echoes what is traded and who gets traded (traited?). What is the lesson? The figurine evokes the seriousness of play, the deep attention to craft, and the emptiness of those who would consume "race" in the form of an object.

Our third rebellion fueled by capitalist exploitation takes place one hundred years after Bacon's Rebellion and almost one hundred years after the Pueblo Revolt. The American Revolution was sparked in part by the colonists' desire for more trade partners beyond Great Britain; debt incurred by the French and Indian War, which the monarchy used the colonies to finance through heavy taxation; and treaties made with First Nations peoples that halted westward expansion in exchange for their role in the success of Great Britain in the war against France. John Singleton Copley's portrait of the proud supporter of the American Revolution unintentionally inhabits the very tension that Robyn Wiegman wants to explore: the tensions that form and inform the aspirations and priorities of identity objects and the identity knowledges that they produce (see fig. 4). The portrait was a self-conscious and self-fashioned statement that sought to prioritize a nascent "Americanness." Portraits like that of Elkanah Watson produce their own feedback loops and ways of writing about them that are as normalized and ubiquitous as their existence. The biography of the sitter meets the biography of the artist; they have an encounter in which a likeness is produced; the biography of the sitter becomes the explanation of the portrait. The tautology is complete when an engraving of Copley's portrait was used as the frontispiece for the second edition of Watson's autobiography, *Men and Times of the Revolution; or, Memoirs of Elkanah Watson*, published in 1857 (as a point of interest, around the time that Drake made the storage jar in Princeton's collection).[26] Even as Watson celebrated the story of his liberation from a tyrannical empire, Drake was enslaved by the very entity that assured Watson of his freedom and belonging. What did Watson inherit from the previous rebellions? In part, he inherited the relational, performative, and participatory identity of "Whiteness" as "Americanness" that the portrait struggles so mightily to normalize and authenticate.

There is another word about which I teach my students in the vocabulary lesson. The word is "authenticity"

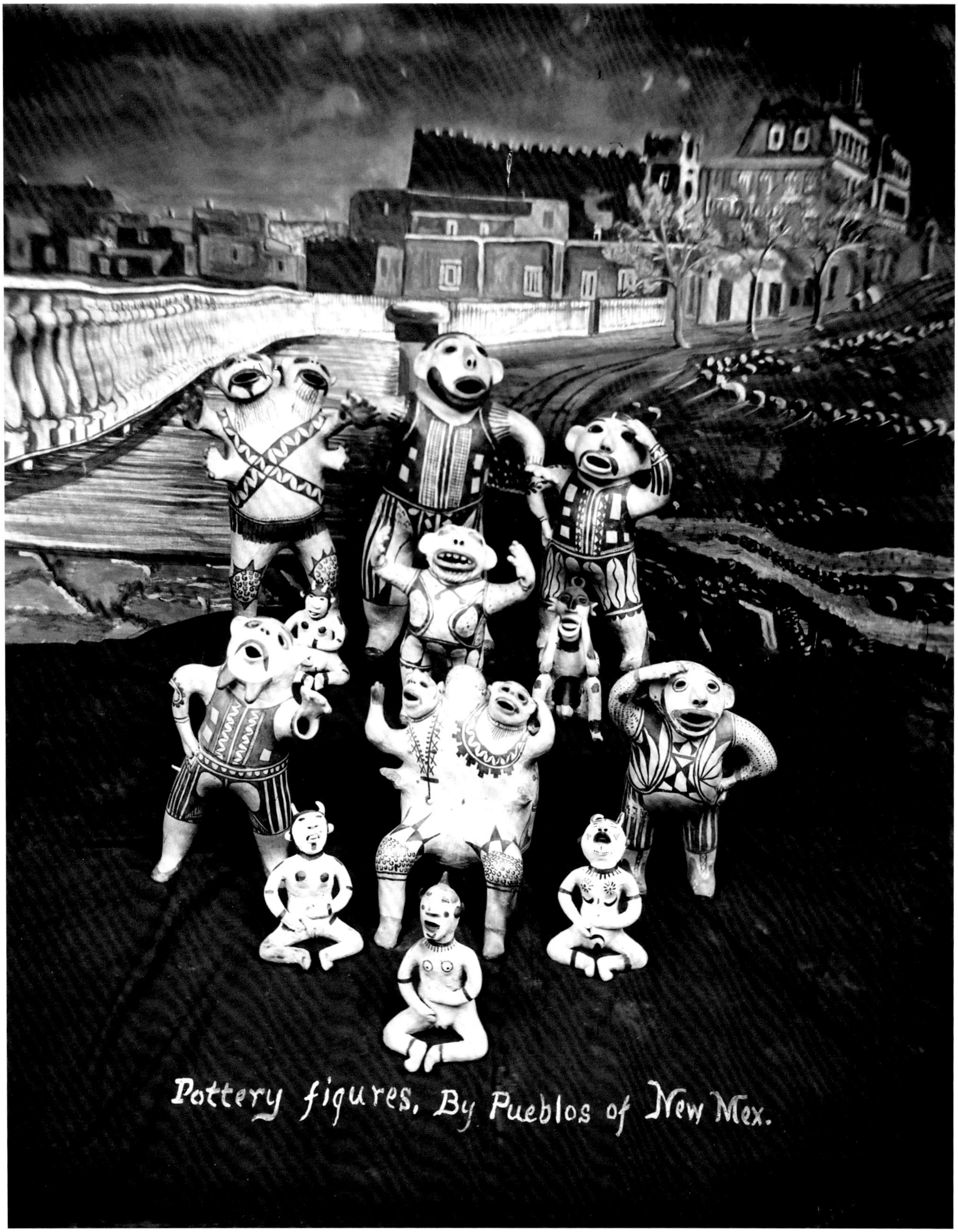

Pottery figures, By Pueblos of New Mex.

and its many derivations and how notions of the authentic rely on and attach to materials and objects. Drake's storage jar and the Cochiti Pueblo figurine are truly "vessels" in that regard, vessels that hold racial content and the racialized identities of their makers. "Place" is also a significant factor for each, Drake's "place" as an enslaved laborer not on a plantation but in a pottery factory and the Cochiti artist's place in the pueblo. They are also significant of place because work in clay is a form of landscape representation. Adolph Reed is clear about the function of the "authentic": "The idea of the authentic is always hortatory rather than descriptive. It is an attempt to impose a boundary on the intrinsically fluid, syncretic, pragmatic processes that are the substance of human social existence. Notions of cultural authenticity reify culture by construing it as a set of properties whose ownership is established by proof of origination (though 'cultural borrowing' may, in some tellings, confer rights of usufruct)."[27] The authentic, in effect, helps to construct identity objects that, through convention and repetition, present themselves as obvious and reducible to lists of attributes and traits as the origin of the authentic itself. The explanation is circular because in locating origins, the oppressive structures that give rise to identity objects are invariably elided. This is not to discount Drake's authorship and the value that his uniqueness holds for history, which is reflected in museum collecting practices. But the workings of authenticity can be less obvious in storage jars or in figurines mocking White souvenir hunting and tourism until we begin to understand how authorship becomes the content. In each instance, "White ownership" structures the "Blackness" or "Indianness" contained therein. Authenticity, as in Reed, seeks to persuade rather than describe; it is a strategy deployed to construct, police, and control boundaries of differentiation. All of which brings us back to the "portrait encounter" that is our third "object lesson"—this time, an encounter between an intrepid Irish English artist (twenty years older than his subject) and an English American businessman who was visiting England in 1782.

Theodore Allen begins volume one of his two-volume opus, *The Invention of the White Race*, with what he describes as "a long look into an Irish mirror" as the origin of the paramount issue in American history. According to Allen, "Irish history presents a case of racial oppression without reference to alleged skin color, or, as the jargon goes, 'phenotype.'"[28] Allen argues that, historically, racial oppression has always been an option rather than an inevitability and that at certain points in colonial and later US history could have been displaced but was renewed by deliberate ruling-class decisions. "Race" or "racial oppression" as a category of practice is what concerns him: "However one may choose to define the term 'racial,' it concerns the historian only as it relates to oppression (subordination, subjugation, exploitation) of one set of human beings by another."[29] He is unconcerned about assumptions of innate differences or feelings about superiority. Those don't define an oppressor, he argues. Racial slavery was an entrenched system of social control. Empire turned its hungry eyes to Ireland in the twelfth century, and between 1536 and 1691 Ireland was successfully colonized by first the English and later the British Empire.[30] Just as the English in colonial Virginia and the Spanish in colonial New Mexico transformed economic exploitation into racial(ized) oppression, the English in Ireland did the same and extended the treatment to the Irish in the colonies. Allen, in exploring the analogy as practice, suggests the Irish became the standard of savage or outlandish social behavior for interpreting African and Indigenous societies. Through the Empire's exploitation of Irish people, England had developed "race" without the convenience of "color." However, color would prove to be an invaluable instrument in transforming "racism" (as a category of practice) into the explanation of "race" as the reason for the severity of oppression once their oppression of the Irish reached the colonies. Ironically, resistance to oppression meant that the oppressed were disqualified from Christian civilization and it increased the severity of the oppression.[31]

Born into this context and to parents who were recent Irish immigrants to America (only three years

FIGURE 7 George Benjamin Wittick (1845–1903; born Huntington, PA; died Fort Wingate, NM), Pottery figures, Pueblos of New Mexico, ca. 1880–90. New Mexico History Museum, Santa Fe. Palace of the Governors Photo Archives, Ben Wittick Collection (130750)

before his birth in 1738), John Singleton Copley had a lot to prove. The small family settled in Boston, where Richard Copley worked as a tobacconist and Mary Singleton Copley raised their one and only child. By the mid-1740s, Richard was dead; and by 1748, Copley's mother had married Peter Pelham, who was an artist, engraver, and schoolmaster.[32] Copley had ambitions beyond his class, beyond his race, but not beyond his talent. Every face of an Englishman or woman whose likeness he took added to his cachet and propelled him toward something that he desired, which was to live his life in England and in the manner of an English gentleman. And he did exactly this in 1774. Thus, the Museum label for the portrait of Elkanah Watson is inadequate to the job of reflecting the complexities of the encounter and the men's various identificatory strategies: "John Singleton Copley, American" is not quite accurate, while the portrait sitter's name cannot encompass (although it pretends to do so) the intricacies of "distinctions, differentiations, and disidentifications" that it attempts to capture both for the subject *and* the artist. Like the storage jar and figurine, the (racial) content is in the object; but in the case of the portrait, the identities that get traded are Irish for English as Copley transgresses the boundaries of race(ism) and English for American as Watson takes on a new identity that is grounded (like Englishness) in both nation and race.

To return to our third rebellion, Kevin Phillips contextualizes the English Civil War (1640–1649; 1688), the American Revolution (1775–1783), and the US Civil War (1861–1865) as a series of conflicts among "Puritan cousins" and explores them as the pangs of Anglo-American expansion. Consistently, the outcomes saw Native Americans, African Americans, and Irish people as successive losers beset by the triumph of New England and the sequence of three phases of "Puritanism."[33] When Watson, the newly minted American, traveled to England, he stopped by the studio of the old Loyalist, who was by now enjoying life as an English gentleman. Watson commissioned Copley to paint his portrait, which is three-quarters length. He stands in a contrapposto pose while holding a sheaf of letters in his left hand and a tricorn in his right. He wears a fine red coat, a cream waistcoat, and a white shirt with an intricately tied cravat. And like the visionary he imagines himself to be (and certainly was), he stares with confidence into the future. There are also the usual massive columns, swirls of dramatic drapery, and, beyond the table filled with books and correspondence and an inkwell, a view out the window, where the sun creates a prismatic effect over a departing ship. Watson was particularly proud of that view, explaining, "The painting was finished in most admirable style, except the back-ground, which Copley and I designed to represent a ship, bearing to America the intelligence of the acknowledgment of independence, with a sun just rising upon the stripes of the Union, streaming from her gaff. . . . This was, I imagine, the first American flag hoisted in old England."[34] Directly below this patriot's view out the window is a piece of legible writing on one of the papers that cover the table—a signature from "John Brown / Providence." Between 1774 and 1779, Watson was indentured to Brown, who was a slave trader and merchant, and who was instrumental in the founding of Brown University (previously known as the College of Rhode Island), which now bears his family's name. Watson was active in all aspects of Brown's business, including the Atlantic slave trade. At the end of Watson's indenture, he continued as an employee in Brown's mercantile firm and, during the Revolutionary War, carried dispatches from Brown to Benjamin Franklin, who was in France working to secure French support in the war effort. During this period, Watson sat for Copley.

Certain of his own significance to history, Watson had begun writing his autobiography in 1821. His various careers and his vision for the new nation were certainly impressive: he was a developer, helping to dispossess and secure for the government in New York land originally owned by the Iroquois nation but lost to them with the defeat of the British Empire; he proposed the creation of the Erie Canal and formed a company to build it; he founded the State Bank of Albany; he traveled extensively; and, in his waning years, he turned to agricultural pursuits before his death in 1842. As an "American," Watson remains clear in his writings about his opinions of "Negroes" and "Indians." He generally characterized enslaved Black people as naked and uncivilized.[35] His opinion of First Nations peoples was no better. In September of 1788, Watson, representing the interests of the state of New York, met Peter Ostequett,

Chief of the Oneidas, who during treaty making signed away the Oneida portion of eight million acres of land between Lake Ontario and the Susquehanna River. The Oneidas and the Onondagas received in return a promise to share one hundred square miles of land, to retain fishing and hunting rights everywhere, to reserve large swaths of land along the rivers to use as they would, and to receive one thousand French crowns in money, two hundred pounds in clothing, and an annuity of five hundred dollars in silver that could be paid in the value of clothing. Of course, what the Oneidas understood was different from what the government intended. New York officials later pretended that they had purchased exclusive ownership of the land and that the people could be removed whenever necessary.[36] About Ostequett, Watson wrote,

> A young Indian, named Peter Ostequett, a Chief of the Oneidas, was attending this Treaty. He had just returned from France, having been in that country for several years, under the patronage of the Marquis de La Fayette, by whom he was taken when a boy. He is probably the most polished and best educated Indian in North America. He speaks both French and English, correctly; is familiar with music and many branches of polite and elegant literature; and, in his manners, is a well-bred Frenchman. He is, however, a striking instance of the moral impracticability of civilizing an Indian. There appear to exist natural impediments to their amelioration. While visiting the Catawba Indians, a year since, I became acquainted with a young Indian, who had been educated at a prominent college; but had already fallen into the degradation of his native savage habits, and was to all intents an Indian. It is noticed that each year, in its progress, wears off the European polish of Ostequett, and brings him nearer to the savage.*
>
> *I have since been assured, by a young gentleman who knew Ostequett near the close of his life, that he actually degenerated below the ordinary level of savages. His refined education in France, commencing when a boy, had divested him of those masculine virtues which are engrafted on the Indian character. Having lost these, he possessed no high qualities to su stain him, and, abandoning himself to the bottle, he ultimately became a vagabond.[37]

You don't clear the forests once. You must keep clearing them so that civilization can thrive. Like forests, the process of civilizing "Indians" must be sustained and never ending lest the veneer of progress peel away, leaving only the savage. Even as Copley's Watson stands complete in his racial certainty, Watson's autobiography must do the work of differentiation, disidentification, and distinction that defines and racializes the uncivilized "negroes" and "Indians" who populate his adventures. While Watson's "rebellion" may have made him into an "American," African Americans and Native Americans were left in a permanent state of non-belonging and no-place through theft and dispossession.

LANDSCAPE AS IDENTITY OBJECT

Because you don't clear the forests once, here are two propositions: we must extend our conceptualization of the "colonial period" to encompass the US government's relations and actions around Indigeneity, territorial expansion, racialization, conquest, labor exploitation, and extermination; and we must consider the role that landscape representation played (plays?) in the translation of concepts such as identity, citizenship, and belonging, as well as the "not there" (having no legally defined presence on or right to property) and the "nowhere" (land that has yet to be commodified) and "no one" (designated as neither alien nor citizen) according to national priorities. Place does not produce nor confirm identity. However, in any given context, our spatial relations can tell us about our social relations relative to gendered, classed, and racialized hierarchies. In the imperial project of US formation, the first quarter of the nineteenth century marked two watershed moments, each codified in landscape representation: the Doctrine of Discovery deployed by the Supreme Court to transfer land from First Nations peoples to the federal government; and the beginning of domestic tourism. (The frontier was a much older invention that morphed into something new with the embrace of Manifest Destiny.)[38] In their essay "Beyond 'Identity,'" Brubaker and Cooper warn against the temptation to view place as identity object or view place as the thing that produces identities,

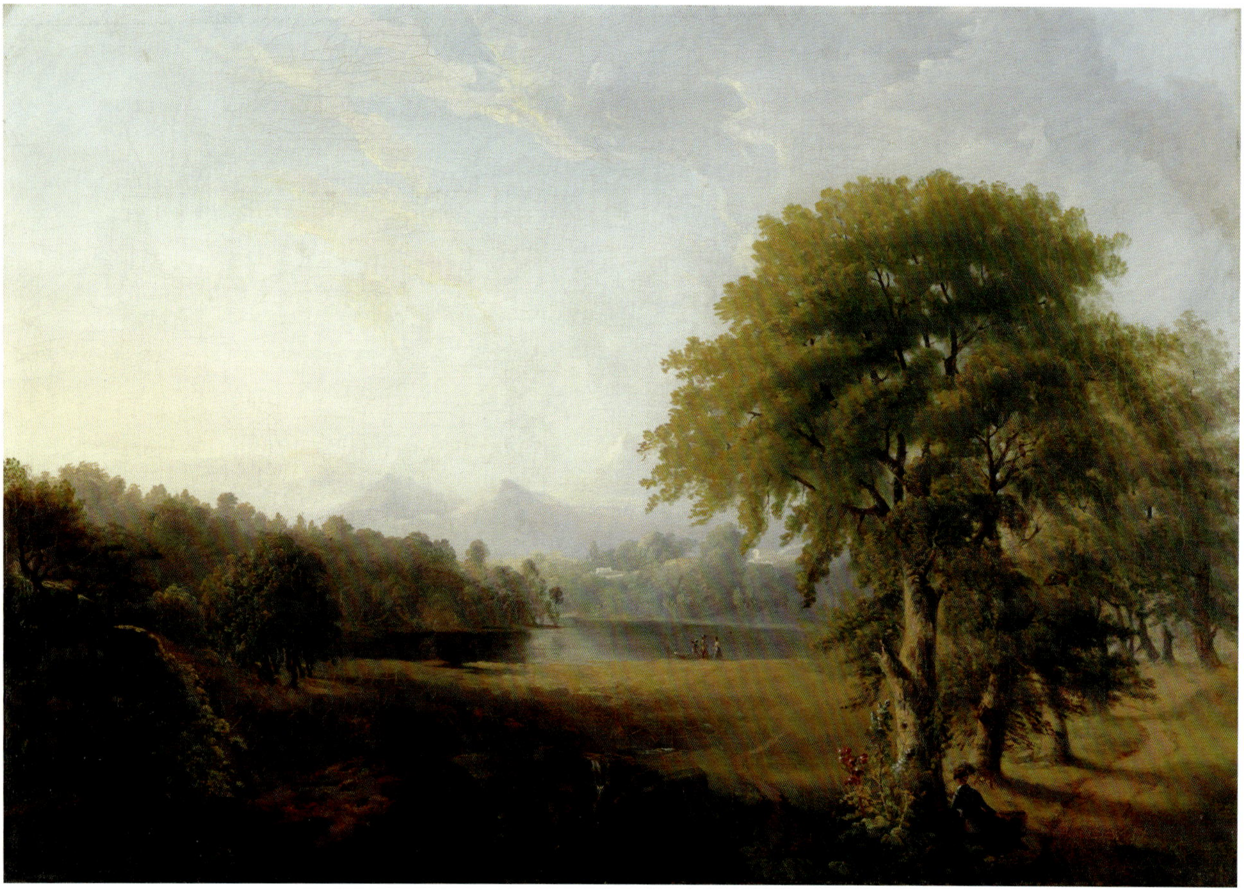

FIGURE 8 Robert Seldon Duncanson (1821–1872, born Fayette, NY; died Detroit, MI), *Untitled (Landscape)*, late 1850s. Oil on canvas, 61 × 66 cm. Princeton University Art Museum. Museum purchase, Kathleen Compton Sherrerd Fund for Acquisitions in American Art and Mary Trumbull Adams Art Fund (2011-107)

which is the exact work that landscape representation asks us to do: "To a greater extent than the forms of domination that preceded it, colonial rule attempted a one-to-one mapping of people with some putatively common characteristic onto territory. These imposed identifications could be powerful, but their effects depended on the actual relationships and symbolic systems that colonial officials—and indigenous cultural entrepreneurs as well—had to work with, and on countervailing efforts of others to maintain, develop, and articulate different sorts of affinities and self-understanding."[39] The caution that Brubaker and Cooper inveigh against colonial rule's attempts at a "one-to-one mapping of people with some putatively common characteristic onto territory" is what makes Robert Seldon Duncanson's landscape in Princeton's collection extraordinary—and the painter himself extraordinarily perspicacious (fig. 8).

Born a free man of color in Fayette, New York, Robert Seldon Duncanson (1821–1872) worked as a house painter before moving to Cincinnati, Ohio, which was known both for its dynamic art scene and as a hub of antislavery activity. Influenced by the Hudson River School of American artists, Duncanson's successes included an 1850 commission to paint a series of murals in what is now the Taft Museum of Art in Cincinnati. Duncanson also toured his landscape paintings throughout Europe. His large-scale masterwork, *Land of the Lotus Eaters*, inspired by Alfred Lord Tennyson's poem, was purchased by the King of Sweden, and won praise from Tennyson himself. The significance of landscape representation can be measured by how few people of color and White women were known as landscape artists. Landscape representation was largely restricted to those who could understand it aesthetically (as symbol) and

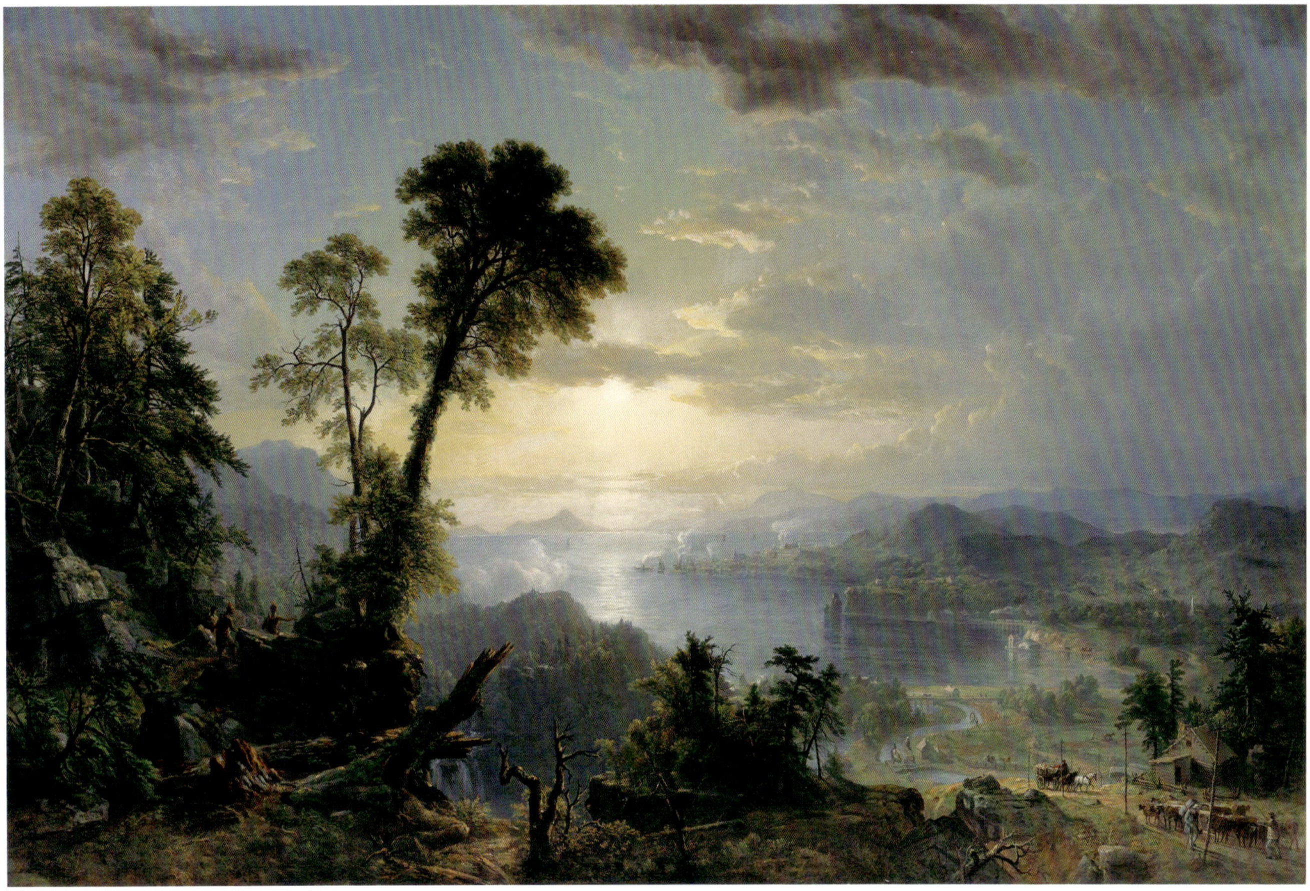

FIGURE 9 Asher B. Durand (1796–1886; born Jefferson, NJ; died Maplewood, NJ), *Progress (The Advance of Civilization)*, 1853. Oil on canvas, 148.4 × 208.9 cm (framed). Virginia Museum of Fine Arts, Richmond. Gift of an anonymous donor (2018.547)

who could own it outright (as resource). During the nineteenth century, property ownership was predominantly White and male, as were artists. Landscape was also how the nation represented itself to itself; the nation's territorial ambitions, its normalization of extermination and labor exploitation, and its ability to "sell" the West to the public are just some of the burdens placed on landscape. It is why scholars like W. J. T. Mitchell name the function of landscape as an instrument and agent of power and ask us to expand our understanding of it not as a noun but as a verb and as a process rather than a thing.[40] Duncanson's landscape is a serene rendering structured along the traditional lines of landscape, with a foreground, middle distance, and background. The eye is directed to a central lake that is a gathering place for three figures who are symbolically colored black, red, and white. They are not separated and segregated to parts of the space rendered "obvious" by conventions that associated the figures as identity objects locatable to place. There are no plantations (inhabited by the enslaved), nor wildernesses (with Indians vanishing into the distance of prehistory), nor bustling towns (busily traversed by White settlers). Instead, Duncanson presents us with landscape as a shared space, a space of interchange rather than conflict, a "peaceable kingdom" for humanity. By contrast, Asher Brown Durand's contemporaneous landscape fulfills the more popular function of the genre, which was to aestheticize belonging for some and normalize extermination and labor for others.

Asher Brown Durand (1796–1886) had a storied career. A self-proclaimed successor to Thomas Cole, Durand also served as president of the National Academy of Design in New York. He is perhaps best known for two works: *Kindred Spirits* (1849), which represents the friendship to be found in nature and between the poet

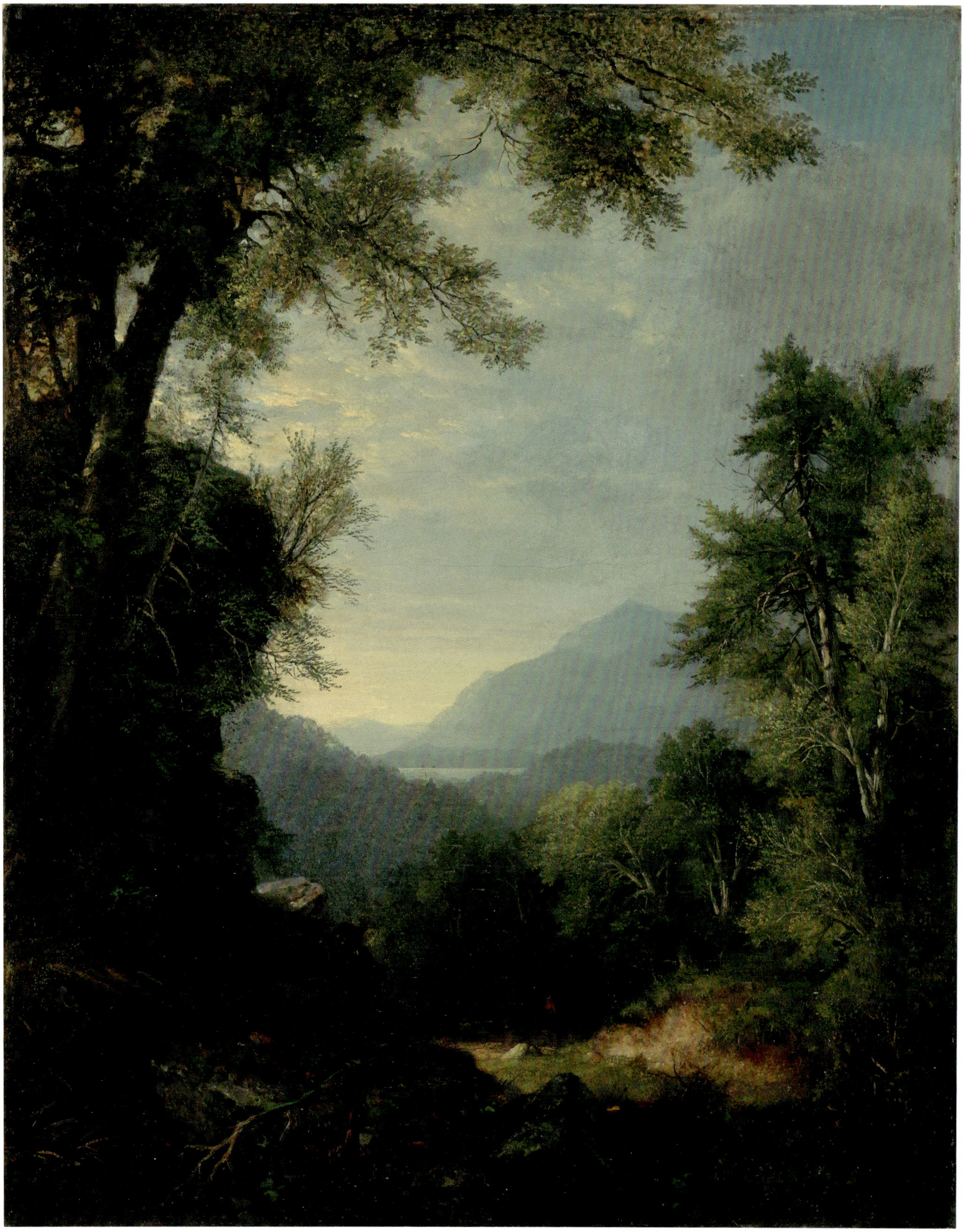

William Cullen Bryant and the painter Thomas Cole; and *Progress (The Advance of Civilization)* (fig. 9). *Progress* puts Manifest Destiny on full display: "Indians" occupy the wilderness in the left foreground, while a log cabin built by a White man occupies the right foreground. In front of the cabin, oxen are being moved, a wagon is bringing supplies, and a reference to Thomas Cole's famous "Oxbow" painting is just to the left of what will be a bustling town. In the middle distance, trains, factories, a harbor, and a city represent the fulfillment of the two opposing scenes in the foreground. Durand's landscape in Princeton's collection is more subtle but no less nationalistic (if we define nationalism—a category of practice—by who is excluded). Into the moody wilderness of Durand's 1859 *Landscape* (fig. 10), a figure clothed in symbolic red (shirt), white (hat), and blue (pants) walks purposefully into a dense massing of trees. But we know the outcome of this story; in his wake will be "civilization." Such representations of nationalistic aesthetics were accompanied by the theory and practice of "associationism," which Angela Miller so helpfully recovers. "Through the second quarter of the nineteenth century," she writes, "the associational power of images reinforced a developing nationalist ideology. While preserving nature's totemic function, it simultaneously placed it in service of the powerful colonizing energies of American settlement and industry by linking landscape to a specific cultural narrative. . . . The primary tenet of associationism was that aesthetic pleasure proceeded not from the inherent qualities of images but from the ideas attached to them." Those who were equipped to have an aesthetic experience of and in the landscape (whether painted or in nature and understood to be White and male) could thereby translate visual experience into "social and moral values."[41] Landscape/property was therefore vested with nationalistic and racializing imperatives and filled with empathetic exchanges and reciprocities that excluded the nation's original inhabitants from identification with their own land.

Property, however, was no settled matter during the first quarter of the nineteenth century. Eric Cheyfitz finds parity in two pieces of writing from two separate narrative traditions, one judicial ("legal fiction," as he describes it) and the other fiction. In his essay "Savage Law," Cheyfitz maintains that the Supreme Court's ruling in *Johnson and Graham's Lessee v. M'Intosh* and James Fenimore Cooper's *The Pioneers* ground both of their imperialist claims on the disappearance of the "other," which necessitated the construction of First Nations peoples as undifferentiated "Indians," as "absolutely oppositional, completely homogeneous, and ultimately superfluous figure, rather than as figures in a possible dialogue of equals, figures with which one is implicated."[42] Such a position is made clear in Elkanah Watson's writings; his contempt for the enslaved and his work in the slave trade; and his efforts in the dispossession of First Nations peoples' land. Watson was an effective agent of political, cultural, and social contempt and exploitation. "This is the moment when," Cheyfitz continues, "in 1823, the genre of the Western . . . and the edifice of federal Indian law first appear as distinct yet . . . interlocking and inseparable institutions."[43] From there, Cheyfitz identifies the historical narrative and "legal fiction" of the Doctrine of Discovery, in which the federal government grounds its claim to transfer and hold title to Indigenous lands. As the Doctrine elucidates, only Europeans are capable of acts of discovery even as it distorts and misrepresents Indigenous understandings of property, kinship structures, and title. Indigenous peoples were acknowledged to "be here" but to be nonexistent before the law. The distortion of Native American kinship structures, the misrepresentation of their understanding of land, and the invention of "discovery" as a state only available to Europeans were a violent translation that I would argue extends to landscape representation, despite the benignity of their appearance (or perhaps because of it). Throughout the nineteenth century, and on both sides of a tumultuous civil war, landscape continued its work as the handmaid of imperialism because of artists like Albert Bierstadt (1830–1902). Bierstadt was born in Germany and his parents immigrated to the United States when he was one. He studied painting in Düsseldorf, showed work at the National Academy of Design, ran a photography business with his brother in Virginia, and was renowned as a major interpreter of western landscapes. Bierstadt accompanied

FIGURE 10 Asher B. Durand, *Landscape*, 1859. Oil on canvas, 77 × 61.5 cm. Princeton University Art Museum. Gift of J. O. MacIntosh, Class of 1902 (y1955-3249)

several survey parties in the exploration of the West and Canada. His sketches and paintings provided the necessary aesthetic gloss of expansion, which meant careful distortions and manipulations to create the most convincing experience rather than the most accurate. W. J. T. Mitchell once described landscape as the "dreamwork of imperialism," and Bierstadt makes it apparent.[44] In *Mount Adams, Washington* from 1875 (fig. 11), like other landscapes that include them, Bierstadt depicts Native Americans as unsettled and on the move. In this fantastical rendering of the land, Native Americans are there but not for long. Painted to attract the patronage of Jay Cooke, developer of the Northern Pacific Railway, Bierstadt's rendering of Mount Adams represents the prehistory of the country. Like the landscape, the "Indians" are the unfinished business of empire; they are placeholders and a promise to the White landowners to come. Here, the painter's brush stands in for a reconstructed army, which now included Black soldiers, and for armed settlers who, through violent conflict, would sweep Indigenous peoples away in government-sanctioned extermination policies to uphold the nation's investment in "property" as a racialized weapon of removal.

I close this section with a contemporary landscape representation made by an artists' collective formed in 2007 by Raven Chacon (Diné), Cristóbal Martínez (mestizo of the Genízaro, Pueblo, Manito, and Chicano people of Northern New Mexico), and Kade L. Twist (Cherokee). Postcommodity describe their practice as rooted in Indigenous futurism to create work that is unified in vision and voice. In recognition of the past and the various processes of economic, social, and cultural efforts that have destabilized communities and geographies, their work offers alternatives for our shared present and future survival. As their name suggests, they envision a future beyond capitalism, beyond the forces that made David Drake a "slave," beyond that which inspired the painfully humorous Cochiti figure, and beyond that which made Elkanah Watson a cruel and rapacious predator of African labor and Indigenous lands. They offer a healing similar to that envisioned by Duncanson, I believe. Postcommodity's installation from 2015 is titled *Repellent Fence / Valla Repelente* (fig. 12) and was made of twenty-six helium-filled balloons that they floated at regular intervals along a two-mile line perpendicular to and crossing the border near Douglas, Arizona, and Agua Prieta, Sonora. With thirteen balloons situated in the United States and thirteen in Mexico, they highlighted the arbitrariness of geopolitical borders and the harm that those borders wreak on the environment. Each balloon is ten feet in diameter and colored a bright yellow with a glaring eye on four sides of the structure, replicating an ineffective bird-repellent product but on a scale that is outsized. The regular intervals and repetition of forms created a menacing and watchful presence over the landscape. Moreover, the symbolism of the eye was not empty (like that of the Cochiti figurine); the artists explain that they used imagery long associated with Indigenous spiritual power in the Americas.[45]

Postcommodity's twenty-six helium balloons also evoke the discovery of the horizon, first in nautical terms that made the "discovery" of the "New World" possible and that later served as the organizing principle for the very landscape representations that worked to make extermination achievable. Stephan Oettermann in *The Panorama: History of a Mass Medium* affirms, "It is no accident that the discovery of the horizon and the first successful balloon flights occurred at about the same time. One could almost believe the balloonists' ascents were fueled by people's craving to experience the horizon."[46] One year after Elkanah Watson sat for his portrait, the first officially confirmed flight of an unmanned hot-air balloon took place in France on June 5, 1783. Named after its inventors, the brothers Joseph-Michel and Jacques-Étienne Montgolfier, the *montgolfière* symbolized yet a new era and yet another type of conquest—this time of the sky (fig. 13). In nautical terms, the horizon provided sailors with a way of fixing their position and thus offered precision in navigation. The "variable constant" of the horizon "enables sailors to take a 'piece of home' with them everywhere, so to speak. If what lies beyond the horizon is unknown and frightening, then by implication everything enclosed by it is familiar and not threatening."[47] The technology of the hot-air balloon aided in strategies for stitching together multiple views and reconciling them along one horizon line so that it appears to be unified and persuasive and familiar. In a haunting echo of the promise of the horizon line, Postcommodity states that it is

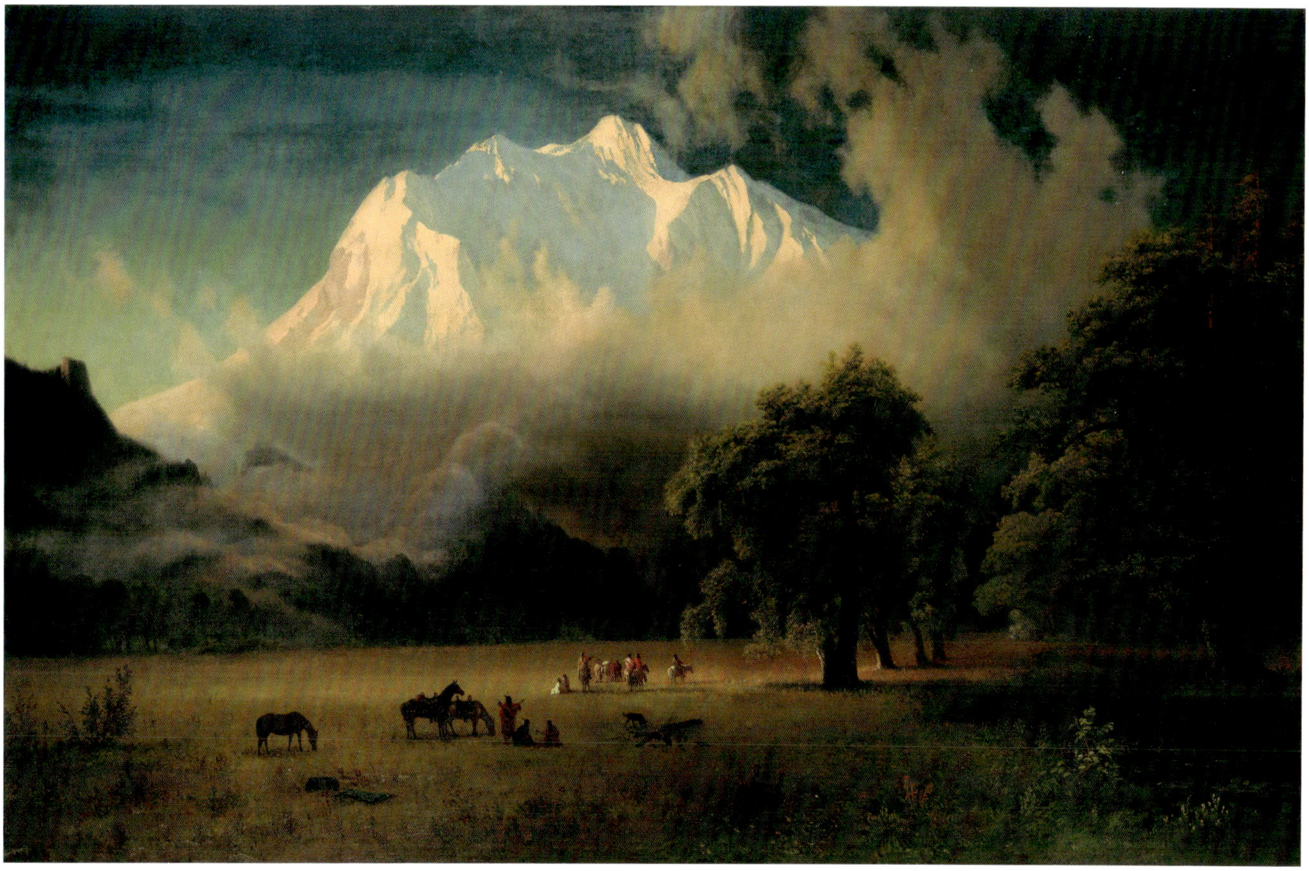

FIGURE 11 Albert Bierstadt (1830–1902; born Soligen, Germany; died Irving, NY), *Mount Adams, Washington*, 1875. Oil on canvas, 138 × 213 cm. Princeton University Art Museum. Gift of Mrs. Jacob N. Beam (y1940-430)

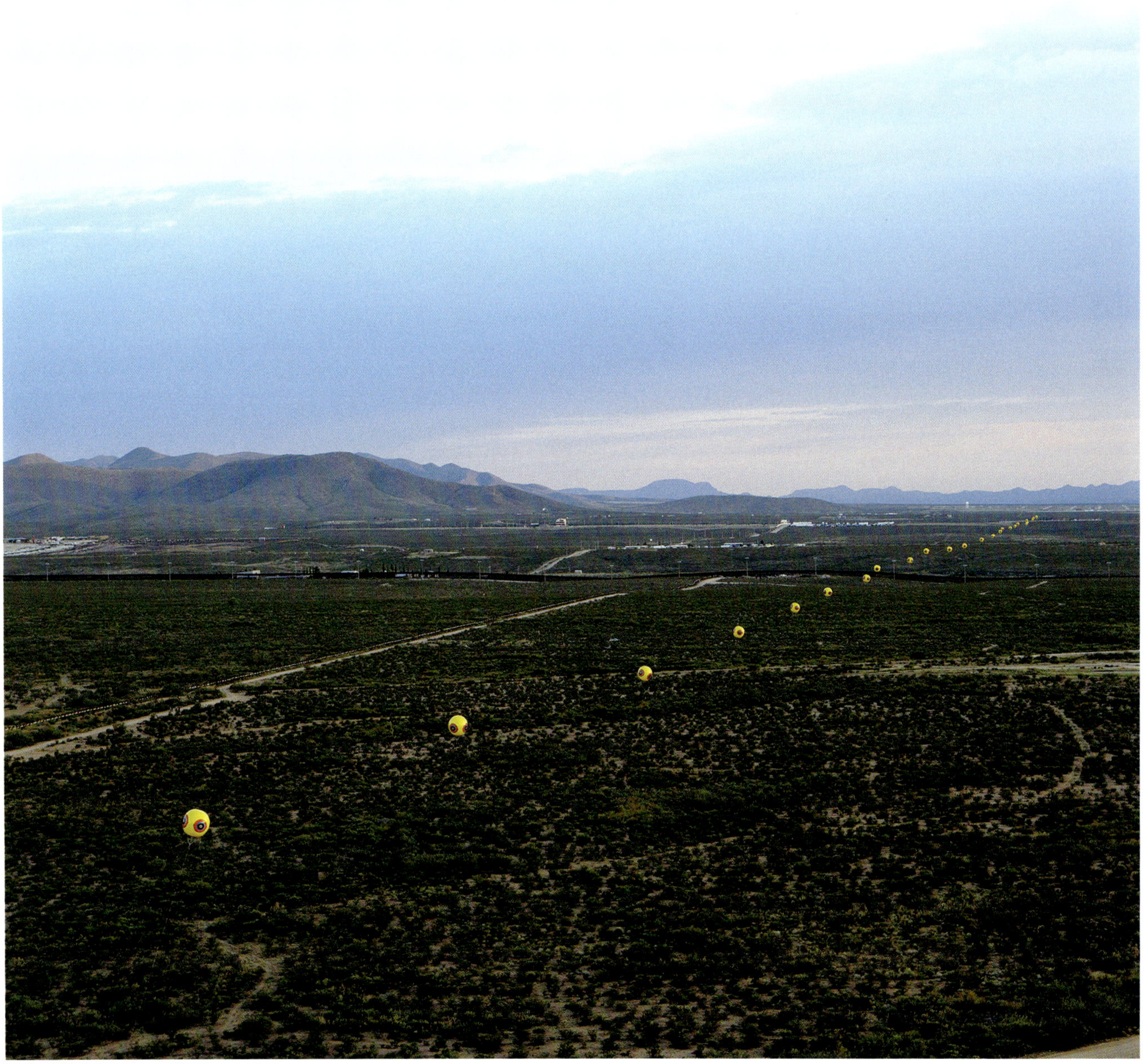

FIGURE 12 Postcommodity (active 2007–), *Repellent Fence / Valla Repelente*, 2015. Installation view at the US-Mexico Border, Douglas, Arizona–Agua Prieta, Sonora, 2015. Courtesy of Postcommodity and Bockley Gallery, Minneapolis

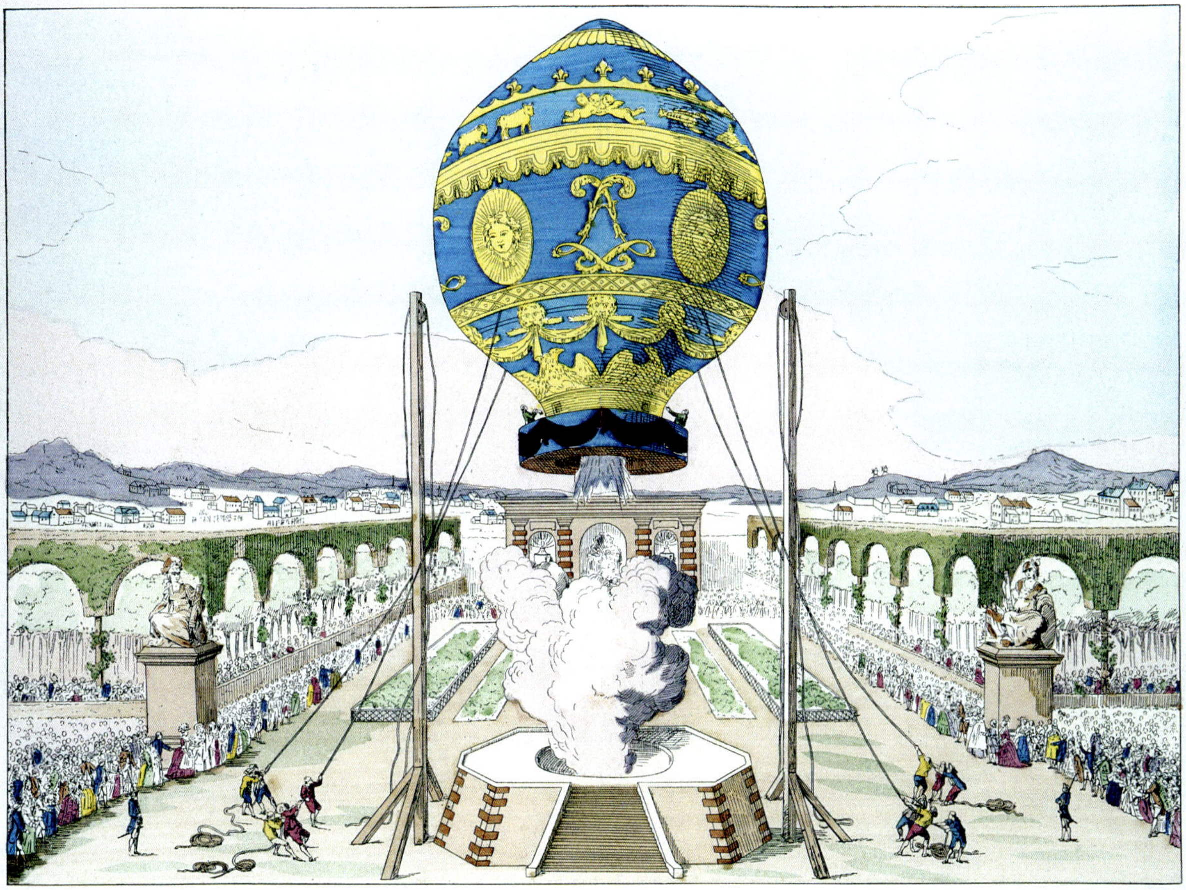

ASCENSION CAPTIVE EXÉCUTÉE PAR PILÂTRE DE ROZIER DANS LE JARDIN DE RÉVEILLON AU FAUBOURG SAINT-ANTOINE A PARIS, LE 17 OCTOBRE 1783.

FIGURE 13 Jean-François Pilâtre de Rozier (1754–1785), *Ascent in a tethered balloon at the Jardin de Réveillon, Paris, October 17, 1783*, illustration in Gaston Tissandier, *Histoire des ballons et des aéronautes célèbres: 1783–1800*, vol. 1 (Paris: H. Launette & Cie, 1887)

their purpose to "bi-directionally reach across the U.S./Mexico border as a suture that stitches the peoples of the Americas together—symbolically demonstrating the interconnectedness of the Western Hemisphere by recognizing the land, indigenous peoples, history, relationships, movement and communication."[48] One could argue that the horizon line was as revolutionary as one-point perspective. Certainly, horizons functioned in landscapes of the "untamed" West to render them as panoramic perspectives. Even as nineteenth-century landscape enacts strategies of differentiation, disidentification, and distinction that render First Nations peoples temporary subjects, Postcommodity refuses that erasure. They refuse borders and, in a powerful move, relocate Indigeneity to the sky with the intention and attention to heal the damage that the horizon line and the panorama helped facilitate. As Timothy Mitchell instructs, "Colonising refers not simply to the establishing of a European presence but also to the spread of a political order that inscribes in the social world a new conception of space, new forms of personhood, and a new means of manufacturing the experience of the real."[49] "Race" as identity object remains a series of deliberate choices rather than inevitable; it created and creates new forms of personhood and manufactures and conditions how we experience reality. The British, Spanish, and US colonizing experiments gave us identity objects (individuals who must conform to the narrowest of subject positions) in the form of "White people," "slaves," and "Indians" and fixed them to and in "place." We remain in an ongoing struggle and negotiation with imperialism and its disciplinary powers.

"FAMILY LORE ABOUT RACISM AND PROPERTY . . ."

It is fitting to conclude with Princeton's own bit of institutional family lore about racism and property. In the recent reckoning that colleges and universities are conducting through Land and Labor Acknowledgments as well as ongoing efforts to recover histories of their various entanglements with extermination and enslavement, Princeton is to be lauded for its self-exploration.[50] Understanding the compelling nature of the visual, Princeton has also opened its art collection for reconsideration through exhibitions and through single works of art. One such opportunity was the commissioning of a contemporary artist of African descent to directly engage a work in the collection. Titus Kaphar (1976–) was born in Kalamazoo, Michigan, and received his BFA from San José State University and MFA from Yale University. Given his interest in history and his captivating reinterpretations of historical subjects such as Thomas Jefferson and Sally Hemings, Kaphar was uniquely suited to the project. After exploring the archives, Kaphar chose the portrait of Princeton's fifth president, Samuel Finley, painted by Charles Walker Lind after the eighteenth-century original by John Hesselius (fig. 14). Lind's copy was created in 1870 (around the time of David Drake's death). Finley (re)appears as the somber minister that he was, with white wig and collar. President of Princeton from 1761 to 1766, Finley was a theologian, a scholar, and an enslaver. Some of those in bondage to him worked at Maclean House, the president's campus residence. In *Ebony and Ivy: Race, Slavery, and the Troubled History of America's Universities*, Craig Steven Wilder reveals the early purpose of the American college and how it became rooted in the slave economies of the colonial world: "Colleges arrived in the Americas in response to European nations' attempts to seize territories and hold off rivals. European powers deployed colleges to help defend and regulate their colonial possessions and they turned to African slavery and the African slave trade to fund these efforts."[51] Beyond the manual labor that enslaved African people provided, American colleges trained their personnel and cultivated the ideas that "accelerated and legitimated the dispossession of Native Americans and the enslavement of Africans."[52] Their vision, their horizon line, was a future in which the entirety of the world would undergo processes of differentiation under the guise of reason, science, and logic; and we would live out the abstractions of identity that convince us that race, gender, class, et cetera, are real and fixed and coherent. Kaphar centers on the moment in Princeton's history during the dispersal of President Finley's estate, when

FIGURE 14 Charles Walker Lind (active United States, 1850–75; died 1882), after John Hesselius (1728–1778; born Philadelphia, PA; died Prince George's County, MD), *Samuel Finley,* 1870. Oil on canvas, 76 × 63.5 cm. Princeton University. Gift of Samuel Finley Breese Morse (PP11)

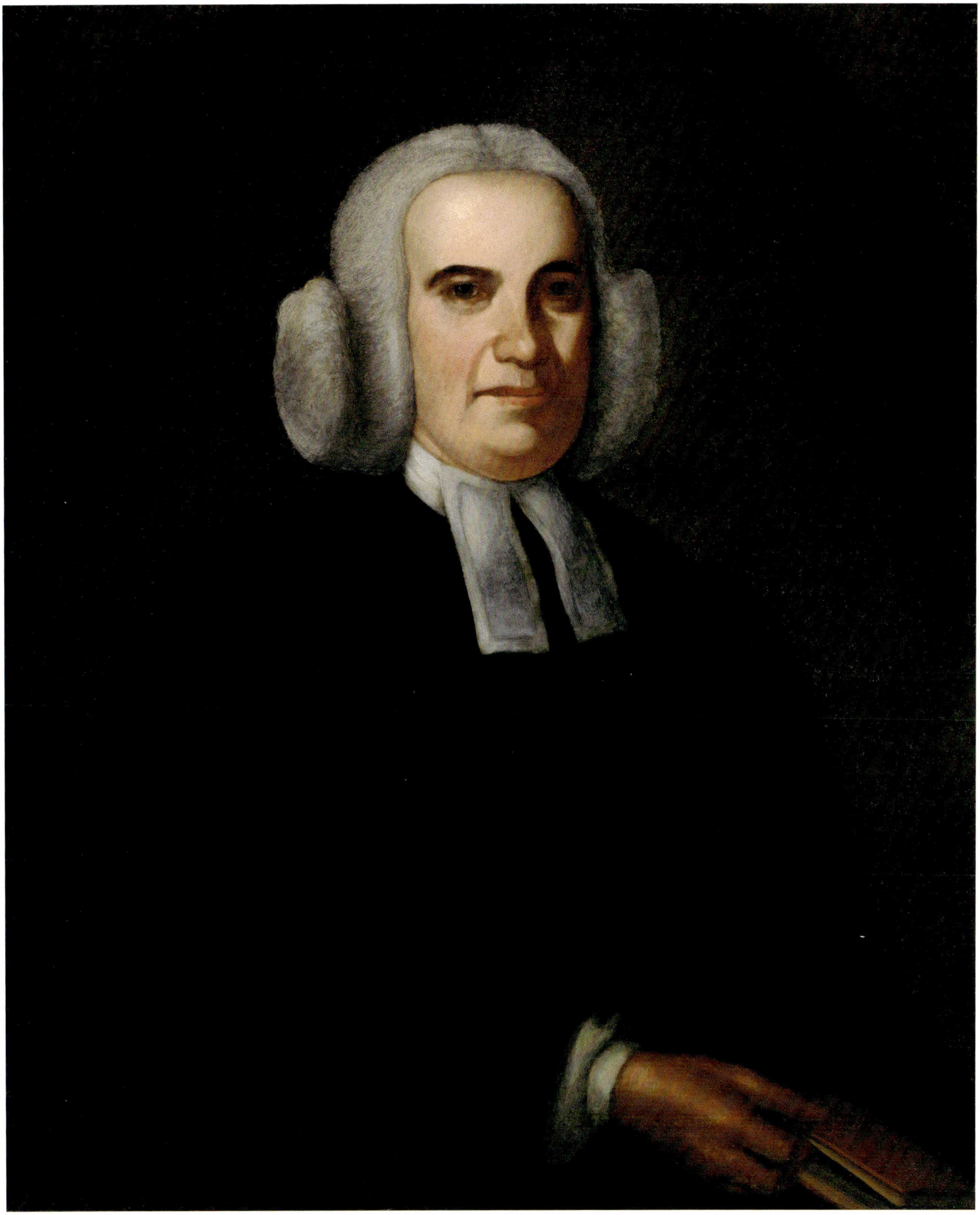

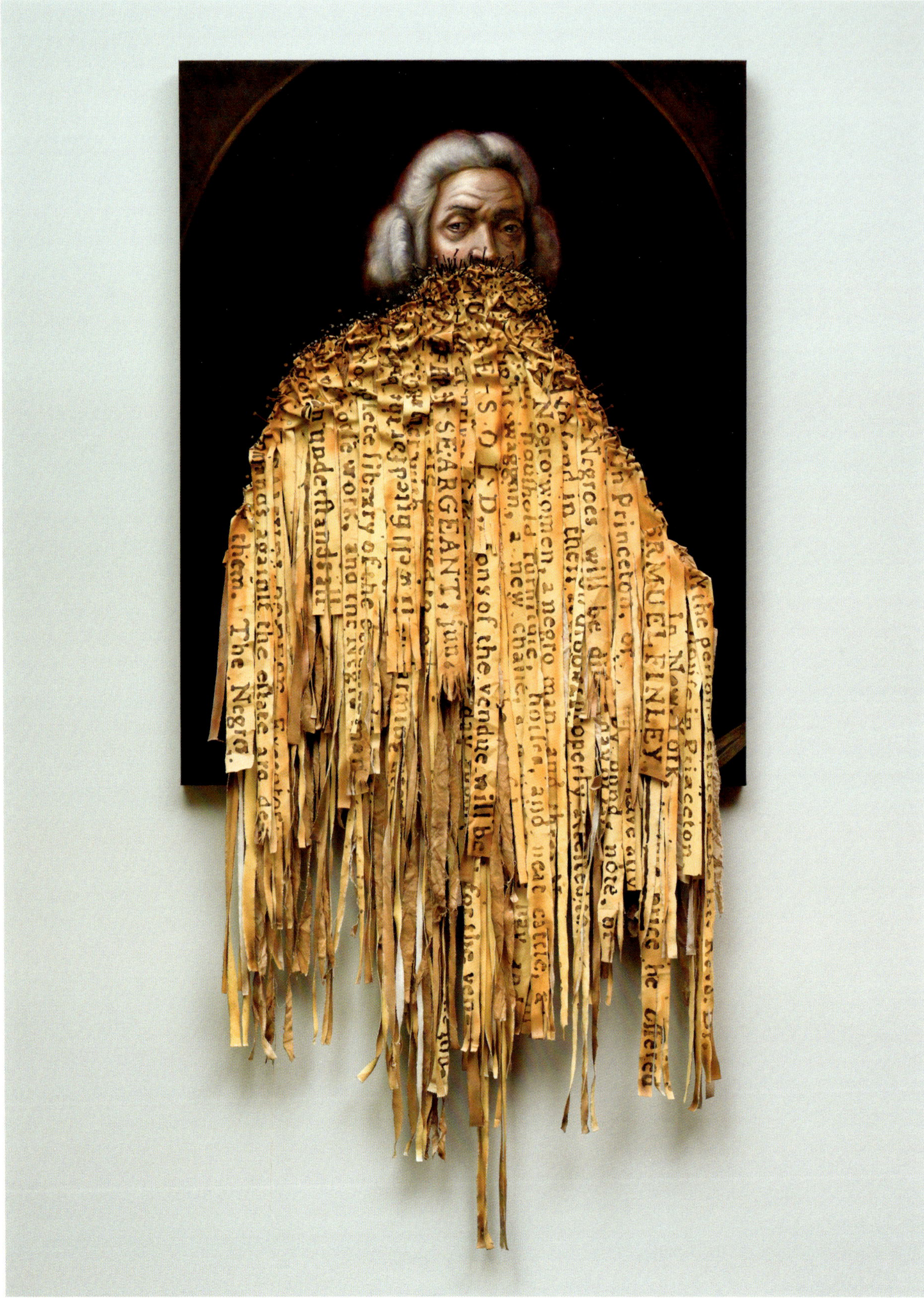

it was advertised that six slaves were to be sold (fig. 15). Kaphar gives us a distorting, Dorian Gray–like rendering of Finley's face. Onto his corrupted countenance are affixed tattered strips of painted canvas announcing the sale of human property. The canvas strips are gold and represent the value of the enslaved and the monstrousness of capitalism. Finley seems to vomit the gold and be engulfed by it simultaneously. Kaphar reminds us that the task of forgetting can be countered by the imperative to remember. In the midst of Land and Labor Acknowledgments, I think again about my grandfather and about property—how capitalism and its obsessions turn us all into invaders of Indigenous land.

FIGURE 15 Titus Kaphar (born 1976, Kalamazoo, MI; active New Haven, CT), *To Be Sold*, 2018. Oil on canvas with rusted nails, 152.4 × 121.9 × 8.9 cm. Princeton University Art Museum. Museum purchase, Fowler McCormick, Class of 1921, Fund (2018-83)

NOTES

1. Maxwell Williams, "This Is the Earliest Known Photograph of Slaves in the US—and It Challenges Our Understanding of History," *Artnet News*, December 5, 2019, https://news.artnet.com/art-world/nelson-atkins-earliest-slavery-daguerreotype-1724079.
2. Hilarie M. Sheets, "Unseen Wyeth," *New York Times*, May 1, 2022, 36; Kristi Eaton, "Beyond Black Wall Street: These Experts Are Unearthing Historically Black Towns Lost to History," *Fast Company*, April 4, 2022, https://www.fastcompany.com/90737451/beyond-black-wall-street-these-experts-are-unearthing-historically-black-towns-lost-to-history.
3. It was Stephen Daniels and Denis Cosgrove who wrote, "A landscape is a cultural image, a pictorial way of representing, structuring or symbolising surroundings." Denis Cosgrove and Stephen Daniels, "Introduction," in *The Iconography of Landscape: Essays on the Symbolic Representation, Design and Use of Past Environments*, ed. Denis Cosgrove and Stephen Daniels (Cambridge: Cambridge University Press, 1988), 1.
4. In the late 1980s and early 1990s, feminist scholars like Kimberlé Crenshaw and Elsa Barkley Brown argued for the intersectional and relational framing of human experiences in order to complicate simplistic belongings reconfirmed in things like the census. First introduced in 1989 by Crenshaw, intersectionality is an analytical framework that considers how multiple forms of inequality or oppression (racism, sexism, ableism, classism, etc.) can compound and create different modes of discrimination or disadvantage. Kimberlé Crenshaw, "Demarginalizing the Intersection of Race and Sex: A Black Feminist Critique of Antidiscrimination Doctrine, Feminist Theory and Antiracist Politics," *University of Chicago Legal Forum* 1989, no. 1 (1989): 139–167, https://chicagounbound.uchicago.edu/cgi/viewcontent.cgi?article=1052&context=uclf. In 1992 Elsa Barkley Brown launched an early challenge to the roll call of diversity and demonstrated that our experiences of difference rely on and are related to an entire spectrum of experiences that are relational and contingent. Her most effective example is simply "not all women have the same gender." She explains that recognizing and including difference is not enough; "middle-class white women's lives are not just different from working-class white, Black, and Latina women's lives. It is important to recognize that middle-class women live the lives they do precisely because working-class women live the lives they do." Elsa Barkley Brown, "'What Has Happened Here': The Politics of Difference in Women's History and Feminist Politics," *Feminist Studies* 18, no. 2 (Summer 1992): 295–312, quoted at 298.
5. A note about language: I capitalize "White" and "Whiteness" deliberately to reflect the racializing processes of identity and the contingent nature of ideologies or categories

of practice. "Indigenous," "Black," and "African American" could only be made meaningful by and to the construction and maintenance of "White" as a racial category. To write it in lowercase, therefore, is to normalize it. To be consistent with all my work, I choose to call attention to the abstraction of "race."

6. Robyn Wiegman, *Object Lessons* (Durham, NC: Duke University Press, 2012), 122, 343.

7. Rogers Brubaker and Frederick Cooper, "Beyond 'Identity,'" *Theory and Society* 29, no. 1 (February 2000): 1–47; Hope Reese, "Adolph Reed Jr.: The Perils of Race Reductionism," *JSTOR Daily*, April 28, 2021, https://daily.jstor.org/adolph-reed-jr-the-perils-of-race-reductionism/.

8. Henry Glassie, *Material Culture* (Bloomington: Indiana University Press, 1999), 194.

9. I derive my vocabulary lesson for students in part from the following sources: Karen E. Fields and Barbara J. Fields, *Racecraft: The Soul of Inequality in American Life* (New York: Verso, 2012); Judith Butler, "Performative Acts and Gender Constitution: An Essay in Phenomenology and Feminist Theory," *Theatre Journal* 40, no. 4 (December 1988): 519–31; Benedict Anderson, *Imagined Communities: Reflections on the Origin and Spread of Nationalism*, 2nd ed. (New York: Verso, 2016); Wiegman, *Object Lessons*; and Kirsten Pai Buick, "Monu*ment*ality: Edmonia Lewis, Meta Fuller, Augusta Savage and the Re-Envisioning of Public Space," in *Augusta Savage: Renaissance Woman*, ed. Jeffreen M. Hayes (Jacksonville, FL: Cummer Museum of Art and Gardens, 2018), 40–57.

10. Ethan A. Schmidt, *The Divided Dominion: Social Conflict and Indian Hatred in Early Virginia* (Boulder: University Press of Colorado, 2015).

11. *The Oxford Dictionary of Proverbs*, ed. John Simpson and Jennifer Speake (Oxford: Oxford University Press, 2008; current online version 2009), https://www.oxfordreference.com/view/10.1093/acref/9780199539536.001.0001/acref-9780199539536-e-650.

12. Susan McCulley and Jen Loux, "Bacon's Rebellion," Historic Jamestowne, National Park Service, June 1987, revised November 1995, https://www.nps.gov/jame/learn/historyculture/bacons-rebellion.htm.

13. Theodore W. Allen, *The Origin of Racial Oppression in Anglo-America*, vol. 2 of *The Invention of the White Race* (London: Verso, 2012); also see Barbara Jeanne Fields, "Slavery, Race and Ideology in the United States of America," *New Left Review* 1, no. 181 (May/June 1990): 95–118.

14. John Michael Vlach, *The Afro-American Tradition in Decorative Arts* (Athens: University of Georgia Press, 1990), 76–81.

15. Vlach, *Afro-American Tradition*, 76–81.

16. Leonard Todd, *Carolina Clay: The Life and Legend of the Slave Potter Dave* (New York: W. W. Norton, 2008), 61.

17. Todd, *Carolina Clay*, 61.

18. Andrés Reséndez, *The Other Slavery: The Uncovered Story of Indian Enslavement in America* (Boston: Mariner Books, 2016), 163–71, quote at 165.

19. Reséndez, *Other Slavery*, 167.

20. Reséndez, 167–69. Jorge Cañizares-Esguerra argues that there is a striking resemblance between Spanish and Puritan discourses of colonization as "exorcism" and as spiritual gardening. He reasons that it is more fruitful to think of Puritan endeavors as a continuation of Iberian models rather than a radically different enterprise. See Jorge Cañizares-Esguerra, *Puritan Conquistadors: Iberianizing the Atlantic, 1550–1700* (Stanford, CA: Stanford University Press, 2006), 14–34.

21. Jonathan Batkin, "Some Early Curio Dealers of New Mexico," *American Indian Art Magazine* 23, no. 3 (Summer 1998): 69. Batkin's article is especially important for the light that it sheds on Pueblo dealers in curios, which forces us to rethink the market, and how and for whom it functioned.

22. See Karl Jacoby, "'The broad platform of extermination': Nature and Violence in the Nineteenth Century North American Borderlands," *Journal of Genocide Research* 10, no. 2 (June 2008): 249–67; and Kirsten Pai Buick, "Narrative Structure as Secular Judgment in Thomas Crawford's *Progress of Civilization*," in *Race and Vision in the Nineteenth-Century United States*, ed. Shirley Samuels (Lanham, MD: Lexington Books, 2019), 169–81.

23. Ruth B. Phillips, *Trading Identities: The Souvenir in Native North American Art from the Northeast, 1700–1900* (Seattle: University of Washington Press, 1998), 29.

24. Such figurines have been made famous by the contemporary artist Virgil Ortiz, who makes similar forms based on the work of his nineteenth-century ancestors. See his *Cochiti Pueblo Two Headed Seated Male Pottery Figurine*, item #C4268B, Native American Art Online (accessed October 24, 2022), https://www.nativeamericanartmagazine.com/shows/280/tradition-and-innovation-in-cochiti-figurative-pottery.

25. Barbara A. Babcock, "By Way of Introduction," in "Inventing the Southwest," special issue, *Journal of the Southwest* 32, no. 4 (Winter 1990): 384.

26. Elkanah Watson, *Men and Times of the Revolution; or, Memoirs of Elkanah Watson, Including His Journals of Travels in Europe and America, From the Year 1777 to 1842*, ed. Winslow C. Watson, 2nd ed. (New York: Dana, 1857).

27. Adolph L. Reed Jr., *W. E. B. Du Bois and American Political Thought: Fabianism and the Color Line* (New York: Oxford University Press, 1997), 132.

28. Theodore W. Allen, *Racial Oppression and Social Control*, vol. 1 of *The Invention of the White Race*, 2 vols. (London: Verso, 2012), 22–23.

29. Allen, *Racial Oppression*, 27.

30. Livia Gershon, "Britain's Blueprint for Colonialism: Made in Ireland," *JSTOR Daily*, January 29, 2022, https://daily.jstor.org/britains-blueprint-for-colonialism-made-in-ireland/.

31. Allen, *Racial Oppression*, 31.

32. Carrie Rebora, "Chronology," in Carrie Rebora et al., *John Singleton Copley in America* (New York: Metropolitan Museum of Art, 1995), 325–27.

33. Kevin Phillips, *The Cousins' Wars: Religion, Politics, and the Triumph of Anglo-America* (New York: Basic Books, 1999), xi–xv, 480–89.

34. "Elkanah Watson, 1782," Princeton University Art Museum, accessed May 17, 2022, https://artmuseum.princeton.edu/collections/objects/29121.

35. Watson, *Men and Times of the Revolution*, 33, 41, 44, 63. Later in the autobiography, Watson laughingly relays an anecdote about English people's confusion over the complexions of children born in Boston. "One remarked to the other, 'I have seen a wonderful sight,—a little girl born in a place called Boston, in North America: and, what is very astonishing, but I pledge my word is true, she speaks English as well as any child in England; and, besides, she is perfectly white!' 'Is it possible!' exclaimed the other, in no counterfeit astonishment at the recital. Many of the people of England suppose us to be a nation of Indians, negroes, or mixed blood." Watson, *Men and Times*, 218.

36. Jeremy Dupertuis Bangs, *The Travels of Elkanah Watson: An American Businessman in the Revolutionary War, in 1780s Europe and in the Formative Decades of the United States* (Jefferson, NC: McFarland, 2015), 162.

37. Watson, *Men and Times of the Revolution*, 315–16.

38. The function of landscape representation within the Doctrine of Discovery, domestic tourism, concepts of wilderness/West/frontier, "nowhere" and "no one," and nonbelonging can all be found here: Eric Cheyfitz, "Savage Law: The Plot Against American Indians in *Johnson and Graham's Lessee v. M'Intosh* and *The Pioneers*," in *Cultures of United States Imperialism*, ed. Amy Kaplan and Donald E. Pease (Durham, NC: Duke University Press, 1993), 109–28; Eric Purchase, *Out of Nowhere: Disaster and Tourism in the White Mountains* (Baltimore: Johns Hopkins University Press, 1999); Dona Brown, *Inventing New England: Regional Tourism in the Nineteenth Century* (Washington, DC: Smithsonian Institution Press, 1995); Nicole Eustace, "The Sentimental Paradox: Humanity and Violence on the Pennsylvania Frontier," *William and Mary Quarterly*, 3rd series, 65, no. 1 (January 2008): 29–64; and Alan Heimert, "Puritanism, the Wilderness, and the Frontier," *New England Quarterly* 26, no. 3 (September 1953): 361–82.

39. Brubaker and Cooper, "Beyond 'Identity,'" 24.

40. W. J. T. Mitchell, "Introduction" and "Imperial Landscape," in *Landscape and Power*, ed. W. J. T. Mitchell (Chicago: University of Chicago Press, 1994), 1–34.

41. Angela Miller, *The Empire of the Eye: Landscape Representation and American Cultural Politics, 1825–1875* (Ithaca, NY: Cornell University Press, 1993), 79–80.

42. Cheyfitz, "Savage Law," 109.

43. Cheyfitz, 110.

44. Mitchell, *Landscape and Power*, 10.

45. Alan C. Braddock and Karl Kusserow, "Introduction," in *Nature's Nation: American Art and Environment*, ed. Karl Kusserow and Alan C. Braddock (New Haven, CT: Yale University Press, 2018), 35.

46. Stephan Oettermann, *The Panorama: History of a Mass Medium*, trans. Deborah Lucas Schneider (New York: Zone Books, 1997), 13–14.

47. Oettermann, *Panorama*, 8.

48. Quoted in Braddock and Kusserow, "Introduction," 35.

49. Timothy Mitchell, *Colonising Egypt* (Berkeley: University of California Press, 1991), ix.

50. See, e.g., "The Princeton & Slavery Project: An Exploration of Princeton University's Historical Ties to the Institution of Slavery," accessed July 15, 2022, https://slavery.princeton.edu.

51. Craig Steven Wilder, *Ebony and Ivy: Race, Slavery, and the Troubled History of America's Universities* (New York: Bloomsbury Press, 2013), 9.

52. Wilder, *Ebony and Ivy*, 10.

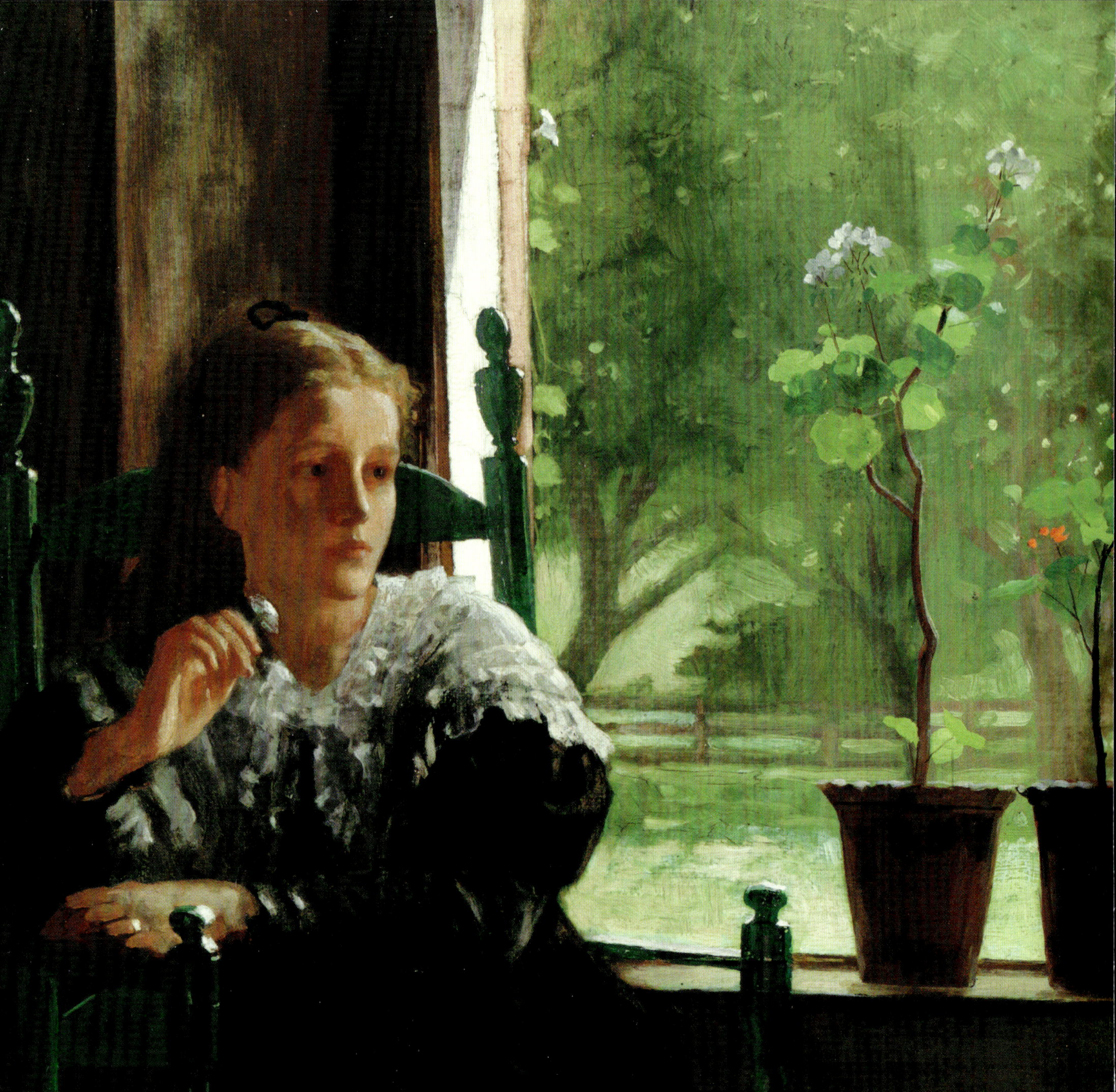

Ellery E. Foutch

Looking Back and Looking Forward: A Feminist Lens on a Collection of American Art

Museums—and their catalogues—are decidedly Not Neutral.[1] Over the past several decades, scholars of critical museum studies have analyzed systems of power and privilege, oppression and expression, authority and status as they pertain to or are manifested in art museums.[2] This exhibition catalogue seeks to consider works from Princeton's canonical collections of art of the United States with these critical lenses. As a feminist art historian and as an art historian who is a feminist, I approach such a task by thinking not only about the individual works of art on the exhibition's checklist, but also about the broader cultural and structural contexts that led to the development, display, and reception of this collection and this museum, its audiences, and its creators. What follows are several case studies of these varied aspects of works of art, across genres and chronological spans, as well as of the actions or decisions of collectors who helped to shape the collection.

Anyone researching art, archaeology, or art history of any era at Princeton University will quickly become acquainted with the Marquand name, inscribed on the architecture of its art library and on the bookplate of every volume within it. Many of those very volumes derive from the private library of Allan Marquand,

Detail, figure 16

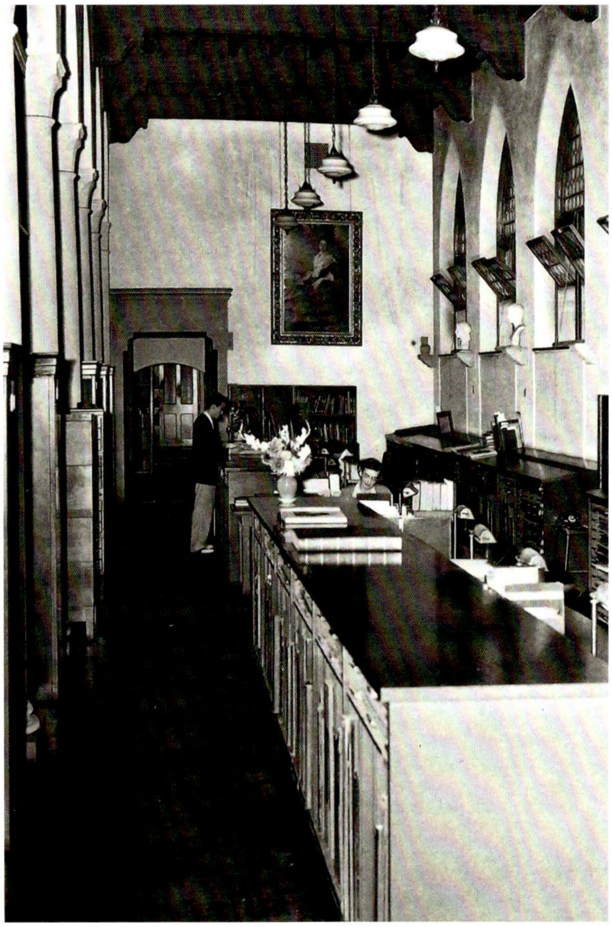

FIGURE 1 Interior of first Marquand Library of Art and Archaeology, ca. 1940, from *The Marquand Library* (Princeton, NJ: 1951). Princeton University Library, Department of Special Collections

Princeton class of 1874 and professor of art from 1882 to 1910, whose family was instrumental in the collecting and scholarship of art not only at Princeton but also in the United States more broadly. A portrait bas relief of Allan Marquand has long graced the Marquand Library of Art and Archaeology, featuring a bold Latin inscription: "*avctoris / stvdiorum nostrorvm / hvivsqve bibliothecae / conditoris*," reminding library patrons of Marquand's role as the "author and leader of 'our studies,' creator and founder of this library."[3] For a period of time, a large oil painting in an elaborate gilded frame also kept watch over the reference desk: John Singer Sargent's portrait of Elizabeth Love Allen Marquand, Allan Marquand's mother, is visible in an undated photograph (fig. 1; the library patron seen in the image, a slender young white man wearing saddle shoes, and two female employees seem to wear the fashions and hairstyles of the 1940s, while the rotary telephone resembles the "300" type desk telephone introduced by Western Electric about 1937, even though the portrait was not officially donated to the Princeton University Art Museum until 1977). How might this imposing, and imposingly displayed, picture help us think about gender and art history in Princeton's collection of American art?

THE "DIGNIFIED LADY" AND THE "SAWDUST HEROINE": MRS. MARQUAND AND MADAME X

In the autumn of 1887, painter John Singer Sargent was on his way to Newport, Rhode Island. The investor, philanthropist, and art collector Henry G. Marquand had hired the artist to paint a portrait of Mrs. Marquand—the same Elizabeth Love Allen Marquand, his wife. The resulting likeness is one of restrained refinement, an image of mature, self-contained femininity (fig. 2). Mrs. Marquand is seated in a warm interior, turning to meet our gaze with reserved friendliness. Her simple black dress evokes New England modesty, even as bountiful white ruffles of translucent lace emerge from her sleeves and are wrapped about her shoulders as a fichu. Brilliant flecks of white evoke the luminosity of a shimmering pearl necklace and earrings, while the graceful fingers of her left hand display a sizeable ring, elements that might derive from her husband's family jewelry business, Marquand & Co. Her right hand loosely holds a fan, with Sargent's quick brushstrokes of ivory, brown, and gray conveying its frothy feathers juxtaposed against its smooth ivory sticks and rivet. There is weariness but also warmth in Mrs. Marquand's eyes, as the sixty-year-old matron holds our gaze.

The portrait is a striking departure—or perhaps retreat—from Sargent's infamous *Madame X*, exhibited only a few years earlier at the Paris Salon of 1884, even as the two pictures share a restrained palette of blacks, browns, and whites.[4] In that picture, Virginie Amélie Avegno Gautreau defiantly turns away from the viewer, exposing the graceful lines and flesh of her long arms, neck, and décolletage, leaving us to contemplate her haughty profile, set against a mottled background of browns and golds (fig. 3). Viewers of the period had been shocked by this display of Sargent's bravura painting of aloof femininity—and by the immodesty of both. Writing in the *Art Amateur*, one such critic exclaimed, "In the whole great exhibition, where nude and semi-nude figures so abound, there is not a more indelicate canvas . . . its immodesty is so conspicuous that groups of 'gommeux' and 'flaneurs' pose themselves beside it to watch and grin at its first effect upon young girls as they unconsciously catch sight of it."[5] This reviewer emphasized not only the embarrassment and shame he presumed Gautreau must (or should) feel—"if the unlucky lady who is thus exhibited could hear the comments made upon her by the passing throng, she would cut it from the walls at any cost"—but also the discomfort of female visitors to the Salon, whose imagined chagrin would be amplified by the leering young men around them; the gendered and sexualized atmosphere of the Salon thereby accentuated the policing of women's bodies and women's comportment in this historical moment, as was the case in numerous settings, both urban and rural. Dozens of articles mocked Sargent's painting, emphasizing the ways in which both the artist and the subject had transgressed accepted bounds of propriety; as the *Art Amateur* suggests, these indiscretions were multiplied over the course of its exhibition, as viewers scrutinized the reactions of unsuspecting young women and ogled not only the painting, but also their fellow exhibition-goers. The painting and the dynamics of the Salon thereby reinforced concepts of propriety and impropriety, demonstrating the bounds of both feminine behavior and artistic expression.

There were consequences for Sargent for his transgression, as well. Writing to his friend Emma-Marie Allouard-Jouan, the painter noted his commissions had declined precipitously in the aftermath of the 1884 Paris Salon; Sargent attributed his waning popularity to "the effect of the Gautreau disaster."[6]

In contrast, when Sargent's portrait of Mrs. Marquand was exhibited in 1888, viewers marveled at its restraint. Writing to *salonnière* Henrietta Reubell, Henry James noted, "Mrs. M. will do him great good with the public—they will want to be painted like that—respectfully honourably, *dignement*. It is a noble portrait of an old lady."[7] As a mutual friend of Sargent's living in Paris, Reubell would have been acutely aware of Sargent's tenuous reputation in the aftermath of the *Madame X* scandal, and one might read a slight archness of tone in James's assessment of the aristocracy's desire "to be painted like that." Posed on a distinctive mahogany Chippendale chair and clad in black and white, Mrs. Marquand evokes a subtler version of the Colonial Revival aesthetic that so many late nineteenth-century Americans embraced, while her jewels and the sensuous textures of her feathered fan indicate her wealth and stature, a departure from puritanical emphases on thrift and denial of earthly pleasures.[8] The praise from most outlets was unqualified. The *Leeds Mercury* extolled "the brilliancy of Mr. J. S. Sargent's portrait of Mrs. Henry Marquand . . . a dignified lady in a rich dress, in which the curiously limited range of the painter's colours is brought out."[9] We might imagine Sargent's calibrated creation and selection of this work as a rebuttal to critics' disparagement of *Madame X*, which had been pilloried as a "female clown" or "sawdust heroine" rendered in "atrocious color."[10]

Another reviewer, for *The Graphic*, applauded both of Sargent's 1888 contributions to London's Royal Academy, praising a portrait of Mrs. Edward Darley Boit (Mary Louisa Cushing) as "painted with remarkable facility and firmness." This same critic averred, "a still better work by him is the portrait of a lady of more mature age, 'Mrs. Marquand' . . . it is an admirable rendering of character, and more restrained in style and infinitely more harmonious in colour than anything we have seen by him."[11] The two Sargent portraits of Boit and Marquand were singled out by several critics as "the most artistic and exquisite works in the Academy," and viewers praised the vivacity and modesty of the works: "Seated on a Chippendale chair, dressed in black, with white lace collar and a *gorgerette*, in which is placed a yellow rose . . . the face of the lady is full of life and light, and the half-smiling expression that plays over the features seems to illuminate the whole picture. How delicately the face is modelled, and how refined the artist's vision, words cannot describe. . . . These two portraits simply kill all the pictures hung near them."[12] Sargent's reputation was thus secured, and his dalliance with *Madame X*, with its "coarse sensationalism" and "willful exaggeration," seemed forgiven, if not forgotten.[13] The repeated

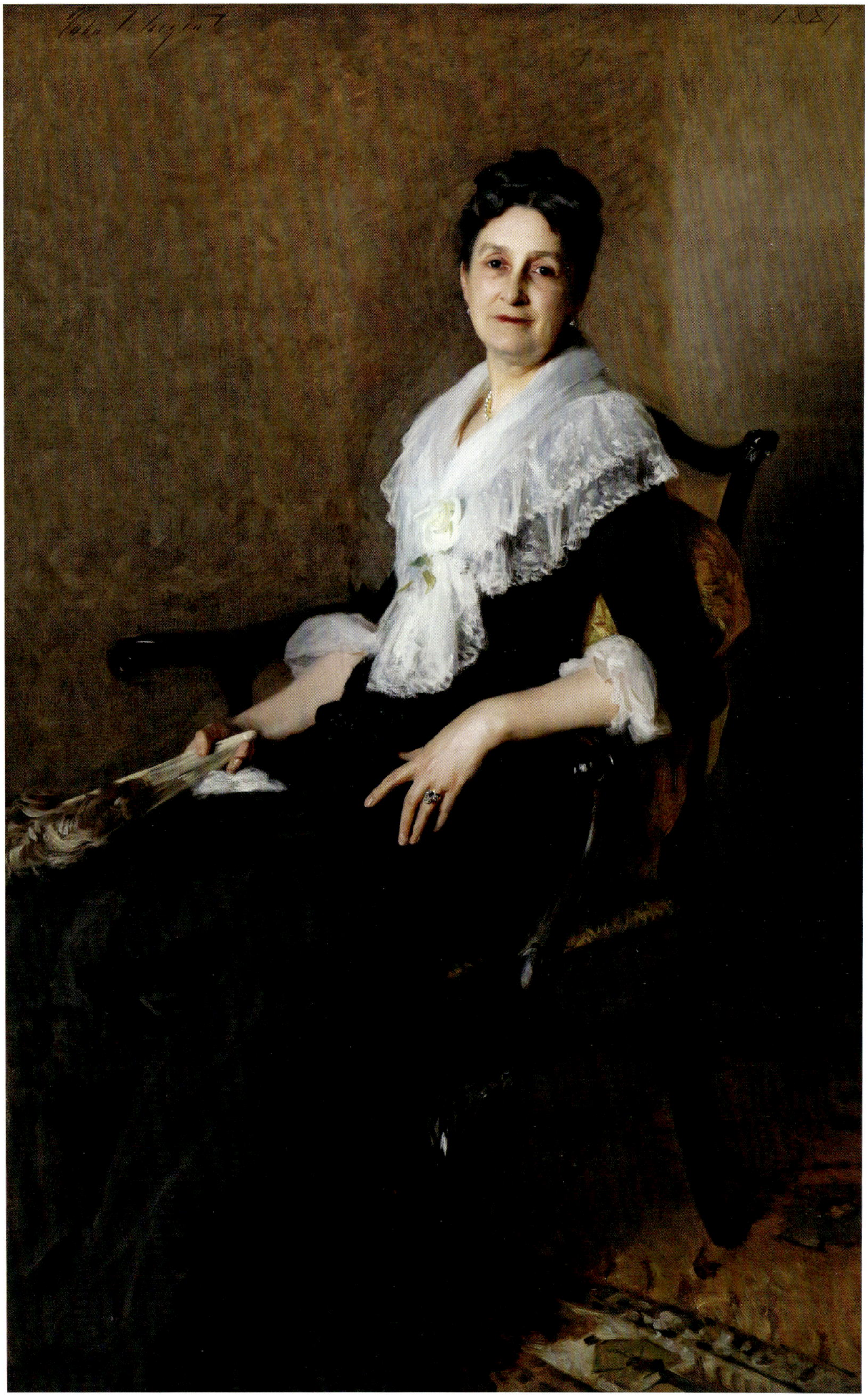

references to Marquand's liveliness are in striking contrast to critics' previous descriptions of Gautreau's "pallor" and appearance of deathly decay, while the violence implied in the pictures' victorious "kill[ing]" of all other works in the gallery bristles with tension.[14]

Sargent himself could recognize the success of the painting and its reception. In the aftermath of the 1888 Royal Academy exhibition, he wrote to Henry G. Marquand in appreciation for lending the portrait, noting, "It has stood me in very good stead at the R.A. and I again thank you and Mrs. Marquand most heartily for having spared it."[15] The artist later reflected, in another letter to Marquand, "My going to America to paint Mrs. Marquand's portrait was a turning point in my fortunes for which I have most heartily to thank you."[16] While *Elizabeth Allen Marquand*, the portrait, might have secured his reputation, the artist credited Mr. Marquand, the person and patron, as well.

A little less than ten years after the success of *Elizabeth Allen Marquand*, the Metropolitan Museum of Art commissioned Sargent to paint a portrait of Henry G. Marquand, the president of their board of trustees (fig. 4). Like his wife, Marquand is dressed in black and white, seated in a mottled dove gray and brown interior; one arm is slung over the back of an ecru chair, while he rests his other elbow atop an Empire-style table, bringing his fingers to his temple and almost seeming to raise his left eyebrow at us. Although the left side of the composition is shrouded by a olive green curtain, the subdued and muted interior suggests he might be in the same room as the previous portrait of Mrs. Marquand; both can be imagined turning from conversation with each other in order to face the viewer who has recently entered their shared interior. Marquand's dark suit is accentuated by the whiteness of his collar and cuffs, and Sargent carefully delineates further embellishments: gold cufflinks, the loop of a long trail of a watch fob and its watch, and a ring on the graceful fingers of his left hand. Indeed, to at least one reviewer of the era, the ring was the basis for the picture's palette, an indication of its centrality: "a chrysoprase or other greyish stone worn in a ring on a finger of the left hand—sets the key for the color scheme."[17] Might the Met trustees have hoped that the Marquand family would also donate Sargent's portrait of Mrs. Marquand, reuniting pictures of husband

FIGURE 2 John Singer Sargent (1856–1925; born Florence, Italy; died London, United Kingdom), *Elizabeth Allen Marquand*, 1887. Oil on canvas, 169 × 107 cm. Princeton University Art Museum. Gift of Mrs. Eleanor Marquand Delanoy, granddaughter of the sitter (y1977-77)

FIGURE 3 John Singer Sargent, *Madame X (Madame Pierre Gautreau)*, 1883–84. Oil on canvas, 208.6 × 109.9 cm. The Metropolitan Museum of Art, New York. Arthur Hoppock Hearn Fund, 1916 (16.53)

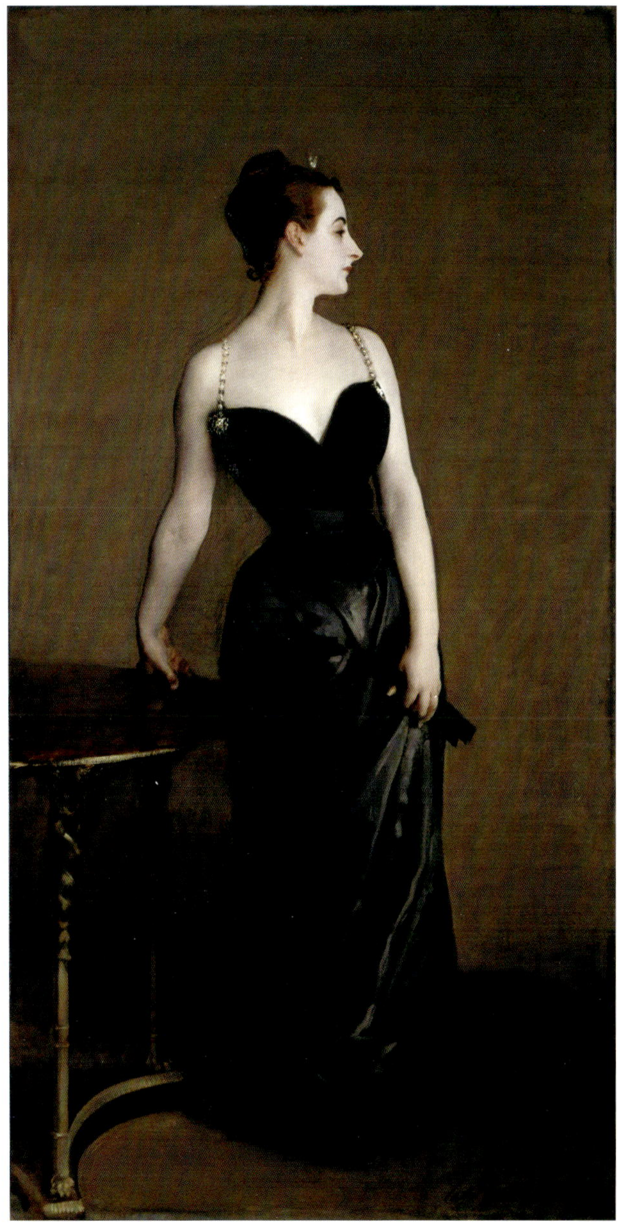

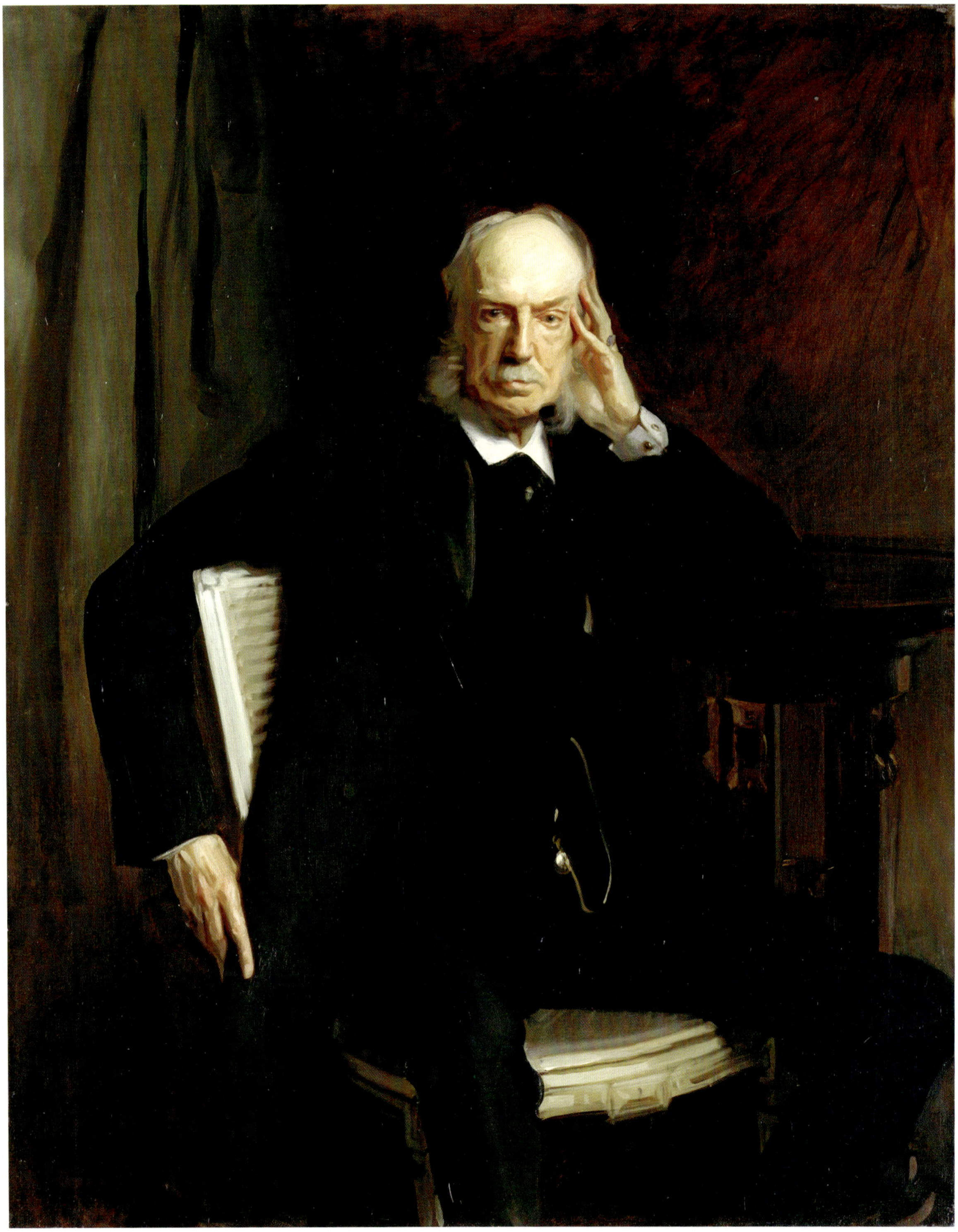

FIGURE 4 John Singer Sargent, *Henry G. Marquand*, 1897. Oil on canvas, 132.1 × 106 cm. The Metropolitan Museum of Art, New York. Gift of the Trustees, 1897 (97.43)

and wife? In commissioning (and displaying) the portrait of Henry Marquand, another critic noted, the trustees were "breaking their rule not to exhibit the portrait of one of their number," but Marquand's numerous gifts to the museum had also been unprecedented; in addition to his financial donations (including a $1,000 donation in 1870 as one of the museum's original subscribers), Marquand had bequeathed collections of old master paintings, Roman and Venetian glass, ancient bronzes, and plaster casts of sculptures.[18]

In the end, the Marquand family kept Sargent's portrait of Elizabeth Love Allen Marquand in the family for nearly ninety years. The painting was so treasured by the Marquands that it served as the focal point for young Eleanor Marquand's wedding at the family's Guernsey Hall estate in 1927; as the social pages gushingly reported, "The bridal party stood before the Sargeant [*sic*] portrait of Mrs. Henry G. Marquand, grandmother of the bride, around which [were] banked calla lilies, ferns, and palms," evoking a setting that almost transforms the portrait into an altar.[19]

Instead, the family commissioned another portrait of Henry G. Marquand for the family home from John White Alexander, an artist more frequently associated with his paintings of languorously posed women in billowing gowns. Unlike his portraits and allegorical renderings of female subjects, Alexander's portrait of Marquand is restrained and almost austere (fig. 5). Mr. Marquand stands in a dark interior barely suggested by quick and broad strokes of brown, gray, gold, and black. A small, framed print with broad white mat seems to hang on the wall behind him, its glass catching the reflection of light. Marquand holds his spectacles in one hand and folded sheets of paper in the other. Some scholars have surmised these must be the plans for the Metropolitan Museum of Art's planned expansion, but its rectangularity and nestled layers suggest a folded newspaper.[20] Marquand's portrait was donated to Princeton's portrait collection in 1950, and granddaughter Eleanor Marquand Delanoy gave Mrs. Marquand's portrait to the Princeton University Art Museum in 1977; they are reunited in this exhibition.

The spare setting of each of these three portraits gives no indication of Marquand's voracious collecting practices. Sargent's portrait of Mrs. Marquand was painted at the family's Newport estate, Linden Gate, a house that one contemporary writer described as "contain[ing] so many rare and curious things, that Bric-a-Brac Hall has been suggested as a fitting name for it."[21] None of this is evident in Sargent's rendering; the interior dissolves into a haze of brushstrokes beyond the Chippendale armchair with its golden cushions and the faint glimpse of a rug's border. Nor do the portraits of Mr. Marquand evoke the aesthetic interiors he had so painstakingly installed in his Manhattan mansion, such as the elaborate music room commissioned from Lawrence Alma-Tadema, or the ornate fireplace, both of which were illustrated in Elizabeth Alexander's profile of the collector, published in *Harper's Monthly* shortly after her husband, John, had painted Marquand's likeness.[22] Despite all of Marquand's public philanthropy, these portraits keep us at arm's length.

Very little about Elizabeth Love Allen Marquand's life is knowable today.[23] She is almost always referred to in relationship to her male family members—her grandfather Reverend Thomas Allen, known as the "fighting parson,"[24] her husband the famed industrialist and art collector, and her son Allan Marquand, who was so pivotal in the development of Princeton's art department and the Museum that now owns her portrait.[25] Extensive press coverage of Henry G. Marquand's art collections, philanthropy, and social activities frequently refers only to him. Even the rose in Mrs. Marquand's portrait seems to have come from her husband's conservatory, which was frequently singled out for praise in newspaper coverage of the annual Newport Flower Show.[26] The Marquands are inextricably linked with the development of art collections in the United States, especially the establishment of the Metropolitan Museum of Art; their legacy also permeates Princeton, not only due to Allan Marquand's many contributions to the art department, but also owing to Henry G. Marquand's generous donations that supported the building of both a University gymnasium and a chapel, edifices that gave material form to nineteenth-century ideals of "muscular Christianity."[27] Yet in many ways, Elizabeth Marquand remains a closed book. In this very retelling, I have merely made her a foil for Sargent, a means by which another man might try to secure or rehabilitate his reputation. How does this happen?

FIRST THINGS FIRST

One way to begin to answer such a question might be to ask, more broadly, what does it mean to write an analysis—not only of a painting, but of an art collection—from a feminist perspective? In each case, it is a matter of methodological priorities and responsibilities. First, it requires acknowledging that gender, sexuality, and even feminism itself are categories and concepts that are historically contingent and socially constructed, whether they are implicit, unspoken, and generally accepted, or whether their meanings are explicitly debated and hotly contested. It also mandates a recognition of intersectionality—the ways in which each person is a constellation of multiple identity categories and identifications, both self-defined and as perceived or ascribed by others (including race, class, gender, religion, sexuality, and beyond), and as such, each will experience the world in different ways. Writing a feminist essay also might demand an acknowledgment of my own subjectivity and historical position, a departure from the often-authoritative voice of an exhibition catalogue presenting itself as objective.[28] These broader cultural and structural contexts must inform interpretations of authors and readers.

Thinking critically about gender in an art collection thus requires we attend to a multitude of complexities beyond those depicted on canvas or in bronze, including broader currents in social and cultural history as they shape and are shaped by the actors (artists, collectors, patrons, or consumers) and institutions—in this instance, Princeton University—that collectively constitute them. As Griselda Pollock has stated, "Feminist interventions demand recognition of gender power relations, making visible the mechanisms of male power, the social construction of sexual difference and the role of cultural representations in that construction."[29] A feminist reading of a collection requires considerations of the ways in which gender roles, expectations, and legal codes circumscribed or enabled the lives and possibilities of artists who first made the work—and the collectors who bought it, as well as market pressures and gatekeepers who chose to feature some works of art and refuse others. We contend not only with the reception of the work during the artist's lifetime, but also with the continually evolving and developing perception of these works, including the ongoing role of the secondary art market.

THE BUILDING OF PRINCETON'S ART COLLECTIONS

In the case of this particular collection—the Princeton University Art Museum—we must recognize the complicated histories not only of museums but also of universities and institutions of higher education; Princeton's status as an elite institution that assiduously selected its community and engaged in rigorous gatekeeping is a crucial factor.[30] Throughout most of the University's history, that community was limited to men—men who were white or white-passing.[31] The workings of institutions are nonetheless the labor of complicated human individuals: professors and curators and scholars and collectors and alumni—and their wives and daughters and sisters and widows. Browsing the Museum collections' credit lines vividly reveals the degree to which the collections have been shaped by donations from alumni and their family members, their tastes and preferences and lived complexities (the portrait of Elizabeth Marquand, for example, was donated by her granddaughter, Eleanor Marquand Delanoy, the daughter of Princetonian Allan Marquand). The works of art available for our analysis have been filtered by dint of these families' selections.

The historical core of the collections, in particular, reifies official institutional history: Princeton's portrait collection explicitly sought to commemorate and represent those deemed instrumental in the building and continuation of the University.[32] These portraits establish and disseminate images of power and prestige, their gilded frames signifying the valued status of canvases that portray the stern and solemn features of white sitters in their powdered wigs, somberly dressed in black (fig. 6). This collection, begun in 1755, predated the founding of the University's Art Museum by over one hundred years, from the earliest days of the College of New Jersey, when benefactors donated portraits of themselves and of British royalty. After the American Revolution, Charles Willson Peale's monumental portrait *George Washington at the Battle of Princeton* (see p. 12, fig. 1) joined the collection, solidifying the ties between the College and the young nation. As long installed in

FIGURE 5 John White Alexander (1856–1915; born Allegheny, PA; died New York, NY), *Henry G. Marquand*, 1896. Oil on canvas, 198 × 107 cm. Princeton University. Presented by the daughters of Mr. and Mrs. Allan Marquand (PP344)

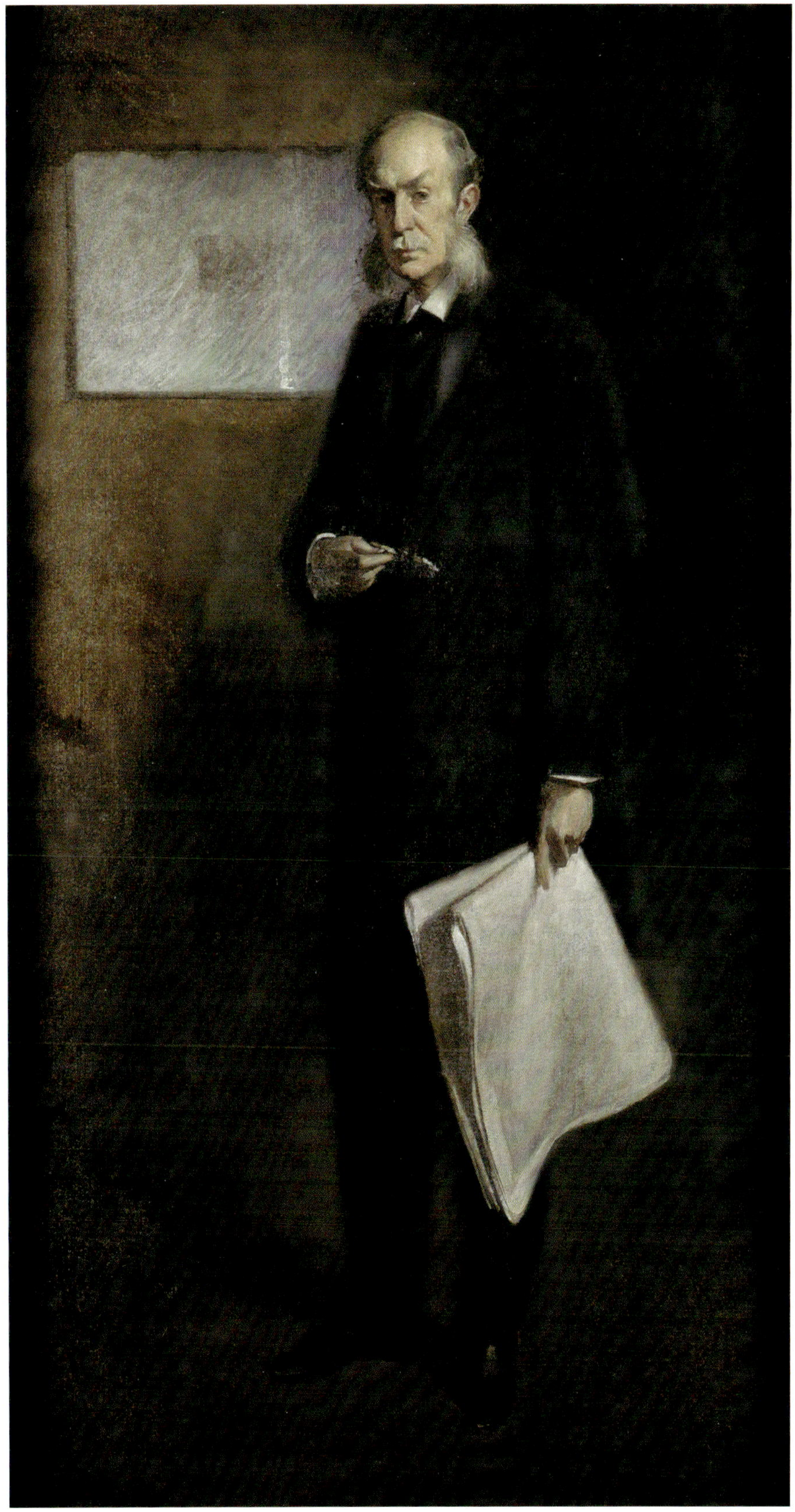

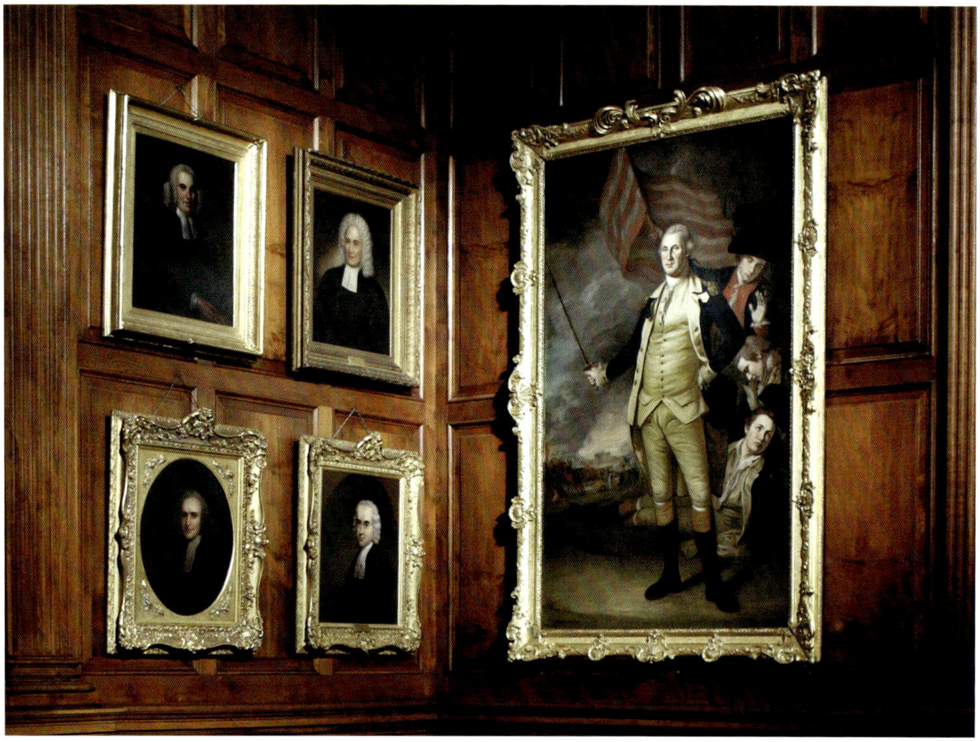

FIGURE 6 Faculty Room in Nassau Hall, Princeton University, 2010

Princeton's Nassau Hall epicenter, Peale's dramatic canvas interrupts the rows of somberly clad theologians and preachers with its swashbuckling scene of composed heroism; it asserts both the artist's and the subject's military experience, emphasizing Washington's controlled command even in the clouds of cannon smoke and the bloodshed on the battlefield.

The collection's rows of elder white statesmen are in striking contrast to the portrait gallery of another, much "younger" institution of higher education, the reading room of Wellesley College's library, which features the portraits of that institution's past presidents, all of whom have been women; visitors to this space are thus surrounded by images of female intellectuals.[33] Once one has been in a space surrounded by *this* vision of leadership, the overwhelming maleness of other collections is all the more conspicuous, as my own father observed on a visit to Wellesley in the 1990s.

Princeton's collections of portraits and artifacts continued to grow over the course of the nineteenth century, often aided by "the liberality of lady friends of the College," indicating women's institutional influence, even as they were still prohibited from enrollment in the University.[34] By the 1880s, then-President James McCosh had begun implementing curricular reforms at Princeton, which included a critical consideration of art's role in society. The report he commissioned, penned by alum and collector William C. Prime with General George B. McClellan, conveys a vision for a mutually interdependent art department and art museum; the pamphlet further articulates an expansive working definition of "art" that transcends the rarefied and embraces the everyday, decades before the conceptualization of the field of "material culture." As they assert,

> Art, in its broad sense, is the product of the human brain and hands. Whatever man has made, of whatever material, is a work of art. Every work of art is a permanent record of a thought or a group of thoughts. . . . The maker has left visible and permanent a purpose, and the object implies not only a maker, but a person or persons for whom it is made. . . . Art is, and has always been, a matter of the ordinary business, commercial, industrial, and social

life of peoples . . . this is equally true, whether the works of art be the simplest objects of common utility, or statues, architecture, and paintings.[35]

In many ways, this is a radical definition of art. It proclaims belief in an object's ability to communicate, educate, and inspire, while illuminating the complex web of meaning-making and interpretation. The report also explicitly welcomes women into the field of intellectual inquiry, hailing these subjects as ones "in which men and women are intelligently interested," a marked departure at a time when most documents addressed only the "sons of Princeton."[36] Prime and McClellan's pedagogical philosophy is also notable for its emphasis on object-based education and the necessity of a teaching collection: "The foundation of any system of education in Historic Art must obviously be in object-teaching. A museum of art objects is so necessary to the system that without it we are of [the] opinion it would be of small utility to introduce the proposed department. . . . The museum . . . gathers all works of art which are in any degree valuable as records of human tastes, desires and habits of life."[37] These emphases on object-based learning and applied arts find a parallel in institutions such as London's South Kensington Museum, founded in the 1850s and renamed the Victoria and Albert Museum in 1899, or Philadelphia's Pennsylvania Museum and School of Industrial Art, founded in 1876.[38] Those institutions sought to educate designers and the public on matters of good design and utopian visions of a society improved by the arts; not coincidentally, both were formed in the aftermath of world's fairs. In contrast, however, Princeton's Museum of Historic Art sought to educate Princeton students in particular, and to illuminate not only the design qualities of the objects on view, but also their humanistic value as well. As Prime and McClellan wrote, "works of art are the only trustworthy record of—not alone the history—but of the tastes, the mental character, and the manners and customs of various people in various ages . . . the works of art of any people are another form of their literature. They are thoughts, purposes, wants, necessities, habits, customs, tastes, recorded not in phonetic or hieroglyphic characters, but in plain objects."[39] If we read capaciously, we might see that Prime and McClellan were arguing for the possibilities of material culture and social history, even before those fields were codified or conceptualized. Although much of Prime and McClellan's text focuses on concepts of "beauty," the acknowledgment of the significance of the applied arts and non-elite objects can be seen as a precursor for some of the important intellectual developments of the twentieth century: thinking critically about everyday objects and the lived experiences of the working class, of women, of marginalized members of society, and connecting objects to larger social and political structures, although these developments would still be decades in the future.[40]

Prime's philosophy reflected one of his primary collecting and research interests, that of pottery and ceramics, and the Trumbull-Prime Collection became the kernel of the Princeton University Art Museum.[41] Significantly, and unlike Henry G. Marquand, Prime credited his wife, Mary Trumbull Prime, as an equal partner in this intellectual enterprise. As he noted in his 1878 book about ceramics, written five years after her death, the Trumbull-Prime Collection was named "in memory of its founder, who was, so far as I know, the first lady, and perhaps the first person, in America who made a special study of ceramic art. . . . Had I the assistance of her superior information, pure taste, and unerring judgment, this would have been a much more valuable book; for to them I owe all that I know of the subject . . . that [memory's] constant presence has made it a labor of love."[42] This passage suggests a willing attribution of intellectual credit and a marriage that was also a collaborative and generative partnership. Mary Trumbull Prime's first name, however, appears nowhere in the book; her identity is still subsumed to her relationship to her husband and to her father (whose collection is also referenced in the book, with objects credited to "Mr. G. Trumbull, of Hartford").[43]

The frontispiece of Prime's book features a cozy domestic scene of a woman reading by a roaring fire in an aesthetic interior whose mantel displays an array of decorative objects (fig. 7). Two landscapes hang over the mantel, further framed by a symmetrical arrangement of ceramic plates and chargers. Prime describes the illustration as "show[ing] the decorative value of a few old plates . . . [and] the excellent taste of a lady who loves art. . . . It is a very easy matter for any one, with patience and taste, thus to make a room brilliant, cheery, and full of bright thoughts."[44] Of course, these are not "a few old plates" but rather a meticulously arranged collection of fine objects from around the globe, assembled by wealthy connoisseurs and scholars, the Trumbull Primes themselves. The woman in the picture does not consider the ceramics nor the viewer; instead, she is absorbed in her reading, whose "HARPER'S" title is faintly discernable. Prime's text echoes the kind of home decorating advice dispensed in countless volumes of the nineteenth century, perhaps most famously in *The American Woman's Home*, a collaboration between Catharine Beecher and Harriet Beecher Stowe first published in 1869 and dedicated "to the women of America, in whose hands rest the real destinies of the republic, as moulded [*sic*] by the early training and preserved amid the mature influences of home."[45] Beyond its main purpose in educating an American audience about ceramics, Prime's book invests in and contributes to the nineteenth-century "cult of domesticity" with its beliefs in the importance of cultivating aesthetic and moral values within the home.[46]

It is important to note that the tastes and triumphs of collectors, especially those who commissioned aesthetic interiors, were seen as separate enterprises or perhaps even conquests from the cozy "decoration" assigned to mothers and housewives. While Prime and his wife (and their collections) were crucial in the formation of the Art Museum, they are dwarfed by the legacies of the Marquands. Yet as noted above, Sargent's and Alexander's portraits of Mr. and Mrs. Marquand do not hint at the extensive art collections or the lavish aesthetic interiors Marquand had commissioned from leading artists of the day.[47] Portraits of collectors were not always portraits of collections. But the selective emphasis or valuation of different kinds of "decoration" is a significant aberration in the period's dogma about the domestic sphere as the domain and purview of women.[48]

Prime's "Home Decoration" finds a parallel in a meticulous drawing by Thomas Charles Farrer, which features a young woman sewing in a brightly lit domestic interior (fig. 8). She, too, sits in profile and perches her feet on a stool, but she is preoccupied with needle and thread; a pair of scissors is balanced precariously on her knee. Farrer carefully delineates all the aesthetic details that have gone into making this house a home. Sunlight streams in from a window only partially obscured by a shade with decorative tassel, illuminating a small vase of flowers and potted plants. Beyond the fabric the woman sews, pulling her needle and thread taut, the room is filled with a variety of textiles with floral patterns: a batik tablecloth with somewhat abstracted vegetal and floral designs, a riotous carpet with fat cabbage roses, drapery that flows and pools behind the seated woman. A rendering of Raphael's *Madonna della Sedia* watches over the room, reminding viewers of the centrality of motherhood in this scene of domesticity, even if

FIGURE 7 "Home Decoration," frontispiece, in William C. Prime, *Pottery and Porcelain of All Times and Nations* (New York: Harper & Brothers, 1878). Smithsonian Libraries

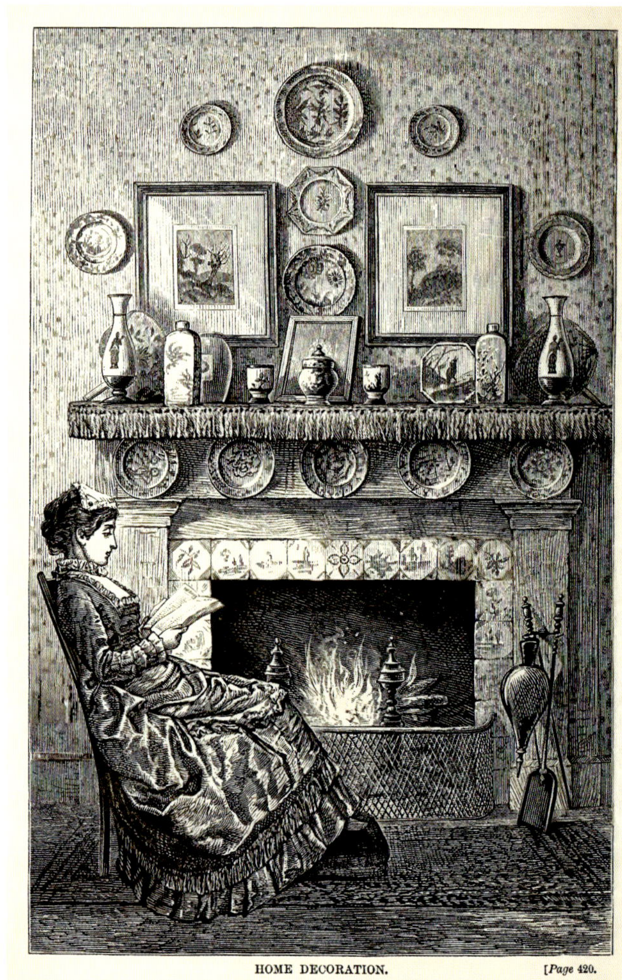

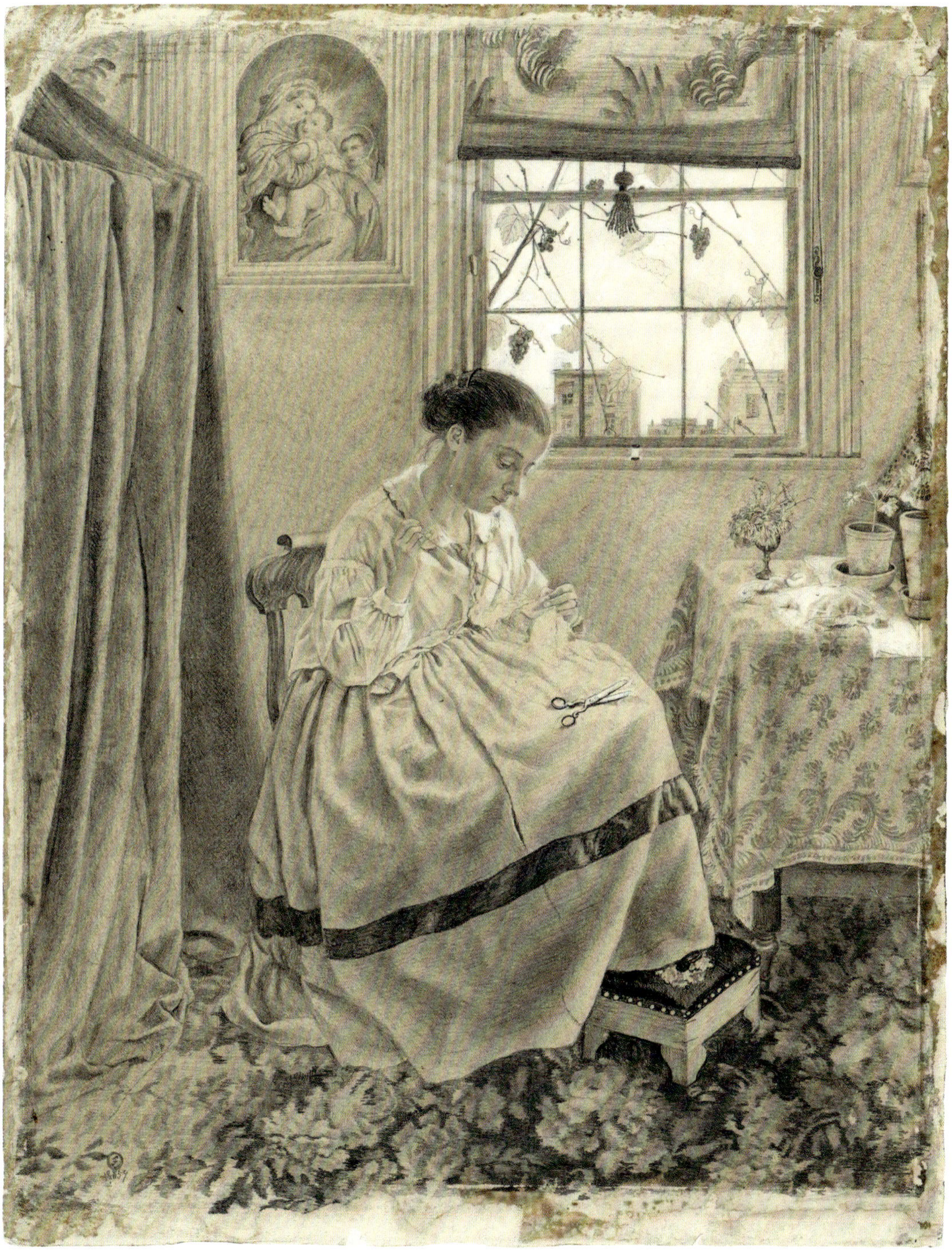

FIGURE 8 Thomas Charles Farrer (1839–1891; born and died London, United Kingdom; active New York, NY), *Woman Sewing*, 1859. Graphite on paper heightened with white gouache, 30.3 × 23.5 cm. Princeton University Art Museum. Gift of Professor Charles Ryskamp in memory of Mr. Gerard B. Lambert, Class of 1908 (x1969-372)

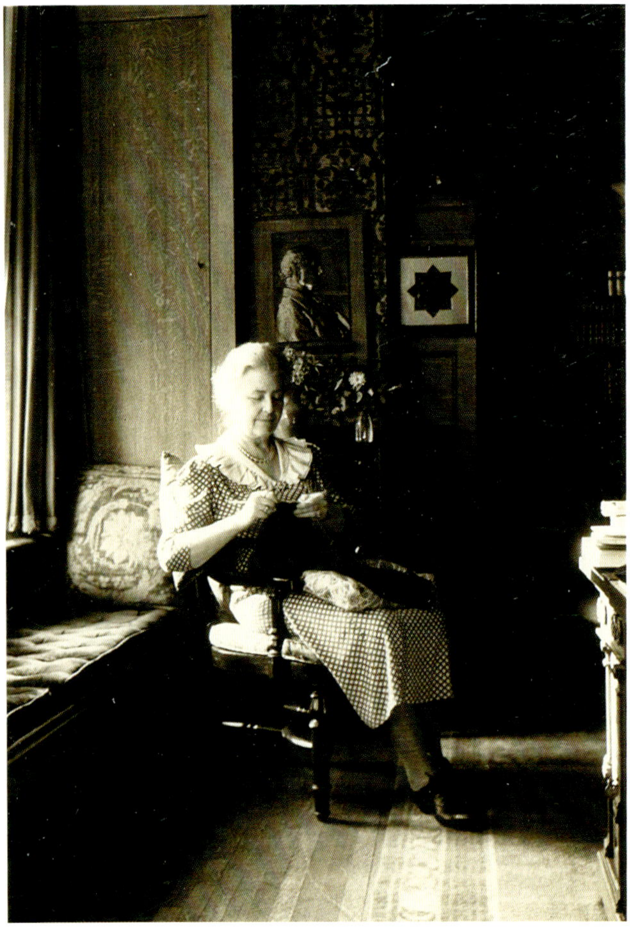

FIGURE 9 Eleanor Cross Marquand, ca. 1940s. Princeton University Library, Department of Special Collections. Princeton University Archives, Honorary Degree Records

no children are present. Raphael's seated Madonna, who so gently cradles the Christ child, adorned the walls of countless nineteenth-century homes, reifying this vision of affectionate and ultimately sacrificial motherhood; Nathaniel Hawthorne had declared it "the most beautiful picture in the world . . . familiar . . . in a hundred engravings and copies."[49] While Farrer's drawing reminds us of the cultivation of "separate spheres" for women and men, with women's roles as mothers being prioritized above all else, it also might remind us of the ways in which many people of the time experienced works of art: circulated as copies, with reproductions of European masterpieces often prized over original works of art, even within the context of the art museum.[50] Another example of Henry G. Marquand's munificence, for example, was the donation of a collection of plaster cast copies of antique sculptures to the Metropolitan Museum.

Almost eighty years after Farrer's drawing, the Marquands' daughter-in-law posed for a photograph with a strikingly similar composition (fig. 9). Eleanor Cross Marquand is seated by a window, also attending to needlework. The vertical folds of the window curtain and wooden paneling frame the left side of the image. A bronze portrait relief of her husband, Allan Marquand, presides over the scene, invoking his presence decades after his death.[51] Vases of flowers are arranged atop the chest of drawers below the portrait, akin to an offering or a shrine. While the *Madonna della Sedia* set a tone of maternal affection and domesticity in Farrer's drawing, Eleanor Marquand's interior evokes her ties to her husband and her aesthetic interests. Next to her husband's portrait, the geometric pattern of an eight-sided star, possibly a medieval Islamic tile or textile, is also visible in the dark interior.

This Mrs. Marquand wears a polka-dotted dress whose ruffled fichu frames a pearl necklace, also calling to mind Sargent's portrait of her mother-in-law; the heavy lines of her wooden armchair, softened somewhat by a cushion, similarly parallel the earlier painting, as does the patterned border of a carpet at her feet. Although Eleanor Cross Marquand was a scholar in her own right, for this photograph she is memorialized in the domestic sphere, with the old-fashioned trappings of another Colonial Revival, depicted as an industrious widow at her sewing.[52] We might look more closely and note the table in the right margin of the picture, though, which suggests a stack of books, or the glinting vertical lines in the right background that indicate shelves full of books with stamped and gilded spines. In the 1940s, Eleanor Marquand was a founding member of the Hroswitha Club, a group of women bibliophiles and collectors, and her academic research focused on the representation and iconography of flowers and floral emblems in art, giving new significance to the vases of flowers gathered under her husband's portrait.[53] Perhaps her intellectual interests are evident in this photograph, after all. In concert with her husband, a curator and professor at Princeton, Eleanor Cross Marquand helped to build Princeton's art department and art collections; she advocated for the education of her daughters, who would in subsequent years donate the Sargent and Alexander portraits of Mr. and Mrs. Marquand to the Art Museum.[54]

GENDER AND THE LIVES OF PRINCETON'S STUDENTS—THE MUSEUM'S PRIMARY AUDIENCE

Who were these collections intended to educate? While official, painted portraits tell one kind of story about the dignified lives of scholars and leaders, looking beyond the scope of Nassau Hall and the Art Museum offers a glimpse of the lives and interests of the students of Princeton, the core audience for the program of art education and the Museum—and the attitudes and expectations that they held about gender.

Although the University did not admit women to its undergraduate program until 1969, there was a brief attempt at women's education in Princeton in the nineteenth century: Evelyn College for Women, the first women's college in the state of New Jersey, founded in 1887, the same year Sargent painted Mrs. Marquand's portrait.[55] During its decade of existence, it primarily enrolled the female relatives of Princeton's male scholars—the daughters or sisters of faculty members, alumni, and undergraduates; classes were taught by Princeton faculty, and the female students were given access to the resources of the libraries and museums. Art Professor Allan Marquand sat on its board of trustees and was an ardent supporter of the institution. Despite the brevity of its tenure, stories and artifacts related to Evelyn College throw issues of gender, as experienced at Princeton, into high relief. As an 1896 *Harper's Bazaar* article noted, "There seems to be a certain deep-rooted conservatism in New Jersey which has made that State slow to recognize the necessity of providing for the higher education of her women . . . [but] in the most conservative town in this most conservative State, right under the shadow of Old Nassau itself, a woman's college has evolved."[56] Advocates for women's education emphasized the intellectual achievements of the students, asserting "young women can do all the work required by the same professors of young men, and can pass the same examination . . . teaching [men] the useful lesson of a woman's possibilities in intellectual work," yet the college struggled for funds.[57] Evelyn College offered a brief glimpse of access and parity, even as proponents hoped that in the distant future, "our country shall come to speak with equal pride of the sons *and of the daughters* of Princeton."[58] The school closed after only ten years, in large part attributed to the lack of financial support, exacerbated by the Panic of 1893 and the death of its founder, Joshua Hall McIlvane.

In one posed portrait of Evelyn College students, a group of young women has gathered in front of a brick and clapboard building on a fair day; leafy vines and the girls' attire indicate warm weather and a pleasant garden (fig. 10). These eleven young women have brought chairs outside to assist in their posing; the heavy leather upholstery of furniture usually seen in a parlor can be glimpsed behind them. They arrange themselves in three rows. Five women are seated, with three standing behind them and three sitting on the ground. A few women look directly at the camera, but many of them are absorbed in one another, their arms intertwined and overlapping. They are wearing an array of patterns and colors: plaids, stripes, checks, with pleats, folds, and ruffles. Some wear simple straw hats, while others have elaborate ribbons, flowers, and complicated brims; three women are bare-headed. Some have sashes that accentuate their narrow waists and suggest the confining corsetry that might be undergirding this effusion of prints and patterns and details of dress. It is a large but still intimate group. Those in the front row rest their arms on the laps of the women sitting behind them. On the right side of the photograph, two duos gaze at each other intently and gently clasp hands. One woman is so consumed in this interaction that she turns fully away from the camera, showing us the back of her head; her long braid parallels the intertwined limbs of the group. We cannot know what they are thinking in this self-contained assembly, but their gestures and gazes convey an intensity of connection that gives visible form to the powerful relationships, friendships, and erotic attachments that often developed at women's colleges.[59] This cloistered atmosphere is belied by stories of harassment and conflict with Princeton students, from tales of a chicken coop set ablaze to the refrain "Eva, Eva, l-y-n! Eva, Eva, let me in!" said to be shouted at the gates.[60] One Princeton student was compelled to write a letter to the University newspaper expressing his concerns about "the rude receptions given . . . to the Evelyn girls" at a recent event: "When Princeton men forget their reputation for

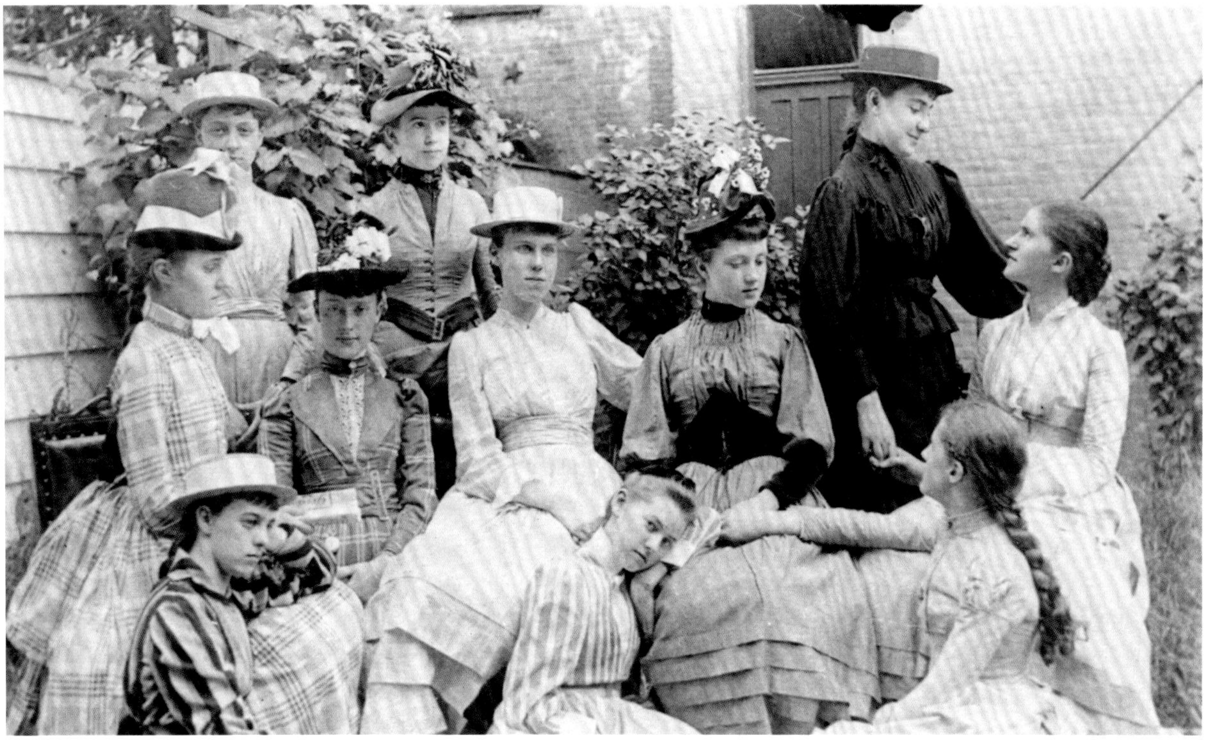

FIGURE 10 Students from Evelyn College, ca. 1887–97. Historical Society of Princeton, New Jersey. Photo Archives (H_5_002)

chivalry so far as to greet ladies with their robust mirth, it is time to call a halt . . . college men should be too far along to plead the immunities of infancy . . . let [these men] consider for a moment how they would enjoy seeing their own sisters walking up the aisle, blushing and painfully embarrassed under the vociferous applause of a thousand cultivated and refined academic gentlemen."[61] These anecdotes echo the leering of the *gommeux* and *flâneur* at young women's reactions to the Paris exhibition of *Madame X*, with the mere entry of women into the public sphere seen as sufficient impetus for harassment and humiliation, another means of regulating female behavior via male misbehavior.

While the women of Evelyn College show their connection by touch and interlocked gazes, a cabinet card of three Princeton students displays the aftermath of an altogether different kind of physical contact (fig. 11). These three boys (identified as members of Princeton's class of 1895) traveled to the Rose Photography Studio of Princeton to commemorate their participation in the annual freshman versus sophomore snowball fight, and they proudly display their wounds.[62] Two of the young men are seated on simple wooden chairs, while a third stands above them; his eyes are nearly swollen shut, and he almost seems to brandish his battered profile to the camera. The trio is dressed nearly identically in rough and rugged clothing: thick corduroy jackets are layered over heavy woolen sweaters, a departure from the suits they often would have worn as Princeton students into a guise we might understand as an appropriation of working-class gear.[63] The young men have seemingly identical haircuts as well, with short-cropped hair that seems dampened from sweat or snow, combed down over their foreheads. They look sullenly at the photographer, or slightly past him—or is it simply that their bruised and battered faces are swollen into these expressions? Their faces bear cuts that are still weeping, traces of blood trickling down their cheeks. But this was not a mug shot taken against their will—they have entered the space of the photographer's studio specifically to record this moment for posterity, prizing its significance and perhaps already anticipating how they will have this record of their conquest or conflict. It is unclear whether they were defeated or whether they emerged the victors, but the indexical signs of their brutal fight are commemorated and preserved for the future. This is a display of masculinity that emphasizes brawn and might, contest and striving, evoking what would come to be known as the "strenuous life," as it was so memorably articulated by Theodore Roosevelt.[64] Indeed, many of Princeton's traditions during the nineteenth century centered around violent physical contests; in addition to the annual snowball fight, Princeton students eagerly anticipated the "Cane Spree," a brawl that was eventually converted into organized athletic competitions and was frequently covered in the *New York Times* and other publications.[65] We see then that Princeton men were swayed by broader trends that have been analyzed by social and cultural historians: seeking the rush of "authentic experience" and physical exertion as fears circulated about a crisis of masculinity, many wealthy men of the period—and those who were considered "brain workers," rather than physical laborers—pursued rigorous exercise programs and hobbies or vacations that emulated and romanticized the rugged labor of ranchers or fishermen, for example.[66]

These students and alumni sometimes also mirrored these activities and anxieties in their art collections and aesthetic interests, joining the late nineteenth-century enthusiasm for nostalgic representations of boyish pluck and innocence, the rugged masculinity and youthful energy seen in John George Brown's terrifically popular series of newsboys, shoe shiners, and street urchins, or the best-selling chromolithographs of Eastman Johnson's *I Was Once a Barefoot Boy* and its evocation of a bucolic, rural boyhood.[67] Indeed, Brown's *Lazy Bones* (fig. 12) was donated to Princeton by Carl Otto von Kienbusch, Class of 1906, as part of the Carl Otto von Kienbusch Jr. Memorial Collection; this diverse collection also encompasses Japanese prints, stained glass, family portraits, and nineteenth-century pictures of fish and fishing, including Junius Brutus Stearns's *The Old, Old Story* (fig. 13).[68] Created about fifteen years after Louis Prang's *Barefoot Boy* chromolithograph and in the midst of its continued popularity, Stearns's painting stages an encounter between a young (and barefoot) boy and a middle-aged man in an allegory of country and city, or youth and adulthood. The two figures are posed beside an idyllic creek, far from the cares of the city, yet the middle-aged man's glossily polished waders and shiny fishing kit

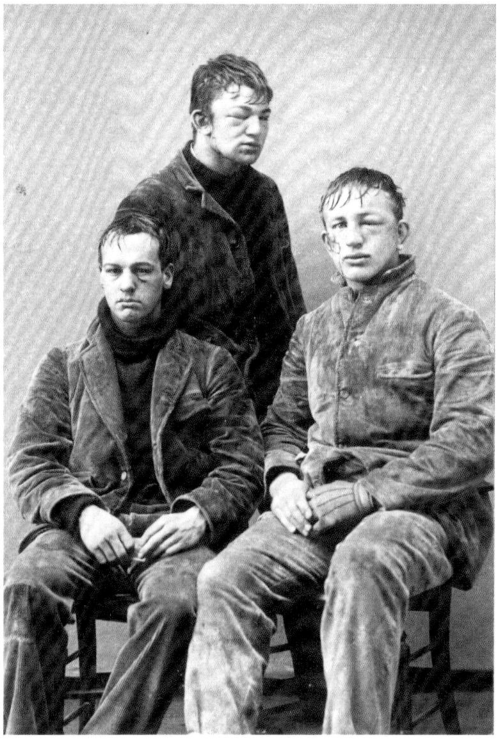

FIGURE 11 Rose Photography Studio (Princeton, NJ), "Snowball fight"; left to right: Darwin R. James (Class of 1895), John P. Poe (Class of 1895), Arthur L. Wheeler (Class of 1895), ca. 1893. Princeton University Library, Department of Special Collections. Princeton University Archives, Historical Photograph Collection

suggest this is not his usual milieu; this is also conveyed by the way in which he almost hides the small, solitary fish he has caught while gazing somewhat forlornly at the young boy's bountiful catch of plump brown trout. The boy's self-fashioned fishing pole, no more than a stick with a line, has proved victorious in this contest.

Princeton's *Lazy Bones* is emblematic of Brown's idealized representations of white urban youth, who, wearing torn and ragged clothes and weather-beaten boots, grin impishly at viewers, belying the dire straits in which many of them lived and worked. In this particular picture, the young boy leans against the scratched and peeling surface of a painted wooden panel. He is seated on the wooden crate that is intended to be his work surface or bench, and his shoe shine kit, with its brushes and polishes, rests unused on the ground next to him. The title underlines or implies his "laziness" rather than his low-paying labor, ascribing his circumstances to his lax

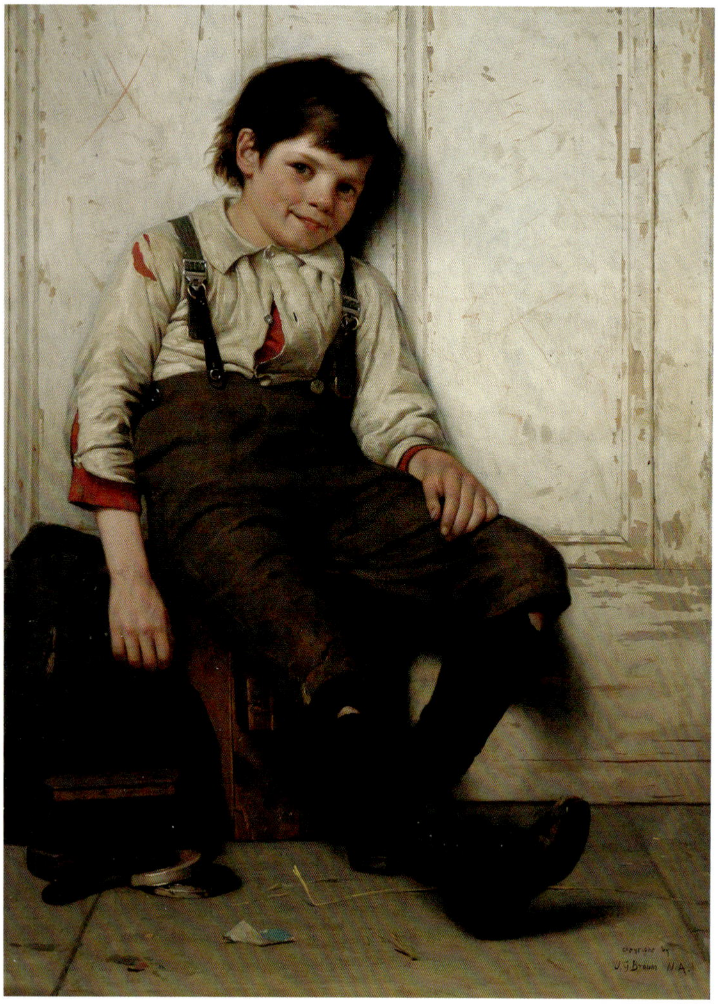

FIGURE 12 John George Brown (1831–1913; born Durham, United Kingdom; died New York, NY), *Lazy Bones*, ca. 1890. Oil on canvas, 112 × 82 cm. Princeton University Art Museum. Gift of Carl Otto von Kienbusch, Class of 1906, for the Carl Otto von Kienbusch Jr. Memorial Collection (y1951-57)

work ethic rather than the complex of structural issues and exploitation in the late nineteenth century. While the actual perils of street life and urban poverty were carefully documented in photographs by Lewis Hine and Jacob Riis, along with dozens of Progressive Era reformers, Brown's paintings romanticize these young boys as carefree and independent, seen from the vantage point of middle- and upper-class comfort and aestheticized as "picturesque and dirty," as one 1899 critic described them.[69]

Hine's *Young Boy at Vegetable Market*, in contrast, is a hard-focus photograph that attempts to convey the lived experiences of an actual child (fig. 14). A young boy with a solemn face grips a basket of vegetables in one hand and a bunch of greens in the other; he has been outlined in white pigment to distinguish him from the dark setting of the market and to assist in cropping and reproducing this detail in another image. Hine was a fervent believer in the power of images, especially photographs, to instigate social change and reform; in addition to teaching at New York's Ethical Culture School, he photographed immigrants arriving at Ellis Island and later the tenement neighborhoods in which they lived.[70] In 1908, he joined the staff of the journal *Charities and the Commons* and began working as an investigator for the progressive National Child Labor Committee,

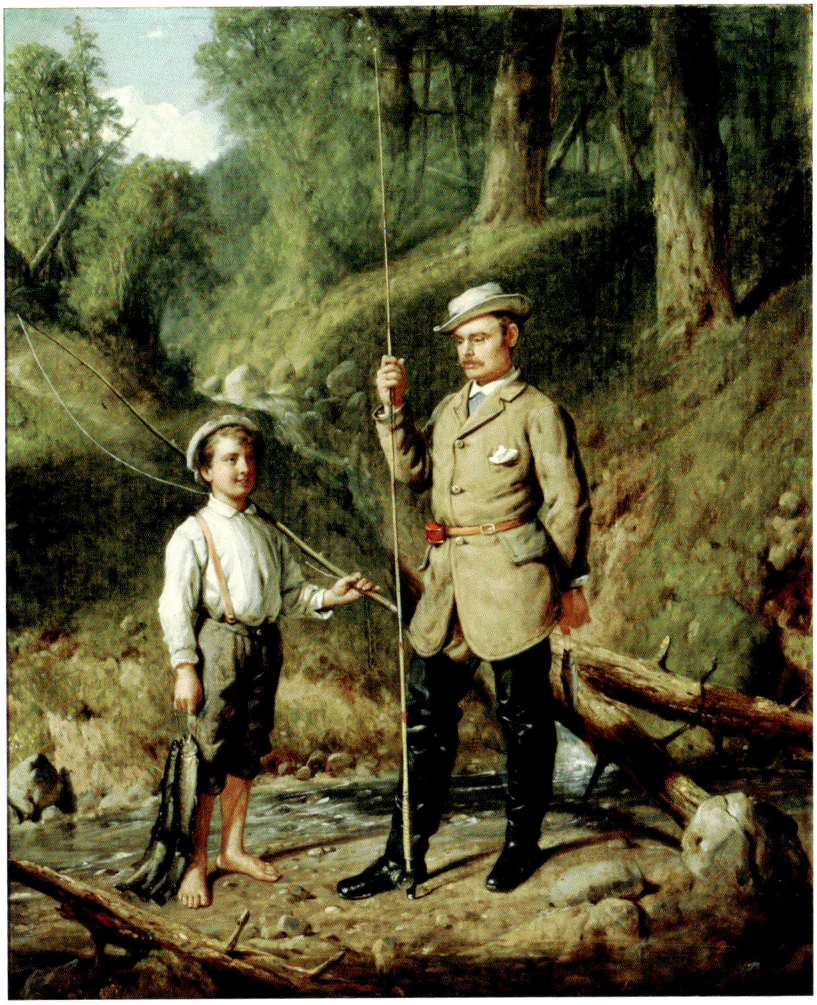

FIGURE 13 Junius Brutus Stearns (1810–1885; born Arlington, VT; died New York, NY), *The Old, Old Story*, 1882. Oil on canvas, 61 × 51 cm. Princeton University Art Museum. Gift of Carl Otto von Kienbusch, Class of 1906, for the Carl Otto von Kienbusch Jr. Memorial Collection (y1964-180)

documenting the factories, mills, streets, and mines where children worked by photographing and interviewing them about their experiences. Hine's photographs were transformed into lantern slides for public lectures and cropped and reprinted in graphic posters and pamphlets for broad circulation as a key strategy in social reform campaigns that advocated for better housing codes and labor laws that would protect children and other workers. The alteration and markup of Princeton's photograph is evidence of Hine's intent to incorporate a detail of the picture—the figure of the young boy holding the market basket—into another format, disseminating the image to sway public opinion and advocate for social change.

J. G. Brown's representations of street youth also achieved widespread circulation, but to very different ends. Attesting to the pictures' popularity, a turn-of-the-century journalist proclaimed, "Everywhere throughout the land, if not throughout the world, in the houses of the highest as well as the lowest, are to be found the originals or copies of Mr. Brown's bootblacks, who have endeared themselves to the hearts of all who know them."[71] While middle- and working-class audiences could obtain reproductions of his work (sold commercially as chromolithographs, engravings, and photographs), wealthy collectors adorned their lavish homes

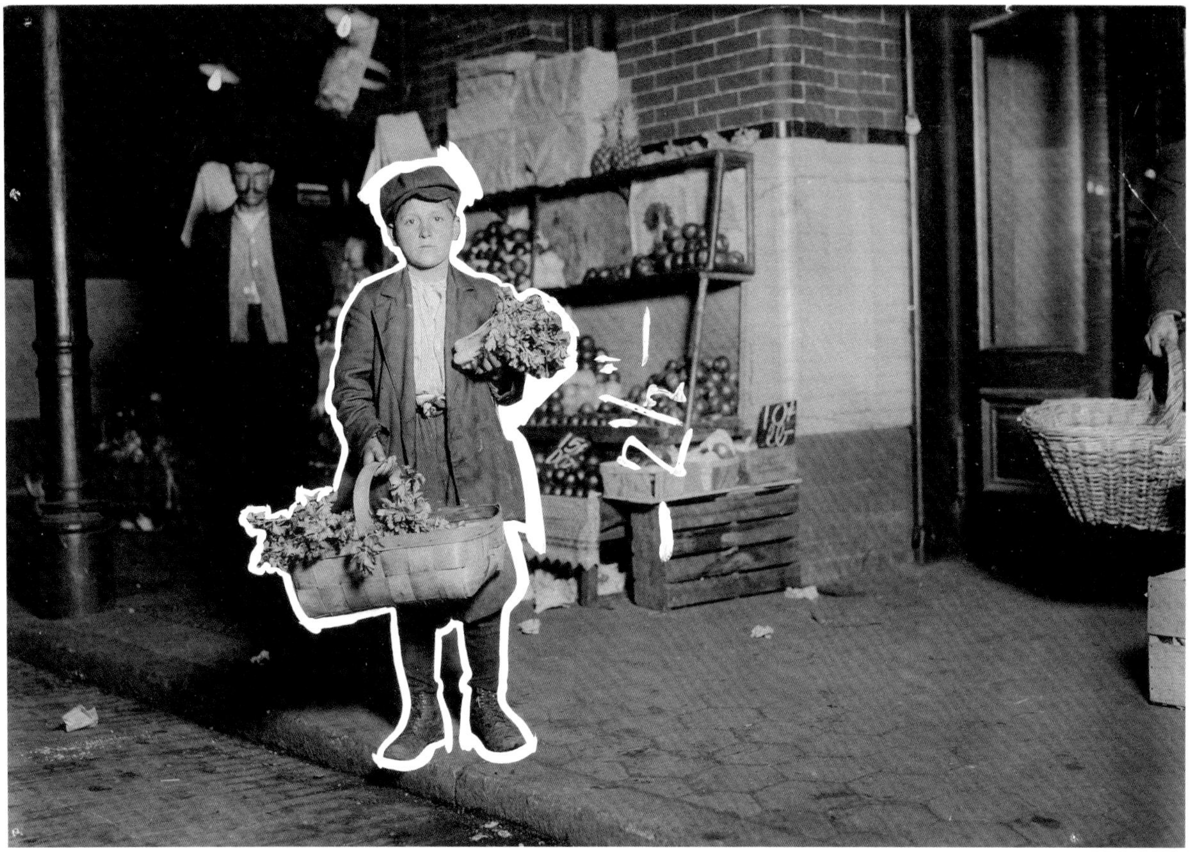

FIGURE 14 Lewis Wickes Hine (1874–1940; born Oshkosh, WI; died Hastings-on-Hudson, NY), *Young Boy at Vegetable Market*, ca. 1910. Gelatin silver print with later paint additions, 11.8 × 16.8 cm. Princeton University Art Museum. Museum purchase, Fowler McCormick, Class of 1921, Fund (2010-58)

with oil on canvas renderings of indigent and exploited children, albeit ones who seemed endearing and content. Brown himself declared, "I do not paint poor boys . . . solely because the public likes such pictures and pays me for them, but because I love the boys myself for I, too, was once a poor lad like them."[72] Economic interests were indeed what motivated Brown's subject matter, and he tailored his output to meet demand, shifting, for example, from painting both boys and girls to featuring boys almost exclusively in his work; as the *Times* journalist noted, "it was early borne in upon Mr. Brown's mind, by pitiless financial evidence, that the boys appealed more to the taste of buyers, and in this way he gradually came more and more to neglect the female urchin and to devote his energies to the bootblack and newsboy."[73] Representations of vulnerable young girls were apparently too unsettling for audiences, who could perhaps still imagine plucky hijinks or rags-to-riches narrative arcs for Brown's young boys.[74] Once he was an established artist with his own financial security, Brown waxed nostalgic for "the ragged, uncared-for gamin [who] is now the exception, where formerly he was almost the rule."[75] The distance from poverty was what made aestheticizing it possible; pictures of young boys as carefree "street urchins" provided an imagined alternative to lives of comfort.

Although much of the visual record of Princeton's culture indicates an investment in rugged conceptions of masculinity, the archive of Princeton's theatrical performances demonstrates students' readiness to play with or subvert gender norms (fig. 15). From its first performance in 1883, the Princeton College Dramatic Association, like many all-male theater troupes, featured actors cast across gender lines, cross-dressing and playing as women. By 1893, the company had evolved into the

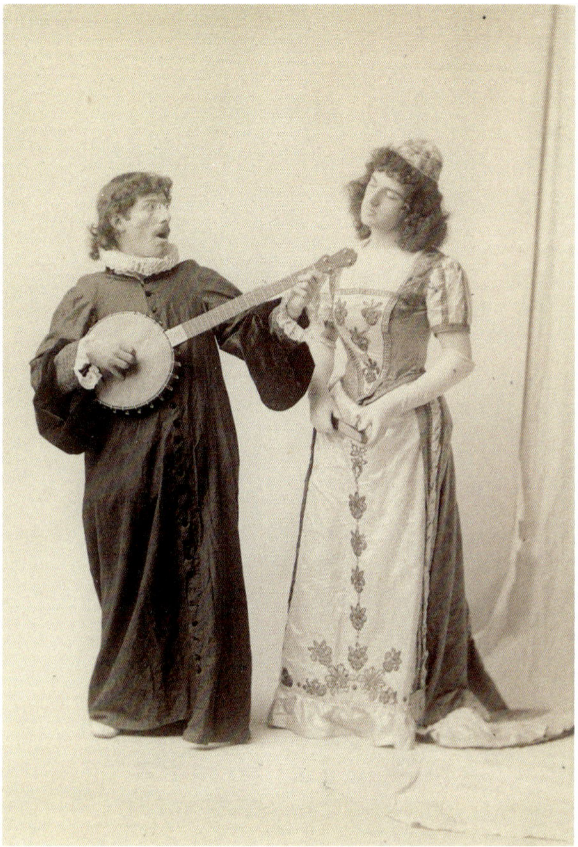

FIGURE 15 Publicity photograph for *Katherine*, 1892. Princeton University Library, Department of Special Collections. Princeton University Archives, Triangle Club Records

Triangle Club, and their performances consistently featured a vaudevillian kickline of enthusiastic, over-the-top camp.[76] Yet these are burlesques. While there might be some sense of experimentation or an exploration of identity, the performances often serve to reinforce binary conceptions of gender, lampooning qualities associated with women or finding humor in the gaps or fissures of the performance, highlighting the distinctions between conventional notions of femininity and masculinity. Princeton faculty often tried to circumscribe Triangle Club's national tour, fearing for the University's reputation; as the *Alumni Weekly* reported in 1908, faculty objected that the performance "does not leave with the audience an impression of that manly quality they like to ascribe to our students, a quality developed by sound minds in sound bodies."[77] Playing with gender, in this context, often reinforced the very binaries it might be thought to subvert.[78]

GENDER AND THE AMERICAN ART WORLD OF THE NINETEENTH AND TWENTIETH CENTURIES, IN CRITICISM AND IN PRACTICE

The women of Evelyn College are perhaps a generation removed from Winslow Homer's *At the Window* of 1872 (fig. 16). In juxtaposition to the connected community of the Princeton women, this canvas features an isolated woman, sitting alone by a window whose glimpsed greenery suggests the same early summer fecundity evoked in the archival photograph. A critic who viewed the painting in 1873 assessed it as "a strongly-painted and admirably drawn interior, with the figure of a young lady seated at an open window. Flowering plants are growing upon the windowsill, and the landscape out of doors appears dressed in the foliage of early summer."[79] Homer scholars often group this work with similar paintings that feature solitary young women who seem lost in their thoughts, all dated to 1872–73: *An Open Window* (Portland Museum of Art), *Reverie*, *Salem (Looking Out to Sea)*, and *Morning Glories* (private collections). Each canvas depicts a lone young woman posed near potted pelargoniums, framed by simple architectural elements that shelter her from the dazzlingly lush summer landscape. With the exception of *Morning Glories*, the young woman wears a dark dress and white fichu whose translucent ruffles drape over her shoulders, attire that many scholars have interpreted as indicating that she is in mourning. Her costume, in fact, is strikingly similar to that of the much older Elizabeth Marquand. In Princeton's *At the Window*, the young woman's hair is tied back with a thin black ribbon; the center part of her hair is accentuated by the contrast of light and shadow that bifurcate her profile. She is almost backlit by the sunny window, which we can surmise is open to the outside world with its warm breezes, as the view is not divided by muntins or panes. In the middle distance, the lines of a rustic fence cut across the scene parallel to the windowsill, where two terracotta or clay pots are perched. Gangly pelargoniums reach skyward, with the distinctive scalloped and lobed leaves of their foliage nearly blending with the greenery of tall trees in the background, whose strong trunks and branches, in turn, echo the stems of the potted

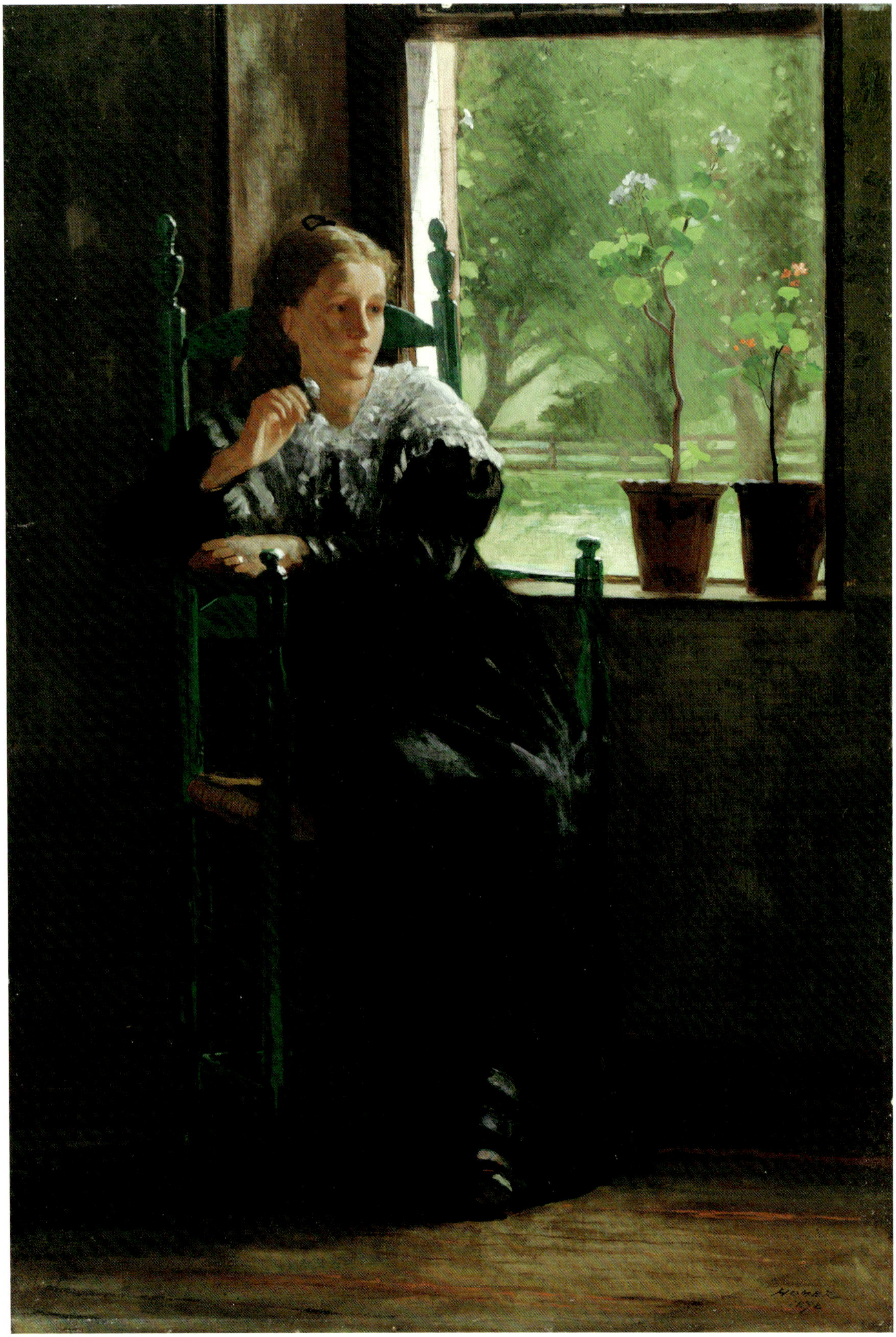
HOMER

plants; their blossoms are conveyed by quick splotches of white and red. Like the young woman, these plants have been cultivated and protected within a domestic interior. Tender pelargoniums cannot survive outdoors in harsh climates, and so they have likely overwintered indoors and continue to be sheltered from the wind or a change of weather. The young woman holds a leaf close to her face, perhaps enjoying its scent. In this dim interior, a glint of gold shines on her left ring finger: a wedding band. To modern viewers, her features perhaps seem too youthful for this marker of adulthood, and in combination with the somber dress and her solemn expression, we might ponder her circumstances. Yet to at least one viewer of the 1870s, empathy with the young woman's interior life seemed impossible. A Boston critic described the painting as "represent[ing] a lady sitting in an old-fashioned chair at an open window, meditating on some of the problems that come to the womanly mind in great force about as she leaves her teens: whether it be the next new dress, the forthcoming necklace, or the tardy lover, it would be impossible to say."[80] To this viewer, a rich intellectual interior life was inconceivable, as he caricatured the woman's concerns as materialistic yearnings or romantic impatience. The young woman's fate was, in fact, tied to the men in her life, as she herself could not own property or have recognized legal standing and autonomy.

Juxtaposing this work with another work of Homer's points to one possible future the young girl might imagine, whether with hope or despair. In *The Family Record*, we recognize the same wooden slat-back armchair with its woven rush seat and distinctive finials turned to resemble urns (fig. 17). In this scene, a young man occupies the chair, his wife at his side; an infant gazes up at them from a nearby cradle, arms outstretched. The couple leans over a thick book, and from the accompanying poem and details of the print, we can ascertain they are entering the infant's name into the family Bible, cementing their kinship relations by creating this textual record. Family genealogy is further invoked by a portrait that hangs in the background of a young boy attired in the garb of the eighteenth century. Scholar Reilly Rhodes has recently linked these pictures and the specificity of these material culture artifacts, tracing them to one particular domestic interior: the Wynkoop family homestead of Hurley, New York.[81] Might *The Family Record* suggest a happy ending, or is it a phantom vision of a never-to-be-realized future, one that a young widow might only dream of? Indeed, the carefully turned finials of the dark green chair in the painting evoke funerary urns and Neoclassical emblems of mourning, silhouetted against the window. Even the Boston critic who had mocked the young woman's presumed concerns noted the stark contrast between the quiet interior and the

FIGURE 16 Winslow Homer (1836–1910; born Boston, MA; died Prouts Neck, ME), *At the Window*, 1872. Oil on canvas, 57 × 40 cm. Princeton University Art Museum. Gift of Francis Bosak, Class of 1931, and Mrs. Bosak (y1985-38)

FIGURE 17 After Winslow Homer, *The Family Record*, illustration in *Harper's Bazaar*, August 28, 1875. Wood engraving. The Metropolitan Museum of Art, New York. Harris Brisbane Dick Fund, 1933 (33.21.9[1])

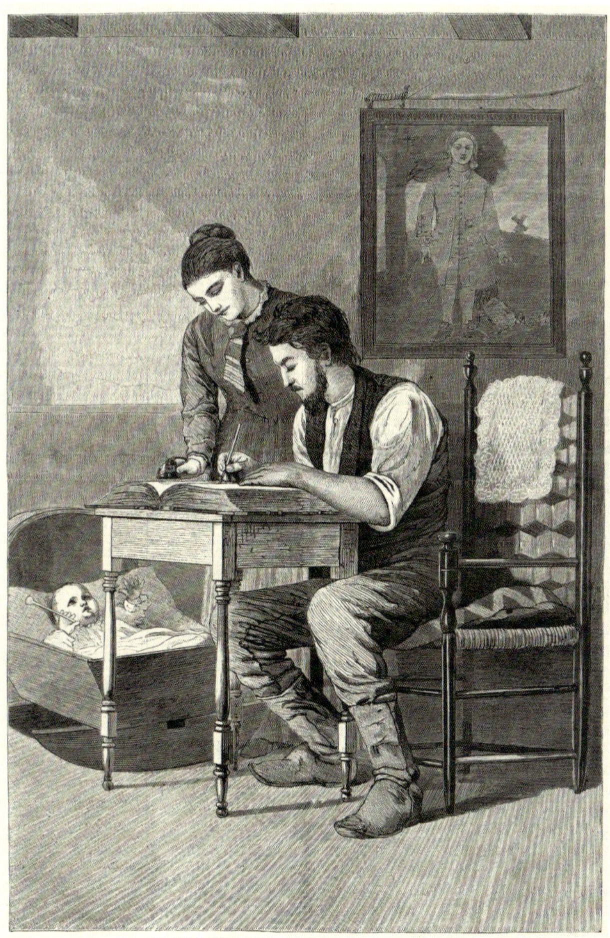

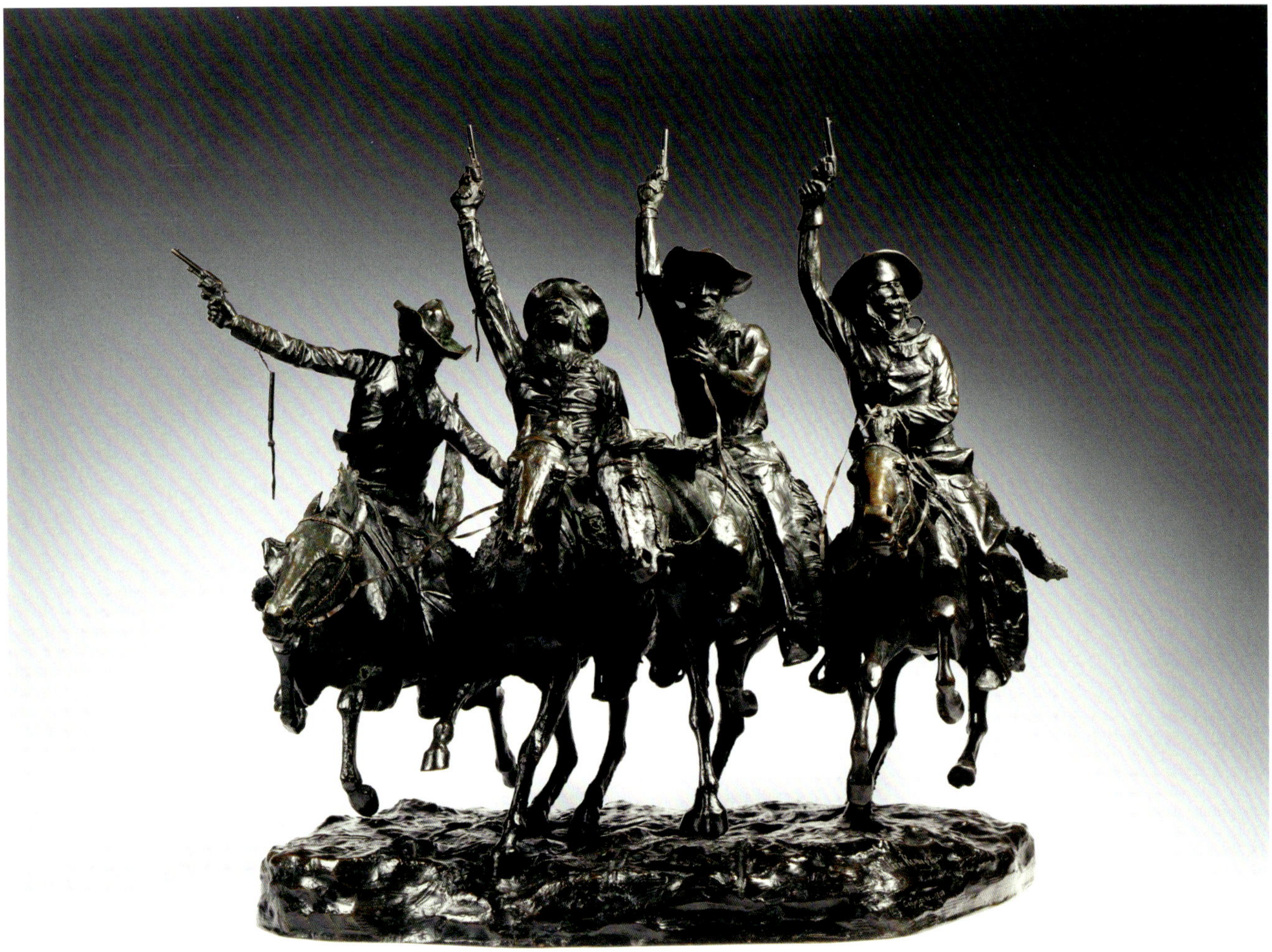

FIGURE 18 Frederic Remington (1861–1909; born Canton, NY; died Ridgefield, CT), *Coming through the Rye*, 1902. Bronze, 73 × 72 × 73 cm. Princeton University Art Museum. Gift of Laurance S. Rockefeller, Class of 1932 (y1991-5)

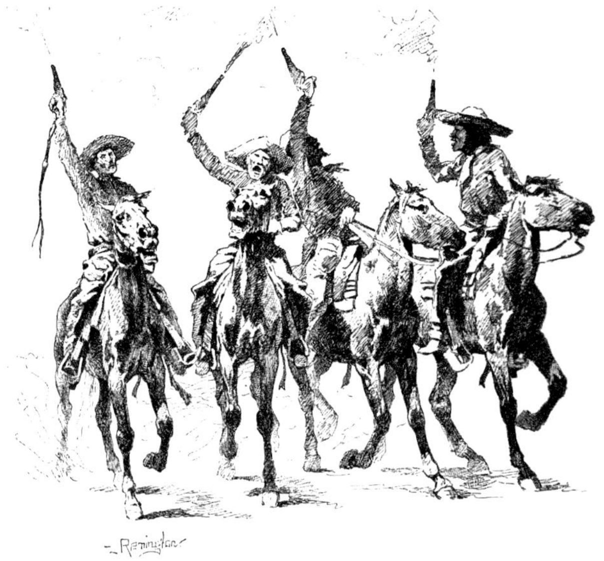

FIGURE 19 Frederic Remington, "Dissolute Cow-Punchers," illustration in Theodore Roosevelt, "Frontier Types," *Century Illustrated Monthly Magazine*, October 1888

outside world rendered by Homer, how its "play of sunlight and shadow disputes with that of the dreamy mood upon her for possession . . . one will not carry away any idea but that of the flesh-and-blood young woman sitting in quiet shadow, while outside the world is gay with rollicking sunshine."[82] In this manner, the critic implicitly acknowledges the conflict between the gay and the somber, the animated and the still, "rollicking" sunshine, living flesh-and-blood versus a cold and unspoken alternative.

This work seems a world removed from Frederic Remington's *Coming through the Rye*, a bronze sculpture featuring a group of boisterous cowboys on horseback, raising their guns in the air as they whoop and holler (fig. 18). Despite the subject matter of the American West, this sculpture, like most of Remington's bronzes, was created and distributed in collaboration with two New York establishments: it was cast by the Roman Bronze Works and exhibited and sold by Tiffany & Co.[83] Remington was a key player in building the mythology of the American West, disseminating romanticized imagery of heroic cowboys and subjugated or combative Indigenous figures in a variety of media including paintings, sculptures, and mass media illustrations.[84] Remington scholars have linked *Coming through the Rye* to two magazine illustrations of the previous decades (fig. 19). In 1888, the same year Mrs. Marquand's portrait was on view in Boston and in London, Remington's illustrations accompanied a series of articles by Theodore Roosevelt entitled "Frontier Types," which rhapsodize about the rugged characters of the American West, presaging Roosevelt's famous "Strenuous Life" speech. As Roosevelt mused, already waxing nostalgic, "The old race of Rocky Mountain hunters and trappers, of reckless, dauntless Indian fighters, is now fast dying out. Yet here and there these restless wanderers of the untrodden wilderness still linger . . . [living] wild, free, reckless lives."[85] This is a man's world, as Roosevelt relates: "The frontier is hard on women and on cattle . . . the grinding toil and hardship of a life passed in the wilderness, or on its outskirts, drive the beauty and bloom from a woman's face long before her youth has left her."[86] Rather than considering the women of the frontier, we are to keep our gaze on the men of the West and their lives of "hardship and adventure."[87] Remington's "Dissolute Cow-Punchers" are a disorderly lot, a raucous grouping of four men on horseback who crow and shout, twisting and turning in their saddles; smoke disperses from their recently shot pistols as their horses stagger under their uneven weight. Roosevelt writes of their carousing with fondness, perhaps mitigating the perceived violence of the illustration:

> In the main, [they are] hard-working, faithful fellows, but of course are frequently obliged to get into scrapes through no fault of their own . . . they exchange the wages of six months' grinding toil and lonely peril for three days' whooping carousal, spending their money on poisonous whisky or losing it over greasy cards. . . . All this is mere horse-play; it is the cowboy's method of "painting the town red," as an interlude in his harsh, monotonous life.[88]

Boys will be boys, Roosevelt seems to aver, denying or suppressing the very real violence that drunken gangs might (and did) commit, especially in this post-Reconstruction era of frequent acts of racialized and extrajudicial violence.[89]

Roosevelt also wished to convey to his readers that the absence of women was not total, even if frontier women were not sufficiently picturesque for his attention or Remington's illustrations. No, Roosevelt's cowboys bashfully tell him of their "sweethearts," asking the writer to post letters for them, "each . . . directed to a girl."[90] In this homosocial world, Roosevelt is quick to emphasize, compulsory heterosexuality still follows suit.

The following year, Remington's illustration of the "Dissolute Cow-Punchers" was slightly adapted for *Harper's Weekly*, featured in a December issue as "Cow-Boys Coming to Town for Christmas" (fig. 20). But this was not a heartwarming holiday tale of peace and goodwill toward men:

> It is at this season that every wild and lawless instinct of the cow-boy seem to have their fullest development. . . . The cow-boy . . . when he "turns loose" in town does it in a thorough way. His animation vents itself in shrieks and yells, the firing of the revolver, and the mad gallop. . . . With the advent of Christmas the cowboys from the surrounding ranches gather in the frontier towns. They come on their most fiery horses, and are dressed in their characteristic picturesque costumes. When they have taken drink enough, to become boisterous, there follows the reckless riding and the shouting.[91]

In Remington's illustration, the cowboys gallop through a snow-covered town, a dog at their heels. The horses are represented in midair, evoking the energy with which they gallop and jump and buck and lunge, jerked about by the boisterous cowboys. A man in an apron stands under a sign labeled "Meat Market," an invocation of the eventual results of the cowboy's labor and the cattle's slaughter, transformed into holiday feasts. The townspeople gathered near the butcher shop seem unperturbed, as though this is a common sight; none of them turn their heads or express alarm, despite the threatened and implied violence.

Coming through the Rye evokes a similar dynamism to the two illustrations, with breathtakingly few points of contact between the horses' hooves and the base of the sculpture (see fig. 18). As Remington himself noted, suggesting satisfaction with the ways in which energy and motion could be conveyed in three dimensions, "Sculpture is the most perfect expression of action."[92] The rarefied air of the Tiffany showroom on Fifth Avenue could not be further from the riotous scenes evoked in *The Century* and *Harper's*, but the company proudly displayed Remington's western bronzes, including them in a lengthy inventory of "Suggestions for Christmas Gifts" in December 1907.[93] Many prominent New York families moved seamlessly between the mansions of Manhattan and the ranches of the American Southwest; Laurance S. Rockefeller (Princeton Class of 1932), who ultimately donated Remington's sculpture to Princeton, also frequented his family's JY Ranch in Wyoming, indicating the family's investment in the romantic myth of the West.[94]

Beyond its multiple lives in print and in bronze, in the homes of magazine subscribers and purchasers of tabletop sculptures, Remington's quartet of carousing cowboys attained monumental scale when it was adapted as a larger-than-life sculpture for the 1904 St. Louis World's Fair celebrating the anniversary of the Louisiana Purchase and US westward expansion. In a stereographic view of the fairgrounds, we can discern two young women dwarfed by the massive sculpture (fig. 21). The cowboys tower over spectators, providing an alarming contrast to the Neoclassical allées and imposing architecture of the Fair. Expanded beyond life size and situated within the heterosocial world of edifying and entertaining exhibitions, the cowboys might seem sorely out of place, a terrorizing presence. Yet organizers of the Fair thought it was fitting, noting, "The frolicsome spirit of this work makes it peculiarly appropriate as an introduction to the lighter merriment of the concessions' street," even as the sculpture was displayed with the title "Cowboys Shooting Up a Western Town," creating a dizzying cognitive dissonance between the

FIGURE 20 Frederic Remington, "Cow-Boys Coming to Town for Christmas," illustration in *Harper's Weekly*, December 21, 1889

FIGURE 21 C. L. Wasson, *"Cowboys off the Trail"—Statuary after painting by Frederic Remington, entrance to pike, World's Fair, St. Louis, Mo.*, ca. 1904. Stereograph card published by International View Co., Decatur, IL. Library of Congress, Washington, DC. Prints and Photographs Division

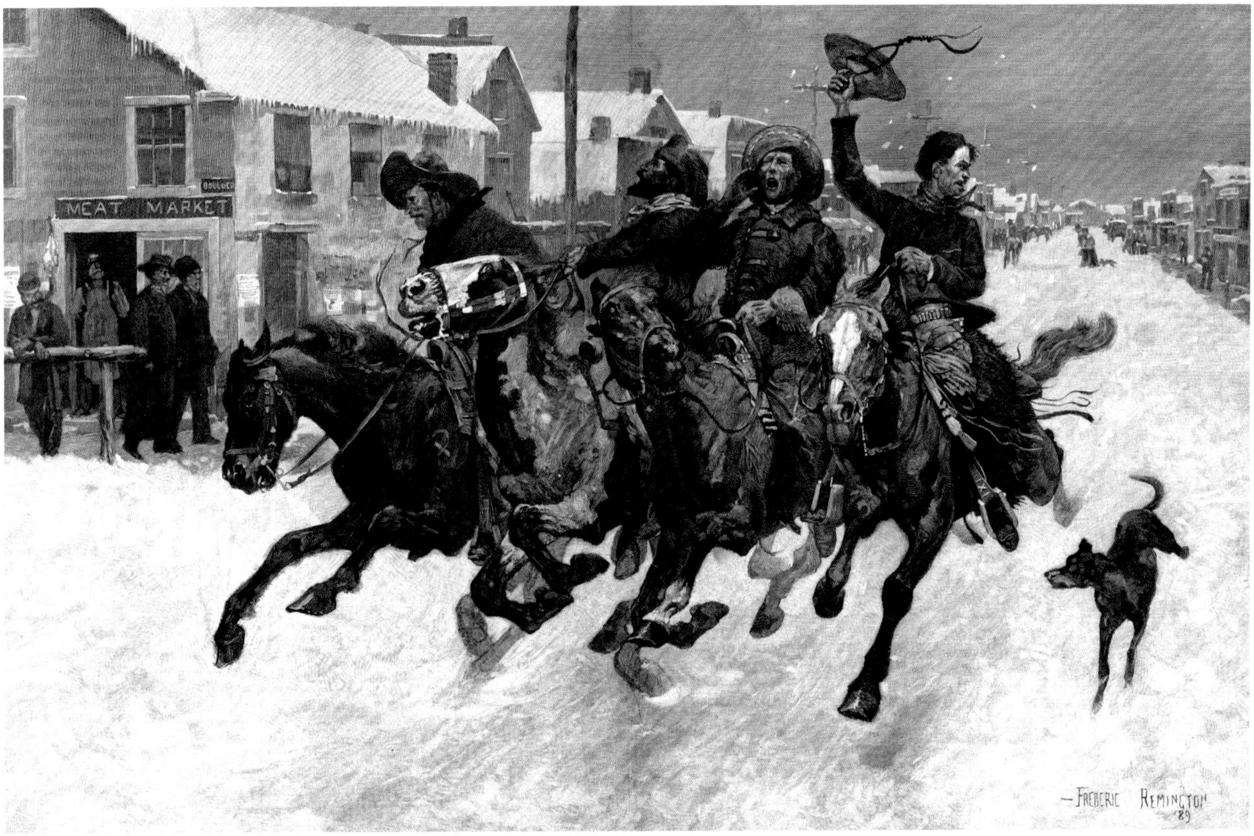
MEAT MARKET
FREDERIC REMINGTON '89

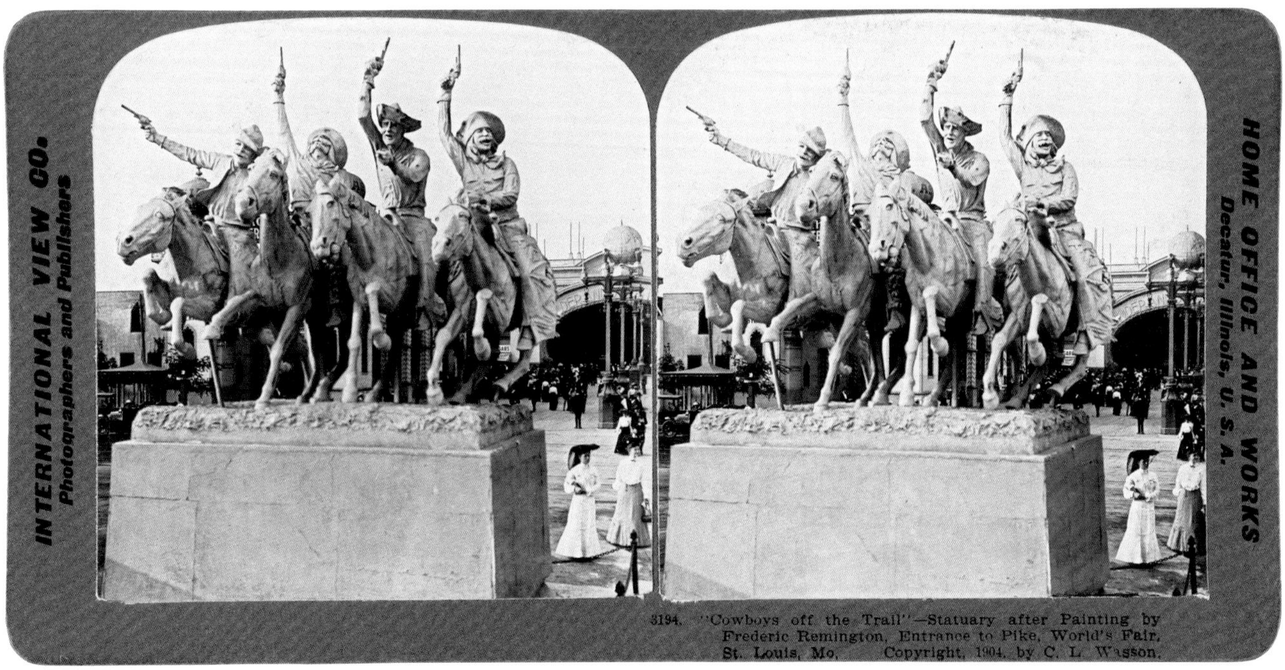
INTERNATIONAL VIEW CO.
Photographers and Publishers
HOME OFFICE AND WORKS
Decatur, Illinois, U. S. A.
3194. "Cowboys off the Trail"—Statuary after Painting by Frederic Remington, Entrance to Pike, World's Fair, St. Louis, Mo. Copyright, 1904, by C. L. Wasson.

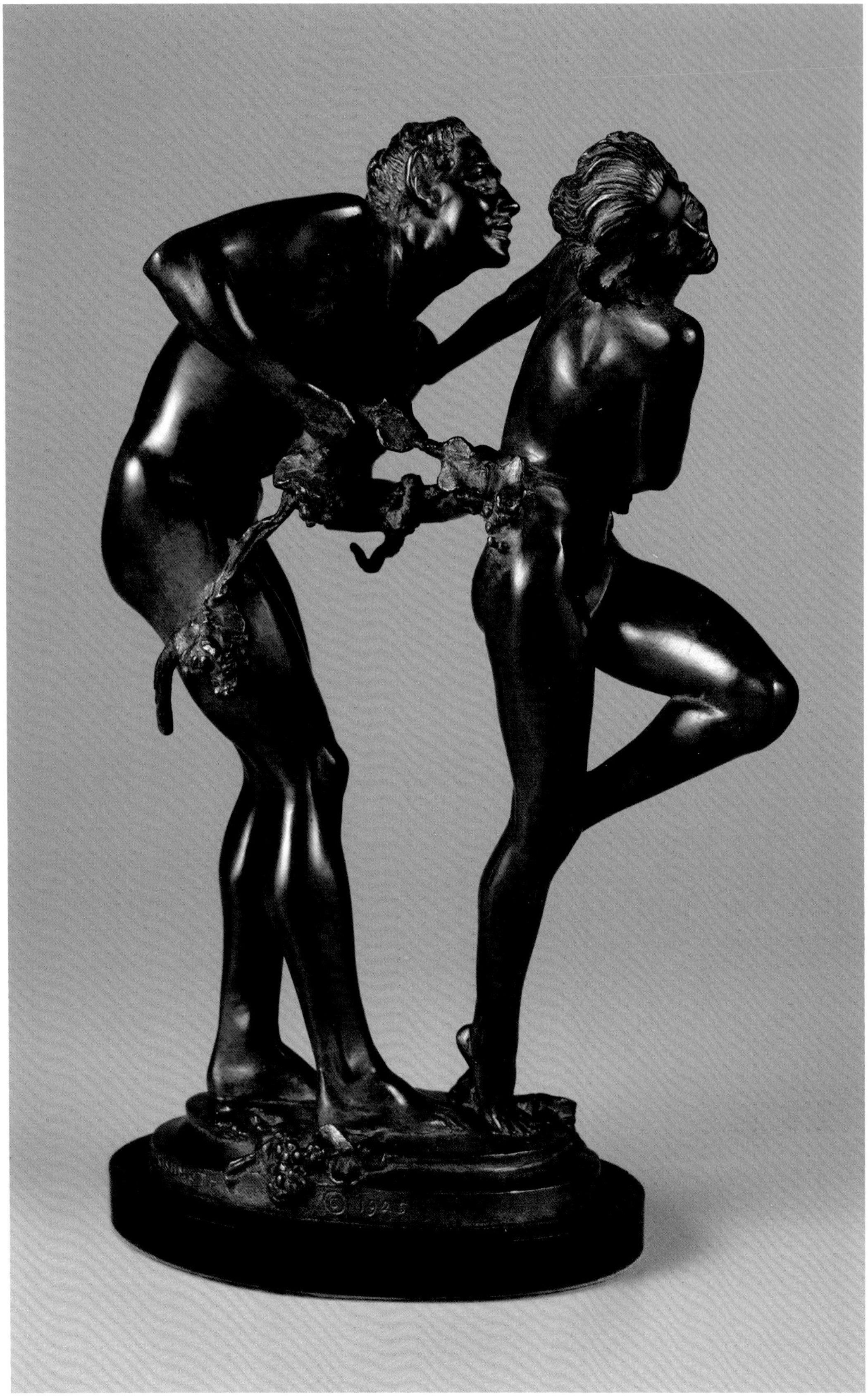

"frolicsome spirit" and "merriment" of leisure activities versus a scene of gun violence and intimidation.[95] The earlier context of the alcohol-fueled rampage conveyed in Remington's illustrations of the quartet had not been lost; one reviewer described the sculpture as "Four [cowboys] riding madly abreast [and] firing their revolvers in the air after firing themselves with liquor. It is a fitting introduction to the gay and reckless Pike, and a tour de force in modeling."[96] Similar to Chicago's Midway, the Pike was an avenue of immersive entertainments including a "Moorish Palace," an "Old Plantation," and, significantly, a bridge to William F. Cody's "Congress of Nations and Rough Riders."[97] As the Fair organizers proclaimed, "The Pike is a story-book land. All creeds and customs are there . . . characters have stepped from the leaves of history, travel and adventurous fiction to salute you in reality."[98] These constructed fantasies were nonetheless populated by very real people who were paid unconscionably low wages to reperform their own subjugation, repeatedly, for primarily white audiences' entertainment.[99] This was all of a piece in a Fair intended to reinforce white settler–colonial domination. In his address at the dedication ceremonies of the exposition, Theodore Roosevelt celebrated the Louisiana Purchase as the spark of a heroic victory carried out by white frontiersmen: "The greatest feat of our forefathers," he crowed, "was the deed of the men who, with pack-train or wagon-train, on horseback, on foot, or by boat, pushed the frontier ever westward across the continent," who "tame[d] the rugged wilderness" with their "manliness and stalwart hardihood."[100]

The sculptural program of the Fair was also designed to reinforce these messages of white male heroism. "The sculpture tells the story of the great event commemorated by the Universal Exposition," the *Official Guide* informed readers, "the sway of liberty from the Atlantic to the Pacific, through the acquisition of the Louisiana territory. . . . The sculpture reflects the larger and grander phases in the adventurous lives of those explorers and pioneers who won the wilderness from its brute and barbarian inhabitants as well as those achievements of later civilization, wrought by the genius of American intellect."[101] Remington's cowboys are thus recast as heroic pioneers, not "brutes," in light of their whiteness—an advance of "progress" rather than terrorism.

Remington's plays with scale, collaborations with luxury retailers, and evocations of a mythical past find a perhaps surprising parallel in the work of Harriet Whitney Frishmuth, whose *Rhapsody* of 1925 was created in collaboration with Gorham Manufacturing Company (fig. 22). In this graceful work, the elegant forms of two nude figures, a nymph and a faun, are balanced in a dynamic dance of attraction and repulsion. The faun leans eagerly toward the nymph, and he has looped a sinuous grapevine around her waist as though to pull her to him; she turns, pushing him away, perching on tiptoe, and raising a knee as though she might leap into the distance. Both figures display beatific smiles, suggesting a playful and flirtatious interaction rather than one of violence and conflict. Still, the faun grasps the vine tightly in his fist, even as the nymph emphatically pushes back against his shoulder and twists away, turning her face from him. Today's viewers might sense her ambivalence at being pursued, notwithstanding that this sculpture features the idealized forms of mythological creatures, indicated by the elongated and pointed ears of the male figure. Is this a playful and willing interaction, fraught with eroticism? Or is there a darker undercurrent of violence and aggression? Whose "rhapsody" is this?

We know that Frishmuth worked extensively with dancers from the Fokine ballet, especially Desha Delteil, and the gracefulness of this suspended pose suggests careful choreography rather than desperation. However, the female figure's effort to extricate herself from the faun's embrace demands to be considered in the context of the art historical aestheticization of rape as the narrative setting for artists to demonstrate their bravura skills in modeling the nude body and intertwined figures.[102] Is this female figure smiling in the pleasures of flirtation, or could this be a de-escalation tactic, a learned behavior of appeasement and amelioration?[103] If the latter, the "Rhapsody" of the title centers the male or faun's perception and experience of sexual pursuit

FIGURE 22 Harriet Whitney Frishmuth (1880–1980; born Philadelphia, PA; died Waterbury, CT), *Rhapsody*, modeled 1925, cast 1926–29. Bronze, 30.2 × 20.6 × 11.1 cm. Princeton University Art Museum. Gift of Frank L. Hohmann III, Class of 1968 (2016-495)

and pleasure, denying or suppressing the potential fear and panic of the female figure and that of any viewer attuned to this possibility. What might this work by an early twentieth-century sculptor offer us about issues of consent, appeasement, or pleasure that persist in the lives of present-day women, and how might our interpretation of it be further inflected by the stories of the young women of Evelyn College, or those visiting the 1884 Paris Salon, or those women who entered a coeducational Princeton in 1969?[104] We might see pleasure, or we might hear nervous laughter.

Frishmuth was featured alongside the work of other female sculptors in a breathlessly enthusiastic 1911 account published in *Good Housekeeping* entitled "Women Sculptors of America: How Many Readers Knew There Were So Many of Them? And So Talented?"[105] The author, Gardner Teall, was at pains to reassure readers about the femininity of these women sculptors, acknowledging the gendered expectations of the medium:

> The sculptor's art is scarcely one that could be called a parlor avocation, or a neat pastime to be casually indulged in with the mere hope of producing something pretty for the pains one may bestow upon it; instead it suggests heroic things, clay beds, marble quarries and the sort of a workshop that the name of Michelangelo brings to mind. Indeed the sculptor's art requires the devotion of a true love for it and a determination to work hard to achieve the results which the mind of the artist conceives, and which the hand of the sculptor must be trained by patient discipline to produce in beautiful form . . . there are in America probably more women sculptors of distinction than men, despite the rougher work the sculptor's pursuit is supposed to entail, work, one would imagine, which would appeal more to the sterner sex.[106]

This passage's brief mention of "parlor avocation[s]" serves primarily to set aside what were traditionally the artistic practices of women who were fortunate enough to have leisure time and means, frequently devalued as "fancywork": needlework and embroidery, hairwork, small-scale sculptural arrangements of seashells or wax, albums of seaweed, moss, or pressed flowers arranged in intricate forms.[107] Like many fine art museums, the Princeton University Art Museum does not include many works of this genre or in these varied media in its collections; these productions have been consistently undervalued and denigrated, in contrast to the "heroic" works of marble or bronze sculpture highlighted by the author.

The article offers capsule biographies of each artist, referring almost always to them by their married names and reassuring readers of their femininity *despite* the quality of their work: "Miss Theodora Ruggles, and her study with Henry Hudson Kitson, the Massachusetts sculptor, developed the pretty romance that led to her becoming Mrs. Kitson . . . she has always managed to find time for social pleasures, knowing that all work and no play is no more the thing for Jill than it is for Jack."[108] Teall's discussion of "Mrs. Harry Payne Whitney" (Gertrude Vanderbilt Whitney) is especially heavy-handed, conveying a scene of a studio where "her dear little children, Barbara, Flora and 'Sonny' play at 'making things like mama makes.' Mrs. Whitney is a devoted mother; even her art cannot lead her to neglect her children; she would desert it instantly if there were any such danger."[109]

These effusive assurances are in stark contrast to the curt description of Frishmuth, who, the author notes, "finds little time for anything but her work, with which she permits nothing to interfere."[110] Frishmuth was indeed unmarried at the time of the *Good Housekeeping* article, and Teall may have also been intending to convey Frishmuth's queerness to readers who were attuned to what was left unsaid. In this era, after all, a woman's single-minded pursuit of her career—or her single status—was seen as an aberration and a threat. An article in *Arts and Decoration*, written later in the same decade as Teall's terse assessment of Frishmuth, illuminates this attitude: "There is one thing preeminently that a woman can create, and that is her child. To create that child is the greatest aspiration of her life, and when she can do that she rightly cares for nothing else. . . . That is why women have never been great painters, even as they have never been great musical composers."[111] Arthur Edwin Bye was willing to concede a few exceptions, however, observing, "We know of plenty of cases where a woman's whole life is wrapped up in her career. Rosa Bonheur, the most prominent example of a woman painter, has been cited as of this type, but she was what in German is termed an 'Urninge' and scarcely can be classed among women painters."[112] In this quick acknowledgment and subsequent dismissal of Bonheur as an artist and as a woman, respectively, Bye invokes a derogatory and now-archaic German sexological term that connotes homosexuality and collapses gender and sexual orientation, proceeding to assert Bonheur's disqualification as a "real woman."[113] By the 1940s, Frishmuth and her partner, Ruth Talcott, began living together in a cozy domesticity they would share until Frishmuth's death in 1980, but this relationship was still often referred to only elliptically, with Talcott labeled as Frishmuth's "companion-secretary."[114] We might imagine a further layer of complexity at play in the small bronze sculpture of *Rhapsody*, with its heterosexual pairing, or the tight-lipped smile with which Frishmuth might have endured slights and outright insults and slurs.

More than thirty years after Frishmuth's inclusion in *Good Housekeeping*, Georgia O'Keeffe was experiencing similar conflicts with incredulous journalists, one of whom committed the following interaction to print: "'Don't call me Mrs. Stieglitz,' corrected Miss O'Keeffe. 'I've had a hard time hanging onto my name, but I hang onto it with my teeth. I like getting what I've got on my own.'"[115] O'Keeffe's *From a New Jersey Weekend II* depicts the delicate silhouettes of two headstones rendered in tones of pink, their slanting forms overlapping amid a snowy ground; meandering but intersecting lines in the background suggest a sagging fence (fig. 23). Tree trunks with leafless branches reach toward the sky, in contrast to the sinuous forms of nearly baroque gravestones whose surfaces are tempered with delicate tonal gradations, conjuring the striations of weathered stones whose inscriptions have likely been abraded over time. The two stones tilt and lean toward each other, evoking the aged couple who might be buried beneath, the wife's name subsumed to that of her husband.

The painting was first exhibited the year after its creation in O'Keeffe's winter 1942 exhibition at An American Place, the New York gallery run by her husband, Alfred Stieglitz. O'Keeffe and Stieglitz often visited friends Esther Underwood Johnson and J. Seward Johnson at their Oldwick, New Jersey, home, including at Christmas holidays.[116] Photographs of their home in the Library of Congress show a comfortably appointed house furnished with elegant antiques and a stable archway that echoes the silhouettes of the early nineteenth-century gravestones.[117]

O'Keeffe's 1942 exhibition was dominated by her landscapes—scenes of the environs of Abiquiu, New Mexico, where the artist had been spending her summers since 1929.[118] Yet the two canvases of New Jersey gravestones held their own, capturing the attention of art critics and serving as the publicity image in at least one review. As *Art Digest* noted, including a photograph of *From a New Jersey Week End, No. 1* (fig. 24), "Georgia O'Keeffe went to New Jersey for a weekend and came back, not with an impression of the neat patch-work fields or the immaculate dairy barns of the Garden State, but of two old tombstones, one pearly white and the other pearly pink. At Miss O'Keeffe's exhibition of 1941 canvases . . . these two strangely alive canvases are bewitching in their poetic conception and their effortless creation."[119] Preoccupations with liveliness and death simmer throughout the reception of these works as well as her paintings of animal bones and skulls, reactions stimulated not only by the subject matter but also by the impending war. Henry McBride's assessment of the exhibition invoked this explicitly: "[O'Keeffe] herself, like heroic Gen. MacArthur, is staying on. The wear and tear of nature, to her, is not frightening. Death is not disconcerting. Whatever happens, some time after the event, the remains take on a varnish. There is no real loss. . . . To the artist, [O'Keeffe] says, disaster is just the beginning and often it's merely the prelude to creation."[120]

CONCLUSION: ABSENCE AND PRESENCE

In her canonical 1971 essay, "Why Have There Been No Great Women Artists?," art historian Linda Nochlin searingly analyzes the structural conditions of the nineteenth-century art world, illuminating the ways in which art and educational institutions systematically excluded and denied access "to all those, women among them, who did not have the good fortune to be born white, preferably middle class and, above all, male."[121] While Nochlin's article served as a call to arms for scholars to shift their analytical and methodological considerations to incorporate these structural barriers, Alice

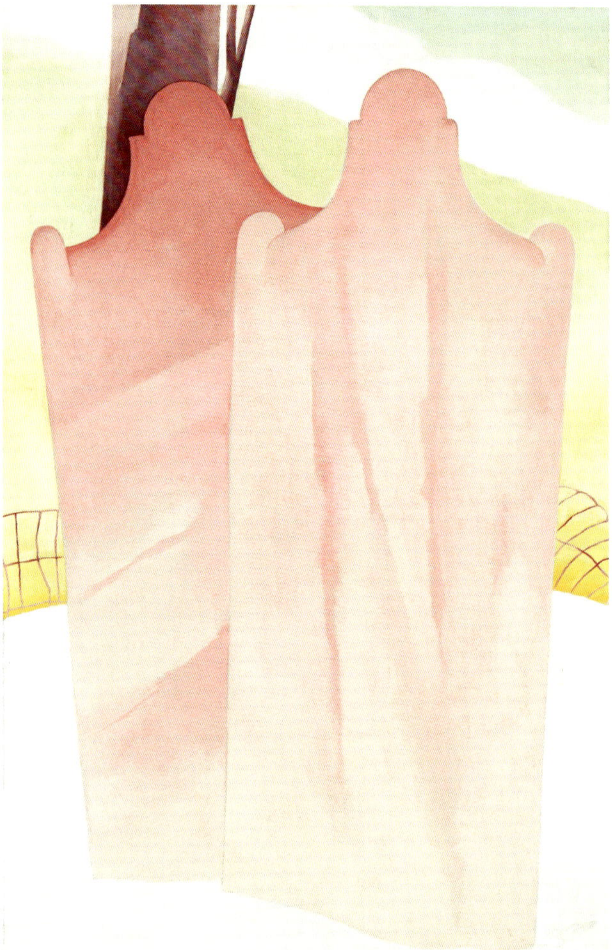

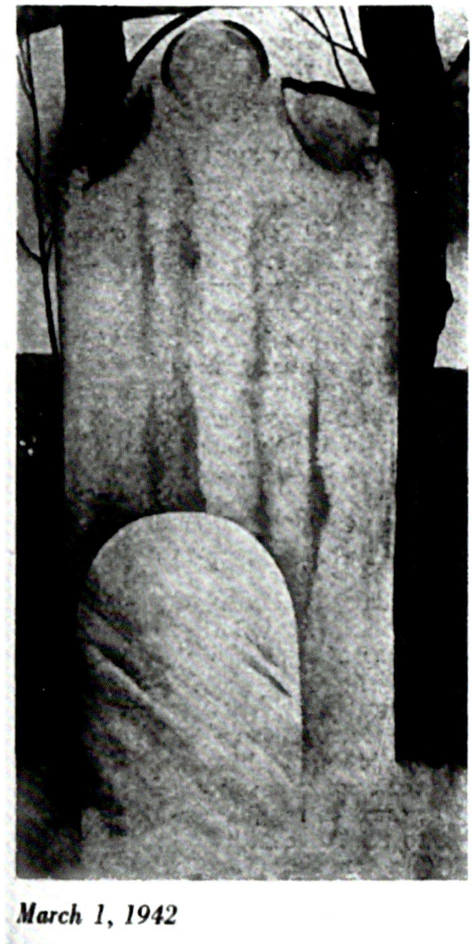

FIGURE 23 Georgia O'Keeffe (1887–1986; born Sun Prairie, WI; died Santa Fe, NM), *From a New Jersey Weekend II*, 1941. Oil on canvas, 91.5 × 61 cm. Princeton University Art Museum. Gift of the Georgia O'Keeffe Foundation (y1994-136)

FIGURE 24 Reproduction of Georgia O'Keeffe's *From a New Jersey Week End, No. 1*, in "Steadfast O'Keeffe," *The Art Digest*, March 1, 1942

Walker, writing in 1974, encouraged readers to imagine the artists of the past whose work could never come into being amid social and legal restrictions. "What did it mean for a black woman to be an artist in our grandmothers' time? In our great-grandmothers' day?," she asks. "It is a question with an answer cruel enough to stop the blood . . . these grandmothers and mothers of ours were not Saints, but Artists; driven to a numb and bleeding madness by the springs of creativity in them for which there was no release."[122] It is haunting and harrowing work. Walker's imaginative empathy helps us recognize and envision both lasting and ephemeral expressions that achieved physical or visible form. "We have constantly looked high, when we should have looked high—and low," she writes, conjuring examples of gardens, of textiles, of meals cooked with inventiveness and care—objects that we might consider within the framework of material culture studies, or even within William Prime and George McClellan's definition of art with which the formal study of art at Princeton—and this essay—began: "the product of the human brain and hands. Whatever man [or woman] has made, of whatever material, is a work of art. Every work of art is a permanent record of a thought or a group of thoughts."[123]

Turning to a quilt in the galleries of the Smithsonian, Walker recalls the label that credits "an anonymous Black woman in Alabama." As Walker muses, "If we could locate this 'anonymous' black woman from Alabama . . . she would turn out to be one of our grandmothers—an artist who left her mark in the only materials she could afford, and in the only medium her position in society allowed her to use."[124] While reading Walker's work, one imagines all the works that *might* have been, or those that were not recognized as such and cast aside. I think of all the creative works we can never know, and I grow discouraged. And yet in the years since Walker's essay was published, the quilts of Alabama artists have achieved great acclaim; when the *Quilts of Gee's Bend* exhibition came to New York's Whitney Museum of American Art in 2002, critic Michael Kimmelman proclaimed them to be "some of the most miraculous works of modern art America has produced."[125] Meticulous family records and the advocacy of the Souls Grown Deep Foundation have ensured that these works are *not* anonymous but rather carefully documented, their creators properly named and credited.[126] In 2021, Princeton University Art Museum acquired a selection of Gee's Bend quilts, including Henrietta Pettway's "Housetop" quilt, crafted around 1925 (fig. 25); the quilt features rhythmic geometric arrangements of rectangular panels of cloth punctuated by white stitching. An off-white border creates a frame of sorts for this work, evoking, to a modern eye, the format of a Polaroid picture. A thick band of purple fabric forms a square frame for four blocks of "log cabin" variations, gathered from a variety of textiles whose predominant colors are white, navy, and gray. In addition to the solid-color fabrics, there are glimpses of prints: the evocation of a vegetal or floral pattern in soft pinks and grays, tiny yellow roses, the pink veins of a leaf design on a mottled ground of gray and black, the shock of a red, black, and white plaid, whose rectilinear and intersecting forms echo the syncopated squares and rectangles of pieced fabric. We might imagine the irregular pieces in the "log cabin" as representing the rough wooden walls of many of the original dwellings of Gee's Bend, with the floral prints evoking carefully tended gardens surrounding these rustic log cabins—calling to mind the gardens planned and planted by Minnie Tallulah Grant Walker, lovingly described in her daughter's essay. The quilts of Gee's Bend, at least, are starting to take their rightful place among celebrated works of American art, even if many of us are still left to imagine "our mothers' gardens."

When we muse on Walker's evocations of societally imposed limits, we recognize, however, that these apply not only to artists of the past, but also to those of the present. Artist Ruth Cuthand has written about her own selection of media and aesthetic style as a means of exposing the status and treatment of Canada's First Nations peoples while also celebrating the survivance of Indigenous peoples. Cuthand recalls some of her earliest experiments with materials, emphasizing their utility and availability, while offering a glimpse of the inventiveness with which she transformed these cast-offs from medical exams into works of art: "As a child, my first art materials included the orange paper that was discarded in the processing of the Polaroid chest x-rays that we were subjected to annually . . . in routine tuberculosis screenings; they collected the peculiar-smelling 18-inch squares of paper and gave them to my Anglican minister father for use in Sunday school."[127] With a practice that now also encompasses beadwork and textiles, Cuthand notes, "Maintaining the anti-aesthetic principles on which my practice was founded, I have traded crudeness of style for materials and techniques that have long been denied status as serious art."[128]

Alongside ongoing works of recovery and research, Princetonian Toni Morrison has encouraged us to look forward and ahead. Writing in 2010 of the hallowed space of Nassau Hall's Faculty Room with its wood-paneled walls and gilded frames, Morrison saw not only the artifacts of the past, but also the promise of the future. As she observes, "Universities play a powerful mnemonic role. . . . But they are not memorabilia or mausoleums." Acknowledging the ways in which Princeton's history and leadership have been enshrined in the historic portrait collection, she anticipates the changes that are to come. "What may suggest stasis in the gender and racial monopoly on display in the Faculty Room will eventually be eclipsed by the inevitable inclusion of President Shirley Tilghman's presence as well as future luminaries not exclusively white or male," Morrison asserts. "The Faculty Room is not a tomb. It is a womb."[129] With this profoundly gendered and generative metaphor, Morrison shifts our thinking from the past to the future, from a place of death and decay to one of new life. Indeed, in

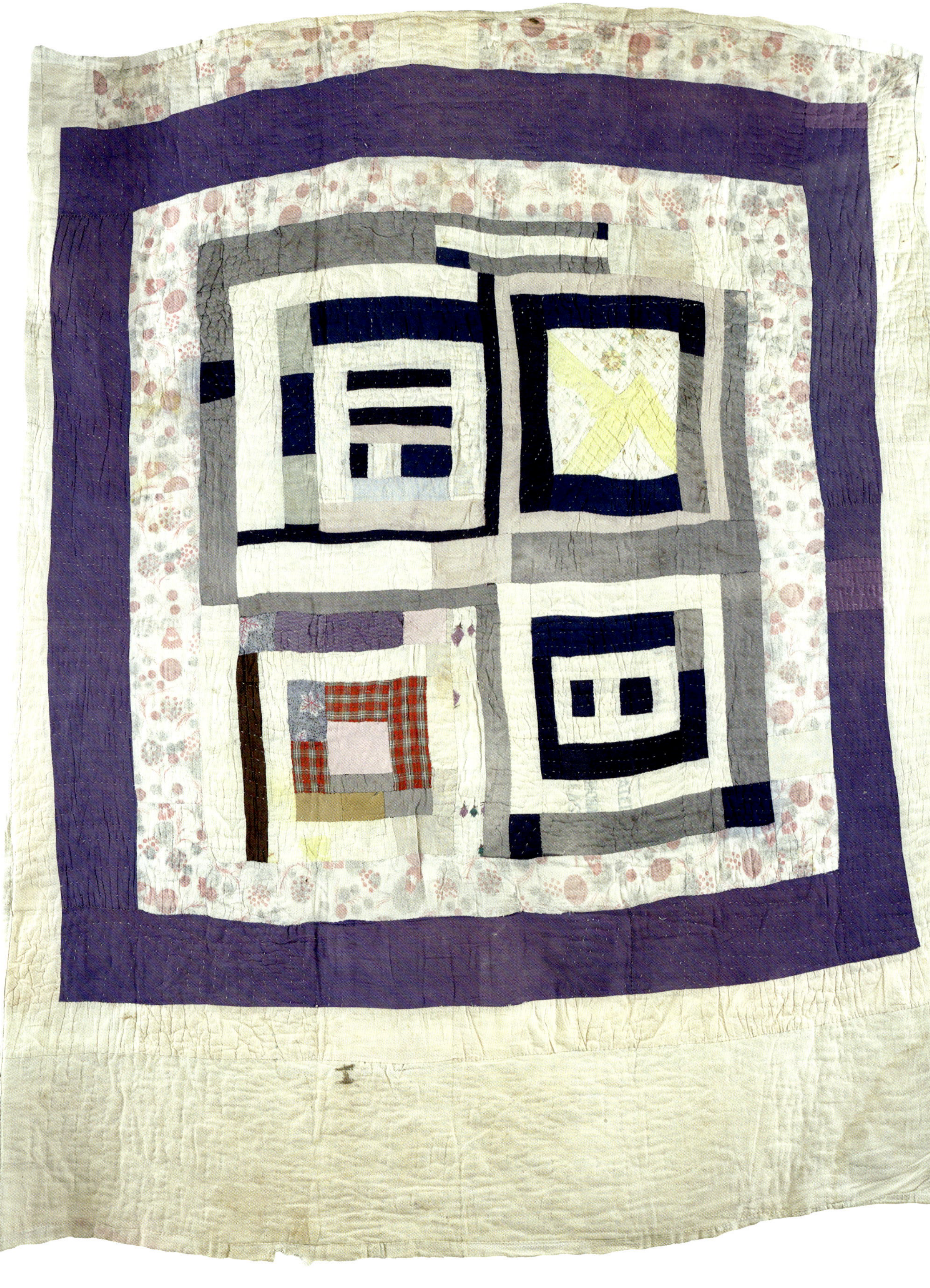

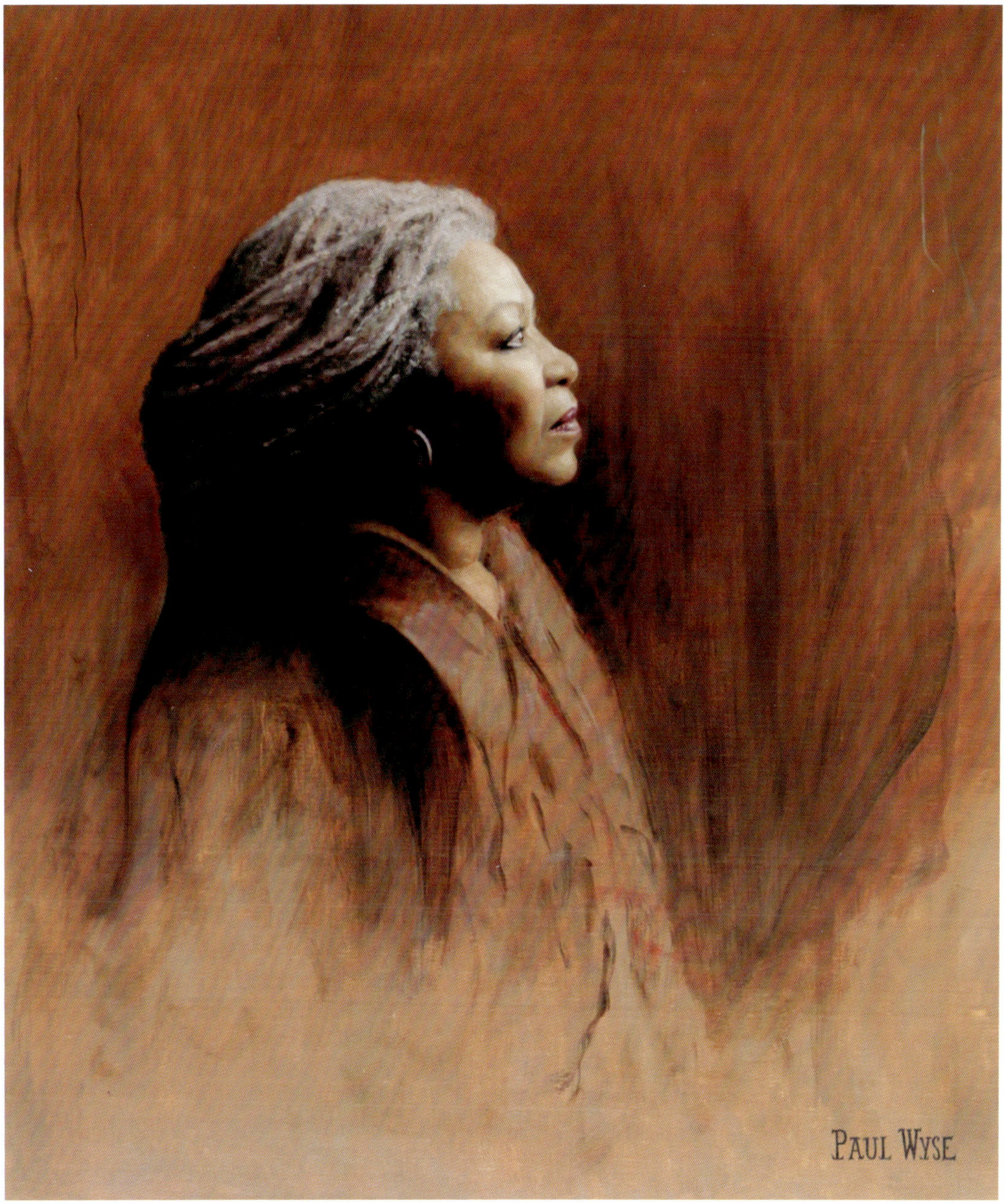

FIGURE 25 Henrietta Pettway (1894–1971; active Boykin, AL), Quilt ("Housetop" pattern with "Log Cabin" variation), ca. 1925. Cotton clothing and sacking, 218.4 × 188 cm. Princeton University Art Museum. Museum purchase, Mary Trumbull Adams Art Fund, and gift of the Souls Grown Deep Foundation (2021-50)

FIGURE 26 Paul Wyse (born 1970, Portland, ME; active Cleveland, OH), after a photograph by Timothy Greenfield-Sanders (born 1952, Miami Beach, FL; active New York, NY), *Portrait of Toni Morrison*, 2017. Oil on canvas, 78.7 × 68.6 cm. Princeton University (PP720)

recent years, Princeton has begun deliberately reconsidering its portrait collection and associated questions of representation, inclusion, and acknowledgment, establishing a Campus Iconography Committee in 2017; the University also established the Princeton Histories Fund to assist in the necessary research of "aspects of Princeton's History that have been forgotten, overlooked, subordinated, or suppressed."[130] Notably, this work includes a Portraiture Nominations Committee, whose labor has revivified the portrait collection by soliciting suggestions of individuals whose likenesses should be displayed on campus to honor their legacies.[131] One of the first commissions featured Toni Morrison herself, represented in a luminous painting by Paul Wyse (fig. 26). Morrison is depicted in profile, her face bathed in light; she seems to be looking toward that bright future she evoked. Her gray locs are gracefully swept back into a braid; although her features are delineated with striking illusionism and focus, her body dissolves into the merest evocations of painterly brushstrokes that fade in turn into a warm-colored ground, echoing a camera's depth-of-field optical phenomena. Morrison has already been joined by portraits of Princetonians Alan Turing, Robert Rivers, Denny Chin, and Supreme Court Justice Sonia Sotomayor, among others, representing a more inclusive institution. In addition to the ongoing commissions for Princeton's portrait collection, the Art Museum continues to diversify its collections, including through partnerships such as the one with Souls Grown Deep Foundation, which led to the acquisition of Pettway's quilt. With Morrison's generative metaphor of the womb, we might look to the future of Princeton's art collections, all the artists yet to be born, and what they might imagine and create; we might muse on the pictures and objects that will join *Elizabeth Allen Marquand* on the walls, and what they, and the circumstances surrounding them, can tell us about American art and society.

NOTES

1. See Museums Are Not Neutral, https://www.museumsarenotneutral.com/. Also see La Tanya S. Autry and Mike Murawski, "Museums Are Not Neutral: We Are Stronger Together," *Panorama: Journal of the Association of Historians of American Art* 5, no. 2 (Fall 2019), https://doi.org/10.24926/24716839.2277.
2. See, e.g., Artists Meeting for Cultural Change, *An Anti-catalog* (New York: Catalog Committee of Artists Meeting for Cultural Change, 1977); Paul DiMaggio, "Cultural Entrepreneurship in Nineteenth-Century Boston: The Creation of an Organizational Base for High Culture in America," *Media, Culture & Society* 4, no. 1 (January 1982): 33–50; Fred Wilson, "The Silent Message of the Museum," in *Global Visions: Towards a New Internationalism in the Visual Arts*, ed. Jean Fisher (London: Kala Press, 1994), 152–60; Carol Duncan, *Civilizing Rituals: Inside Public Art Museums* (New York: Routledge, 1995); Tony Bennett, *The Birth of the Museum: History, Theory, Politics* (New York: Routledge, 1995); and Alan Wallach, *Exhibiting Contradiction: Essays on the Art Museum in the United States* (Amherst: University of Massachusetts Press, 1998).
3. The scope of the library, with its genesis in Marquand's own collection, is discussed in W. Frederick Stohlman, "Special Collections at Princeton: I. The Marquand Art Library," *Princeton University Library Chronicle* 1, no. 1 (November 1939): 9–14; the inscription is quoted on page 14. I am grateful to Melissa Haynes for a discussion of the meanings and possible translations of the inscription.
4. Richard Ormond and Elaine Kilmurray, *John Singer Sargent: The Early Portraits*, vol. 1, *Complete Paintings* (New Haven: Yale University Press, 1998); Susan Sidlauskas, "Painting Skin: John Singer Sargent's 'Madame X,'" *American Art* 15, no. 3 (Autumn 2001): 8–33; Marc Simpson et al., *Uncanny Spectacle: The Public Career of the Young John Singer Sargent* (New Haven, CT: Yale University Press, 1997); Trevor Fairbrother, *John Singer Sargent: The Sensualist* (New Haven, CT: Yale University Press, 2001).
5. "Eccentricities of French Art," *Art Amateur* 11, no. 3 (August 1884): 52. *Gommeux* (or *gomineux*) and *flâneurs* were understood as Parisian "types" of the era: dandies and modern urban spectators, respectively, who were key players in nineteenth-century life of the city, articulated most famously by Charles Baudelaire (*The Painter of Modern Life*, 1863) and later Walter Benjamin (see "The *Flâneur*" in Benjamin, *Charles Baudelaire: A Lyric Poet in the Era of High Capitalism*, trans. Harry Zohn [New York: Verso, 1983], 35–66); also see Susan Buck-Morss, "The Flaneur, the Sandwichman and the Whore: The Politics of Loitering," *New German Critique* 39 (Autumn 1986): 99–140. The figure of the *gommeux* was featured in Bertall's *La Comédie de Notre Temps*, compared to *les beaux fils* and the dandy: "At each period of French history, a more or less whimsical name has

been used to designate those whom elegance, pretension, or success, or chic, according to the modern expression, particularly highlighted . . . [he] who is in full view, who shines, who is envied for his toilet, his position, his *genre* and his *chic*, is a *gomineux*" (translation mine, from Bertall's *La Comédie de Notre Temps*, vol. 1 [Paris: Plon, 1874], 111, 115).

6. Transcribed as "l'effet du désastre Gautreau" and translated by the Museum of Fine Arts, Boston, which also attributes the undated letter to 1885. John Singer Sargent to Emma-Marie Allouard-Jouan, undated, The Museum of Fine Arts, Boston, The John Singer Sargent Archive, SC.SargentArchive.7.8, https://www.mfa.org/collections/john-singer-sargent-archive/letters/SC-SargentArchive-7-8.

7. Punctuation and spelling have not been changed from the letter as it was transcribed in *Henry James: Selected Letters*, ed. Leon Edel (Cambridge, MA: Belknap Press, 1987), 222 ("Henry James to Miss Reubell, 1 April 1888"). See Paul Fisher, "The Lost Ambassador: Henrietta Reubell and Transnational Queer Spaces in the Paris Arts World, 1876–1903," in *Foreign Artists and Communities in Modern Paris, 1870–1914: Strangers in Paradise*, ed. Karen L. Carter and Susan Waller (Abingdon, UK: Taylor & Francis, 2015), 199–212; and Paul Fisher, "'Her Smoking Was the Least of Her Freedoms': Henrietta Reubell, Miss Barrace, and the Queer Milieu of Henry James's Paris," *Henry James Review* 33, no. 3 (Fall 2012): 247–54.

8. See Bridget A. May, "Wearing and Inhabiting the Past: Promoting the Colonial Revival in Late Nineteenth- and Early Twentieth-Century America," in *Performance, Fashion and the Modern Interior: From the Victorians to Today*, ed. Fiona Fisher et al. (New York: Berg, 2011), 45–58; Beverly Gordon, "Dressing the Colonial Past: Nineteenth Century New Englanders Look Back," in *Dress in American Culture*, ed. Patricia A. Cunningham and Susan Voso Lab (Bowling Green, OH: Bowling Green State University Popular Press, 1993), 109–39; and Beverly Gordon, "Woman's Domestic Body: The Conceptual Conflation of Women and Interiors in the Industrial Age," *Winterthur Portfolio* 31, no. 4 (Winter 1996): 281–301.

9. "The Royal Academy," *Leeds Mercury*, May 16, 1888.

10. "Eccentricities of French Art," 52.

11. "The Royal Academy," *The Graphic*, May 26, 1888, 551.

12. "The Royal Academy Exhibition," *New York Sun*, May 20, 1888, 7.

13. "Eccentricities of French Art," 52.

14. For more on Gautreau's skin and critics' responses to it, see Sidlauskas, "Painting Skin."

15. John Singer Sargent to Henry G. Marquand, September 5, [1888]. Archives of American Art, Robert C. Graham Collection of Artists' Letters, Box 1, Folder 24. Although no year is inscribed on the letter, Sargent discusses the impending closure of the Royal Academy exhibition and indicates the letter was written in Calcot-Reading, where he lived in 1888; see Evan Charteris, *John Sargent* (New York: Charles Scribner's Sons, 1927), 98.

16. John Singer Sargent to H. G. Marquand, March 18, [no year], quoted in Ormond and Kilmurray, *John Singer Sargent: The Early Portraits*, 199.

17. "Mr. Sargent's Portrait of Mr. Marquand," *The Critic* 28, no. 821 (November 13, 1897): 286.

18. Sophia Antoinette Walker, "Fine Arts: The Fall Exhibition at the Metropolitan Museum," *The Independent*, November 11, 1897, 7. On Marquand's extensive support of the Metropolitan Museum of Art, see Esmée Quodbach, "Collecting Old Masters for New York: Henry Gurdon Marquand and the Metropolitan Museum of Art," *Journal of Historians of Netherlandish Art* 9, no. 1 (Winter 2017), DOI: 10.5092/jhna.2017.9.1.2; Calvin Tomkins, *Merchants and Masterpieces: The Story of the Metropolitan Museum of Art*, rev. ed. (New York: Henry Holt, 1989); Ernest Knaufft, "Henry G. Marquand as an American Art Patron," *American Monthly Review of Reviews* 27, no. 2 (February 1903): 172–76; and Daniëlle O. Kisluk-Grosheide, "The Marquand Mansion," *Metropolitan Museum Journal* 29 (1994): 151–81. I am grateful to Melody Barnett Deusner for sharing her extensive research files on Henry G. Marquand with me.

19. "Miss Eleanor Marquand, Bride of G. H. Forsyth, Jr.—Brilliant Reception Follows Wedding Ceremony at 'Guernsey Hall,'" *Princeton Herald* 4, no. 19 (February 11, 1927): 5.

20. Mary Anne Goley, "John White Alexander's Princeton Legacy," *Princeton University Library Chronicle* 75, no. 2 (Winter 2014): 265–85.

21. Charles H. Dow, *Newport: The City by the Sea* (Newport, RI: John P. Sanborn, 1880), 76.

22. E. [Elizabeth] A. Alexander, "Mr. Henry G. Marquand," *Harper's New Monthly Magazine*, March 1897, 560–71. On Marquand's commissioned interiors, see especially Melody Barnett Deusner, "Building a Reputation: Henry Gurdon Marquand's New York Mansion," in *Orchestrating Elegance: Alma-Tadema and the Marquand Music Room*, ed. Alexis Goodin and Kathleen M. Morris (New Haven, CT: Yale University Press, 2017), 37–61; and Melody Barnett Deusner, "'In Seen and Unseen Places': The Henry G. Marquand House and Collections in England and America," *Art History* 34, no. 4 (September 2011): 754–73.

23. "Elizabeth Love Marquand," *New York Times*, February 4, 1895, 8. This death notice is only three sentences long and gives little information about her life. On the challenges of finding women in the archive and for broader historiographic questions and literature, see Laurel Thatcher Ulrich, *Well-Behaved Women Seldom Make History* (New York: Vintage Books, 2008).

24. "Henry Gurdon Marquand," in Lyman Horace Weeks, *Prominent Families of New York* (New York: Historical Company, 1897), 396. Also see Richard D. Birdsall, "The Reverend Thomas Allen: Jeffersonian Calvinist," *New England Quarterly* 30, no. 2 (June 1957): 147–65.

25. See especially Deusner, "'In Seen and Unseen Places,'" 754–73; Quodbach, "Collecting Old Masters for New York"; and Betsy Rosasco, "The Teaching of Art and the Museum Tradition: Joseph Henry to Allan Marquand," *Record of the Princeton University Art Museum* 55, no. 1/2 (1996): 26–42.

26. See, e.g., "Newport Flower Show," *New York Times*, July 2, 1885, 1.

27. See Clifford Putney, *Muscular Christianity: Manhood and Sports in Protestant America, 1880–1920* (Cambridge, MA: Harvard University Press, 2001). The Bonner-Marquand Gymnasium opened in 1870, and Marquand Chapel (designed by Richard Morris Hunt, who also designed Henry G. Marquand's Madison Avenue and Newport, Rhode Island, houses) was dedicated in 1882 and lost to fire in 1920. Sarah E. Bush and P. C. Kemeny, "The Princeton University Chapels: An Architectural and Religious History," *Princeton University Library Chronicle* 60, no. 3 (Spring 1999): 317–52, esp. 329–30.

28. The collaboratively written *An* Anti-*catalog* brilliantly analyzes, exposes, and occasionally satirizes the medium of the lavishly illustrated exhibition catalogue preoccupied with emphasizing a collection's "quality"; see Artists Meeting for Cultural Change, *An* Anti-*catalog*.

29. Griselda Pollock, *Vision and Difference: Femininity, Feminism and Histories of Art* (New York: Routledge, 1988), 9.

30. For my understanding of Princeton's social and intellectual history, as well as the establishment of its Art Museum, I am drawing on Alexander Leitch, *A Princeton Companion* (Princeton, NJ: Princeton University Press, 1978); Karl Kusserow, ed., *Inner Sanctum: Memory and Meaning in Princeton's Faculty Room at Nassau Hall* (Princeton, NJ: Princeton University Press, 2010); Marilyn Aronberg Lavin, *The Eye of the Tiger: The Founding and Development of the Department of Art and Archaeology, 1883–1923, Princeton University* (Princeton, NJ: Department of Art and Archaeology and the Art Museum, 1983); James Axtell, "The Tiger's Eye," in *The Making of Princeton University: From Woodrow Wilson to the Present* (Princeton, NJ: Princeton University Press, 2006), 487–529; John Wilmerding, "American Art at Princeton," in *American Art in the Princeton University Art Museum*, vol. 1, *Drawings and Watercolors* (Princeton, NJ: Princeton University Press, 2004), 3–48; Rosasco, "The Teaching of Art and the Museum Tradition," 7–52; Barbara T. Ross, "The Mather Years 1922–1946," *Record of the Princeton University Art Museum* 55, no. 1/2 (1996): 53–76; Donald Drew Egbert, *Princeton Portraits* (Princeton, NJ: Princeton University Press, 1947); Thomas Jefferson Wertenbaker, *Princeton: 1746–1896* (Princeton, NJ: Princeton University Press, 1946); and Don Oberdorfer, *Princeton University: The First 250 Years* (Princeton, NJ: Princeton University Press, 1995).

31. Princeton became a coeducational institution in the fall of 1969, although women had enrolled in courses about the critical analysis of pictures—photogrammetry—during World War II. See William K. Selden, *Women of Princeton: 1746–1969* (Princeton, NJ: Princeton University Press, 2000); Catherine Keyser, *Transforming the Tiger: A Celebration of Undergraduate Women at Princeton University* (Princeton, NJ: Office of Printing and Mailing Services, Princeton University, 2001); and Nancy Weiss Malkiel, *"Keep the Damned Women Out": The Struggle for Coeducation* (Princeton, NJ: Princeton University Press, 2016). On photogrammetry and the military analysis of photographs at Princeton, see Axtell, *The Making of Princeton University*, 143–45; Robert K. Root, *The Princeton Campus in World War II* (Princeton, NJ: self-published, 1978); and April C. Armstrong, "'The New Order': How Japan's Attack on Pearl Harbor (Briefly) Led to Women Enrolling in Classes at Princeton University," Mudd Manuscript Library Blog, December 7, 2014, https://blogs.princeton.edu/mudd/tag/women-at-princeton/page/4/.

32. See especially Egbert, *Princeton Portraits*, 3–10.

33. Patricia Ann Palmieri, *In Adamless Eden: The Community of Women Faculty at Wellesley* (New Haven, CT: Yale University Press, 1995); Helen Lefkowitz Horowitz, *Alma Mater: Design and Experience in the Women's Colleges from Their Nineteenth-Century Beginnings to the 1930s*, 2nd ed. (Amherst: University of Massachusetts Press, 1993).

34. *Catalogue of the College* (1875–76), 35, quoted in Rosasco, "The Teaching of Art and the Museum Tradition," 13.

35. William C. Prime and George B. McClellan, *Suggestions on the Establishment of a Department of Art Instruction in the College of New Jersey* (Trenton, NJ: W. S. Sharp, 1882), 3–5, https://catalog.princeton.edu/catalog/9930372353506421.

36. Prime and McClellan, *Suggestions*, 5. The "sons of Princeton" are repeatedly hailed in much nineteenth-century literature, including in the lyrics of Princeton's alma mater, "Going Back to Nassau Hall," written by Kenneth S. Clark, Class of 1905 (Cincinnati, OH: John Church, 1910); also see Jon Elmer Hedges, "The Annual Dinner of the New York Princeton Club," *University Magazine*, March 1890, 55–61.

37. Prime and McClellan, *Suggestions*, 7, 8.

38. See Steven Conn, *Museums and American Intellectual Life, 1876–1926* (Chicago: University of Chicago Press, 1998); Julius Bryant, *Creating the V&A: Victoria and Albert's Museum (1851–1861)* (London: Lund Humphries, 2019); and Leslie W. Miller, "The Work of the Pennsylvania Museum and School of Industrial Art," *Annals of the American Academy of Political and Social Science* 33, no. 1 (January 1909): 105–10. On broader intellectual and pedagogical contexts of

object-based teaching, see Sarah Anne Carter, *Object Lessons: How Nineteenth-Century Americans Learned to Make Sense of the Material World* (New York: Oxford University Press, 2018).

39. Prime and McClellan, *Suggestions*, 4.

40. See, e.g., Jules David Prown, "Mind in Matter: An Introduction to Material Culture Theory and Method," *Winterthur Portfolio* 17, no. 1 (Spring 1982): 1–19; Jules David Prown and Kenneth Haltmann, eds., *American Artifacts: Essays in Material Culture* (East Lansing: Michigan State University Press, 2000); Rozsika Parker, *The Subversive Stitch: Embroidery and the Making of the Feminine* (London: Women's Press, 1984); and Carter, *Object Lessons*, 138–43.

41. Rosasco, "The Teaching of Art and the Museum Tradition," 17–22.

42. William C. Prime, *Pottery and Porcelain of All Times and Nations* (New York: Harper & Brothers, 1878), 7.

43. Prime, *Pottery and Porcelain,* 120.

44. Prime, 420–21.

45. Catharine E. Beecher and Harriet Beecher Stowe, *The American Woman's Home: or, Principles of Domestic Science, Being a Guide to the Formation and Maintenance of Economical, Healthful, Beautiful, and Christian Homes* (New York: J. B. Ford, 1869).

46. Classic texts on these themes are Barbara Welter, "The Cult of True Womanhood: 1820–1860," *American Quarterly* 18, no. 2 (Summer 1966): 151–74; Nancy F. Cott, *The Bonds of Womanhood: "Woman's Sphere" in New England, 1780–1835* (New Haven, CT: Yale University Press, 1977); and Linda K. Kerber, "Separate Spheres, Female Worlds, Woman's Place: The Rhetoric of Women's History," *Journal of American History* 75, no. 1 (June 1988): 9–39.

47. See especially Goodin and Morris, *Orchestrating Elegance*; Deusner, "'In Seen and Unseen Places'"; and Melody Barnett Deusner, "The Impossible *Exedra*: Engineering Contemplation and Conviviality in Turn-of-the-Century America," in *Housing the New Romans: Architectural Reception and Classical Style in the Modern World*, ed. Katharine T. von Stackelberg and Elizabeth Macaulay-Lewis (New York: Oxford University Press, 2017), 153–89.

48. See Lauren Lessing, "Un-Domesticating the Ideal: William Wetmore Story and The Metropolitan Museum of Art," in *New York: Art and Cultural Capital of the Gilded Age*, ed. Margaret R. Laster and Chelsea Bruner (New York: Routledge, 2018), 139–59; and Dianne Sachko Macleod, *Enchanted Lives, Enchanted Objects: American Women Collectors and the Making of Culture, 1800–1940* (Berkeley: University of California Press, 2008).

49. Nathaniel Hawthorne, *Passages from Hawthorne's Note-Books in France and Italy*, 1858 (Cambridge, MA: University Press, 1872), 16. On the popularity of Raphael in the United States, see David Alan Brown, *Raphael and America* (Washington, DC: National Gallery of Art, 1983); and Inge Reist, "Sacred Art in the Profane New World of Nineteenth-Century America," in *Sacred Possessions: Collecting Italian Religious Art, 1500–1900*, ed. Gail Feigenbaum and Sybille Ebert-Schifferer (Los Angeles: Getty Publications, 2011), 224–40.

50. See Dorothy Moss, "Translations, Appropriations, and Copies of Paintings at the Dawn of Mass Culture in the United States, ca. 1900" (PhD diss., University of Delaware, 2012); and Alan Wallach, "The American Cast Museum," in *Exhibiting Contradiction: Essays on the Art Museum in the United States* (Amherst: University of Massachusetts Press, 1998).

51. John Flanagan's 1917 portrait of Marquand is reproduced in Egbert, *Princeton Portraits*, 124–25 and fig. 83; two versions of it are in the collection of the Princeton University Art Museum (PP83 and PP675).

52. Academic accomplishments and biographical information are included in "Mrs. Allan Marquand Succumbs in Hospital after Long Illness," *Daily Princetonian*, February 28, 1950, 1. In 1948, Eleanor Cross Marquand was awarded an honorary master of arts degree from Princeton, only the sixth woman in the University's history to receive one; see "A Daughter of Princeton," *Princeton Herald*, June 16, 1948, 4. Some of Marquand's scholarly papers are now in the collection of the LuEsther T. Mertz Library of the New York Botanical Garden.

53. See, e.g., Eleanor Cross Marquand, "Plant Symbolism in the Unicorn Tapestries," *Parnassus* 10, no. 5 (October 1938): 2–8, 33, 40. The Hroswitha Club's papers are now in the collection of the Grolier Club, New York, NYGG05-A10019.

54. John White Alexander's portrait of Henry Gurdon Marquand was "Presented by the daughters of the late Mr. & Mrs. Allan Marquand in 1950 after death of Mrs. Marquand," while Sargent's portrait of Elizabeth Allen Marquand was a 1977 "Gift of Mrs. Eleanor Marquand Delanoy, granddaughter of the sitter." In 1910, Eleanor Cross Marquand joined the Princeton Borough Board of Education (see "Mrs. Allan Marquand Succumbs"); her daughter Eleanor Marquand Delanoy, donor of the Sargent painting, attended Bryn Mawr College and was active in Princeton's civic life, helping to found the Princeton chapter of the NAACP Legal Defense and Educational Fund, for example. See "Eleanor Marquand Delanoy, Rights Advocate, 91," *New York Times*, February 5, 1988, 103; and "Obituaries: Eleanor Marquand Delanoy," *Town Topics* (Princeton, NJ), February 10, 1988, 26.

55. Frances Patricia Healy, "A History of Evelyn College for Women, Princeton, New Jersey, 1887 to 1897" (PhD diss., The Ohio State University, 1967); Frances P. Healy, "Notes on Evelyn College," *Princeton University Library Chronicle* 52, no. 1 (Autumn 1990): 139–45; "Women's Colleges—Evelyn College," *Harper's Bazaar*, November 17, 1888, 781; Adaline W.

Sterling, "Evelyn College," *Harper's Bazaar*, September 26, 1896, 806–7.

56. Sterling, "Evelyn College," 806.

57. Sterling, 807.

58. Emphasis mine. "Women's Colleges—Evelyn College."

59. The erotic attachments of the "smash" and the "crush," in addition to the intensity of friendships, are discussed in Horowitz, *Alma Mater*, esp. 166–67.

60. The cheer was already reported in "Women's Colleges—Evelyn College," 784; also see Stan Pieringer, "'Eva, Eva, l-y-n! Eva, Eva, let me in!'—1890's Cheer: Girls' School Bloomed Half-Mile down Nassau Street," *Daily Princetonian*, December 9, 1968, 1, 5.

61. "Editors of the Princetonian," *Princetonian*, November 20, 1891, 1.

62. See "Snowball Fight at Princeton," *New York Times*, January 13, 1892, 1.

63. This interpretation is influenced also by the present-day popularity of workwear brands like Carhartt among college and university students (and in high fashion); see Garrett W. Nichols, "Rural Drag: Fashioning Rurality and Privilege," *QED* 4, no. 3 (Fall 2017): 41–66; and Jennifer Craik, *Uniforms Exposed: From Conformity to Transgression* (London: Berg, 2005).

64. Roosevelt delivered "The Strenuous Life" speech to a Chicago men's club in April of 1899 and later published it in a collection of speeches; Theodore Roosevelt, *The Strenuous Life: Essays and Addresses* (New York: Century, 1900). Important analyses of this vision of nationalistic masculinity are Gail Bederman, *Manliness and Civilization: A Cultural History of Gender and Race in the United States, 1880–1917* (Chicago: University of Chicago Press, 1995); Putney, *Muscular Christianity*; John F. Kasson, *Houdini, Tarzan, and the Perfect Man: The White Male Body and the Challenge of Modernity in America* (New York: Hill and Wang, 2001); and Alan Trachtenberg, *The Incorporation of America: Culture and Society in the Gilded Age* (New York: Hill and Wang, 1982).

65. "Cane Sprees," in Henry McAlpin, *The Messenger: A History of the Class of 1881, of Princeton College* (New York: Horace Holden, 1881), 32–34; "Princeton Boys Pleased: The Revival of the Old Midnight Cane Spree," *New York Times*, November 4, 1895, 10. The tradition was also illustrated as "The Annual Cane Fight on the Campus between Freshmen and Sophomores" in the article "Princeton College," *Scribner's Monthly*, March 1877, 637.

66. S. Weir Mitchell, *Wear and Tear, or Hints for the Overworked* (Philadelphia: J. B. Lippincott, 1871); George Beard, *American Nervousness: Its Causes and Consequences* (New York: G. P. Putnam's Sons, 1881); Cheryl Leibold, "Thomas Eakins in the Badlands," *Archives of American Art Journal* 28, no. 2 (1988): 2–15; Tom Lutz, *American Nervousness, 1903: An Anecdotal History* (Ithaca, NY: Cornell University Press, 1991); Sarah Burns, "Revitalizing the 'Painted-Out' North: Winslow Homer, Manly Health, and New England Regionalism in Turn-of-the-Century America," *American Art* 9, no. 2 (Summer 1995): 21–37; Barbara Will, "The Nervous Origins of the American Western," *American Literature* 70, no. 2 (June 1998): 293–316.

67. See Michael Clapper, "'I Was Once a Barefoot Boy!': Cultural Tensions in a Popular Chromo," *American Art* 16, no. 2 (Summer 2002): 16–39; and T. J. Jackson Lears, *No Place of Grace: Antimodernism and the Transformation of American Culture, 1880–1920* (Chicago: University of Chicago Press, 1981), especially his discussion of the "martial ideal," chap. 3. On the popularity of J. G. Brown's "street urchins," see Jennifer A. Greenhill, "Laughing with J. G. Brown, E. W. Perry, and Thomas Nast," *Playing It Straight: Art and Humor in the Gilded Age* (Berkeley: University of California Press, 2012), 43–76; and Martha Hoppin, *The World of J. G. Brown* (Chesterfield, MA: Chameleon Books, 2011). For more on the ways in which the "crisis of masculinity" and the perceived perils of modernity and urban life inflected art collecting, see Burns, "Revitalizing the 'Painted-Out' North."

68. Kienbusch was also an avid collector of arms and armor, which he donated to the Philadelphia Museum of Art, further evoking Lears's antimodernist analysis of a fascination with "martial ideals" and the culture of knights. On Kienbusch, see Frances Follin Jones, "Carl Otto von Kienbusch, Class of 1906," *Record of the Princeton University Art Museum* 36, no. 2 (1977): 22–23; and C. Otto von Kienbusch, "The Kretzschmar von Kienbusch Collection of Armor and Arms," *Philadelphia Museum of Art Bulletin* 73, no. 318 (September 1977): 1, 4–24. On Princeton's bequest, see *The Carl Otto von Kienbusch Jr. Memorial Collection* (Princeton, NJ: Princeton University Art Museum, 1956).

69. "A Painter of Street Urchins," *New York Times Illustrated Magazine*, August 27, 1899, 4. On Riis, Hine, and social documentary photography, see Maren Stange, *Symbols of Ideal Life: Social Documentary Photography in America, 1890–1950* (New York: Cambridge University Press, 1989).

70. On Hine's career and outlook, see Stange, *Symbols of Ideal Life*, 47–88; Oenone Kubie, "Reading Lewis Hine's Photography of Child Street Labour, 1906–1918," *Journal of American Studies* 50, no. 4 (November 2016): 873–97; and Lewis W. Hine, "Social Photography: How the Camera May Help in the Social Uplift," *Proceedings: National Conference of Charities and Corrections* (June 1909), reprinted in Alan Trachtenberg, ed., *Classic Essays on Photography* (New Haven, CT: Leete's Island Books, 1980), 109–14.

71. "A Painter of Street Urchins," 4.

72. Quoted in "A Painter of Street Urchins," 4.

73. "A Painter of Street Urchins," 5.

74. See, e.g., Richard Weiss, *The American Myth of Success: From Horatio Alger to Norman Vincent Peale* (Urbana: University of Illinois Press, 1988); Carol Nackenoff, *The Fictional Republic: Horatio Alger and American Political Discourse* (New York: Oxford University Press, 1994); and James V. Catano, *Ragged Dicks: Masculinity, Steel, and the Rhetoric of the Self-Made Man* (Carbondale: Southern Illinois University Press, 2001).

75. Quoted in "A Painter of Street Urchins," 4.

76. Oberdorfer includes photographs of productions from 1905–6 and 1906–7, as well as other documents; see Oberdorfer, *Princeton University*, 120–21. Also see D. Marsden, *The Long Kickline: A History of the Princeton Triangle Club* (Princeton, NJ: Princeton Triangle Club, 1968); Danielle Mireles, "College Chorus 'Girls': Drag at Male College and University Campuses during the Progressive Era" (MA thesis, University of California, Riverside, 2017); Margaret A. Nash, Danielle C. Mireles, and Amanda Scott-Williams, "'Mattie Matix' and Prodigal Princes: A Brief History of Drag on College Campuses from the Nineteenth Century to the 1940s," in *Rethinking Campus Life: New Perspectives on the History of College Students in the United States*, ed. Christine A. Ogren and Marc A. VanOverbeke (Cham, Switzerland: Palgrave Macmillan, 2018), 61–90; Sharon R. Ullman, "'The Twentieth Century Way': Female Impersonation and Sexual Practice in Turn-of-the-Century America," *Journal of the History of Sexuality* 5, no. 4 (April 1995): 573–600; and Kathleen B. Casey, *The Prettiest Girl on Stage Is a Man: Race and Gender Benders in American Vaudeville* (Knoxville: University of Tennessee Press, 2015). On period-specific understandings of sexuality and gender identity, also see George Chauncey, *Gay New York: Gender, Urban Culture, and the Making of the Gay Male World, 1890–1940* (New York: BasicBooks, 1994).

77. *Princeton Alumni Weekly*, November 4, 1908, 86.

78. The Triangle Club is currently examining the problems posed by this practice; see more recent debates about the ethics of the kickline and of cross-dressing in David Walter, "Tradition, Tradition," *Princeton Alumni Weekly*, November 9, 2016, https://paw.princeton.edu/article/tradition-tradition.

79. "Art at the Century," *New York Evening Post*, February 3, 1873.

80. Clipping from Homer family scrapbook attributed to a Boston newspaper of 1878, quoted in Lloyd Goodrich and Abigail Booth Gerdts, *Record of Works by Winslow Homer*, vol. 2, *1867 through 1876* (New York: Spanierman Gallery, 2005), 179.

81. Reilly Rhodes, *Winslow Homer's Hurley: An Artist's View* (2021), Hurley Heritage Society, https://www.hurleyheritagesociety.org/museum/winslow-homers-hurley/home-and-village-life/the-family-record/.

82. Quoted in Goodrich and Gerdts, *Record of Works by Winslow Homer*, 179.

83. Michael Edward Shapiro, *Cast and Recast: The Sculpture of Frederic Remington* (Washington, DC: Smithsonian Institution Press, 1981); Lucy D. Rosenfeld, *A Century of American Sculpture: The Roman Bronze Works Foundry* (Atglen, PA: Schiffer, 2002), 69–79; Michael Edward Shapiro and Peter H. Hassrick, *Frederic Remington: The Masterworks* (New York: Harry N. Abrams, 1991).

84. On the mythology of the American Southwest, see William H. Truettner, ed., *The West as America: Reinterpreting Images of the Frontier, 1820–1920* (Washington, DC: Smithsonian Institution Press, 1991).

85. Theodore Roosevelt, "Frontier Types," *Century Illustrated Monthly Magazine* 36, no. 6 (October 1888): 831. This illustration was also reprinted as *Painting the Town Red* in Theodore Roosevelt, *Ranch Life and The Hunting-Trail* (New York: Century, 1918), 92.

86. Roosevelt, "Frontier Types," 842.

87. Roosevelt, 835.

88. Roosevelt, 835, 838.

89. See Ken Gonzales-Day, *Lynching in the West: 1850–1935* (Durham, NC: Duke University Press, 2006).

90. Roosevelt, "Frontier Types," 837.

91. "'Turning Loose' in the Frontier Settlements," *Harper's Weekly*, December 21, 1889, 1024.

92. Quoted in Perriton Maxwell, "Frederic Remington—Most Typical of American Artists," *Pearson's Magazine*, October 1907, 407.

93. "Tiffany & Co.: Suggestions for Christmas Gifts," *New York Times*, December 5, 1907, 9.

94. John D. Rockefeller Jr. purchased the ranch in 1932, and it stayed in the family for nearly seventy years; it is now known as the Laurance S. Rockefeller Preserve of Grand Teton National Park. See Robert W. Righter, *Crucible for Conservation: The Creation of Grand Teton National Park* (Boulder: Colorado Associated University Press, 1982); Lawrence R. Borne, *Dude Ranching: A Complete History* (Albuquerque: University of New Mexico Press, 1983), esp. 153–57; Robin W. Winks, *Laurance S. Rockefeller: Catalyst for Conservation* (Washington, DC: Island Press, 1997); and Laurie Hinck, "Waiting for Wilderness: The Corporate Genesis of Grand Teton National Park, Wyoming, 1927–1956" (PhD diss., University of New Mexico, 2009).

95. Louisiana Purchase Exposition Company, *Official Guide to the Louisiana Purchase Exposition at the City of St. Louis, State of Missouri, April 30th to December 1st, 1904* (St. Louis: Official Guide, 1904), 134. See also Gonzales-Day, *Lynching in the West*.

96. "Exterior Sculpture at the World's Fair," *Monumental News*, July 1904, 427.

97. See Thomas R. MacMechen, *The True and Complete Story of the Pike and Its Attractions, World's Fair, St. Louis, U.S.A.* (St. Louis: Louisiana Purchase Exposition, 1904), 1–35.

98. Louisiana Purchase Exposition Company, *Official Guide*, 134.

99. Coco Fusco, "The Other History of Intercultural Performance," *TDR* 38, no. 1 (Spring 1994): 143–67; Robert W. Rydell, *All the World's a Fair: Visions of Empire at American International Expositions, 1876–1916* (Chicago: University of Chicago Press, 1985).

100. "Address at the Dedication Ceremonies of the Louisiana Purchase Exposition, St. Louis, April 30, 1903," in Theodore Roosevelt, *Winning of the West III* (New York: Charles Scribner's Sons, 1924), 597–606; 599, 604–5. While the dedication ceremonies were held on April 30, 1903, to commemorate the centennial of the signing of the Louisiana Purchase Treaty, most buildings were still unfinished, and the Fair did not officially open until April 1904.

101. Louisiana Purchase Exposition Company, *Official Guide*, 27.

102. See, e.g., Margaret D. Carroll, "The Erotics of Absolutism: Rubens and the Mystification of Sexual Violence," *Representations* 25 (Winter 1989): 3–30; Diane Wolfthal, *Images of Rape: The 'Heroic' Tradition and Its Alternatives* (Cambridge: Cambridge University Press, 1999); and Macushla Robinson, *Every Rape in the Met Museum* (New York: Interstitial Press, 2021).

103. See Nancy M. Henley, "Smile When You Say That: Facial Expression," in *Body Politics: Power, Sex, and Nonverbal Communication* (Englewood Cliffs, NJ: Prentice-Hall, 1977); and Phyllis Randall, "Re-Examining the Smiles of Women," *Women's Studies in Communication* 8, no. 1 (Spring 1985): 1–10.

104. Some firsthand accounts of the experiences of women who enrolled in Princeton in the autumn of 1969 are available at Princetoniana Museum, https://www.princetonianamuseum.org/media/blob/24480c96-f26b-49f5-b900-92f2ec15bfdf/24480c96-f26b-49f5-b900-92f2ec15bfdf.pdf; also see Malkiel, *"Keep the Damned Women Out"*; Paul L. Montgomery, "Tigers Purr as 171 Women Enroll at Princeton," *New York Times*, September 8, 1969, 43; Gregg Lange, "Rally 'Round the Cannon: Then Don't Do That," *Princeton Alumni Weekly*, February 2, 2017, https://paw.princeton.edu/article/rally-round-cannon-then-dont-do; and Dara Birnbaum, *Canon: Taking to the Streets, Part One: Princeton University—Take Back the Night* (New York: Electronic Arts Intermix, 1990), 10 min. Princeton University Library has also assembled a library guide for the research of coeducation at Princeton: https://libguides.princeton.edu/c.php?g=84581&p=543378. The Women's Center Records include numerous files on sexual harassment, safety, self-defense workshops, and Take Back the Night rallies, among other topics: Women's Center Records, AC248, Princeton University Archives, Department of Special Collections, Princeton University Library, https://findingaids.princeton.edu/catalog/AC248_c0410.

105. Gardner Teall, "Women Sculptors of America: How Many Readers Knew There Were So Many of Them? And So Talented?," *Good Housekeeping Magazine*, August 1911, 175–87.

106. Teall, "Women Sculptors of America," 175.

107. Nancy Dunlap Bercaw, "Solid Objects / Mutable Meanings: Fancywork and the Construction of Bourgeois Culture, 1840–1880," *Winterthur Portfolio* 26, no. 4 (Winter 1991): 231–47; Ann B. Shteir, "'Fac-similies of Nature': Victorian Wax Flower Modelling," *Victorian Literature and Culture* 35, no. 2 (2007): 649–61; John Whitenight, *Under Glass: A Victorian Obsession* (Atglen, PA: Schiffer Publishing, 2013); Helen Sheumaker, *Love Entwined: The Curious History of Hairwork in America* (Philadelphia: University of Pennsylvania Press, 2007); L. B. Urbino, *Art Recreations* (Boston: J. E. Tilton, 1863).

108. Teall, "Women Sculptors of America," 176.

109. Teall, 177.

110. Teall, 185.

111. Arthur Edwin Bye, "Women and the World of Art," *Arts and Decoration* 10 (December 1918): 87.

112. Bye, "Women and the World of Art," 87.

113. See Florian Mildenberger, "'Urninge' und 'genetische Weibchen': Karl Heinrich Ulrichs und der Diskurs über Hermaphroditismus," in *Neue Funde und Studien zu Karl Heinrich Ulrichs*, ed. Wolfram Setz (Hamburg: Männerschwarm Verlag, 2004); Yvonne Ivory, "The Urning and His Own: Individualism and the Fin-de-Siècle Invert," *German Studies Review* 26, no. 2 (May 2003): 333–52; and Ina Linge, "German and British Sexual Sciences across Disciplines at the Fin de Siècle: 'Homosexuals', 'Inverts' and 'Uranians,'" in *The Edinburgh Companion to Fin-de-Siècle Literature, Culture and the Arts*, ed. Josephine M. Guy (Edinburgh: Edinburgh University Press, 2022), 381–400.

114. Thayer Tolles, "'Art as the True Expression of Life': Harriet Whitney Frishmuth to 1940," in Janis Conner et al., *Captured Motion: The Sculpture of Harriet Whitney Frishmuth* (New York: Hohmann Holdings), 2006; "Harriet Whitney Frishmuth, American Sculptor," *The Courier* 9, no. 1 (October 1971): 21.

115. Quoted in Carol Taylor, "Miss O'Keeffe, Noted Artist, Is a Feminist," *New York World-Tribune*, March 1945.

116. Hunter Drohojowska-Philp, *Full Bloom: The Art and Life of Georgia O'Keeffe* (New York: W. W. Norton, 2004), 389.

117. *J. Seward Johnson, residence in Oldwick, New Jersey. Through stable arch*, June 12, 1947, Gottscho-Schleisner

Collection, Library of Congress, Prints and Photographs Division. LC-G612.

118. Barbara Buhler Lynes, *Georgia O'Keeffe: Catalogue Raisonné*, vol. 2 (New Haven, CT: Yale University Press, 1999), 1131.

119. "Steadfast O'Keeffe," *Art Digest* 16, March 1, 1942, 15.

120. Henry McBride, "Georgia O'Keeffe's Bones: Readings from Tea Leaves and the Sands of Time," *New York Sun*, February 6, 1942, 32.

121. Linda Nochlin, "Why Have There Been No Great Women Artists?," *ARTnews*, January 1971.

122. Alice Walker, "In Search of Our Mothers' Gardens" (1974), in *In Search of Our Mothers' Gardens: Womanist Prose* (New York: Harcourt Brace Jovanovich, 1983), 233.

123. Prime and McClellan, *Suggestions*, 3.

124. Walker, "In Search of Our Mothers' Gardens," 239.

125. Michael Kimmelman, "Art Review: Jazzy Geometry, Cool Quilters," *New York Times*, November 29, 2002, sec. E, 33.

126. See Bridget R. Cooks, "Back to the Future: The Quilts of Gee's Bend, 2002," in *Exhibiting Blackness: African Americans and the American Art Museum* (Amherst: University of Massachusetts Press, 2011); and John Beardsley et al., *Gee's Bend: The Women and Their Quilts* (Atlanta: Tinwood Books, 2002).

127. Ruth Cuthand, "I'm Not the Indian You're Looking For," undated artist statement, Ruth Cuthand (website), https://www.ruthcuthand.ca/.

128. Cuthand, "I'm Not the Indian You're Looking For."

129. Toni Morrison, "The Place of the Idea, the Idea of the Place: A Meditation on the Faculty Room at Nassau Hall," in Kusserow, *Inner Sanctum*, 22.

130. For more on the History and Sense of Place initiative, as well as the Campus Iconography Committee, see https://inclusivehistory.princeton.edu/about and https://cpuc.princeton.edu/sites/g/files/toruqf1221/files/princeton-history-and-iconography-pre-read.pdf. On the solicitation of community opinions, see Denise Valenti, "Committee on Principles to Govern Renaming and Changes to Campus Iconography Seeks Community Input," Princeton University, News, December 7, 2020, https://www.princeton.edu/news/2020/12/07/committee-principles-govern-renaming-and-changes-campus-iconography-seeks-community.

131. See Jamie Saxon, "University Seeks Recommendations for Expanded Campus Portrait Collection," Princeton University, News, September 26, 2017, https://www.princeton.edu/news/2017/09/26/university-seeks-recommendations-expanded-campus-portrait-collection; Emily Aronson, "Princeton Will Commission New Portraits to Update and Diversify University Collection," Princeton University, News, May 3, 2018, https://www.princeton.edu/news/2018/05/03/princeton-will-commission-new-portraits-update-and-diversify-university-collection; Denise Valenti, "Four New Portraits Serve as 'Visible Expression of Princeton' Today," Princeton University, News, September 25, 2019, https://www.princeton.edu/news/2019/09/25/four-new-portraits-serve-visible-expression-princeton-today.

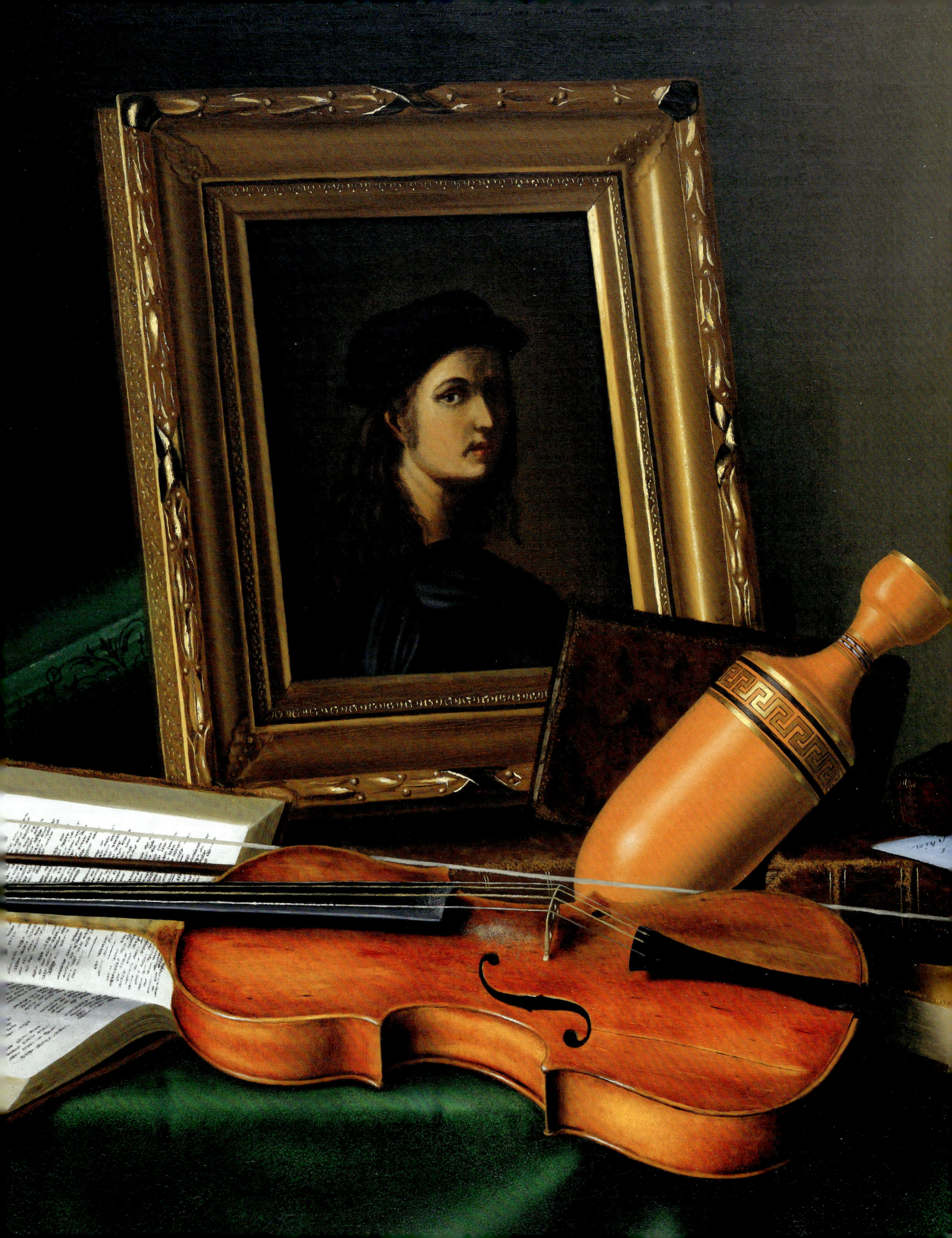

Horace D. Ballard

Oblique Assemblies: Toward Queer Ecologies in American Art

Object Lessons in American Art serves as an astute and important assay and rejoinder for one of the world's great academic collections. Nonetheless, my feelings about the exhibition's thematic groupings are complicated and my attention is divided. I want the exhibition to do three things: to confirm what I think I know about the canon and trajectories of American art; to highlight several works that have become beloved to my eye over years of study; and simultaneously, to offer strategies for remixing, reframing, even discarding all preconceptions of the field. Admittedly, I want the impossible or near impossible. I want the exhibition to *queer* itself; to talk back to itself; to both amplify and eradicate its own need to exist. Akin to our lived experience of ecological fragility and cultural upheaval, I want the exhibition to be a bit more meandering, unruly, singular, and precarious.

As an educator, I believe our shared moment of human history in 2022 asks different things of me and of us in our attention to works of art than before. We are now asked to make legible the principles and assumptions that govern our looking, a process I term "tallying the ethics of our attention." This ethical framework conditions what we study and what we enjoy. My ethics of attention extend beyond accepting or making space for

Detail, figure 2

non-normative identities and experiences; it acknowledges that normality does not exist.

As a queer person and as a curator of eighteenth- and nineteenth-century painting and sculpture, I find myself scanning the checklist for two kinds of queer visual politics: works that visualize evidence of LGBTQIAA+ presence and works that lend themselves to a mode of inquiry and interpretation that is oppositional to canonical narratives and assumptions. To quote Legacy Russell, my role as a queer thinker is "to complicate things, to insist on range, and taking up space, and letting things be sticky and nuanced, and delightful, and catastrophic, and incisive, and baffling all at once."[1] This is what it means to be a queer human and, increasingly, what it means to be a queer curator.

This essay demonstrates the degree to which an ethics of queer ecologies and assembly can open up new pathways for scholarly attention in American painting, especially in the genres of landscape and still life. In my work, I am invested in queer methodologies of assembly, ecology, and coalition and what it means to find possibility and value in interpretations rather than arguments. In the following pages, I aim to model a strategy of close looking within a field somewhat notorious for its limiting precepts in order to claim space for queer presence and to inspire us to continue looking at works we may think we know.

To reflect on the evolution of queer theory and its intersection with the ideological, material, and visual cultures of the Americas is to define what we mean by "queer" and then to ask whether a coherent queer theory exists with a methodological lens through which we can view art. To my thinking, a sense of fecundity (thriving) and questions of futurity are inherent to queer identities. Eight years on, I am still compelled by bell hooks's definition of "queer" as not being about desire but rather "being about the (political) self that is at odds with everything around it and has to invent and create and find a place to speak and to thrive and to live."[2] As to a concrete definition of queer theory, the jury is still out! Aristotle reminds us there can be no unity when synthesizing something as vast and as individually felt as human experience.[3] What can be stated perhaps is that the assemblage of methods and suppositions that perhaps aggregate to queer theory (or perhaps not) posit possible futures as their end. If we hold these constructions of queer and queer modes of fashioning identity in mind, then we must also consider the ways in which imminent ecological disaster either forecloses or inspires the futurities of the human species and its creations.

In recent conversations with students, I have found it instructive to ask them to think of queer methods of attention to a text (visual or otherwise) as a kind of still life assemblage. Queer modes of reading offer us a disparate kitchen pantry of various frameworks accrued from over the years—a raucous set of assembled, commonplace, and systemic frameworks for the investigation of humanist form that, when brought together and viewed collectively, say something about memory, possibility, anxiety, desire, vanity, skepticism, and even the futility of archives, arguments, or stable interpretations. Drawing from American studies, anthropology, biology, comparative literature, demography, disability studies, environmental sciences, feminist studies, film studies, gender studies, history, history of art, Indigenous studies, law, Native cosmologies, NDN wisdom, philosophy, physics, political science, postcolonial theory, psychology, religious studies, sexuality studies, womanist studies, and the theoretical intersections around and between these disciplines allows queer methodologies to be as elastic, wild, and unbounded as a life. Queer theory (if it exists) transgresses and defies all senses of assimilation and the inevitable. Queer scholarship moves the field by transgressing expectations of advancement and disregarding the niceties. The authentic essence of mutable interpretations and possibilities count as much, if not more so, than concise arguments.

For many, the "birth" of queer studies dates to 1990 with the queer studies conference organized by Teresa de Lauretis of University of California, Santa Cruz. The subsequent efforts of its participants and first-generation rejoinderers, such as Lauren Berlant, Judith Butler, David Halperin, Adrienne Rich, and Michael Warner, are cited as setting the critical discourses of the field aflame. Twenty years later, José Esteban Muñoz ushered a new generation of activists, artists, and scholars into the conversation when he drew on the fields of philosophy and hermeneutics to call for a queer phenomenology and a mode of cultural analysis transmogrified into "a structuring and educated mode of desiring that allows us to see and feel beyond the quagmire of the present."[4]

In his articulation of queer futurity (and the role art and artists play in transmuting a progressive vein throughout culture), Muñoz wrestles with Heidegger, who, in turn, is wrestling with Hegel. In opposing Hegel's sense that art provides certainty and absolute truth, Heidegger suggests that art's "truth" is the internal revelation in a viewer the truth of being in multiplicity, what Heidegger terms the "unconcealed-ness of entities as entities."[5] Muñoz, much like Ian Thomson, Phillipe Lacoue-Labarthe, and others, interprets this dialectic between Hegel and Heidegger as one of modernity versus postmodernity, or between totalizing narrative versus the increasing complexity of experience. Muñoz then situates this dialectic as a lens through which queer methodologies can be formulated, especially around the experiences of acculturation, desire, and encounter. Looking at the United States within the capacity of the thirty-five nations, fourteen territories, and five occupied islands that form the Americas, Muñoz predicted a "queer turn" in American culture before we reach the red zone of extractive, imperial civilization. For Muñoz, the goal was a kind of open-source network of queer signifiers that he terms "the aesthetic": "blueprints and schemata for a forward-dawning futurity."[6] The nature of queer phenomenology in Muñoz's wake is a condition of constant and eternal becoming; queering something is a process, not a goal. As I tell my students, while queer studies is a field, and queering can be a methodology, the discipline of queer theory, and thus a queer canon in any art form, is still in formation.

There is much still left to define, but you can tell a queer read and, therefore, a work that is queer(ed) when you experience it.[7] Allow me to give an example from *Objects Lessons in American Art*.

In Georgia O'Keeffe's painting *From a New Jersey Weekend II* (1941), two elongated centrifugal forms emerge in tandem from an enclosed circular field (fig. 1). Behind them, in the upper third of the composition, a svelte, forked passage of contrasting vertical shades leads the eye up and out. The field (for all intents and purposes) is white. The snuggled forms, legible in outline as Baroque-era tablet stones, each with a tripartite-scrolled silhouette, are modeled in a gradient from ash to pale rose. The upper half of the composition, indicative of a sky, glissades from pale pea green to goldenrod as the light warms and falls toward the horizon. An orthogonal swath, the same color as the field and perhaps representing a stratus cloud, gives suggestive balance to the geometric weight of the composition. In the contained reality of the painting, it is winter. It is perhaps early morning. And Georgia O'Keeffe—in the moment of the scene's graphic fixation in her mind and in the focused composition she provides us—is at play.

Gravestones. A bare tree. A fence slightly bent, perhaps sagging under the weight of snow. A chaff-chartreuse sunrise. Nothing we see is modeled with flourish. Everything is purposive and spare. Everything is at work. Even the headstones in their binary arrangement, split center and mark the inevitability of death. And yet, the dual gradients of shifting color and the mirroring of the ground in the cloud is a clue. Something else besides the finite binary of life in death is being expressed. Something else, beyond form, proves to be the painting's subject.

I think it is the light. Everything is suffused with light. Light is everywhere in this work. Light illuminates every surface with nuance and specificity. O'Keeffe has provided us with a hybrid formulation: a landscape that plays on the edges of its genre; a still life of arranged and expected objects that present themselves in sublime novelty. It is as if O'Keeffe was taking a morning walk and glanced over and found the light dancing among the stones and found her eyes enchanted and her fingers tingling and her brain curious and electric.

We are, after all, in Jersey. Anything is possible. Perhaps, just perhaps, a quick meander into a churchyard to get closer, to see if the mirage holds, might make a gift of the morning, and provide a way forward in life, as well as a scene she could capture in the viscous propensity of oil, the material of light set aflame, long ago, by her beloved Titian. Perhaps she walked or jogged over with hands stuffed deep in corduroy pockets, hair loose or in a bun, listening for errant bird song or the chittering of a squirrel. Perhaps the light awakened her to the truth we all know but sometimes need to be in nature and open to the state of nature to see: that winter is a moment of dormant rest necessary for the ecological abundance of spring.

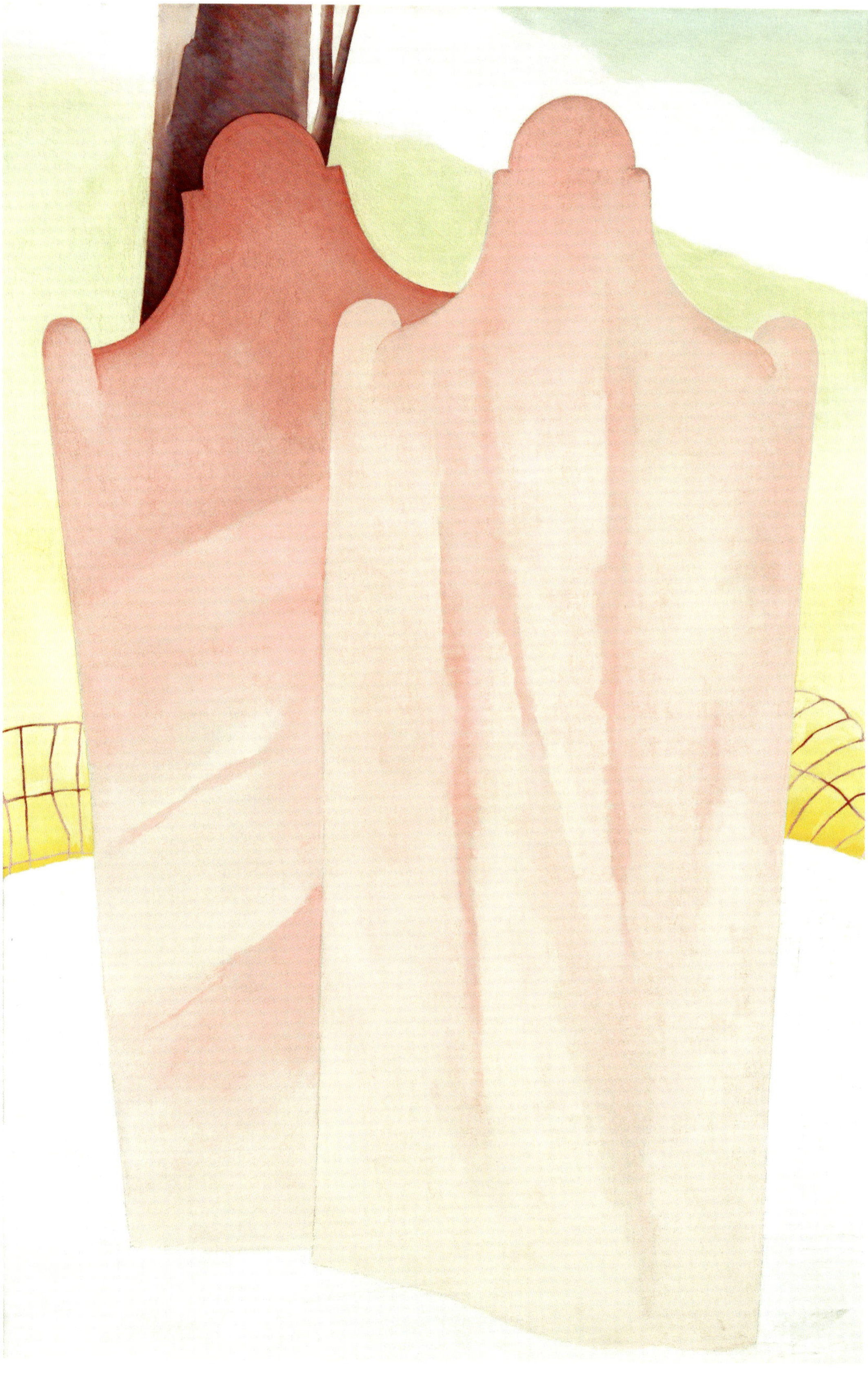

To my eye, *From a New Jersey Weekend II* is a still life depicting an interior landscape, a personal and geospatial interiority. O'Keeffe's iconic depth of field is nonexistent. We are only given a hint of one side of the fence. The fence (perhaps with a gate, perhaps not) that the artist and thus the viewer has overcome to be in the presence of these two stones has been traversed by need. Objects carefully composed in the image's shallow but intimate field of vision provide sensual harmony. This arrangement of stationary forms and light is not only what O'Keeffe potentially saw and wished to capture on a weekend in New Jersey (perhaps back East for her nearly annual show at Stieglitz's gallery). This is what she felt.

I start with the O'Keeffe to model what it feels and sounds like to think queerly about a visual text. To read queerly is to meander: a mode of informed and attentive drifting, humility, thinking, and vulnerability between disciplinary systems. I also start with the O'Keeffe to demonstrate another aspect of queer subjectivity, which is to argue that queerness is not inherently about sexual desire. In the popular imagination, O'Keeffe's visual ruminations on natural forms, especially flowers, are routinely associated with sexuality, though she consistently denied those interpretations as the sole interpretations and intentions of her artistic choices. To be queer, or, rather, to attend to the world queerly, is to think about an assembly of meanings and of peoples and the aggregate of collective, some might even say political, presence. It is to situate the communal and the chosen against the individual or the assumed.

Underlying my thinking about O'Keeffe's painting and its affective assembly as a ruminative and queer mode of composition is my sense that still life as a genre of painting is a kind of meta-argument on assembly. A still life is an arrangement about arrangement; an entity composed of entities; a composition about composition. In such multilayered compositions, the formal elements of mass, shape, and volume become their own semiotic and spatial metaphors. As objects, paintings are also discrete ecologies of interdependent organic and inorganic matter. Paintings breathe and they change, becoming more or less porous, more or less translucent, over time. I find the correspondence between, say, a pigment and the use of that pigment, mixed with a binder, in the graphic representation of something that is that same pigment, enchanting. The miracle of the artifice of painting never gets old. For these reasons, I locate in the painted genre of still life an active queer instigation to referentiality and envisioning other possible futures. As Susan Merriam and Claudia Tobin both suggest in their respective art historical writings, it is in the allegories and metaphors still life affords where political visions of the present, the yearning for future social transformations, and artistic agency aggregate into a worldview.[8]

The object lessons the genre of still life painting provides us with is something akin to what Eileen Myles terms "the real and irregular news" of nature.[9] In still life, the ordinary becomes extraordinary, the extraordinary becomes metaphor, and the young grape and the decaying cheese resound the operatic nature of life. Every day can be an epic if we look at what we are given. Still life is a pathway into the material world of empirical experience. In the sense that a still life is a demonstration of artistic ability, it is also meaningless as a place of theory. It is a low stakes exercise—the more authentic to nature the more jejune the talent; innovation and abstraction coming later, coming through the vehicle of still life to get at something else: still life is a stage for human interpretations. Its juxtaposition of objects connoting mordant humor, disgust, frivolity, wealth, beauty, pleasure.

Let us turn to a particular still life that jumped out at me from the exhibition with such candor and transdisciplinary modalities of queer intention that I was compelled to keep looking and keep questioning and, in so doing, upend my own assumptions about an artist's practice that I thought I knew.

In William Michael Harnett's *Still Life with Portrait by Raphael* (1878), a coalition of objects is represented in a triangular composition atop a ruched field of emerald cloth (fig. 2). In the foreground, a violin and bow are devised orthogonally to a tumbling cadre of leather-bound books, a particularly askance lekythos, and an opened letter. Atop a large folio and above the assembly, a rectangular gilt, bay-leaf frame contains a symbiotic

FIGURE 1 Georgia O'Keeffe (1887–1986; born Sun Prairie, WI; died Santa Fe, NM), *From a New Jersey Weekend II*, 1941. Oil on canvas, 91.5 × 61 cm. Princeton University Art Museum. Gift of the Georgia O'Keeffe Foundation (y1994-136)

mash-up of two portraits by Raffaello Sanzio da Urbino: a presumed self-portrait of about 1503 and the legendary 1515 portrait of Bindo Altoviti.

The title of this natty ecosystem of objects tells us this is a still life. Yet, nothing here is still. It is as if there has been a knock at the door and the violin and bow were hastily set down on an open book of verse, still warm from the hands of the musician, who in haste knocked the souvenir-trade lekythos akimbo. The violin dances precariously on its sliding perch, splitting center the portrait. The trompe l'oeil effect is not so much breaking the fourth wall as pointedly invoking the sense of sound; the movement and the crash that might soon ensue is almost audible in the image itself. In the absence of a human subject whose eyes and fingers animate and control the haptic and entropic possibilities of the scene, the viewer is invited to play within and against the futurity of cacophony. The askew lekythos, almost too pristine in its facture and tubularity, will soon be chipped or shattered in its fall. In a future moment, the present will more resemble the artifacts and ruins of the past. In such a composition, Harnett is questioning the very possibility of the existence of a still life. Nothing is "still" or fixed here, everything is in a momentary suspension of natural rustling, sliding, slipping, falling, fracturing. Yet here we are. We are caught in this moment, a moment for breath in a maelstrom of emotional haste.

What caused this haste? Where was the musician, and what were they thinking, just before this moment? The opened letter gives a clue; the indeterminate, open book of verse (Keats? Shelley? Shakespeare? The Bible?) gives another.[10] We are in the emotive space of sentiment and revelry and formal feelings in poetic language. We are in the interior temporalities of the human soul. The violin atop the book of verse offers a cautious third. A single person could not be reading a letter, playing a violin, and reading poems simultaneously. There must be a progression from one to another; some reason why all the objects are set down, expectant; why our "host" has left the room. Unless more than one person was at the table. We do not know but we can imagine a possible scenario for our mind's eye: an ensemble was chillaxing and an ensemble *exeunt*-ed, leaving behind a coterie of hastily placed things. We do not know; but what we are presented with is this scene *in medias res*: a place where transition, in the lives of persons and things, is happening; where the future of one is mirrored and determined by the future of the other. This mutually symbiotic relationship between objects and "host" strikes me as uncanny, messy, deeply ecological, and deeply queer.

This sense of plurality in the collative metaphoric forms of Harnett's painting are the semantic and activistic traces of a queer ethics. Queer prefers a narratological texture that is profuse, slippery, sweaty, and emerging. Thus, queer readings of the visual are entropic by nature; they are wild; they are unwieldy in their capacious disregard for answers or explanation and their preference for aggregating questions and possibility. It is understandable how such plurality can lead to some feeling adrift. I assure you: to be a queer theorist is not to be illegible, or intellectually promiscuous with one's judgmental connotations, but rather to be almost cybernetic and networked in the range of cultural references and relevancies one can bring to bear in interpreting a work's resonance to our common times and future epochs. It is this interconnected matrix of allusion, analogy, citation, and inquiry that compels me to suture the language of ecologies to queer modalities of close looking and interpretation.

The predicament of queer methodologies is that while they often champion individual aesthetic experience, they sometimes stand apart from the expected ways we write art history. For this reason, I have offered examples of queer modes not as a way of revisioning or intervening in a canon, but to champion the value of close looking. That said, I do believe queer methodologies of attention can redirect our gaze, and thus, our scholarship; though, admittedly, the scale of our intercessions may be different. For example, Nika Elder's recent work on Harnett raises the assertion that Harnett's great aim was the representation of "the nation as a whole." Situating the artist and his early still life paintings within the divisive social milieu of US Reconstruction (1865–1877), Elder casts Harnett in a mode similar to Thomas Eakins as an artist seeking to realign or revolutionize America's academic painting tradition around the years of the nation's centennial and locate within painting's inherent expectation of a future audience a way to elevate "painting above politics."[11]

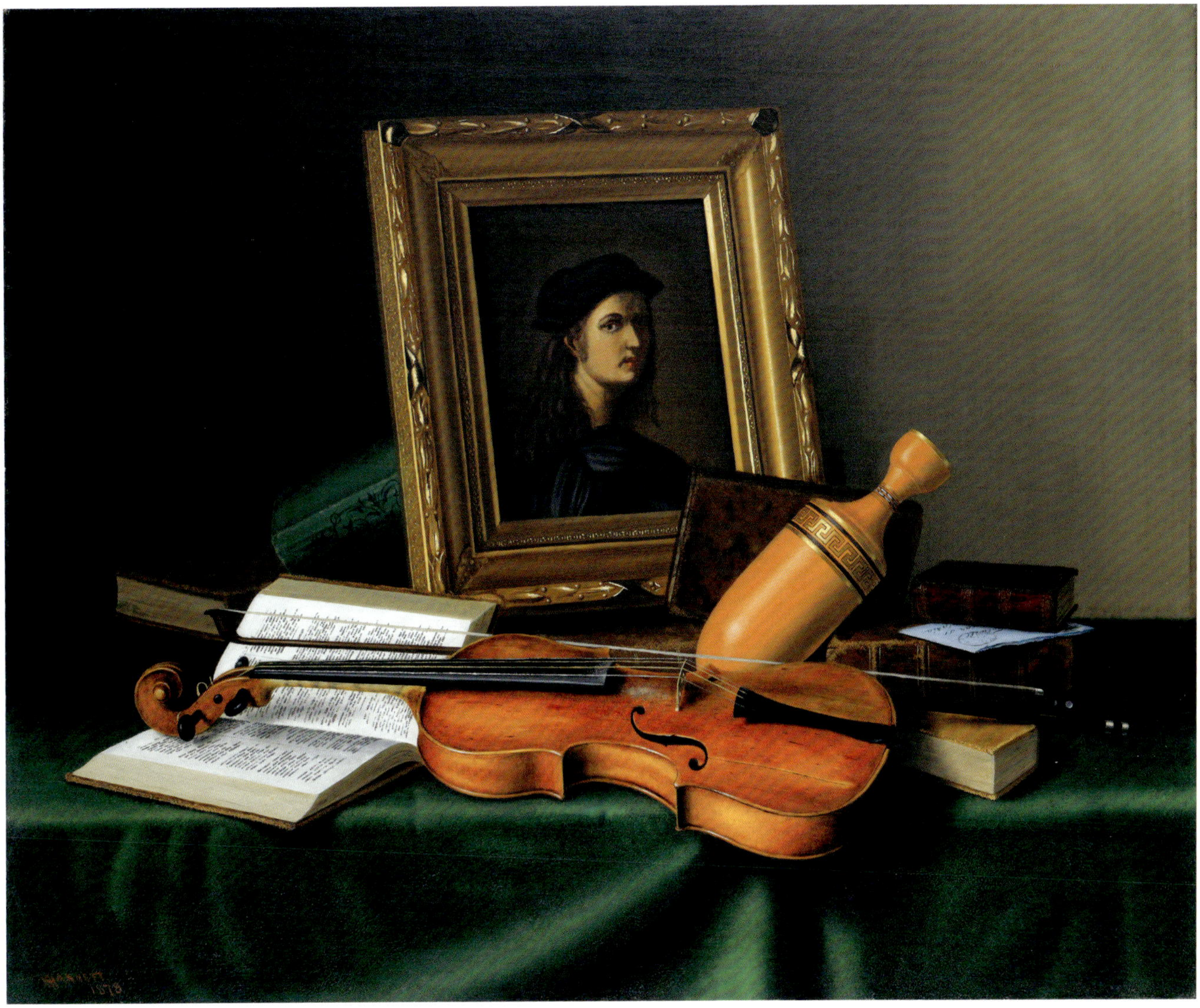

FIGURE 2 William Michael Harnett (1848–1892; born Clonakilty, Ireland; died New York, NY), *Still Life with Portrait by Raphael*, 1878. Oil on canvas, 71.8 × 87 cm. Princeton University Art Museum. Gift of Henry B. Holt and Mary D. Holt (2019-403)

While I do not disagree with Elder, for the purposes of this essay, I might refocus the task of contextualization on what is visually evident and keep the focus on a single work, or a handful of works in a single period. Queer methodologies are meant to emphasize the episodic and singular over the whole and to be discrete and "local" and at the level of the object—rather than affix the artist's practice to narratives of nationalism (that are themselves dynamic). In Harnett's singularly oblique assembly—oblique both in its indirect and unsettled meanings as well as in the diagonal slide toward sonic collision the represented objects seem about to endure—we can visually experience the progression of a queer ontology of becoming, even as the objects eventually clang and clamor to the ground, beyond our sight.

As I look again and again, I notice the painting's central "glitch" at the pinnacle of its central compositional structure. The background of the composite portrait is the same as the background of the larger composition. The portrait could thus be a mirror. The frame within a frame (gilded picture frame of the portrait) within a frame (the short span of Raphael's life) foretells/mirrors Harnett's own short life due to chronic illness. This Victorian Raphael look-alike in Renaissance drag could be, and is, Harnett: a meta-commentary on the artistic life of strong, wild passions, and the glitches, or failures, of representation: no one ever fully sees the intent. The portrait as double portrait as mirror as redoubled self brings citation and performance into futurity. In the words of Jack Halberstam, Harnett's still life can be viewed as a "complex profusion" of creativity in the face of complexity, legacy, and the presence of possible (artistic) failure.And it is in the arrangement and encounter of such high cultural stakes and efforts that are so poignant and fraught with possibility that we turn, again referencing Halberstam, to the queer adage and conceit of "messy."[12]

Still life in the field of American visual culture is a genre ripe for renewed attention. As O'Keeffe and Harnett demonstrate, the genre becomes a bit "messy" with meaning and, as such, queer. At times ironic, satirical, and full of symbolism, at times sensuous, or almost spare, still life, and the power of American artists arranging arrangements, can quickly take on personal and political importance. Compared to the *vanitas* scenes and memento mori arrangements of overladen tables and bodegons of Heda, Heem, Peeters, Romero, or Hamen y León, American still lifes have not been traditionally theorized as holding as high sociopolitical and economic stakes. Harnett compels us to see things differently. *Still Life with Portrait by Raphael* warns of the harm of looking to Europe, of the precarity yet necessity of citation in art, and the seeming impossibility of humanity to imagine itself forward into modernity without the calamity or cacophonous collision of still wishing to claim the inheritance of a European past.

All this complex profusion is indeed messy; yet it offers revelation. Harnett has composed a painting as much about time as arrangement. The viewer in our moment / Harnett's future knows he does eventually go to Europe and knows he does find a modicum of success as a result of that trip. We are asked in our contemporary moment to hold these truths just as we also hold Harnett's present-tense struggle against falling into the cliché of proper academic training (but secret desire for it in support of his own futurity as an artist). This diachronic tension in this most American and most Eurocentric of still life assemblies makes this work a fascinating and messy queer text. There are object lessons we can take away from this work in our own time.

NOTES

1. Legacy Russell, "On Footnotes," lecture, November 29, 2021, The Vera List Center for Art and Politics, The New School, https://veralistcenter.org/events/aica-usa-distinguished-critic-lecture-legacy-russell/.

2. bell hooks, "Are You Still a Slave? Liberating the Black Female Body," panel discussion, May 6, 2014, Eugene Lang College, The New School, https://www.youtube.com/watch?v=rJkohNROvzs.

3. Aristotle, *Poetics*, VII. 5–7, trans. S. H. Butcher (New York: Hill & Wang, 1961), 66.

4. José Esteban Muñoz, *Cruising Utopia: The Then and There of Queer Futurity* (New York: NYU Press, 2009).

5. Martin Heidegger, *Poetry, Language, Thought*, trans. Albert Hofstadter (New York: Harper & Row, 1971), 80–82.

6. Muñoz, *Cruising Utopia*, 1.

7. Yet, it is important to understand that queer texts predate queer theory and queer interpretations. In the literature of the United States, one might locate queer uprising against norms in Thomas Paine's 1776 *Common Sense*. The first consciously queer novel, I would argue, is Robert Montgomery Bird's 1836 *Sheppard Lee, Written by Himself*, a comedic account of a disembodied, enchanting, yet parasitic presence that inhabits bodies across the panoply of gender and race, enslaved and free, South and North, until it finds peace in nature. In art historical scholarship, one might look to Vernon Lee (the nom de plume of Violet Paget) and their introduction of *Einfühlung* (empathy), or aesthetic desire, as a parallax to Winckelmannian desire masquerading as historicism. In modernity's narrative thrall, the queer text par excellence is Virginia Woolf's *Orlando: A Biography* (1928). It is a novel that is queer in the mélange of its genre-breaking origins (bildungsroman, novel, biography) and in its opening scene (a young boy fixated on the image of his ancestry who prefigures his future gender reassignment and immortality at the odd intercession of Purity, Chasity, and Modesty, who all flee before the trumpet of "Truth!").

8. See Susan Merriam, *Seventeenth-Century Flemish Garland Paintings: Still Life, Vision, and the Devotional Image*, 2nd ed. (New York: Routledge, 2016); and Claudia Tobin, *Modernism and Still Life: Artists, Writers, Dancers* (Edinburgh, UK: Edinburgh University Press, 2020). The still life is where the visual texts of America comment on the lost promise of the enterprise. From the watermelons and cherries of Sarah Miriam Peale to the unidentified solider-photographer of the graves south of the Rio Grande in the US annexation and invasion of Mexico in 1848; to Alexander Gardner's photographs of bodies in the Antietam landscape; to Charles Bird King's painted trompe l'oeil of curiosities; to William Harnett's tables, which are sardonic continents; to Grace Hartigan's rejoinders to Matisse; to Ebony G. Patterson's bodies still in the tall woven tapestries of the grasses of her native Jamaica; to Bettina Love's call for the necessary and unapologetic resistance of Black women "resting," *dis-still-ing* life and still life in the visual texts of the United States have always been a compilation of genre: dense yet mutable in its shape and mobilization.

9. My sense of still life as an unfixed and mutable genre is indebted to Maggie Nelson's *On Freedom*. In her discussion of criticism, Nelson writes, "It's also an ethical matter, insofar as Sontag's question reminds us that the world doesn't exist to amplify or exemplify our own pre-existing tastes, values, or predilections. It simply exists. We don't have to like all of it or remain mute in the face of our discontent. But there's a difference between going to art with the hope that it will reify a belief or value we already hold, and feeling angry or punitive when it doesn't, and going to art to see what it's doing, what's going on, treating it as a place to get 'the real and irregular news of how others around [us] think and feel,' as Eileen Myles once put it." Maggie Nelson, *On Freedom: Four Songs of Care and Constraint* (Minneapolis: Graywolf Press, 2021), 86.

10. Harnett, like the American painter Charles Bird King before him, was consistent in making the titles of volumes used in his still lifes legible. To have an illegible folio or volume in a Harnett painting is irregular and important.

11. Nika Elder, *William Harnett's Curious Objects: Still Life Painting after the American Civil War* (Berkeley: University of California Pres, 2022), 3–4.

12. Jack Halberstam, *The Queer Art of Failure* (Durham, NC: Duke University Press, 2011), 10, 92.

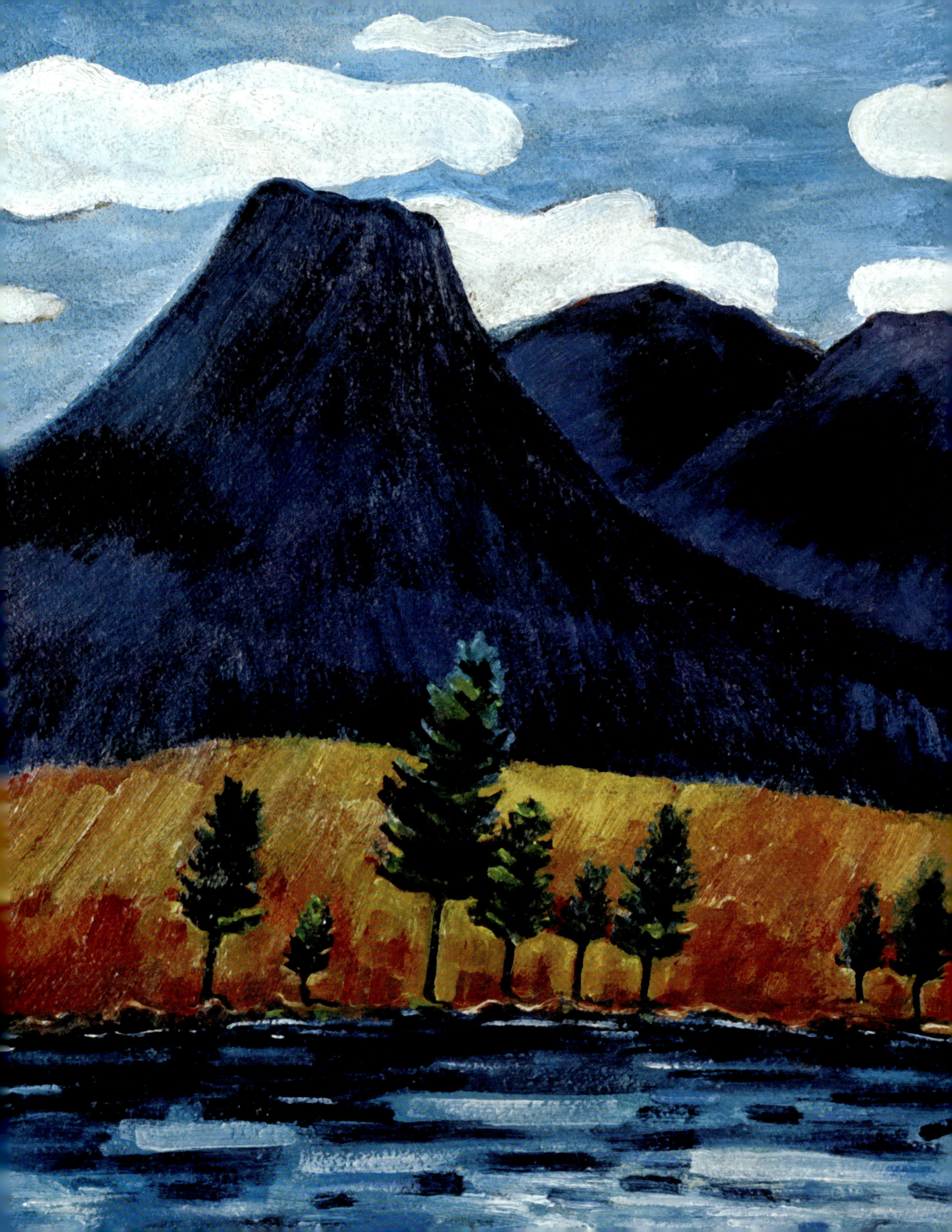

Karl Kusserow

Intimations of Ecology: Varieties of Environmental Experience in American Art

The earliest American landscape painting at Princeton is both a significant and a curious work of art. Small and indistinct, it has the air of being hastily produced, which, as a sketch for a much larger painting, it probably was. Thomas Cole's *Study for The Course of Empire: The Savage State* (fig. 1), like all landscape representation, engages human attitudes toward nonhuman nature, and thus seems a fitting place to begin an essay on the varieties of such engagements in Princeton's collection of American art. Completed in about 1834, Cole's sketch is the only known oil study for the initial work in the artist's *The Course of Empire*, a five-part, defeatist allegory of history, progress, and the nation-state, whose portentous title both suggests its intended contemporary import and anticipates its subsequent distinction in American

---

This essay's title nods to two others, separated by the century that saw the entrenchment of Western industrial attitudes toward nature. William Wordsworth's poem "Ode: Intimations of Immortality from Recollections of Early Childhood," begun in 1802, concerns the human estrangement from the natural world, and William James's monograph *The Varieties of Religious Experience: A Study in Human Nature*, completed one hundred years later, explores the situated pluralism of experience—topics relevant to the various ways different cultures and actors have

Detail, figure 24

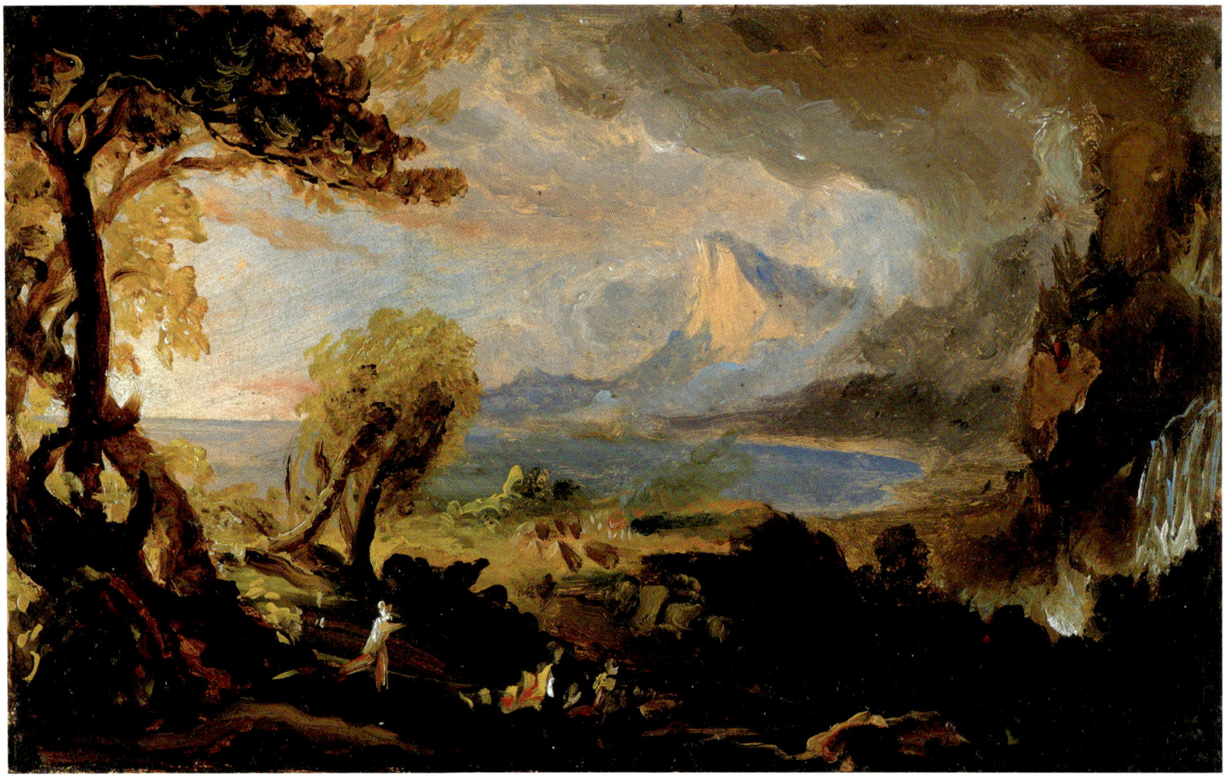

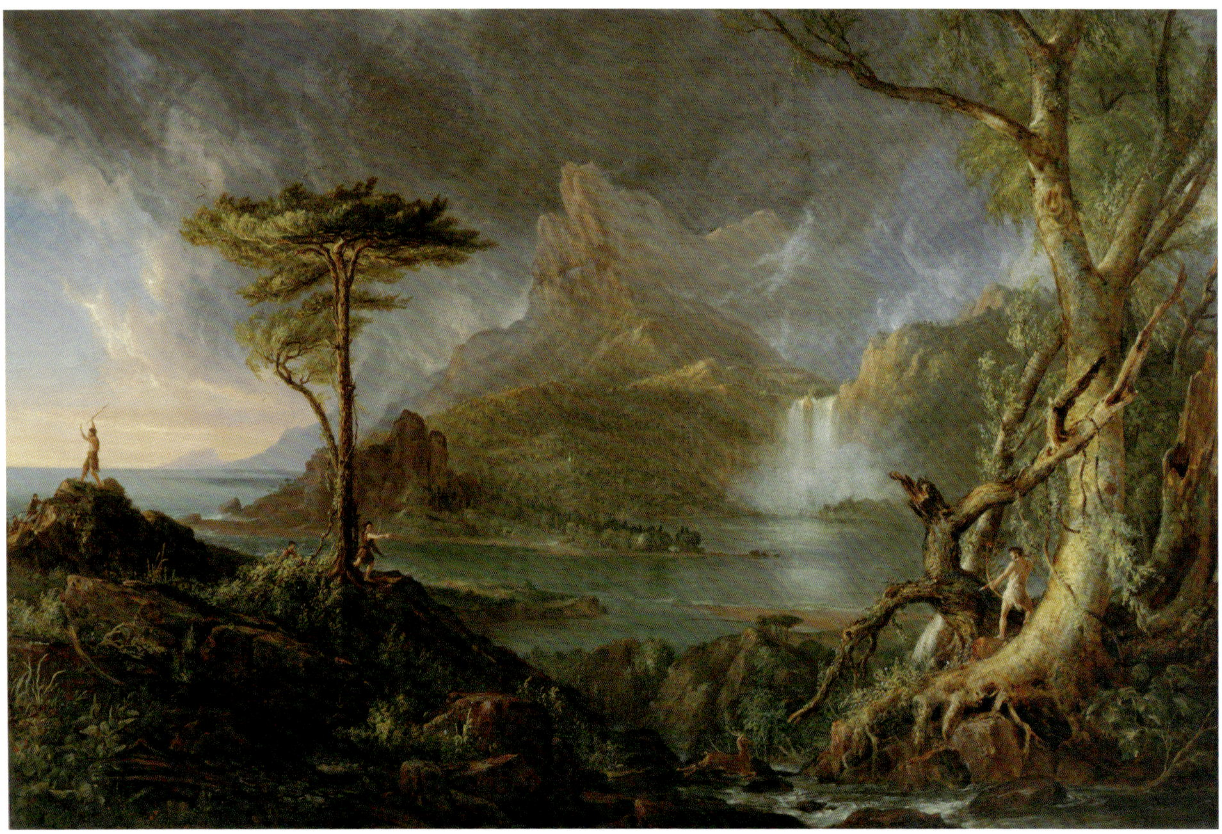

FIGURE 1 Thomas Cole (1801–1848; born Lancashire, United Kingdom; died Catskill, NY), *Study for The Course of Empire: The Savage State*, ca. 1834. Oil on paper laid down on canvas, 16 × 26 cm. Princeton University Art Museum. Gift of Frank Jewett Mather Jr. (y1941-51)

FIGURE 2 Thomas Cole, *A Wild Scene*, 1831–32. Oil on canvas, 129.7 × 194.5 cm. The Baltimore Museum of Art. Purchase with exchange funds from Leonce Rabillon Bequest Fund; and Purchase Fund (1958.15)

art history. At the time of its completion, novelist James Fenimore Cooper considered *The Course of Empire* "one of the noblest works of art that has ever been wrought," and its maker "the highest genius this country has ever produced." Hence, as the emergent expression of Cole's grand opus, the significance, historically at least, of Princeton's small one.[1]

The painting's curiosity resides in its portrayal, unlike virtually all the American landscape paintings that preceded it, of a wholly invented terrain, the depiction not of a particular physical place, but of a mental space through which to engage a topic rather than a topography. Other landscapists at work here before Cole painted similarly generalized views, but these were at least nominally rooted in observed reality, however much they "improved" and otherwise departed from it, also for ideological reasons. Cole's setting for *The Course of Empire*, which portrayed the same invented site as it evolved over time from wilderness to metropolis and back again, was instead wholly the product of his imagination, deployed to make a point about time, human nature, and nature itself. The message seems clear: the one (humanity) advances at the expense of the other (the natural world), but in the end only nature endures.[2]

Cole's sketch was itself based on another, earlier work by the artist. *A Wild Scene* of 1831–32 amounts to a sort of dry run—or rather a false start—for the later *Savage State* (figs. 2, 3). *A Wild Scene* was painted in Florence, where the tradition of invented landscapes with conceptual intentions was more established, notably through the work of Claude Lorrain (1600–1682), a French artist who lived in Italy, and Salvator Rosa (1615–1673), active there at the same time—both of whom Cole admired. It is aptly titled: thunderous skies, crashing waterfalls, and blasted trees conjure a primordial world in which half a dozen fur-clad men, armed with spears and bows, pursue a leaping stag. In the distance, other humans are just discernible on foot and in canoes, apparently come to join the chase, and beyond them wisps of rising smoke suggest a settlement. Despite the human presence, it is a dark and inhospitable environment, aqueous and craggy, affording scant purchase for its inhabitants. And for all its depicted motion, it is also strangely static, the poses of the hunters fixed and statuesque, and the composition's pronounced verticals

construed the human-nature nexus. The essay was written on Nassau Street in Princeton, New Jersey, originally a section of the Assunpink Trail of the Lenni Lenape. The Lenape people's stewardship into the mid-eighteenth century of Lenapehoking—including parts of Delaware, New York, Pennsylvania, and all of New Jersey—was rooted in an animistic perspective that, had it and others like it prevailed instead of extractive anthropocentrism, might have precluded Wordsworth's "Ode," whose second stanza ends, "But yet I know, where'er I go, / That there hath past away a glory from the earth." To affirm the Lenape people's historical and abiding presence in this region thus seems appropriate in this context, while acknowledging that such acts of recognition are not equivalent to redressing their former local sovereignty and coerced removal from the area.

(hunters, trees, paired cataracts) combining at right angles with the pervasive horizontal of the water to fasten image to canvas as if to a grid.

In deciding to set this scene of compositional stasis aside, first in Princeton's study and then in the completed *Savage State*, Cole signaled a desire for a more movemented effect, one specifically oriented to imply a progression from left to right. This he accomplished in both sketch and final canvas through the removal of the rightmost hunter (pentimenti for which are faintly visible in the larger version), whose opposing stance impeded such an effect, and by generally orchestrating landscape, atmospheric, and narrative elements to suggest, like words on a page, a kind of rightward procession. Why? Perhaps because in so doing he could more meaningfully relate this initial work to the other scenes in the series and indicate to viewers of the whole that a narrative is intended. The other compositions support this, each being structured in terms of implied motion according to their relative place in the overall program. In the second and third scenes, *The Arcadian or Pastoral State* and *The Consummation of Empire* (figs. 4, 5), viewers are presented with different manifestations of compositional and narrative equipoise. In the *Pastoral* iteration, humans coexist peaceably with nature, though as the plowman at left and cut stump at right suggest, they have begun to alter it for their own ends. In the grand *Consummation*—larger than the others in the series and intended as its centerpiece—humans have assumed a corresponding centrality, erecting an imperial marble city on the once unoccupied spot. In each painting, a sense of stasis prevails, imparted by the great rooted trees of *Pastoral* and the profusion of weighty, columnar architecture in *Consummation*, lending to each the same fixity as *Wild Scene*. Yet unlike in that abandoned prototype, here it makes sense. In the prevalent logic of anthropocentrism, time and human development are figured in *Course of Empire* as passing quickly (to the right) through their beginning stages, and then, when people predominate and nature appears to exist for them, as standing still. Only when things go awry, as in the series' fourth scene, showing the *Destruction* (fig. 6) of human interests, is compositional movement renewed, but now backward, against time and logic, with the painting's energies reversed and moving emphatically from right to left. When humans no longer prevail, the order of things is subverted.[3]

It is unlikely Cole deliberately set out to portray these effects. Although much has been made of whether he meant in *Course of Empire* to offer an environmental or ecological cautionary tale, in addition to the sociopolitical one, his own words suggest he did not—and in any case, he appears to argue in the series for the significance only of human concerns, not those of everything else. As he wrote to his patron, Luman Reed, his critique was of history and the nation state: "My subject is drawn from the history of the past, wherein we see how nations have risen from the savage state to that of power and glory, and then fallen, and become extinct." In orienting his abiding natural setting fundamentally around the human, the artist conveyed his own anthropocentrism and that of the age, which was to instrumentalize American nature for its own ends, with redounding results.[4]

What has been called "directionality" matters in understanding Cole, especially his most ambitious works. In the midst of creating *Course of Empire* (and on a recycled canvas originally intended for it), the artist painted his masterpiece, *View from Mount Holyoke, Northampton, Massachusetts, after a Thunderstorm—The Oxbow* (fig. 7), in which implied compositional movement also becomes significant—indeed, is central to the work's meaning. The lateral movement of the weather across that canvas draws not only sunshine but also settlement with it, and the small painter nestled among the rocks, surely a self-portrait, approvingly paints the domesticated scene beneath him, not the wild nature at his back. In *Course of Empire*, Cole surfaces similar concerns more subtly, but the import of each is evident. His art reveals not a personal, countervailing indictment of human development at the expense of nature, as often claimed, but rather something more conventional and pervasive in Western culture: the enduring assumption of human primacy in the scheme of things.[5]

Princeton's modest sketch helped set the course for *Course of Empire*, exchanging the stasis of *Wild Scene* for the movement of *Savage State*, and thus critically informing the logic of the whole. Though its meaning depends on the rest of the series to be understood, the study helps make clear what *Course of Empire* is expressing in environmental terms. This small picture underscores how landscape representation has always been essentially anthropocentric, and in this way, ideological. As American landscape painting developed over the succeeding years to express first the ordering logic of settler colonialism and later the more ambitious rhetoric of imperial desire, its exemplars wove into their compositions something equally political and even more fundamental: attitudes about the human relationship to nature, which could not help but be pictured according to the subjective perceptions and concerns of their makers and contemporary audience.

GOD AND MAMMON

The sensibility that caused Cole to linger, compositionally, in the middle works of *Course of Empire*, pausing where the human reigns ascendant, is the same anthropocentric orientation that prompted Europeans to advance their interests and ideologies throughout the Western Hemisphere centuries before Cole picked up his brush—before landscape painting was even invented. In 1619, an English privateer, the *White Lion*, landed at Point Comfort near Jamestown in Virginia, where twelve years earlier colonists had formed the first permanent English settlement in the Americas. Their purpose was commercial: to extract from the "New World" things of value and return them to the "old" one, thus turning a profit. In this they considered they would be abetted by trading fresh provisions with the *Lion*'s crew for the ship's human cargo—some "20 and odd Negroes," seized from a Portuguese slaver, which had in turn seized the Africans from Angola—and setting them to enforced labor "in the service of several planters" growing tobacco for export. Only a year later, another, far more famous ship—the *Mayflower*—whose objective of affording its passengers religious freedom accords more closely with Americans' celebratory self-fashioning of their history, landed at Plymouth in Massachusetts. The Pilgrims' purpose was spiritual, and included proselytizing among Native Americans to advance their beliefs.[6]

These twin arrivals bracket the paired imperatives guiding the Western encounter with both North and South America, where Spanish and Portuguese imperialists already vied for dominance, similarly motivated by religion and revenue. Spanish settlements first established in the Caribbean had, by 1600, spread throughout Central and South America. The wish to practice religion freely and the related urge to proselytize particular forms of belief, and the will to power and riches in the form of territory and the accumulation of valuable natural resources, including people, was pursued on hemispheric scale for centuries, with ruinous consequences for both Indigenous populations and the millions of enslaved Africans forcibly introduced to the West.[7]

What coheres these two elemental impulses, Christianity and capitalism, is an ingrained self-centeredness—respectively, inter- and intra-species—that has in different ways proved harmful not just for disempowered people but for the entire planet. The Judeo-Christian origin story, the biblical Book of Genesis, begins with the command that man, the anointed species, go forth and subdue the earth, and have dominion over the rest of its inhabitants—"over every creeping thing," as the King James Bible put it in 1611. This monotheistic system justified the exploitation of the nonhuman for human ends. Capitalism, in turn, has undermined the virtue of the commons in favor of the individual and valued nature in terms of extractable components rather than as an essential interdependent whole. Around the same time that Charles Darwin was at work on *The Origin of Species* (1859), which enshrined competition as the natural order, Karl Marx theorized in his equally consequential *Capital* (1867) the irreparable "metabolic rift"

FOLLOWING SPREAD

FIGURE 3 Thomas Cole, *The Course of Empire: The Savage State*, ca. 1834. Oil on canvas, 99.7 × 160.7 cm. New-York Historical Society. Gift of the New-York Gallery of the Fine Arts (1858.1)

FIGURE 4 Thomas Cole, *The Course of Empire: The Arcadian or Pastoral State*, ca. 1834. Oil on canvas, 99.7 × 160.7 cm. New-York Historical Society. Gift of the New-York Gallery of the Fine Arts (1858.2)

FIGURE 5 Thomas Cole, *The Course of Empire: The Consummation of Empire*, 1835–36. Oil on canvas, 130.2 × 193 cm. New-York Historical Society. Gift of the New-York Gallery of the Fine Arts (1858.3)

FIGURE 6 Thomas Cole, *The Course of Empire: Destruction*, 1836. Oil on canvas, 99.7 × 161.3 cm. New-York Historical Society. Gift of the New-York Gallery of the Fine Arts (1858.4)

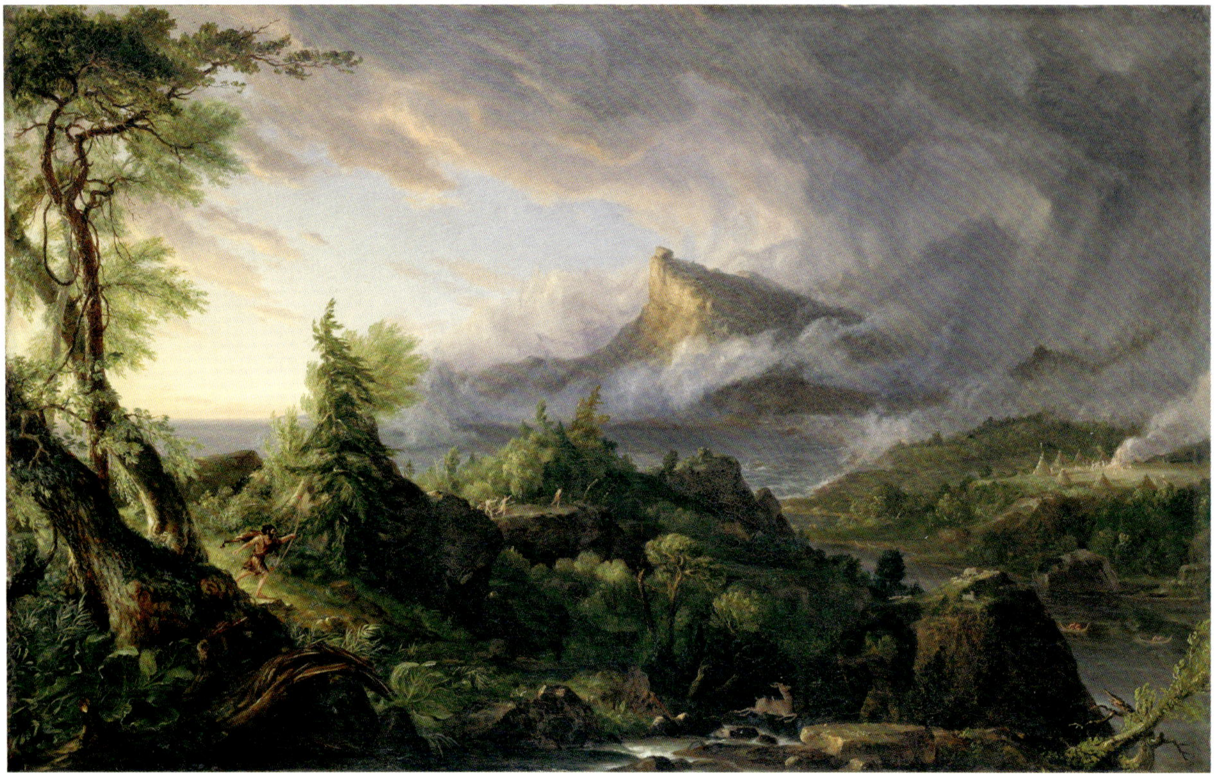

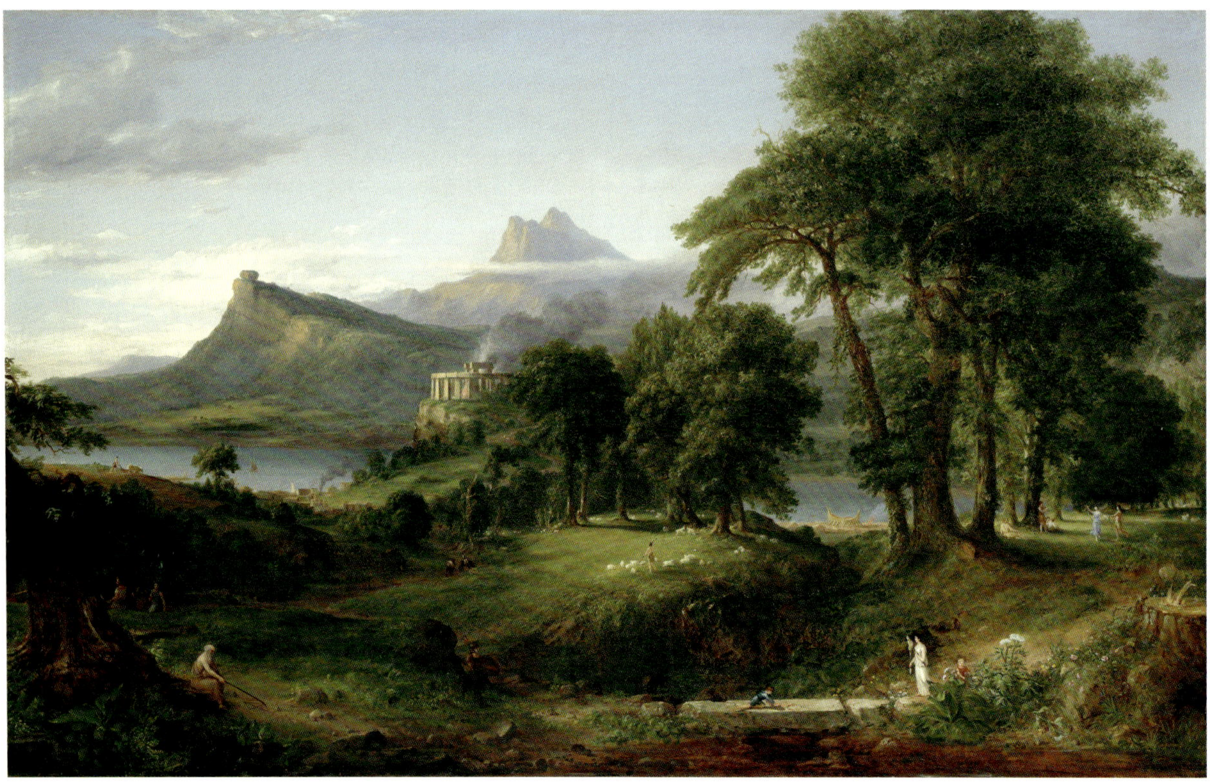

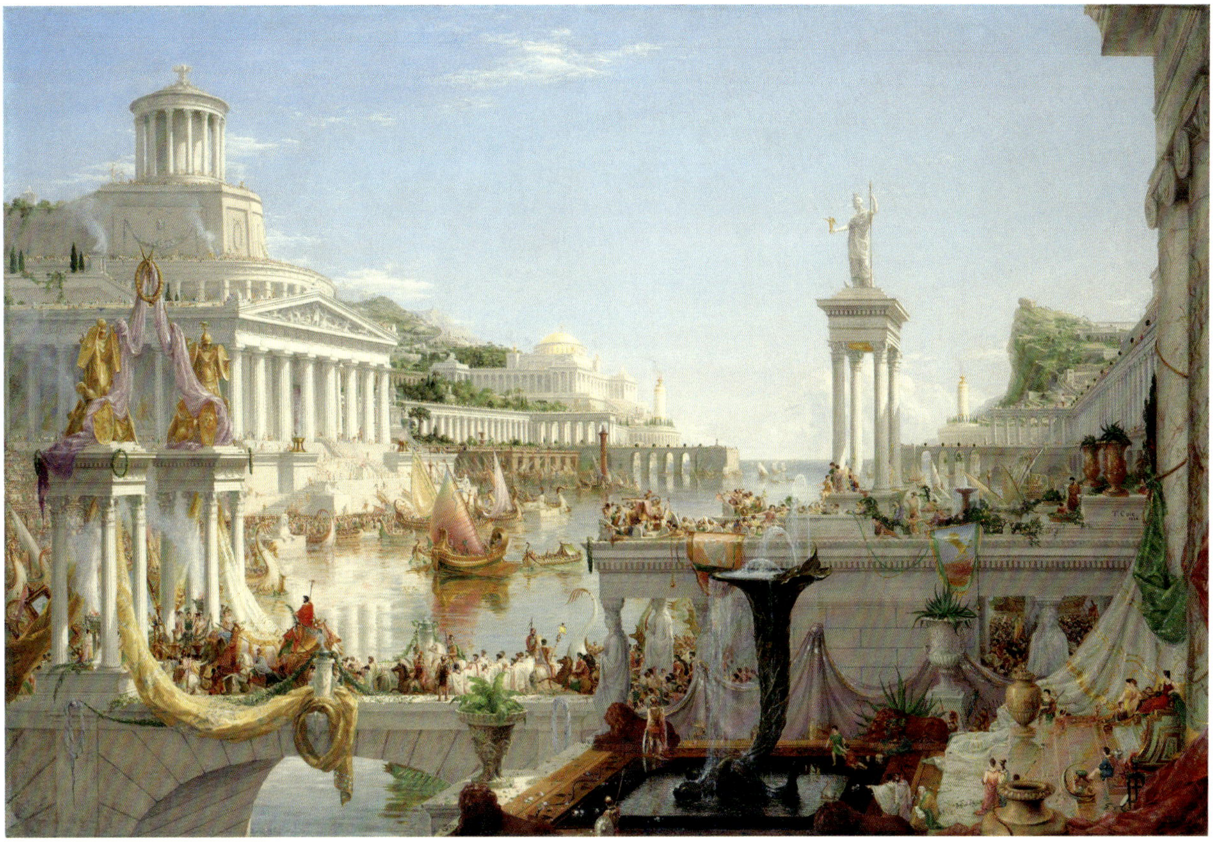

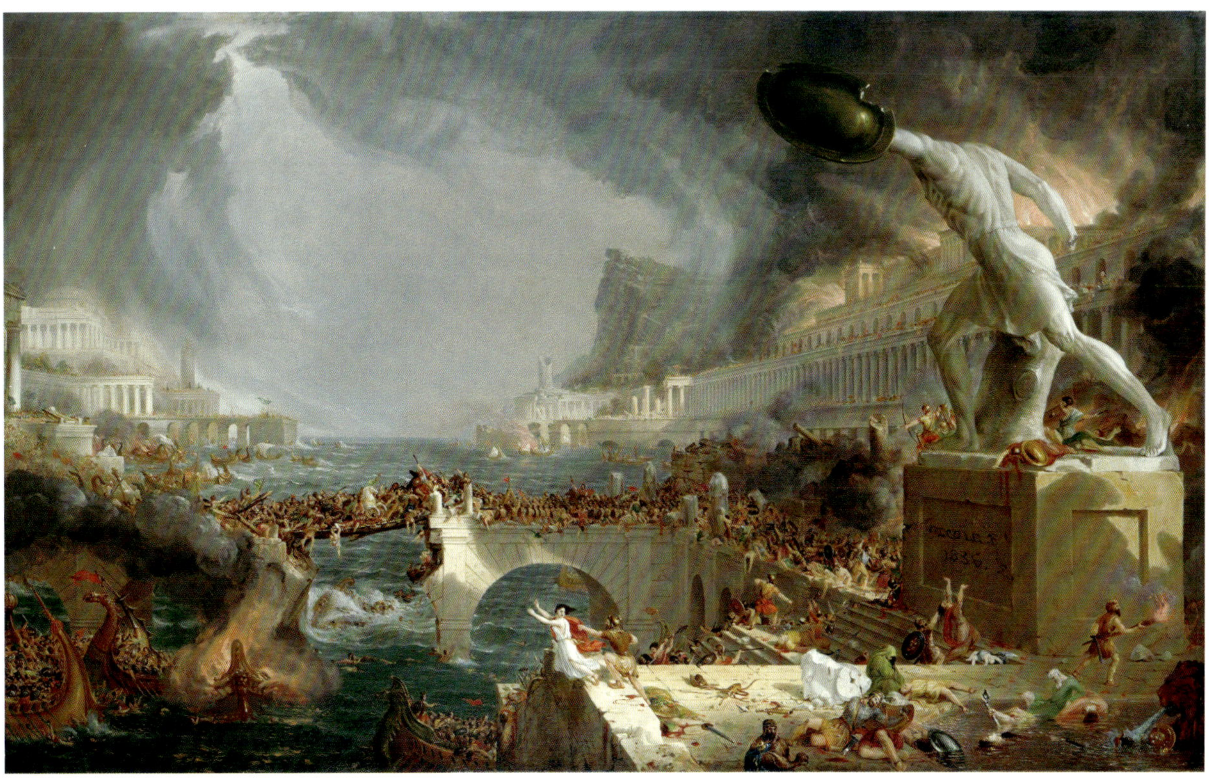

resulting from capitalism's extractive, profit-driven logic, in which essential balances between production, consumption, and regeneration are ignored. The basis for their observations—Darwin's approving, Marx's critical—lay centuries before, in Christian and capitalist orthodoxies that undergirded the spread of Western culture to the hemisphere that shares its name.[8]

In 1579, Diego de Valadés produced *Rhetorica Christiana* (Christian Rhetoric) in Perugia, Italy, the first text ever published by an American-born author. Tellingly, it is an account of Christian evangelization in the Americas and a manual to facilitate the teaching of Catholic missionaries. Written and likely illustrated by Valadés, a Franciscan friar whose mixed-race heritage—his mother was Tlaxcaltec (a Nahua people from the Mexican state of Tlaxcala), his father a Spaniard—*Rhetorica Christiana* underscores the dynamic process of cultural collision and creolization wrought by imperialism. Following a classical humanist education at the school of Santiago Tlatelolco in Mexico City—the oldest European college in the Americas, established primarily to prepare Native American boys for the priesthood—Valadés became the first mestizo to enter the Franciscan Order. Fray Diego subsequently spent two decades converting Indigenous peoples to his father's Catholic faith before moving abroad, serving as Franciscan representative to the Vatican and eventually publishing *Rhetorica Christiana*. His text contains numerous illustrations, in keeping with Valadés's belief that images were indispensable mnemonic devices in the conversion process. Several of the book's illustrations themselves demonstrate this, showing missionaries engaged in instruction using pictorial aids. Valadés's engraving of the *Ideal Atrio* (Ideal Atrium; fig. 8) collapses the process of conversion and practice of the faith into a single allegorical image,

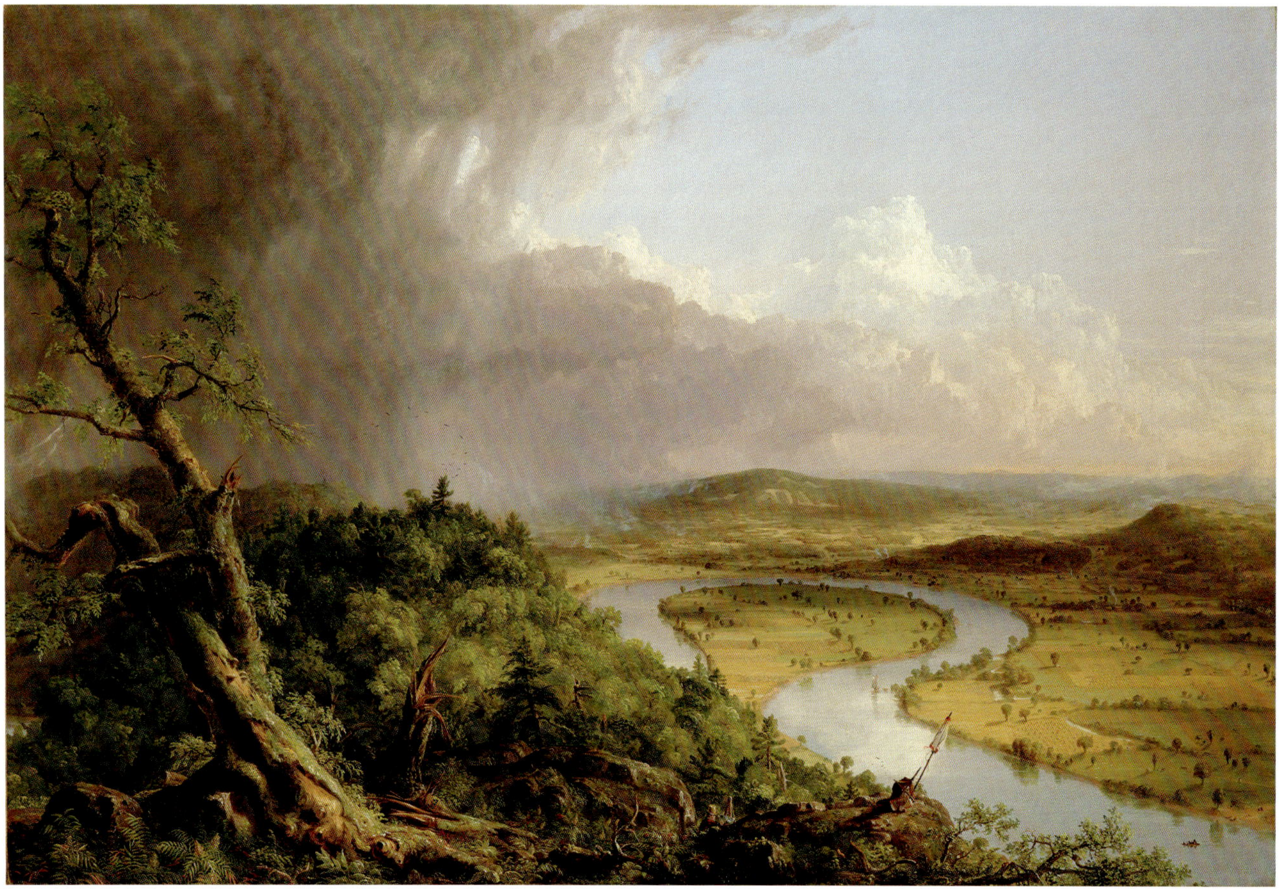

FIGURE 7 Thomas Cole, *View from Mount Holyoke, Northampton, Massachusetts, after a Thunderstorm—The Oxbow*, 1836. Oil on canvas, 130.8 × 193 cm. The Metropolitan Museum of Art, New York. Gift of Mrs. Russell Sage, 1908 (08.228)

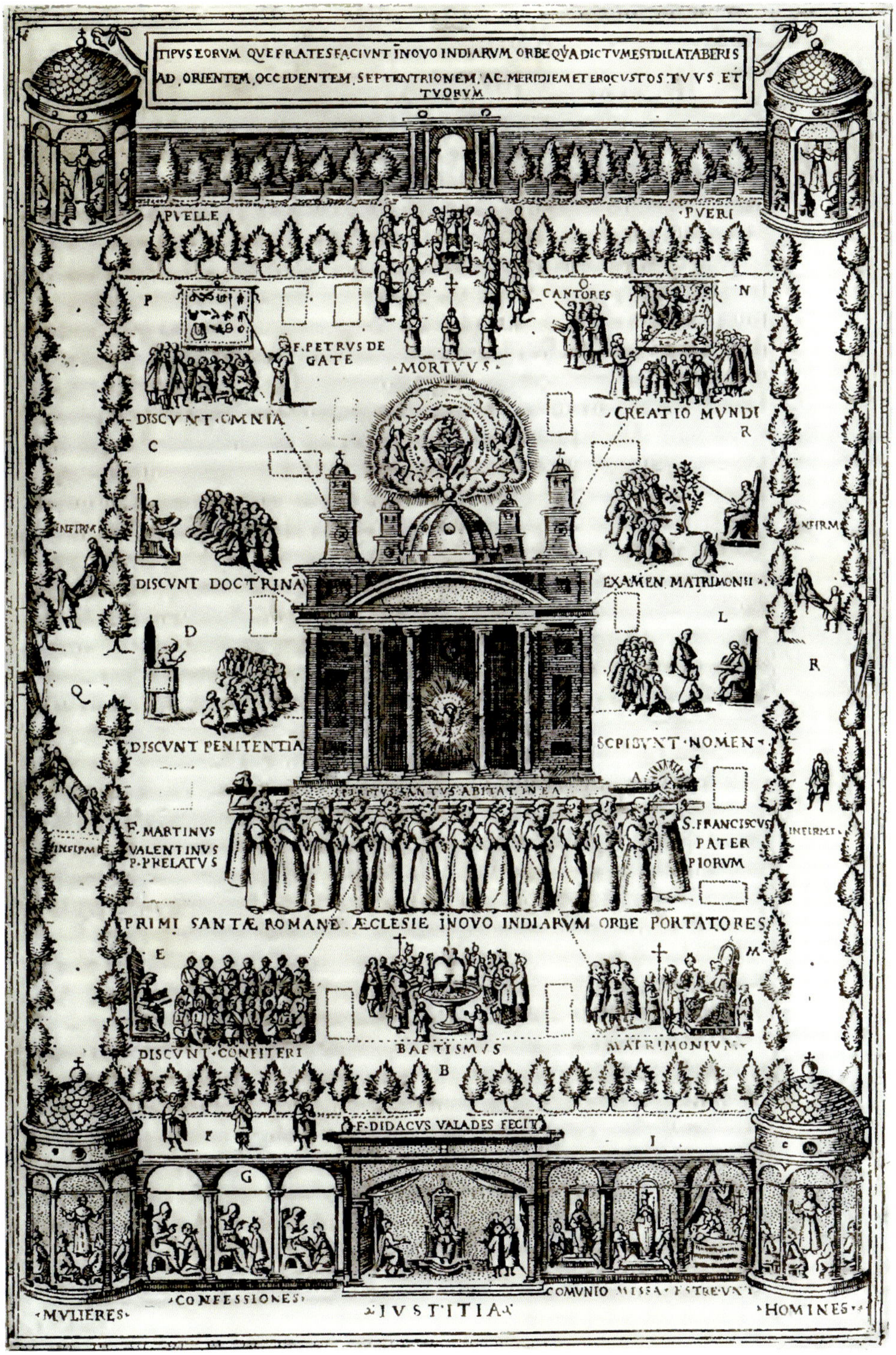

FIGURE 8 Diego de Valadés (Didacus Valades) (1533–1582; born Mexico), *Ideal Atrio*, engraving in *Rhetorica Christiana* (Perugia: 1579). Getty Research Institute, Los Angeles

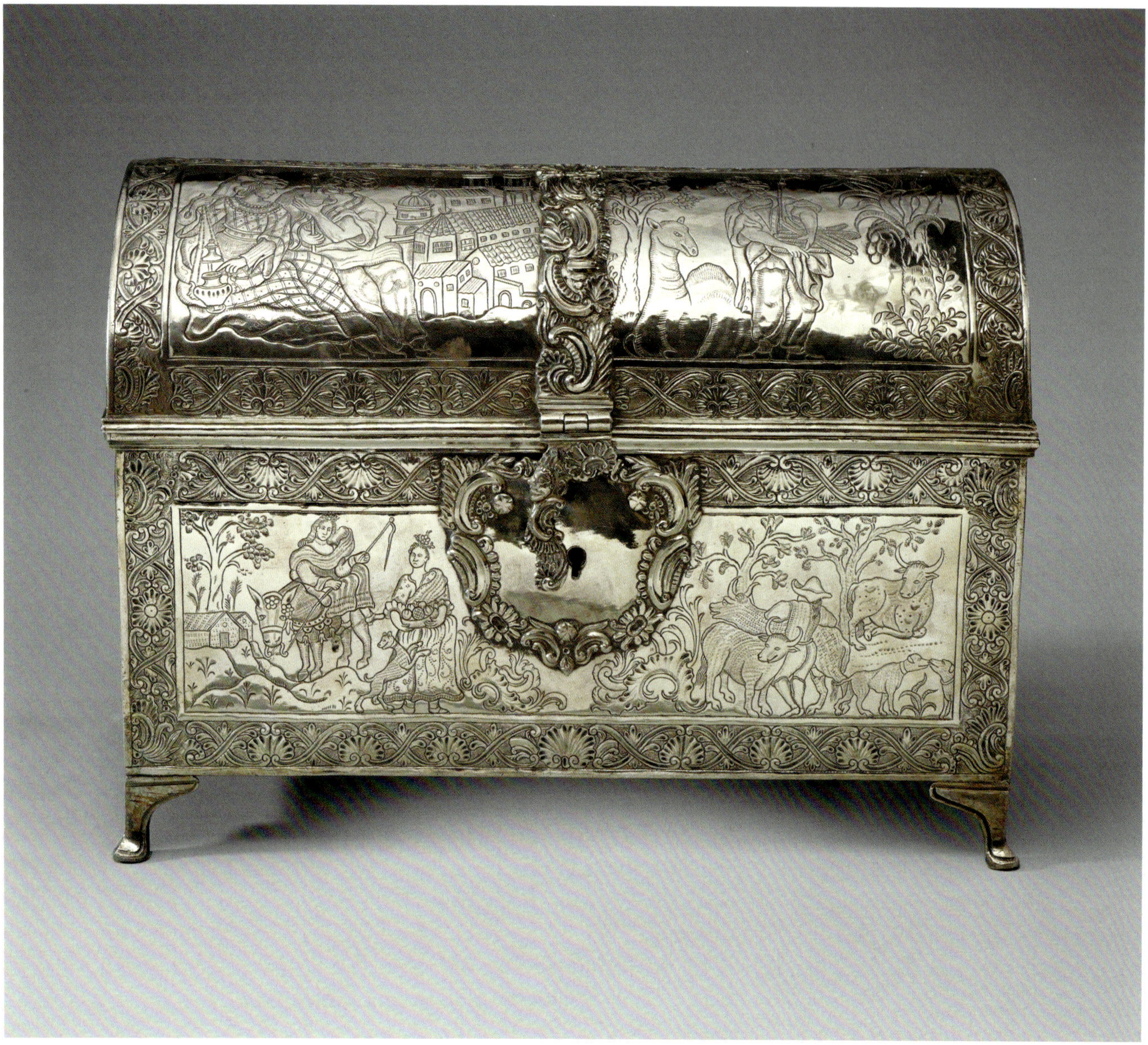

FIGURE 9 Artist unidentified, Viceroyalty of Peru (probably Lima), Chest, ca. 1780. Silver, 28 × 37 × 24 cm. Princeton University Art Museum. Museum purchase, Fowler McCormick, Class of 1921, Fund (2022-50)

with vignettes of priests teaching Catholic doctrine and the newly faithful being baptized, married, and giving confession.[9]

The best-known image in *Rhetorica Christiana* is Valadés's visualization of the Great Chain of Being, illustrating a concept with roots in antiquity and sustained in Christian dogma through millennia. It encapsulates a cosmology that situates humans just below divine beings, with tiered ranks of species considered lesser—first fauna, then flora—descending underneath in hierarchical order. Such a metaphysical paradigm accorded well with Christianity's essential anthropocentrism, underscoring the belief that the earthly realm exists above all for humans, and the vast array of other things subsists in service and support of them, like boughs on an ascending tree, topped by the Deity. This construct offered a useful tool in rationalizing, codifying, and disseminating an ideology in which resources—from (non-Christian) human life to organic to inorganic materials—might be utilized for (Christian) human ends, without particular regard for the implications beyond them.[10]

A silver Peruvian *arqueta*, or chest (fig. 9), made probably in Lima about 1780, speaks to the material wealth extracted from Viceregal Spain, and its costs, across three centuries, from Hernán Cortés's defeat of the Mexica (Aztecs) in 1521 and Francisco Pizarro's conquest of the Inka in 1534, until the viceroyalties of Peru and New Spain dissolved into independent republics about 1820. Tabletop chests such as this were popular in Spanish America throughout the period in both ecclesiastical and domestic contexts; the secular iconography and soft interior lining of this one suggests it was originally a jewel box. Unlike European examples of the type, fashioned from bronze, pewter, or silver plaques nailed to a wooden core, the Peruvian chest is made entirely of sturdy silver plates, bespeaking the regional abundance of the precious metal. The silver used to produce it undoubtedly came from the mines of nearby Potosí, in present-day Bolivia, where the Cerro Rico (Rich Mountain), site of the world's largest silver deposit, loomed materially and metaphorically over the city, which in its heyday was larger and more prosperous than London and Paris. From 1550 to 1800, Latin American silver accounted for 80 percent of global production, crucially abetting the growth and power of the Spanish Empire.[11]

The diverse iconography of the chest, drawn widely from circulating print sources, attests to the cultural cosmopolitanism of Viceregal Spain. In the scene on the back, a finely engraved carriage procession features individuals dressed like French aristocrats, while on the front of the domed lid a turbaned male courts a woman before a mosque with a seated camel opposite. The chest's main face adds local flavor to the varied compositions: a woman on a donkey and a servant girl, both dressed in what would have been recognized as "Amazonian" fashion, populate a landscape in which a peasant tends cattle nearby. In between them, the chest's hinged clasp features a remarkable hybrid figure, a male with feather headdress and curved body that transforms into swirling rocaille, in a loose interpretation of the caryatid-like *indiatides* representing Indigenous peoples found in local architecture. The inclusion of such iconography seems ironic, considering it was the toil of Indians under appalling conditions that produced the silver for the wealthy lady's jewel chest. Indeed, the placement of the figure over its keyhole supplies an apt metaphor, since Indigenous labor was the critical means by which the Spanish accessed the wealth of their "New World." Hundreds of thousands of Amerindians, conscripted to work in Potosí's dangerous mines and noxious refineries, in a malign adaptation of the Inkan mit'a system of tribute labor, perished from accidents, disease, and exposure to the mercury used to amalgamate silver via the toxic process to which the Spanish resorted as the declining quality of available ore obviated smelting—already difficult due to the millions of acres of forests denuded for fuel. Extensive use of enslaved African labor only added to the horrific mix. The human and environmental devastation of the silver industry throughout Spanish America went hand in glove with the proselytizing church and the extractive, capitalistic state. As the narrator in German filmmaker Harun Farocki's video installation *The Silver and the Cross* (2010) bluntly intones, "The Spaniards brought the cross and took away the silver. In doing so, they almost exterminated the Indigenous population."[12]

The material wealth and potential of North America similarly beckoned for English, French, Dutch, and again Spanish imperialists. In 1590, the artist and publisher Theodor de Bry issued a group of images illustrating

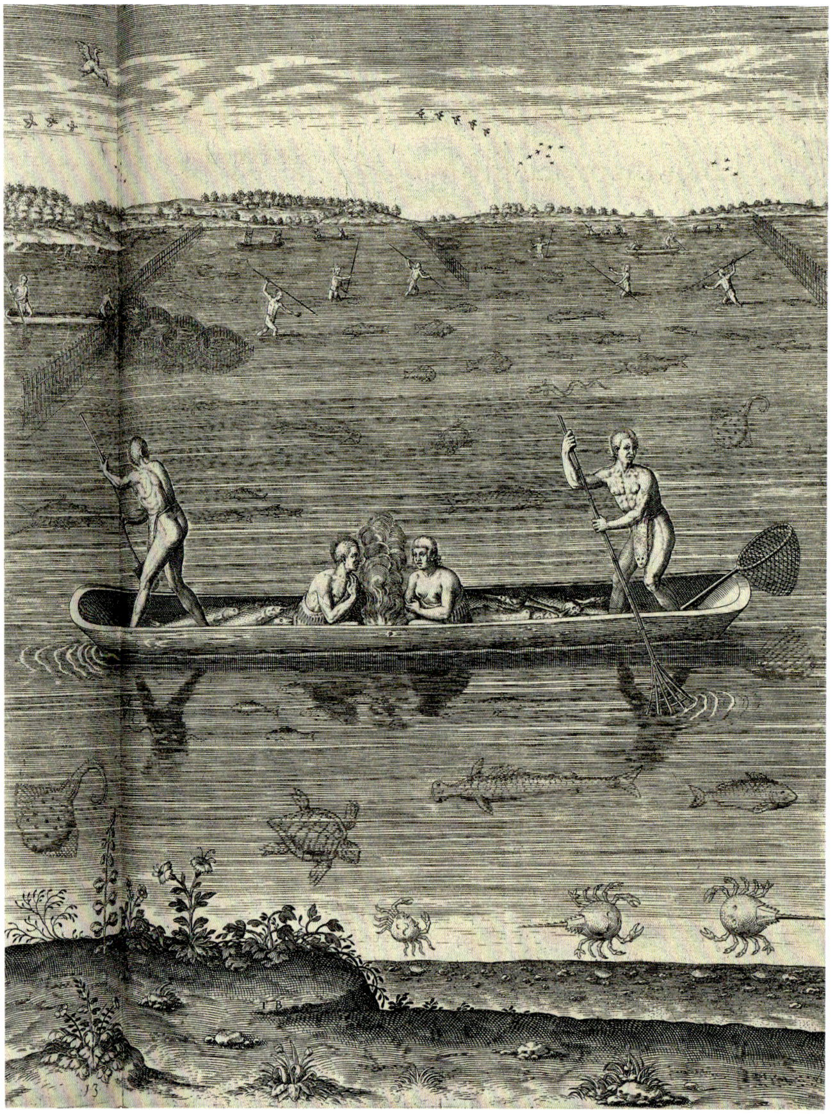

FIGURE 10 Theodor de Bry (1528–1598; born Liège, Belgium; died Frankfurt, Germany), after John White (ca. 1540–ca. 1593; born England; active Virginia), *Their manner of fishynge in Virginia*, engraving in Thomas Hariot, *A Briefe and True Report of the New Found Land of Virginia* [. . .] (Frankfurt: 1590). Princeton University Library, Department of Special Collections. Rare Books Division

Thomas Hariot's *A Briefe and True Report of the New Found Land of Virginia*, written by a member of Sir Walter Raleigh's second expedition to coastal North Carolina (1585–86), and significant as the earliest English account of North America. Raleigh and his patron, Elizabeth I of England, hoped his exploration would identify available riches in the uncharted territory, encouraging settlement and establishing a base for raids on Spanish ships transporting silver and other valuables from Potosí and elsewhere. Accordingly, the engravings collectively present an optimistic vision of America as a place of both great exoticism and promise, in keeping with the fundamentally promotional, expansionist aims of Hariot's text.

Several of de Bry's images picture resource extraction, underscoring America's perceived environmental abundance. *Their manner of fishynge in Virginia* (fig. 10) depicts Roanoke or Secotan people harvesting fish in various ways from the manifestly plentiful waters off the Virginia shore. The engraving is structured as a stable grid, with horizontal elements bisected at regular

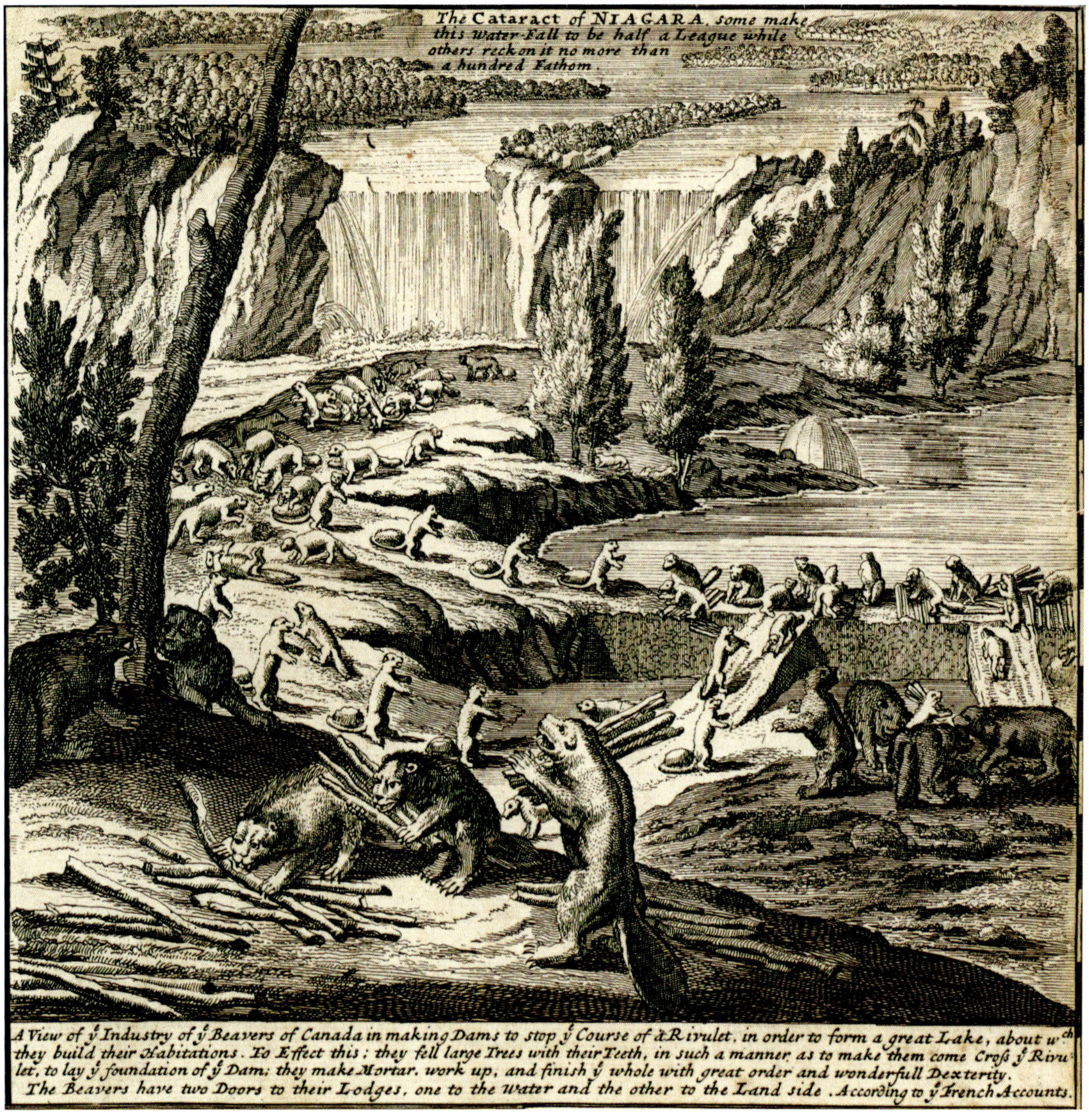

FIGURE 11 Herman Moll (ca. 1654–1732; born Germany; active London, United Kingdom), after Nicolas de Fer (1646–1720; born and died France), *A View of ye Industry of ye Beavers* [. . .], engraving in *A New and Exact Map of the Dominions of the King of Great Britain on ye Continent of North America* [. . .] (London: T. Bowles, 1715). Library of Congress, Washington, DC. Geography and Maps Division

intervals by vertical ones, conveying a sympathetic sense of order while supplying through generalized icons easily understood representations of available resources. The overall effect is to render a wholly new environment as not only comprehensible and nonthreatening but also plentiful and inviting.[13]

Later images did similar work. Among the most well-known maps of eighteenth-century North America is the so-called beaver map, named for its inclusion of an inset engraving depicting dozens of strangely humanoid beavers busily engaged in construction before the cataracts of Niagara (fig. 11). Originally featured in a 1698 map of the Western Hemisphere by French cartographer Nicolas de Fer also intended to promote settlement, the vignette reappeared at greater scale in Herman Moll's rendering of British possessions in North America about 1713. Its prominent incorporation of sedulous beavers working in organized, humanlike fashion in front of the Niagara dynamo transmitted messages of both exceptional natural abundance (beaver pelts were enormously important in the colonial economy) and the beneficial transformation of resources possible through industry.[14]

By the time Moll's map was published, the symbols of religion and religious conversion sometimes appearing on early Spanish maps had given way to a more frank avowal of the real estate and resources fundamentally at stake in the vast new territory. But the spiritual justification for colonization—consistently downplayed in subsequent accounts of US history for the political basis of throwing off Britain's imperial yoke—remained powerfully present, not least in the learned institutions the colonists established once firmly rooted. Of these, Harvard was first, in 1636, profoundly informed by the Calvinism of the Puritans and named for one of its ministers. Congregationalist Yale (1701) and Presbyterian Princeton (1746) followed, each like Harvard founded explicitly to train the ministry, many of whom were in turn charged with spreading the faith to the Indigenous uninitiated, thereby rationalizing ongoing settlement and the expropriation of land and materials that were not theirs.

At Princeton (originally the College of New Jersey), the first academic exercise held at its new Nassau Hall nexus was a prayer service. Every day thereafter, students and faculty gathered before dawn and again in the evening in its prayer hall—by far the largest room in the building—to avow their devotion according to the evangelical Presbyterianism that had ushered the college into existence. The prayer hall gave material expression to the school's pronounced religiosity. Although much has been made of Princeton's early accommodation of both religious and secular education, were it not for the need to train Presbyterian ministers to propagate the beliefs of the fervent "New Sides"—adherents, unlike their conservative "Old Side" counterparts, of the evangelizing First Great Awakening—Nassau Hall would never have been built. Founding trustee Ebenezer Pemberton, himself a minister, wrote that "our great Intention was to erect a seminary for educating Ministers of the Gospel," and Princeton's first president, Jonathan Dickinson, similarly noted, "Our Aim in the Undertaking is to promote the Interests of the Redeemors Kingdom; and to raise up qualified Persons for the sacred Service."[15]

Nassau Hall must have initially functioned something like a cloister, the entire school bound up in a single austere building, and largely devoted to the ministry. The earliest painted representation of the College dates from 1807 (fig. 12), but it is a copy by amateur artist (and, again, minister) Jonathan Fisher of a print by Henry Dawkins featured in the first chronicle of the school, Samuel Blair's *An Account of the College of New-Jersey*, published in 1764 "with a Prospect of the College Neatly Engraved." A few years earlier, the first known image of Nassau Hall anywhere appeared in the March 1760 issue of the *New American Magazine*, printed nearby in Woodbridge, New Jersey, and perhaps engraved by the same Henry Dawkins (fig. 13). It expresses Princeton's initial religious orientation clearly, showing a structure still recognizable in its rudiments today beneath a pair of cherubs holding aloft a banner bearing the college's motto, *Dei sub numine viget* (Under God's power she flourishes). Centered directly above the cupola of Nassau Hall, the motto trumpets the explicit causal link between the Deity and the new institution's strength and progress. Also pictured above Nassau Hall, but off in a corner, boxed and contained in its own mediating frame, is a vignette displaying the tools of earthly knowledge—microscope, dividers, telescope, sextant, globe, and books—illuminated through the clouds by the sun's rays. The relationship between the vignette, with its artifacts of secular humanism, and the banner, tying the college's purpose and future to divine sovereignty, is a telling expression of the artist's impression of the young college. The only two compositional embellishments of the otherwise matter-of-fact illustration, they suggest that while there is room in the picture for the emerging light of reason, in the world Princeton College was constructing, God held center stage.[16]

Princeton's third president, renowned theologian Jonathan Edwards, served little more than a month in 1758 before succumbing to smallpox, but his evangelical beliefs were in keeping with—and meaningfully informed—the ethos of the College. His close follower was David Brainerd, a Presbyterian missionary from Connecticut who, with support from the Society in Scotland for Propagating Christian Knowledge, proselytized extensively among the Mohicans and later the Lenape in New Jersey, near Princeton. He died young of tuberculosis in 1747, while in the care of Edwards and his family, and bequeathed to them, and thus to Princeton,

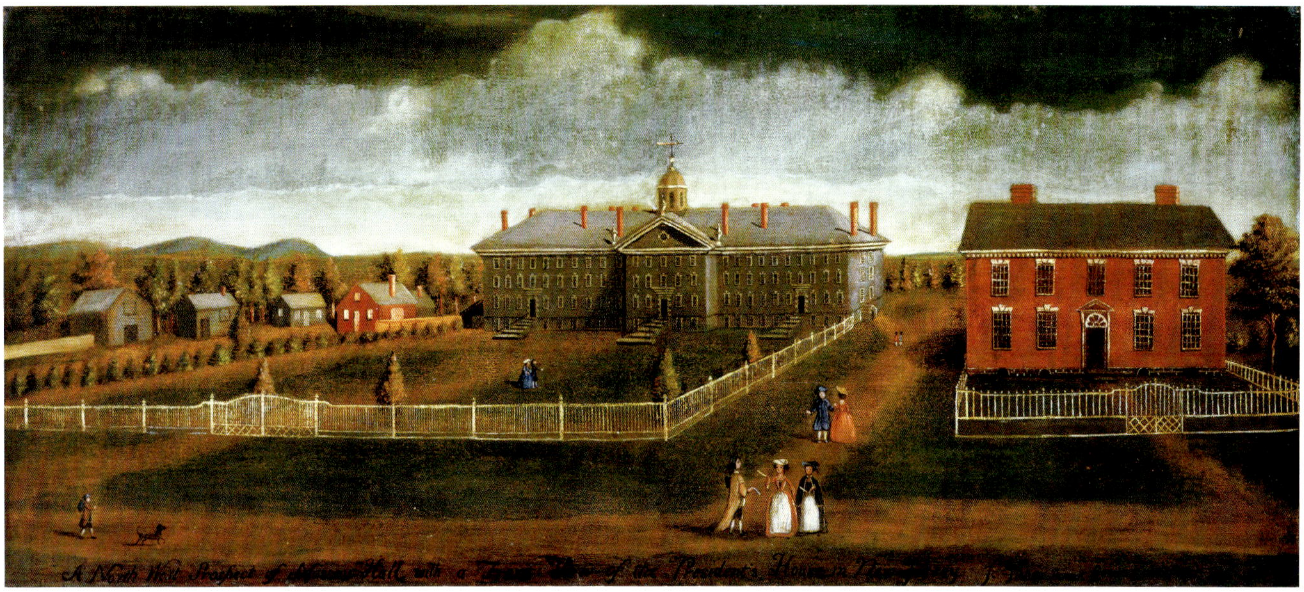

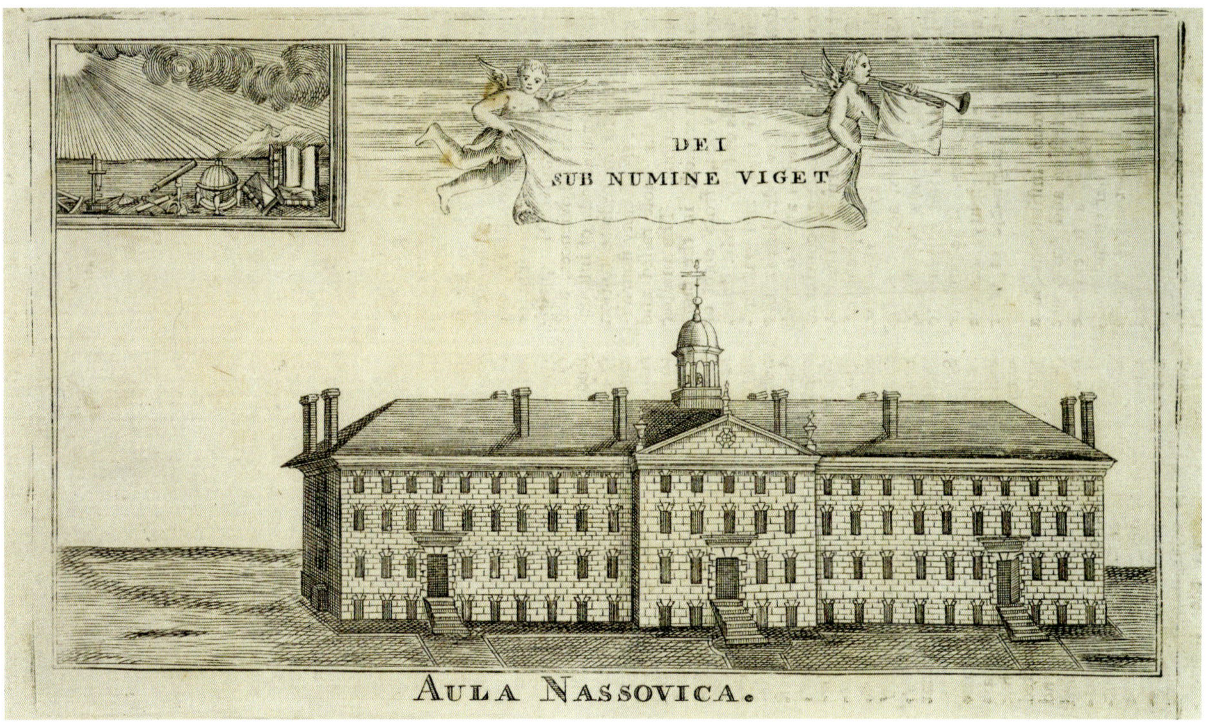

FIGURE 12 Rev. Jonathan Fisher (1768–1847; born New Braintree, MA; died Blue Hill, ME), after a ca. 1794 engraving by Henry Dawkins (active ca. 1753–86, New York, NY, and Philadelphia, PA), *Nassau Hall, a North West Prospect*, 1807. Oil on canvas, 66.6 × 150.8 cm. Princeton University. Presented by alumni headed by A. E. Vondermuhll, Class of 1901 (PP395)

FIGURE 13 *Aula Nassovica (Nassau Hall)*, engraving in *The New American Magazine*, March 1760. Copperplate engraving, 9.5 × 15.9 cm. Princeton University Library, Department of Special Collections. University Archives, Nassau Hall Iconography

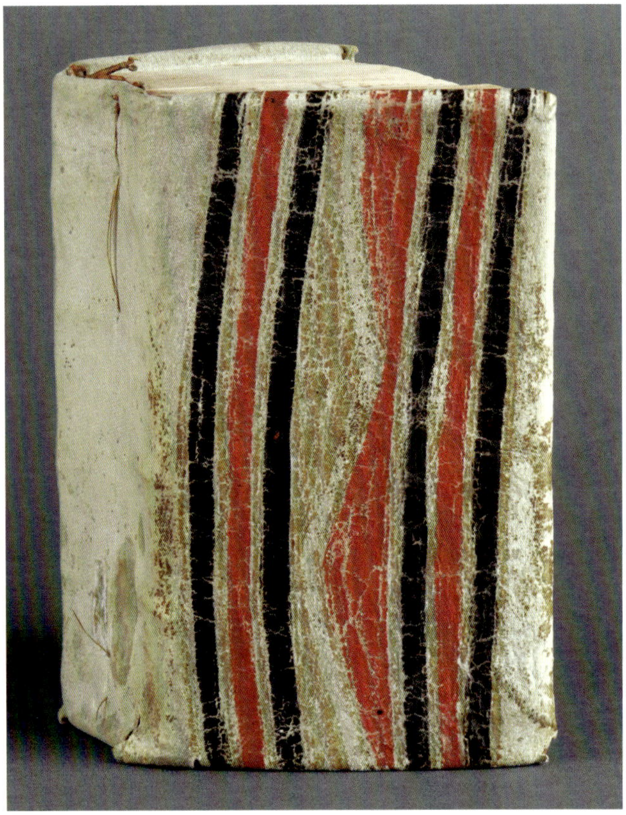

FIGURE 14 Lenape artist, Otterskin binding on a copy of Johann Buxtorf (1564–1629), *Lexicon hebraicum et Chaldaicum* (Basil: 1645). Princeton University Library, Department of Special Collections. Rare Books Division

an old Hebrew lexicon bound in otterskin by a Lenape artist, apparently made for Brainerd as a gift (fig. 14). The book, used in service of his efforts to bring Yankee Christianity to Lenape animism, is an extraordinary artifact of the physical juncture of those disparate worlds, and its parts materially bespeak their differences, the one produced in multiples an ocean away by technological means, the other unique and fashioned locally by hand. Each reflects the environmental sensibility that produced them—mass-produced and anthropocentric in the case of the Christian book, singular and organic in the case of its wrapping. These qualities are in turn indicative of broader cultural mindsets that, for most settler colonists, construed the human–nature relationship as a matter of short-lived exploitation rather than sustained equilibrium, with nature viewed more as an expedient for achieving human ends than something with intrinsic merit and standing. Together, the two pieces of Brainerd's book can be seen as embodying divergent philosophies of how to live in and with the world.[17]

"ALL OUR RELATIONS"

The Lakota phrase *Mitákuye Oyás'in* means "all our relations," or "we are all related," and expresses the belief that all things—those considered both animate and inanimate in Western ontological constructs—are connected in ways meriting consideration and respect. Lately voiced by diverse Native American peoples, the phrase speaks to widely held Indigenous principles regarding the fundamental relationality of life, a concept that supplies the basis of the modern Western discipline of ecology, which it anticipates by centuries.[18]

Because such thinking has clear environmentalist implications, Native peoples throughout the world have often—particularly in a time of environmental duress—been subjected to a simplifying, trans-Indigenous rhetoric insisting on their preservationist values and conservationist credentials. Universalizing constructs flatten the diversity, complexity, and evolution of tremendously varied cultural convictions and impute "enlightened," "modern" attitudes toward the environment (the West having previously disregarded them across millennia) that deny Indigenous peoples their own agency. The critique of the "ecological Indian" has afforded more nuanced understandings, including recognition of extended Indigenous intervention in environments, guided as much by a desire for biodiversity and maintenance of healthy subsistence resources as idealized systems of belief. And yet these systems of belief, which often eschew the distinction between spiritual and economic precepts characteristic of the West, are informed by profound comprehension of local ecologies, with the result that "environmentalist" principles are immanent throughout, and social practices have emerged around them that foster their sustenance.[19]

"Everything depends on everything else," states a traditional maxim of the Haida people, who for thousands of years have lived on Haida Gwaii, formerly known as the Queen Charlotte Islands, off the coast of what is now British Columbia. Like other First Nations peoples of the Northwest Coast—including the nearby Tlingit and Tsimshian—Haida lifeways have been

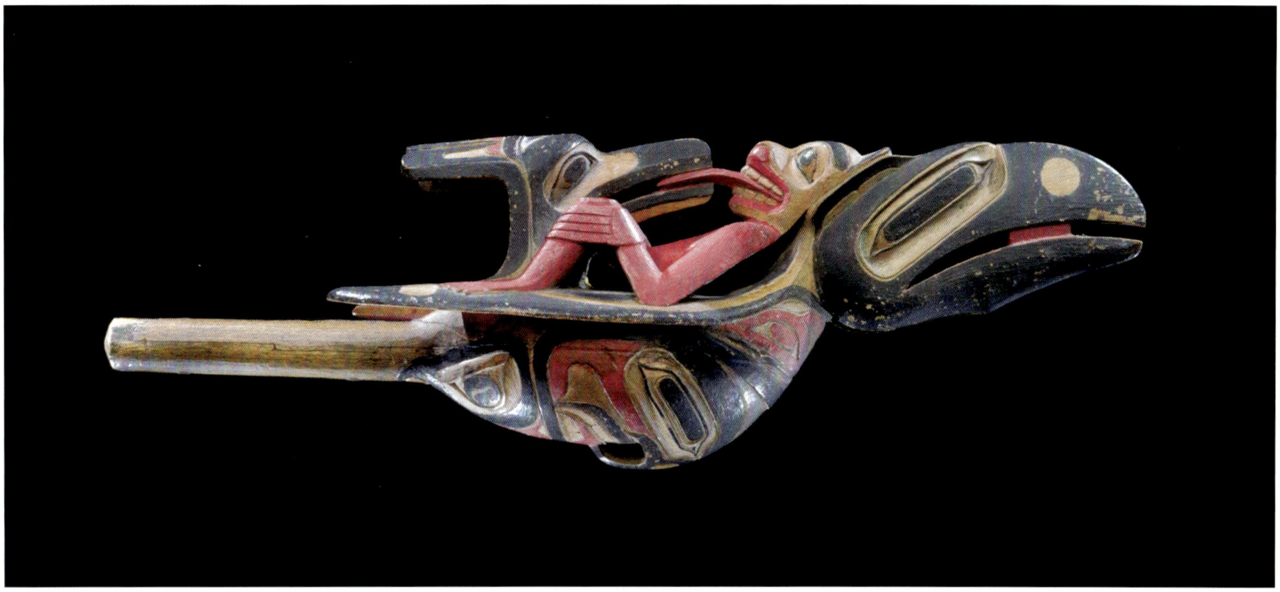

FIGURE 15 Tsimshian artist, Rattle, before 1878. Wood and paint, 9.8 × 31.5 × 9.7 cm. Canadian Museum of History, Gatineau, Canada (VII-C-2149)

informed by the surrounding temperate, littoral environs, which historically afforded not just plentiful resources but also supplied the basis of much of their cultural practice and sacred belief. Indeed, in contrast to the Judeo-Christian tradition of a world created first, and for, humans, Haida cosmogony envisions the genesis of the human species from the Raven, the trickster figure common throughout Northwest Coast peoples and the most powerful among Haida mythical beings, who draws forth the first people from out of a clamshell, to keep him company. Animals are understood to have existed before humans, and to possess unique and indispensable knowledge, though humans, considered comparatively poor communicators, know little about them. An essential means of accessing animal sapience is the shaman, who transgresses mortal bounds of time and place to mediate worlds of human and animal, life and death, and health and sickness to secure the physical and spiritual well-being of individuals and the larger community. Common among hunter-gatherer societies, shamanism is regarded as the world's oldest religion, its respect for animals considered an expression of their relative significance in preagricultural societies.[20]

Shamans commune with and even transform into other, often animal, beings, crossing realms of consciousness rather than interpreting divine edict or stricture in the way of priestly religions. Their knowledge and power devolve from intimate encounter and exchange with nonhuman life and forces. Shamanic worldviews are thus essentially interconnected, and the Haida's distinctive visual culture (the separate realm of "art" as such being foreign to Haida artisans prior to contact with the West) embodies this principle. The totem pole, perhaps the most familiar example of Northwest Coast visual culture, is accordingly as much about relations and transfers of power among the depicted animal and human forms as ancestry or lineal descent. Representations of shamans in Haida, Tlingit, and Tsimshian cultures often directly evince communication and power exchange between the two, as in a carved and painted Tsimshian rattle, likely intended for use by a chief, with a shaman lying on the back of a raven and linking tongues with a kingfisher to symbolize both connection and transfer (fig. 15).[21]

An even more integral connection is expressed using similar iconography in a figure by Haida carver Simeon Stilthda (*sdiihldaa* in Haida orthography) of a shaman in midtransformation, with wings protruding from the subject's back and a bird's head emerging from his chest (American Museum of Natural History, New York), part of a remarkable group of more than a dozen shaman figures produced by Stilthda about 1880. Five of these portray deceased shamans, laid out for ritual burial, two with their tools in their hands, including an especially expressive example whose unpainted condition amplifies the gauntness and emaciation—perhaps intended to signify a liminal state between life and death—evident in each of them (fig. 16). Stilthda, whose work has long been confused with other Haida carvers, was also likely a chief, not uncommon among shamans and indicative of their status within the social structure of Haida communities. Whereas most Haida were traditionally cremated after death, shamans were buried above ground in special mortuary structures elevated by poles and set apart from others.[22]

Such realistic portrayals of shamans are unusual among Northwest Coast peoples and suggest those by Stilthda resulted from a very different sort of connection and exchange—that between Native Americans and Western traders beginning in the eighteenth century, and becoming more prevalent with the arrival of missionaries after 1830. Indeed, Stilthda's depictions of deceased shamans, in particular, appear to be unique and are thought surely to have been produced for foreigners, for whom a shaman's actual paraphernalia would not be considered appropriate for trade. There is a certain irony in Princeton's example being in fact collected by a prominent Presbyterian missionary, Sheldon Jackson, whose very presence among the Haida and other Northwest Coast peoples constituted a serious challenge to both their way of life and their visual culture traditions. Jackson established over one hundred missions, churches, and schools among Indigenous North Americans, actively suppressing their languages, customs, and beliefs while acquiring a great trove of artifacts from them, in a characteristic instance of what is now called "salvage anthropology"—the collection of cultural objects from a place or people considered in danger of imminent collapse—even as in this case he acted as its agent. In a further irony, however, foreign interest in Haida and other visual cultures of the Northwest Coast produced a market for their commodified products that helped sustain ancient artistic heritages endangered by the population collapses wrought by imported disease, while stimulating new modes of artistic expression such as the Princeton shaman. Haida artists today manifest the vibrancy of an abiding visual culture at once informed by tradition and regenerated through innovation and social change.[23]

The shamanic attributes of transformation, interconnection, and mediation between worlds resonate as well in the formally distinct but similarly affecting work of contemporary arts collective Postcommodity, often with an added focus on geopolitics and political ecology. Self-described as "a shared Indigenous lens and voice to engage the assaultive manifestations of the global market and its supporting institutions," the group—currently comprising original members Cristóbal Martínez (Mestizo) and Kade L. Twist (Cherokee)—seeks to "forge new metaphors capable of rationalizing our shared experiences within this increasingly challenging contemporary environment; promote a constructive discourse that challenges the social, political and economic processes that are destabilizing communities and geographies; and connect Indigenous narratives of cultural self-determination with the broader public sphere."[24]

The 2009 site-specific installation *Do You Remember When? (Tempe)* in Arizona, reprised with modifications for "All Our Relations," the themed Biennale of Sydney of 2012, involved cutting away the gallery floor to reveal the earth underneath, in both cases originally tribal land, thereby creating "a spiritual, cultural and physical portal—a point of transformation between worlds—from which emerges an Indigenous worldview engaging a discourse on sustainability" (fig. 17). A microphone suspended over the opening and a concealed audio loop brought a sonic dimension to the work, at once capturing the ambient sounds of the gallery and, metaphorically, the earth below it, while broadcasting a recording produced by the artists of a Pee Posh social dance song that introduced the voice of the local Indigenous group into the space (in Sydney, an Aboriginal song was used). In this way, Postcommodity brought Native perspectives on environmental reciprocity powerfully to the fore and, in suggesting they emanated from the recovered earth, underscored both their essential legitimacy and their primacy in relation to later settler cultures.[25]

The transborder installation *Repellent Fence / Valla Repelente* has been of particular significance for Postcommodity since the formation of the collective in 2007—indeed, Twist attributes the group's inception to a shared desire to realize the project. Eventually

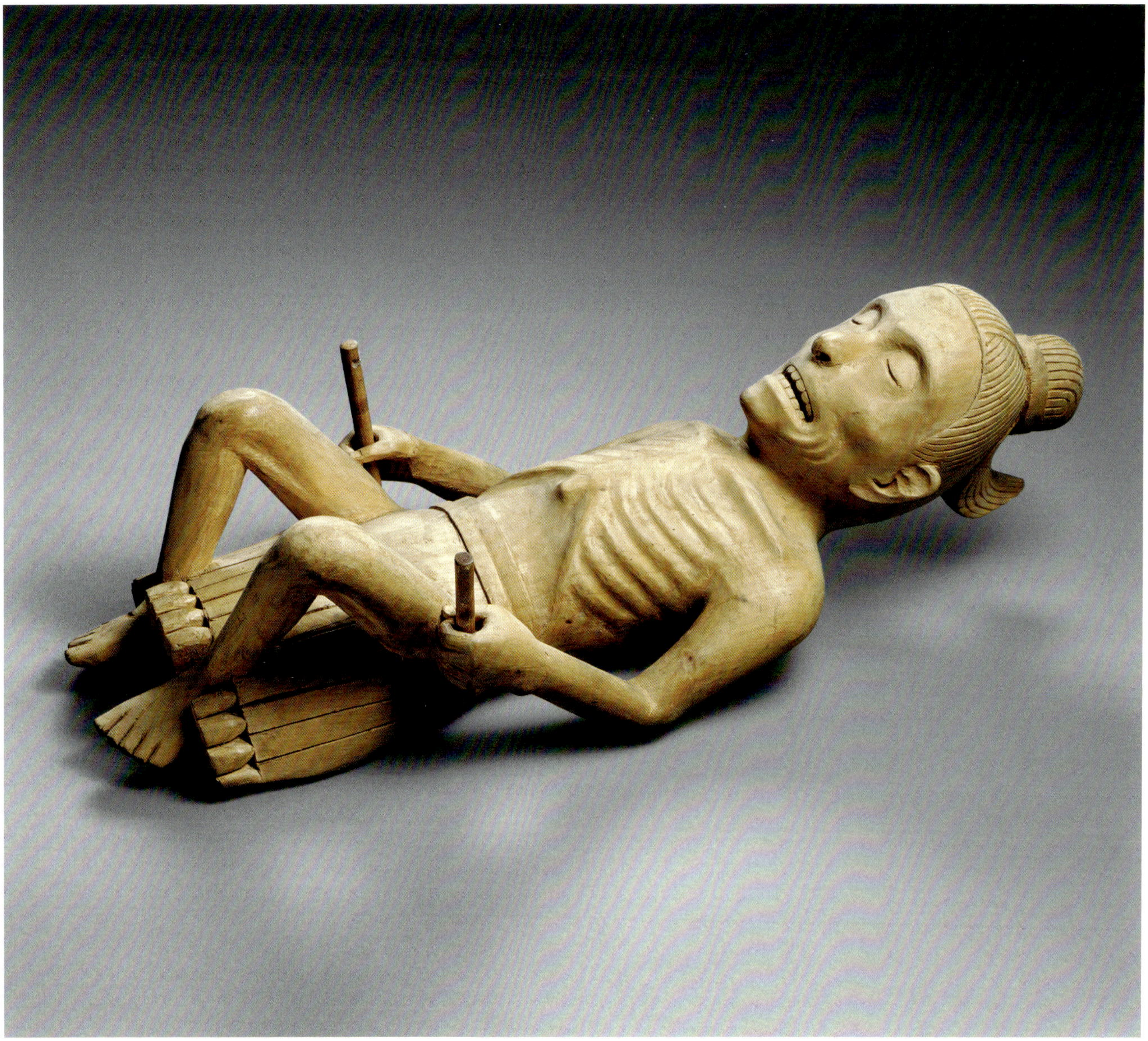

FIGURE 16 Simeon Stilthda (Haida, ca. 1799–1889; born Yan, Haida Gwaii, British Columbia, Canada; died Masset, British Columbia), Deceased shaman, ca. 1880. Alder wood with pigment, 17.1 × 58.4 × 21.6 cm. Princeton University. Department of Geosciences (PU 5160)

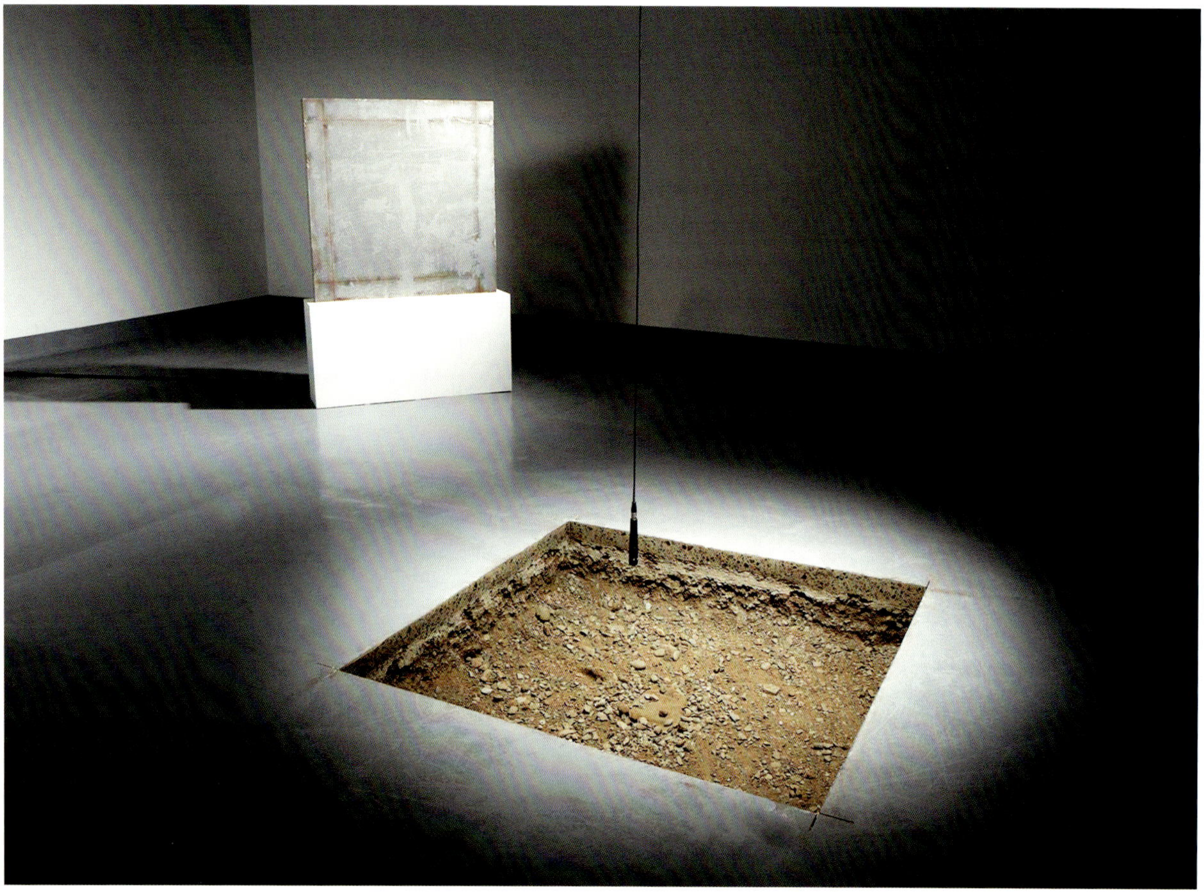

FIGURE 17 Postcommodity (active 2007–), *Do You Remember When? (Tempe)*, 2009. Site-specific intervention and mixed-media installation (cut concrete, exposed earth, light, sound). Courtesy of Postcommodity and Bockley Gallery, Minneapolis

completed in 2015, *Repellent Fence* was a radically collaborative effort involving a host of individuals, communities, organizations, officials, agencies, and ultimately two sovereign states in the establishment of a large-scale temporary monument near Douglas, Arizona, and Agua Prieta, Sonora (fig. 18). Consisting of twenty-six helium-filled balloons, each ten feet in diameter, tethered at regular intervals one hundred feet above the desert landscape along a two-mile vector bisecting the US–Mexico border, *Repellent Fence* both foregrounded the cultural and ecological artifice of geopolitics and figuratively resolved it, acting, in the group's description, as a "suture that stitches the peoples of the Americas together—symbolically demonstrating the interconnectedness of the Western Hemisphere by recognizing the land, Indigenous peoples, history, relationships, movement, and communication."[26]

The title *Repellent Fence* is multivalent, referring most overtly to the large ocular motif repeated four times on each of the balloons, a wry reference to "scare eye" bird repellents of similar design widely available commercially at smaller scale, but also an evocation of Native medicine colors (yellow, red, black, and white) and the oblong, concentric circles of Indigenous "open eye" iconography prevalent throughout the Western Hemisphere. In another sense, the surveillant eyes floating above the desert allude to the militarized border below, even as the evanescent and wholly permeable nature of Postcommodity's "fence"—itself oriented to bisect and thus transgress the border, rather than reinforce it by paralleling its course—questions and gently mocks the artifice of such arbitrary demarcations. In at once ironizing current geopolitical actualities and poetically affirming the possibilities of realizing our essential interconnectedness, *Repellent Fence* offered a timely

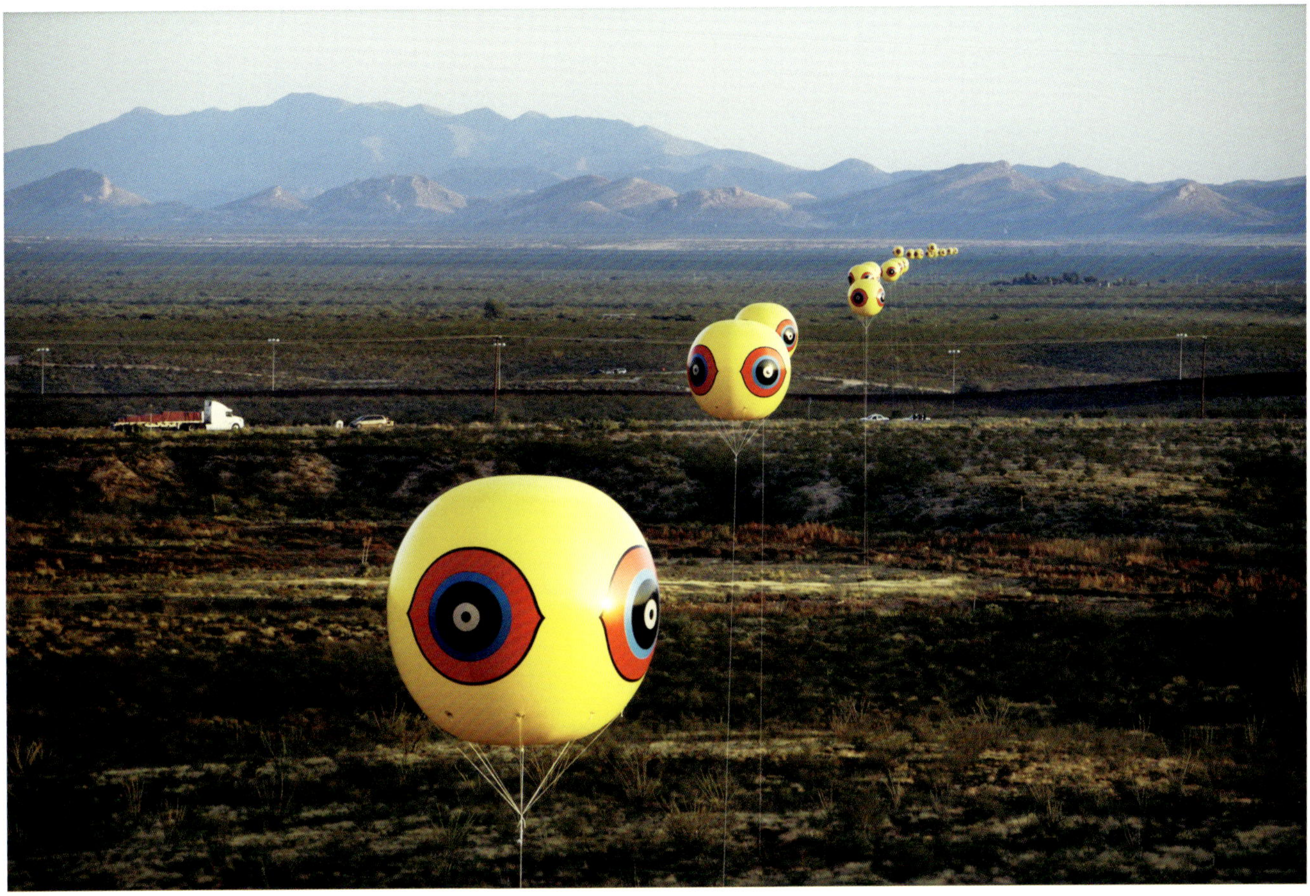

FIGURE 18 Postcommodity, *Untitled (Repellent Fence / Valla Repelente)*, 2015, printed 2019. Printed by Benjamin Brown at Color Space Art and Imaging, Minneapolis. Inkjet print, 121.9 × 182.9 cm. Princeton University Art Museum. Museum purchase, Fowler McCormick, Class of 1921, Fund (2019-149)

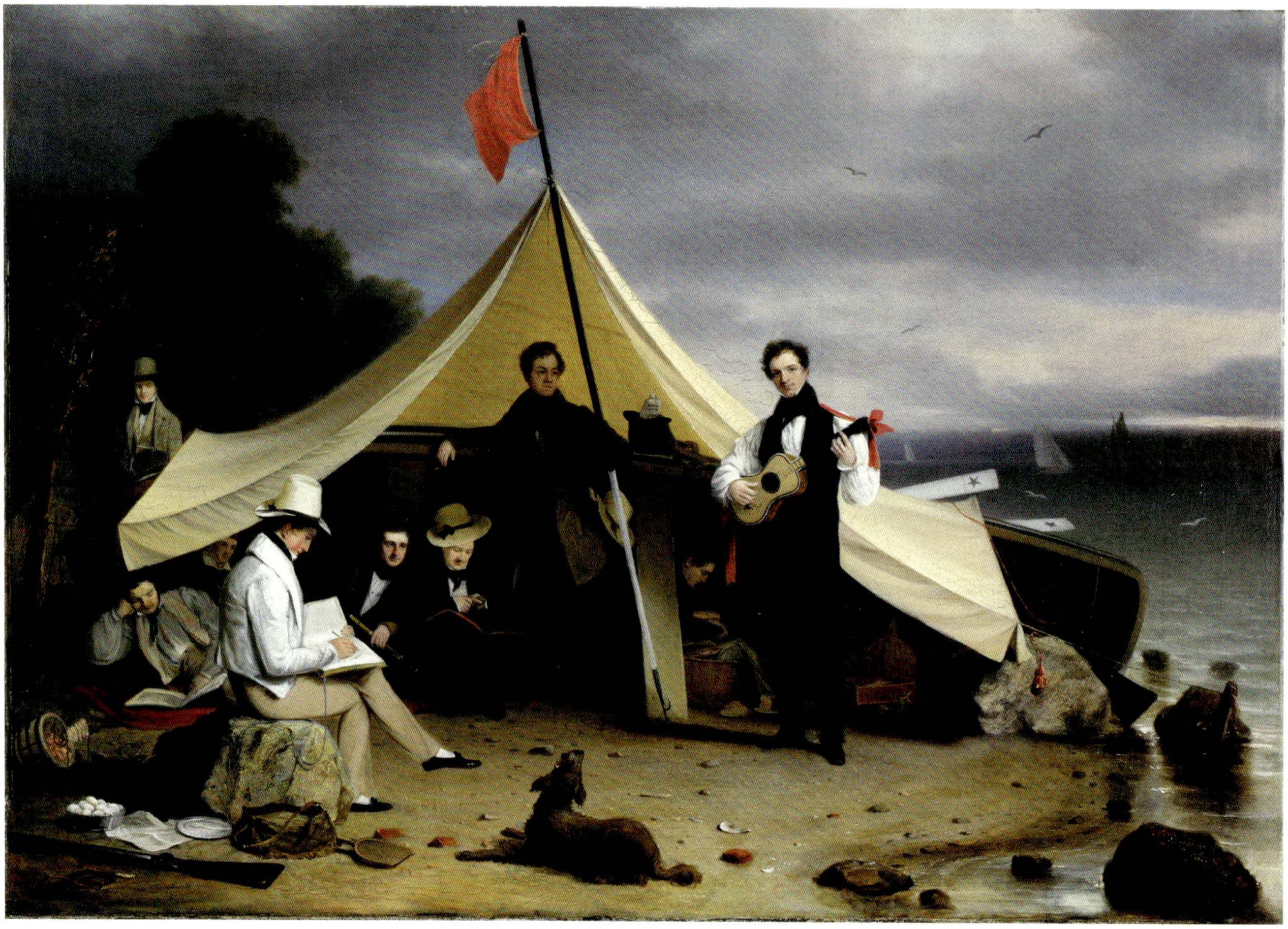

FIGURE 19 Robert Walter Weir (1803–1889; born and died New York, NY), *The Greenwich Boat Club*, 1833. Oil on canvas, 54 × 77.5 cm. Princeton University Art Museum. Museum purchase, Fowler McCormick, Class of 1921, Fund and Kathleen Compton Sherrerd Fund for Acquisitions in American Art (2009-1)

meditation on broad questions of politics, Indigeneity, migration, ecology, and the issue of justice as it relates to each.[27]

Repellent Fence shares with *Do You Remember When?* and much contemporary Indigenous site-specific art a wish to recall and reestablish prior realities and relationships among land, people, and other living things before the imposition of often abstract, and always anthropocentric, colonial constructs. Yet whereas *Do You Remember When?* was literally an excavation, oriented to the recuperation of the past, *Repellent Fence* seems more attuned to the future, gesturing both in its buoyant, ethereal aspect and its realization through community engagement toward the prospect of new political and environmental paradigms. Indeed, the relational aesthetics that characterize the work's creation supply an apt metaphor for the relational world it conjures. However, as suggested in *A Very Long Line*, a Postcommodity video completed shortly after *Repellent Fence* in which images of the actual, fortified border are endlessly screened in a reverse, and perverse, corollary to the earlier work, now it is fences of steel—not air—that mediate our world.[28]

ROMANCING CONTAGION

Just as environmental perceptions differ crucially among different people, so, too, do lived experiences of environmental conditions. In the early 1980s, the concept of environmental justice arose in the United States to confront the escalating inequity, amid globally accelerating industrialization, of the unjust distribution of environmental harms among the poor and disenfranchised. Although long recognized, and combatted sporadically since the civil rights era of the 1960s, environmental justice as a movement began in the poor and overwhelmingly Black county of Warren, North Carolina, a place designated in 1982 to accommodate a large hazardous-waste landfill for thousands of imported truckloads of toxic, PCB-laced soil. Residents protested, ultimately in vain, but recognition of the environment as another aspect of the struggle for justice within the broader campaign for civil rights endured, and has proliferated worldwide. The United States Environmental Protection Agency now codifies environmental justice as "the fair treatment and meaningful involvement of all people regardless of race, color, national origin, or income with respect to the development, implementation and enforcement of environmental laws, regulations and policies," and since 1994 has been empowered to enforce the concept via Executive Order No. 12898, "Federal Actions to Address Environmental Justice in Minority Populations and Low-Income Populations."[29]

Of course, environmental injustice has been ongoing for centuries, if not millennia. Yet its manifestations are varied and often veiled. Consider Robert Weir's appealing group portrait, *The Greenwich Boat Club* (fig. 19). The painting is on one level a celebration of bourgeois homosociality in ascendant Jacksonian America, reflecting in its portrayal of professional men apparently at leisure the transition from the Revolutionary patrician culture of noblesse oblige to an era of expanded suffrage (for Euro-Americans) and market economics, in which education and expertise abetted social advancement as much as birthright. Although not ostensibly "environmental," Weir's picture turns out to have everything to do with political ecology and the history of environmental justice—specifically an epidemic of cholera that plagued New York during the summer of 1832. Due to the unusually well-documented circumstances surrounding the painting's creation, we know the names of each of the depicted individuals (who include the artist himself, standing directly beneath the flagpole) and understand that, despite their carefree appearance, these nine white men have gathered together in an effort to "escape the pestilence," as Weir put it, by fleeing Manhattan—the Greenwich (Village) of the work's title—for the New Jersey shore. In this rustic refuge, they pass the time engaged in various intellectual pursuits and entertainments that reflect their respective proclivities and professions—artist, writer, physician, banker, musician. The figure shown seated on a rock is physician James Ellsworth De Kay, who had studied Asiatic cholera in Turkey and later in Quebec, where the North American outbreak began. At the time, the disease was thought to spread through a vaporous "miasma"; the painting's cloudy sky and murky background atmosphere, through which Manhattan is barely suggested, shrouded in haze, evoke such period medical theories. Only in 1854 did the London physician John Snow establish that cholera is a bacterial infection spread by water and food contaminated with human feces.[30]

Such conditions occurred most often in overcrowded urban environments with poor sanitation, like the notorious Five Points slum north of New York's City Hall, where living conditions were squalid. Charles Dickens visited the area in 1842 and observed "lanes and alleys, paved with mud knee-deep, underground chambers, . . . ruined houses, open to the street, whence, through wide gaps in the walls, other ruins loom upon the eye, . . . all that is loathsome, drooping, and decayed is here." Of the thirty-five hundred individuals who perished in the epidemic (from a New York population of about 240,000), a disproportionate number came from the city's fourteen thousand African Americans, many of them resident in Five Points. The slum was built over the old Collect Pond, once the city's reservoir, which had gradually filled with garbage. Yet the Manhattan Company (founded by Aaron Burr and eventually Chase Manhattan Bank, now JP Morgan Chase & Co.), which had been created to provide clean water for the city, dug the well serving the disadvantaged neighborhood directly over the polluted reservoir, supplying its residents with contaminated, deadly water. Still, many upper-class New Yorkers blamed the victims for contracting the disease. John Pintard, a civic leader but from an earlier, patrician generation, had little sympathy for the stricken. The epidemic, he wrote his daughter, "is almost exclusively confined to the lower classes of intemperate dissolute & filthy people huddled together like swine in their polluted habitations," among whom, he continued, "Those sickened must be cured or die off, & being chiefly of the very scum of the city, the quicker [their] dispatch the sooner the malady will cease." A portrait of Pintard by the fashionable artist duo Samuel Lovett Waldo and William Jewett completed the same year as the epidemic shows a dyspeptic individual, his hand on a Bible open to the ninetieth Psalm, which refers to the power of a wrathful God to "sweep men away in the sleep of death" (New-York Historical Society, New York).[31]

FIGURE 20 Asher B. Durand (1796–1886; born Jefferson, NJ; died Maplewood, NJ), *The Durand Children*, 1832. Oil on canvas, 92.7 × 73.7 cm. New-York Historical Society. Gift of the children of the artist, through John Durand (1903.2)

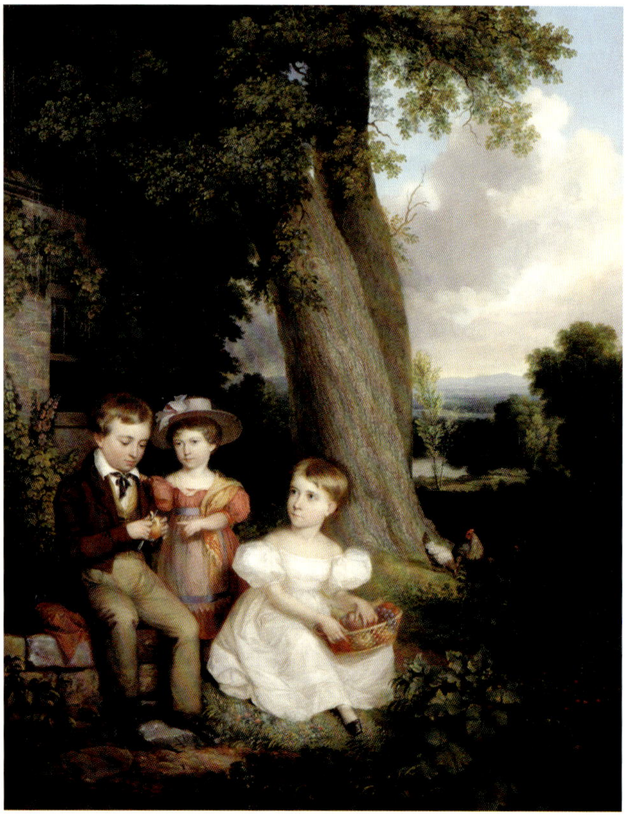

Confirming the dire circumstances, an assistant to the painter Asher B. Durand described the area near the center of the outbreak: "There is no business doing here if I except that done by Cholera, Doctors, Undertakers, Coffinmakers, &c. Our bustling city now wears a most gloomy & desolate aspect." Durand himself was apparently not in a position to make such an observation, having also escaped to New Jersey that summer, where he, too, painted a halcyon outdoor group, in this case showing his three well-dressed children eating from a basket of fruit in front of their country house (fig. 20). The two artists' untroubled representation of what was for many a horrific time contrasts greatly with contemporary images of victims, underscoring how environmental effects are unevenly distributed and experienced among different social groups (fig. 21). In the summer of 1832, it was only those of means—some seventy thousand people, or 30 percent of the city's residents—who were able to flee the contagion and wait it out in safer environs, like, opined the *New York Post*, "the inhabitants of Pompeii fled when the red lava showered down upon their houses."[32]

As a disease that originated in Asia and proceeded westward in waves during the nineteenth century, cholera acquired a reputation as an exotic invader, fostering xenophobia and challenging mythic beliefs about American exceptionalism, while exacerbating moral anxieties regarding cities and class differences. Elite Americans, who initially believed they were immune to what was thought a pestilence of the lower classes, soon learned otherwise, prompting excursions like the one depicted by Weir. Treating the occasion as a kind of bohemian getaway, his painting sidesteps unseemly truths about inequality and environmental justice. When he produced his upbeat visual recollection of the epidemic, thousands had already died, most of them poor.

Variola major, or smallpox, was another exotic invader, and for countless Native Americans, even deadlier. The so-called Columbian Exchange between the "New World" and the "old" following the voyage of Christopher Columbus to the Americas in 1492 included, in addition to flora, fauna, commodities, technology, human populations (both free and captive), and radically disparate worldviews, the transfer of multiple diseases as well. In this as in other instances, the colonists from beyond the Western Hemisphere caused far more damage to its original inhabitants than to themselves, introducing a host of maladies for which Indigenous peoples had no immunity. In the one hundred fifty years following Columbus's arrival, it is estimated that an astonishing 80–95 percent of Native American populations, North and South, were decimated from smallpox, cholera, measles, chicken pox, influenza, typhus, typhoid fever, bubonic plague, diphtheria, scarlet fever, whooping cough, and malaria, among other contagions.[33]

Compounding the devastation, colonists introduced biological warfare by intentionally infecting Indigenous peoples with disease, most notoriously by "gifting" smallpox-laden blankets to Native Americans. Canadian Plains Cree artist Ruth Cuthand's *Extirpate This Execrable Race* (2018) consists of stacks of gray felt blankets, beribboned as if gift wrapped, onto which are affixed enlarged microscopic views of the deadly pathogen made of colorful beads, which, though accurate in appearance, bely their deadly effect. The title of the series references Field Marshal Jeffery Amherst, 1st Baron Amherst, commander-in-chief of the forces in the British Army, who wrote in a letter to a subordinate at the frontier, "You will Do well to try to Inoculate the Indians by means of Blanketts, as well as to try Every other Method that can serve to Extirpate this Execrable Race."[34]

Cuthand elaborates her affiliation of disease and glass beads—trade items similarly imported by European settlers—in three sets of works also deploying dark humor through visually alluring portrayals of viruses and bacteria that disproportionately impact the disadvantaged, Indigenous and otherwise. In *Trading*, which inaugurated the series in 2008, she concentrates on diseases from the early colonial period; in *Reserving: Typhoid Fever*, she focuses on afflictions of the subsequent era during which Native Americans were relegated to reservations (fig. 22); and in the ongoing *Surviving*, recently updated to include COVID-19, she brings the series to the present by foregrounding the enduring nature of contagious disease's unequal impact on those with

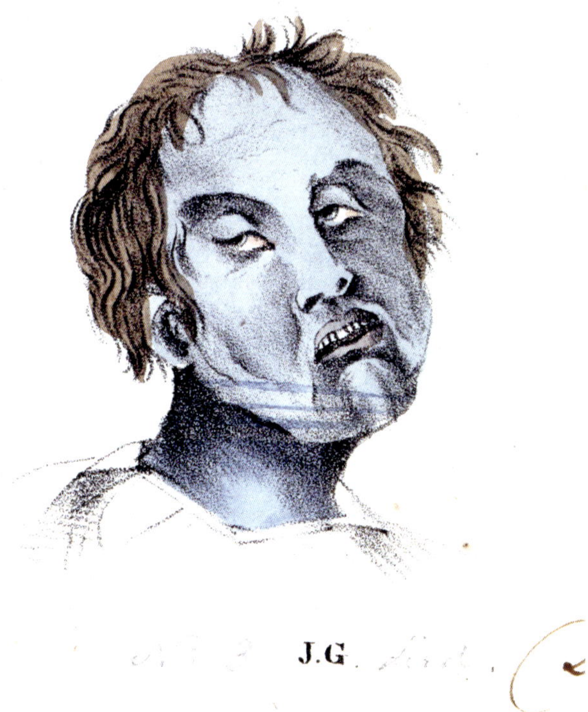

FIGURE 21 "No. 3 J. G. died," illustration in Horatio Bartley, *Illustrations of cholera asphyxia in its different stages: Selected from cases treated at the Cholera Hospital, Rivington Street* (New York: S. H. Jackson, 1832). Lithograph. New-York Historical Society (80488d)

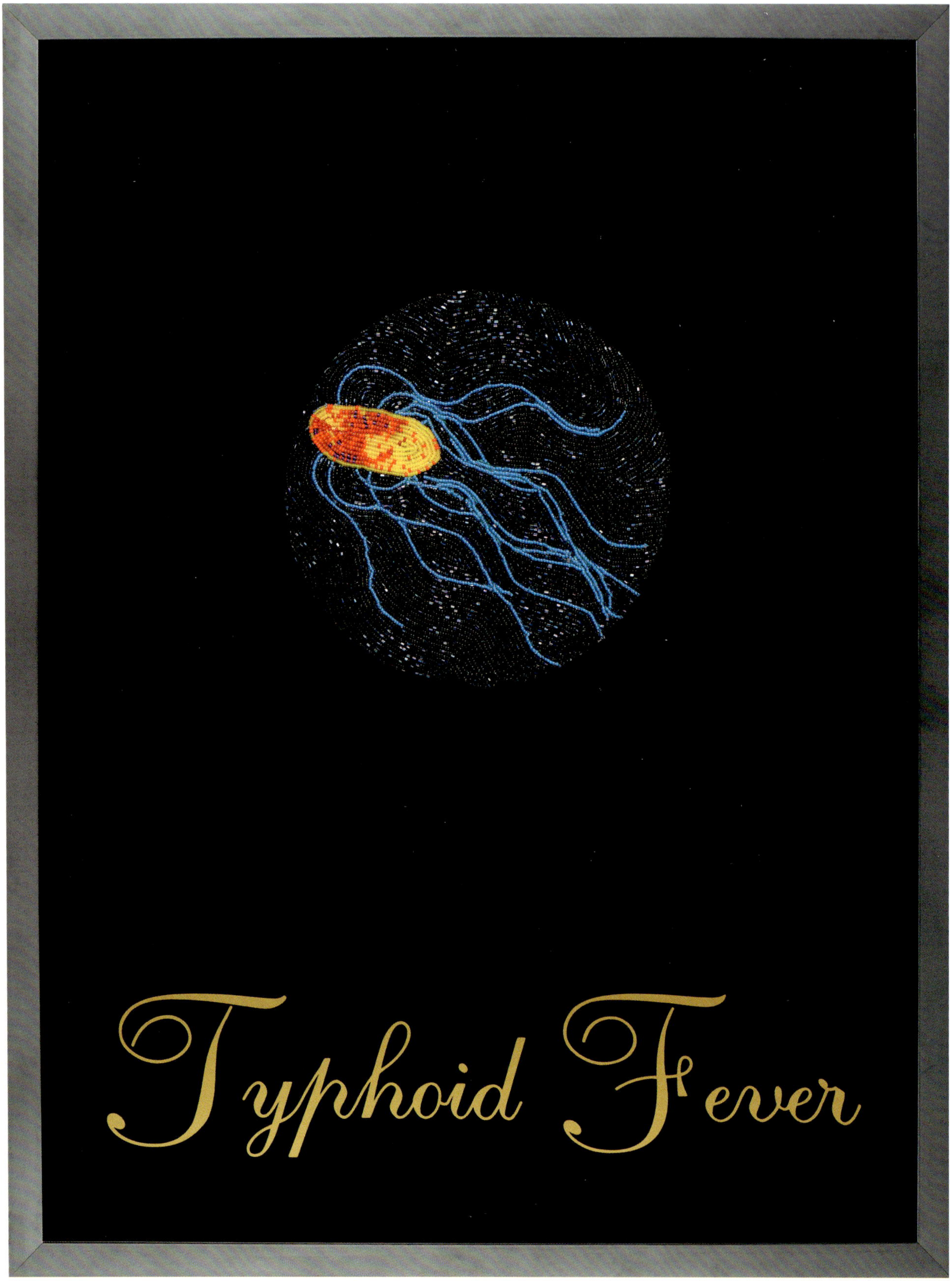
Typhoid Fever

diminished agency. Throughout, Cuthand employs "materials . . . that have long been denied status as serious art," she says, to explore her "fascination with the attractive and repellant subject; the simultaneously beautiful and abhorrent."[35]

THE STUFF OF ART

Ruth Cuthand's use of humble materials to underscore how environmental conditions are unevenly distributed and experienced invites consideration not just of the "attractive and repellent" subjects of her art but of the materials themselves—the nonhuman things, organic and living, inorganic and inert—from which it is made. As the Peruvian chest fashioned from Potosí silver suggests, the resources used to produce art have their own stories to tell. From their origins to the way they were extracted or processed, artistic materials—the stuff of art—raise questions about the environmental impacts, including the human costs, of their production and use, both in themselves and as they exemplify manufactured objects more generally, and as these things in turn relate to broader issues of sustainability, political ecology, and justice.[36]

A gleaming marble statue of a young male fairy, *The Culprit Fay*, epitomizes popular nineteenth-century sculpture created in a quasi-industrial process (fig. 23). Working under the artist's direction, anonymous Italian carvers used marble from local quarries to manufacture copies of this and many other subjects for a growing international market. Pointing machines enabled duplication by transferring the dimensions of plaster casts to marble, which was then finished by the artist or another craftsman. The resulting smooth surfaces of the statues concealed an environmentally and socially destructive infrastructure of mining and backbreaking labor, realities

FIGURE 22 Ruth Cuthand (Plains Cree, born 1954, Prince Albert, Canada; active Saskatchewan, Canada), *Reserving: Typhoid Fever*, 2018. Glass beads, thread, backing, 64.1 × 48.9 × 3 cm. Princeton University Art Museum. Museum purchase, Hugh Leander Adams, Mary Trumbull Adams, and Hugh Trumbull Adams Princeton Art Fund (2019-341)

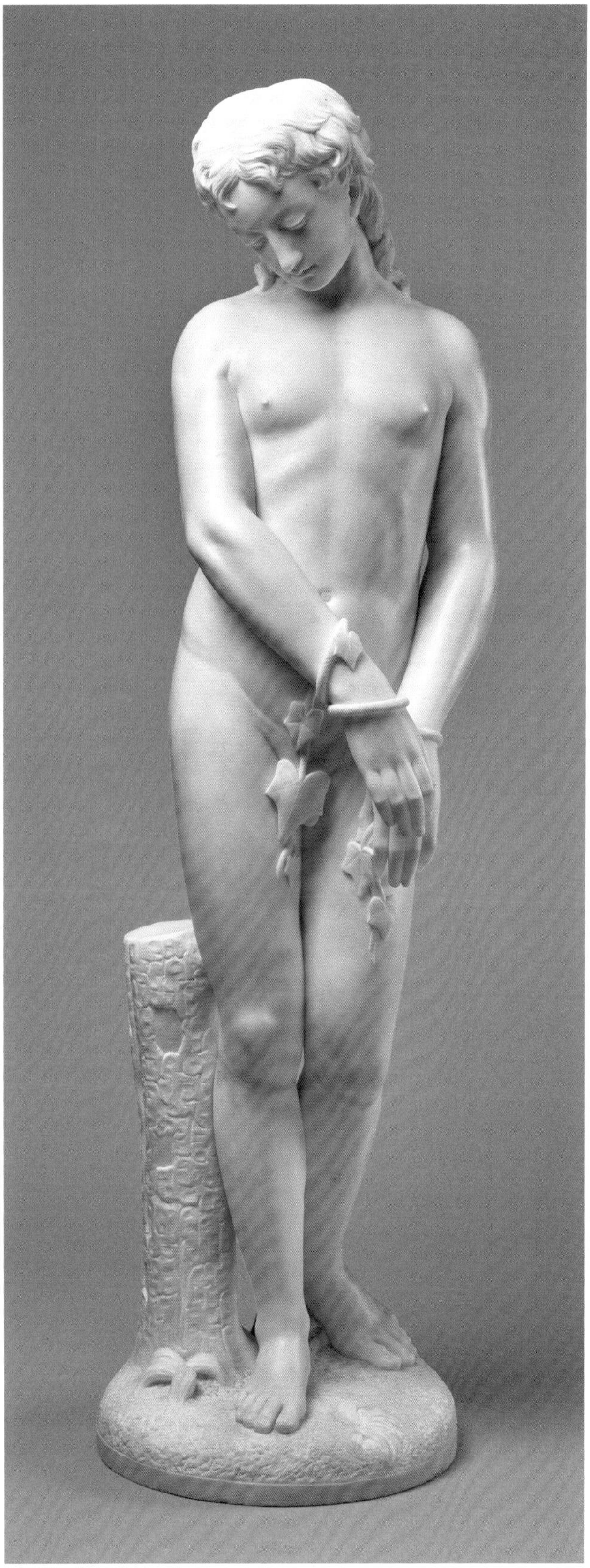

FIGURE 23 John Adams Jackson (1825–1879; born Bath, ME; died Pracchia, Italy), *The Culprit Fay*, ca. 1866. Marble, 95 × 27 × 31 cm. Princeton University Art Museum. Gift of Helen G. Norris (y1953-238)

in conflict with the often idealized and fanciful forms consummately rendered in immaculate stone.[37]

The Culprit Fay is based on a poem of the same name by Joseph Rodman Drake, a member of the Knickerbocker group, the loose affiliation of writers including Washington Irving, James Fenimore Cooper, and William Cullen Bryant active in the early nineteenth century, whose work often appeared in the eponymous literary magazine. "The Culprit Fay" was completed before *The Knickerbocker* published its first issue in 1833, but the lengthy romantic poem about a fairy who lives in the Hudson River Valley and falls in love with a mortal maiden—as punishment for which he must catch a drop of water from a sturgeon's leap and the last spark of a shooting star—accords well with the journal's penchant for imaginary writings extolling life in nature. Especially well known among these was the painter Thomas Cole's "Lament of the Forest," whose two hundred–plus lines appeared in the June 1841 issue. Both Drake's and Cole's poems conjure a beauteous and bountiful natural world, but a transient one, subdued in the end by the break of day in "The Culprit Fay" and by the felling of trees for development in Cole's elegy. In each, the preciousness and fragility of American nature are stressed, and the imperative to preserve it—implicit in "The Culprit Fay," explicit in "Lament of the Forest"—is in keeping with the tenor of the magazine and the sensibilities of its contributors.[38]

It is thus ironic that the marble sculpture created in homage to Drake's work was produced neither in America nor with particular regard for nature or those working in it to extract the prized material. Expatriate artist John Adams Jackson, originally from Maine, sculpted—or rather had sculpted after his designs—numerous copies of *The Culprit Fay* while residing in Florence, where he lived for much of his life. The marble for them surely came from Carrara, on the Tuscan coast some sixty miles away. Carrara marble has been esteemed for its color, luminosity, and soft density since at least the second century BCE, when Romans established quarries in the Apuan Alps above the town. In 1751, Maria Teresa d'Este, a princess of Modena, granted several local families the right to own quarries and mine marble untaxed, reasoning that her ownership of the toll road to the nearby port would produce revenue as trade in the valued material increased. International demand catalyzed modernization and enabled intense growth in production during the mid-nineteenth century, but the working conditions of laborers remained grueling, and the area's environmental devastation continued apace. By the 1880s, not long after Jackson produced his last copy of *The Culprit Fay*, the first Italian anarchist group was formed in Carrara, where, according to a contemporary *New York Times* article, "The workers in the marble quarries are the most abandoned laborers in Italy." In 1894, striking quarriers rose up in the Lunigiana revolt, which culminated with government troops firing into a crowd of protesters outside the town barracks, killing eleven of them—all of which seems far removed from the untroubled fairytale world contrived in Jackson's sculpture. Even today Carrara remains one of Italy's poorest cities.[39]

With advancing industrialization in the twentieth century, artistic materials were increasingly manufactured, as opposed to extracted in the manner of Carrara marble. Like many artists, the painter Marsden Hartley adopted modern industrial materials for his art. Hartley was, like Jackson, from Maine, and similarly lived and worked extensively in Europe. But in 1937, he returned home and announced his intention to become "the painter of Maine." It was a strategic as much as a sentimental move. Despite his great talent, Hartley struggled financially, and identifying himself with the Pine Tree State afforded the prospect of capitalizing on its growing repute as an aesthetic, natural, and tourist attraction. By focusing on portraying Maine's scenic glories, and stressing that "there is no one else so qualified" for the task, Hartley hoped to achieve the public renown and economic security that had long eluded him. Central to his efforts was austere Mount Katahdin (from the Penobscot for "Great Mountain"), Maine's loftiest peak and an icon of regional lore and pride. Katahdin offered an image, "as in a museum, of the most characteristic feature of the Maine woods," according to native enthusiast and promoter Myron Avery, whose *In the Maine Woods* appeared in 1939. Baxter State Park had recently been created encompassing Katahdin, a gift of Percival P. Baxter, after whom the mountain's tallest individual peak was also named. Hartley determined, "I must get that Mt. for future reason of fame and success,"

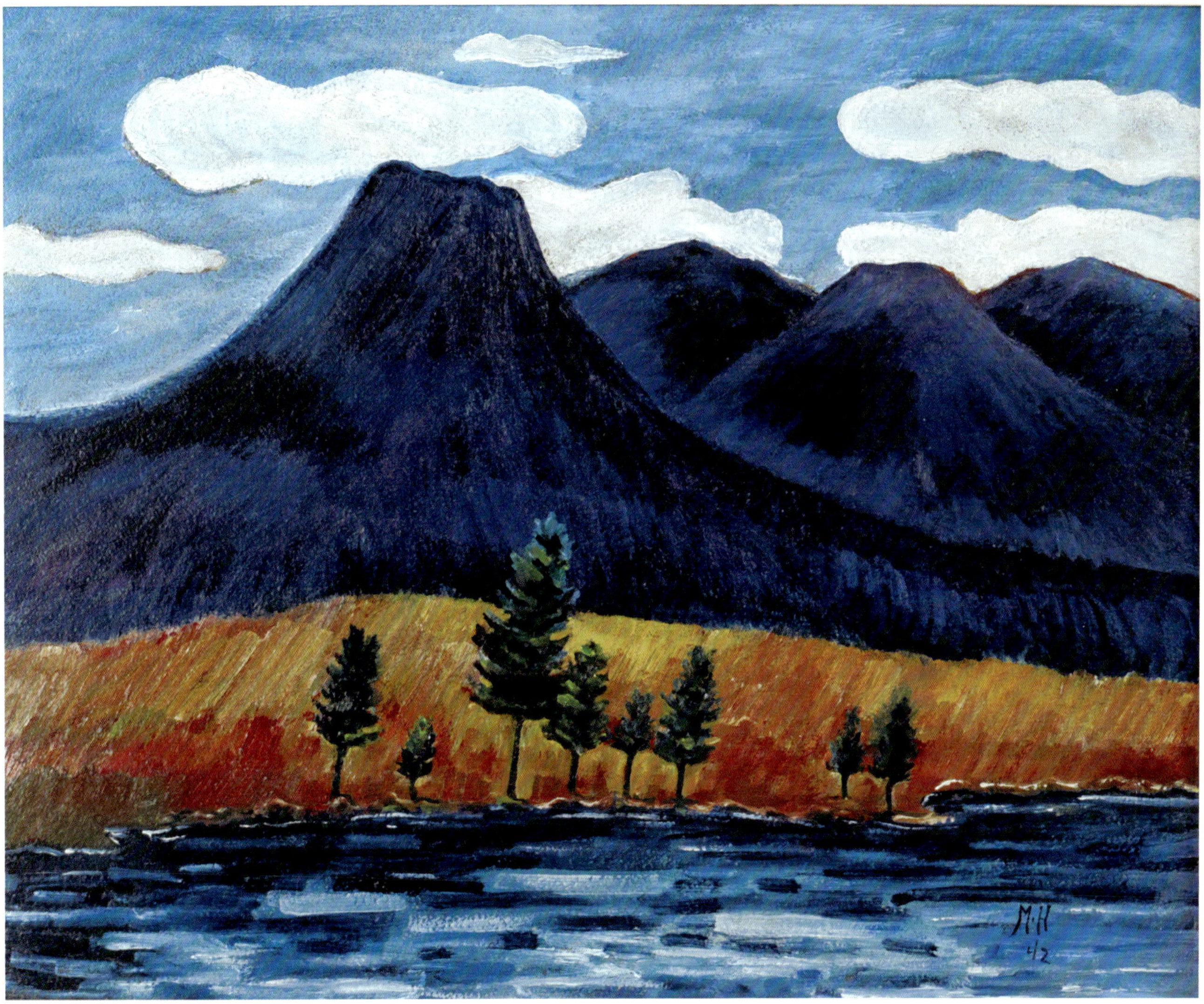

FIGURE 24 Marsden Hartley (1877–1943; born Lewiston, ME; died Ellsworth, ME), *Blue Landscape*, 1942. Oil on fiberboard, 40.6 × 50.8 cm. Princeton University Art Museum. Museum purchase, Fowler McCormick, Class of 1921, Fund and Kathleen Compton Sherrerd Fund for Acquisitions in American Art (2015-6679)

and in the fall of that same year undertook the arduous trek to its base, spending eight days in a hunter's cabin at Cobb's Camp on the south shore of Katahdin Lake and making sketches for what was to become a series of nearly twenty paintings, among them some of the most accomplished works of his career. Collectively, they present a portrait of Katahdin as rugged, raw, and pure—very much in keeping with the more general image of Maine and his art that Hartley sought to project.[40]

Blue Landscape is among the last of the artist's Katahdin pictures (fig. 24). Completed in 1942, by which time Hartley had suppressed Baxter Peak's descriptive ridges, shadows, and other details in favor of elemental forms of pronounced power and effect, the painting was, like approximately half the others in the series, executed not on canvas but on fiberboard of a type used primarily for industrial purposes. The development of this material dates back to 1858, when the first patent was granted for a construction board composed of aggregated wood fiber, but it was not until 1925 that William Mason perfected the process, lending his name to the now-genericized material Masonite. Created through a mechanical process involving wood products and binders, steam, and compression, such products have been

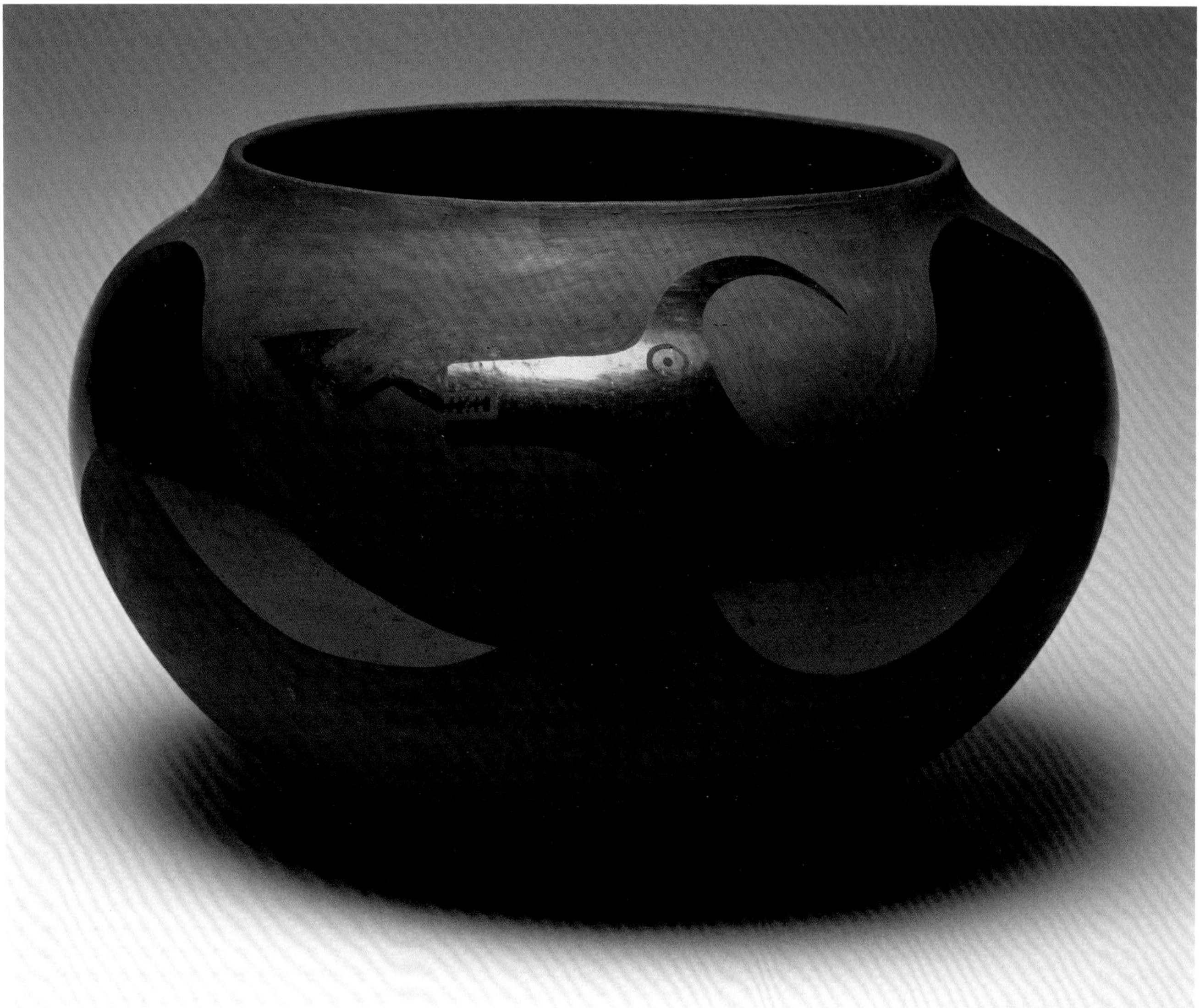

FIGURE 25 Made by Maria Martinez (San Ildefonso Pueblo, 1887–1980; born and died San Ildefonso Pueblo, NM), painted by Julian Martinez (San Ildefonso Pueblo, 1885–1943; born and died San Ildefonso Pueblo, NM), Jar decorated with Avanyu (water serpent), 1919–20. Blackware ceramic, 23 × 33 cm. Princeton University Art Museum. Museum purchase (y1940-431)

promoted as sustainable for utilizing otherwise non-viable wood components, but in fact their production in large "digesters" from a toxic slurry of resin binders like formaldehyde is anything but environmental. Two years before Hartley embarked on his journey into the wilderness to capture views of unspoiled Katahdin, a report on "The Fiber Board Industry" described the various techniques then in use to produce them, which utilized chemicals including "caustic soda" (lye), sulfuric acid, and mercury chloride.[41]

In rendering Katahdin's pristine environs on the modern industrial board, Hartley used a variety of pigments, each with its own environmental profile. The one that would seem least likely to contain harmful additives—pure white, as utilized extensively in the clouds floating above the mountain—in fact incorporates substantial amounts of toxic lead. X-ray fluorescence conducted on the painting confirms Hartley's use of poisonous lead white paint, in spite of the ready availability of the benign alternative zinc white. By the early twentieth century, lead white's harmful effects had caused its manufacture and sale as an artist's pigment to be restricted. Although awareness of the paint's noxious properties—particularly for those involved in its manufacture—dates back to the seventeenth century, its durability, tonal quality, and fast-drying properties outweighed its environmental disadvantages for many artists, including Hartley.[42]

Another orientation to the production of art is evinced by the work of Maria Martinez and Julian Martinez, Tewa potters who in 1919 discovered their signature technique for black-on-black ceramics—reduction-fired objects whose ornamentation relies exclusively on the subtle distinction between areas of polished and matte finish in an otherwise tonally uniform design. Blackware, or black pottery, had for centuries been produced by Pueblo artists, but the Martinezes' innovation—initially, as on Princeton's example, with matte areas predominating, but increasingly featuring polished surfaces—allowed for the development of a new aesthetic vocabulary of abstract and representational decoration. By burnishing the initial slipped form with a polished stone, an overall glossy effect is produced, to which a second slip, applied with a yucca fiber brush, is then added around the desired design, leaving the polished area in reserve. Toward the end of the firing process, the fire is smothered with powdered manure, whose high carbon content turns the pottery black. In this tinaja, or jar (fig. 25), the curved motif of the awanyu, a horned serpent and the Tewa guardian of water, encircles the form, suggesting both flowing water and the lightning that can accompany rain.[43]

Maria Martinez, who made the pots to which her husband, Julian, subsequently added the second slip, sourced the clay herself, rather than acquire the raw material from a supplier in a market exchange. Yet in doing so, she first requested permission to take it, indicating that for her the transaction was with the earth itself. A 1972 documentary on Martinez produced by the National Park Service opens with her gathering clay near her home in San Ildefonso Pueblo, on the Rio Grande in New Mexico. Then in her eighties, she describes her lifelong process: "We do not go and just get the clay; we have to ask the Great Spirit. All the old folks, they do. All the Indians, they do." Her son, Popovi Da (1923–1971 [Maria's Tewa name was Poveka, Julian's was Pocano]), a potter also featured in the film, continues, "We believe in working in harmony with nature. We do not allow ourselves more material than . . . becomes necessary to serve our purpose." Later, Maria adds, "We have to be very careful for the clay. We have to take care of it, because we know how we got it, and we asked them to give [it to] us."[44]

INTIMATIONS OF ECOLOGY

In 1802, English Romantic poet William Wordsworth wrote the first four stanzas of what was to become one of his greatest works, eventually completed in 1804 and initially published simply as "Ode." When the poem reappeared in Wordsworth's 1815 collection *Poems in Two Volumes*, the title had expanded to the one familiar today, "Ode: Intimations of Immortality from Recollections of Early Childhood," whose now eleven stanzas concern the central problem of the narrator's (Wordsworth's) inability to still perceive nature's beauty. The beginning stanza lyrically sets the tone:

> *There was a time when meadow, grove, and stream,*
> *The earth, and every common sight,*
> *To me did seem*
> *Apparell'd in celestial light,*
> *The glory and the freshness of a dream.*
> *It is not now as it hath been of yore;—*
> *Turn wheresoe'er I may,*
> *By night or day,*
> *The things which I have seen I now can see no more.*

Stanza two reinforces the sense of loss, concluding,

> *The sunshine is a glorious birth;*
> *But yet I know, where'er I go,*
> *That there hath past away a glory from the earth.*[45]

Wordsworth's poem has usually been straightforwardly interpreted as the expression of the poet's difficulty—and that of adults, generally—in maintaining, or retrieving, the closeness to nature attributed to youth in the Romantic era. Yet an important part of Wordsworth's larger project was a similarly Romantic critique of industrialization, stemming from his belief in an idealized rural past and its affiliated social and moral relations, in contrast to the bleaker conditions of life in the modern era. Wordsworth matured as the Industrial

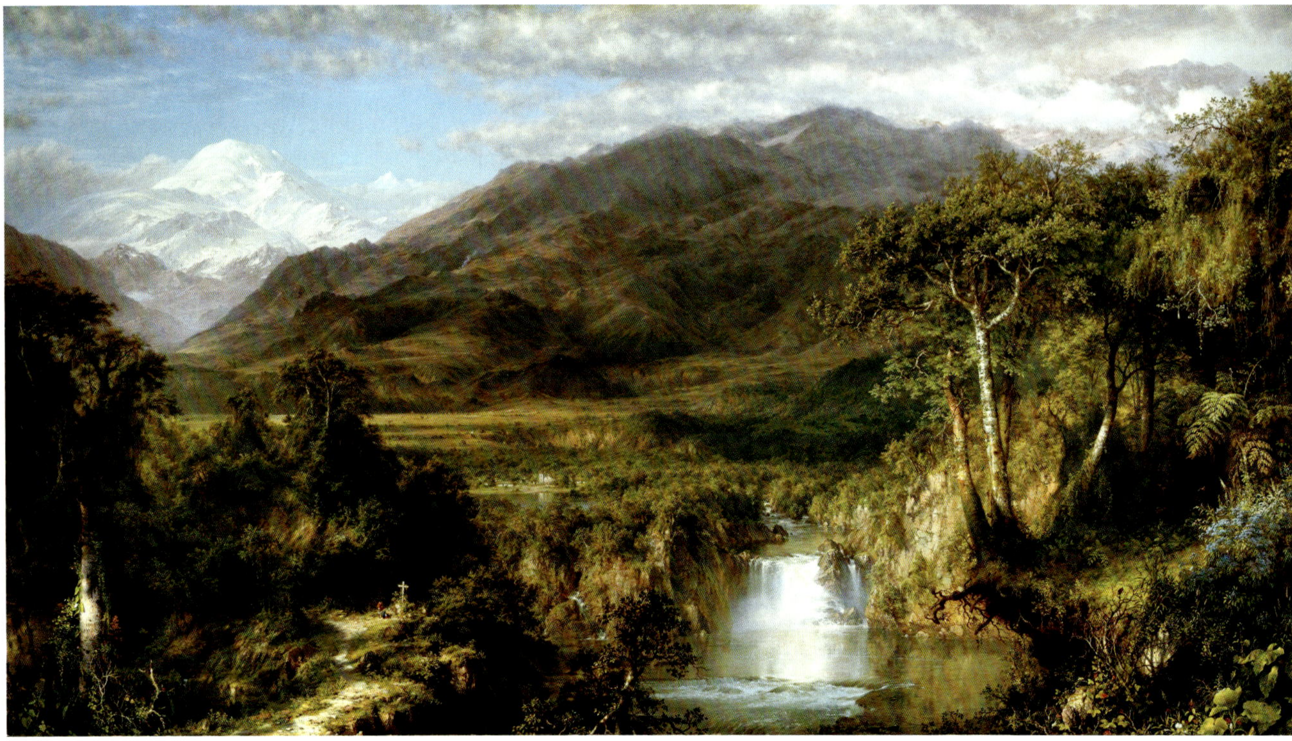

FIGURE 26 Frederic Edwin Church (1826–1900; born Hartford, CT; died New York, NY), *Heart of the Andes*, 1859. Oil on canvas, 168 × 302.9 cm. The Metropolitan Museum of Art, New York. Bequest of Margaret E. Dows, 1909 (09.95)

Revolution in England itself reached maturity, and although he wrote "Intimations of Immortality" in bucolic Grasmere, a village in the midst of England's Lake District, he was little more than sixty miles north of the rapidly industrializing region where Thomas Cole was born the year before he began "Ode," in an area today described as the "Liverpool-Manchester megalopolis." We now understand Cole's sensibilities to have been affected by his early exposure to unchecked industrialization, and considering Wordsworth's own ideas about modernity, it becomes difficult not to see in "Intimations" a broader criticism as well—a lamentation about not only the estrangement of individuals from nature with the advance of age, but also of humans more generally with advancing development.[46]

Cole moved to the United States in 1818, and famously helped develop the Hudson River School, whose subsequent members increasingly depicted the natural world in a way that similarly—and unexpectedly—expressed the human estrangement from nature that Wordsworth elegized, even as they extolled its splendors. Cole had only a few pupils, but one of them, Frederic Church, succeeded him as the Hudson River School's leading artist. Church traveled twice to South America, in 1853 and 1857, and followed up his second trip in particular with a series of grand, operatic canvases, culminating with the massive *Heart of the Andes* (fig. 26). These works, like the similarly outsize productions of his rival, Albert Bierstadt (1830–1902), attempted to capture an entire cosmos—to use the favored term of Prussian polymath Alexander von Humboldt, who greatly influenced Church—representing great swaths of spectacular nature from a disembodied, God's-eye perspective, and evincing a sublime remove that overwhelms as much as it appeals, acquaints, or informs. Seeking to be all-encompassing, these sweeping compositions, rendered in excessive detail, had the counterintuitive effect of distancing viewers from the very familiarity with nature they sought to encourage. Politics instead intruded—imperialism with Church,

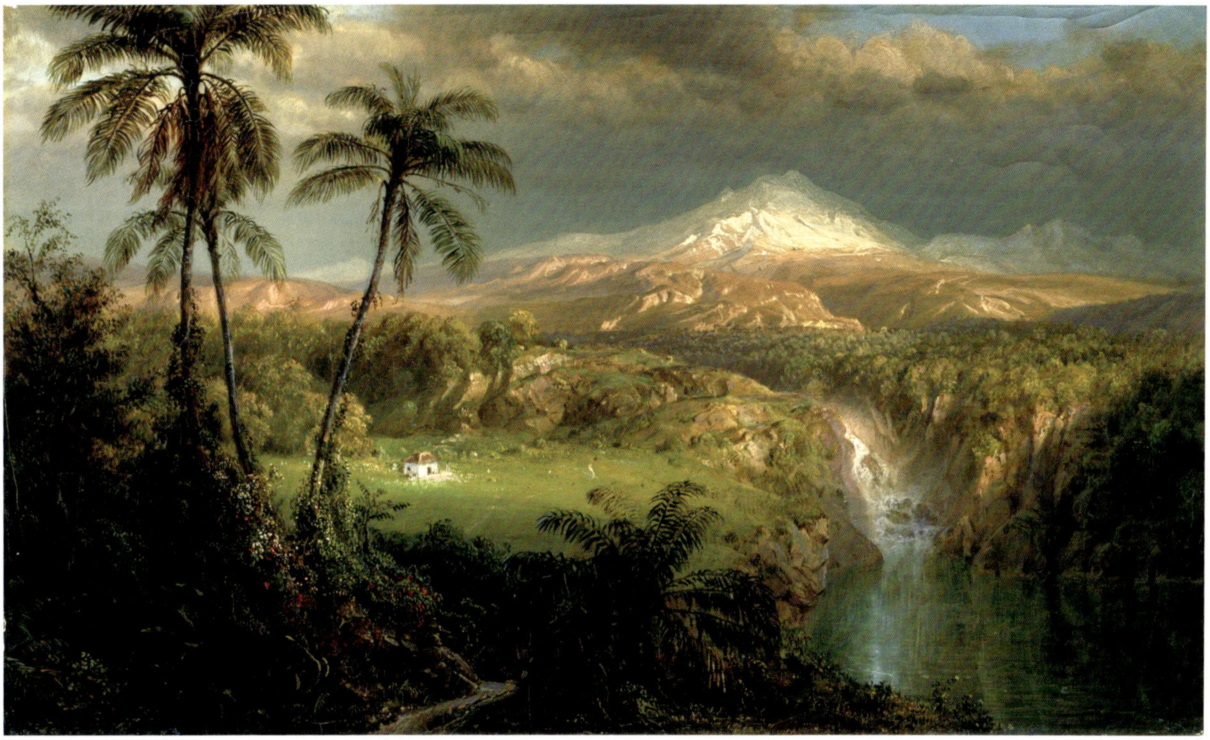

FIGURE 27 Frederic Edwin Church, *Passing Shower in the Tropics*, 1872. Oil on canvas, 31 × 51 cm. Princeton University Art Museum. Museum purchase (y1945-212)

Manifest Destiny with Bierstadt—on the appreciation of nature for its own sake. In thus attempting to bring the natural world under visual and conceptual control, they paradoxically shut it out.[47]

Later, Church produced a number of more modest paintings of Andean subjects that, though diminished in scale, utilized the same expansive pictorial rhetoric. One of them, *Passing Shower in the Tropics* (fig. 27), is a pastiche of previous works—its central peak clearly based on *Cayambe* of 1858 (New-York Historical Society, New York), its middle-ground cataract evoking *Heart of the Andes*. However, by representing in this and other compositions not one particular place but rather a generalized idea of nature, Church belied his professed reverence for its actual, intricately related parts. Moreover, in consistently constructing the natural world as spectacular "other," these artists ultimately separated it from the human realm and reified the notion, entrenched since antiquity, that humans and nature are not part of the same larger whole. Finally, by concentrating on just the extraordinary in nature, they helped rationalize disregard for the rest.[48]

Meanwhile, as if in response, a quieter aesthetic developed among the so-called Luminists, a latter-day neologism introduced to describe pictures displaying an intense preoccupation with light and atmosphere, prevalent in the work of several American artists between 1850 and 1875. Luminism's practitioners evinced an acute awareness of the natural world, captured in works rendered with great subtlety and characteristically evoking a magical stillness. In contrast to the dramatic creations of the Hudson River School, the sparely composed, sparsely peopled, meditative canvases of the Luminists offer quotidian nature, presented not hierarchically, with a particular concentration or focal point, but democratically, with lateral compositions in which interest is apportioned evenly across the picture plane. As a result, attention is devoted less to looking at a discrete, privileged subject—a spectacular peak or rushing cataract—than to observing relations among multiple areas or subjects, a kind of overall orientation that, in both its ecumenism and interconnectedness, seems essentially ecological (fig. 28). Insisting on the equivalent importance of all things observed, Luminist canvases are also implicitly less anthropocentric, instantiating transcendentalist Ralph Waldo Emerson's now famous metaphor for loss of the (human) self in the unity of nature: "Standing on the bare ground,—my head bathed by the blithe air, and uplifted into infinite space,—all mean egotism vanishes. I become a transparent eye-ball; I am nothing; I see all; the currents of the Universal Being circulate through me; I am part or particle of God."[49]

The eldest of Luminism's core practitioners, Fitz Henry Lane was loosely aligned with the philosophical precepts of transcendentalism through his membership in the Unitarian Church, where it originated, and via his affiliation with the Lyceum in his native Gloucester, Massachusetts, where Emerson often lectured. Lane began his painting career producing ship portraits—formulaic images made on commission to record a vessel's appearance—for Gloucester's thriving merchant marine, before expanding his register to include more ambitious harbor and other littoral views. *Ship in Fog, Gloucester Harbor* (fig. 29), completed near the end of Lane's life, is unusual among his crisp and clear-sighted images for its portrayal of their apparent opposite, a world shrouded in fog. The absorbing scene incorporates a variety of seagoing craft, accurately rendered with the detail for which Lane was renowned—contemporary art critic Clarence Cook wrote the artist knew "the name and place of every rope on a vessel." *Ship in Fog* is dominated by a schooner- or hermaphrodite-brig, a common "coaster" plying the ports of New England. At left, a gaff-rigged sloop is positioned before, it appears, two additional, smaller vessels, largely occluded by the fog—the hull of one, three masts, and their sails barely visible. Finally, just above the figures in the foreground rowboat, the rising sails of a topsail schooner leaving the inner harbor and headed to sea are barely suggested in the background, silhouetted beyond the low-lying rise of land, whose indistinct lighthouse identifies it as Ten Pound Island. What Lane's composition thus records is a modest, mundane tableau—a variety of ordinary craft in a significant but now quiet port at the end of a summer day. Its true subject is the fog, the most difficult of atmospheric effects to render, in which light, water, atmosphere, and the interrelation among them assume a poignant primacy. Touching and inflecting everything, the fog exists only as the result of the forces—the exchange of temperature and humidity, the movement

FIGURE 28 Martin Johnson Heade (1819–1904; born Lumberville, PA; died St. Augustine, FL), *Newburyport Meadows*, ca. 1876–81. Oil on canvas, 26.7 × 55.9 cm. The Metropolitan Museum of Art, New York. Purchase, Mrs. Samuel P. Reed Gift, Morris K. Jesup Fund, Maria DeWitt Jesup Fund, John Osgood and Elizabeth Amis Cameron Blanchard Memorial Fund, and Gifts of Robert E. Tod and William Gedney Bunce, by exchange, 1985 (1985.117)

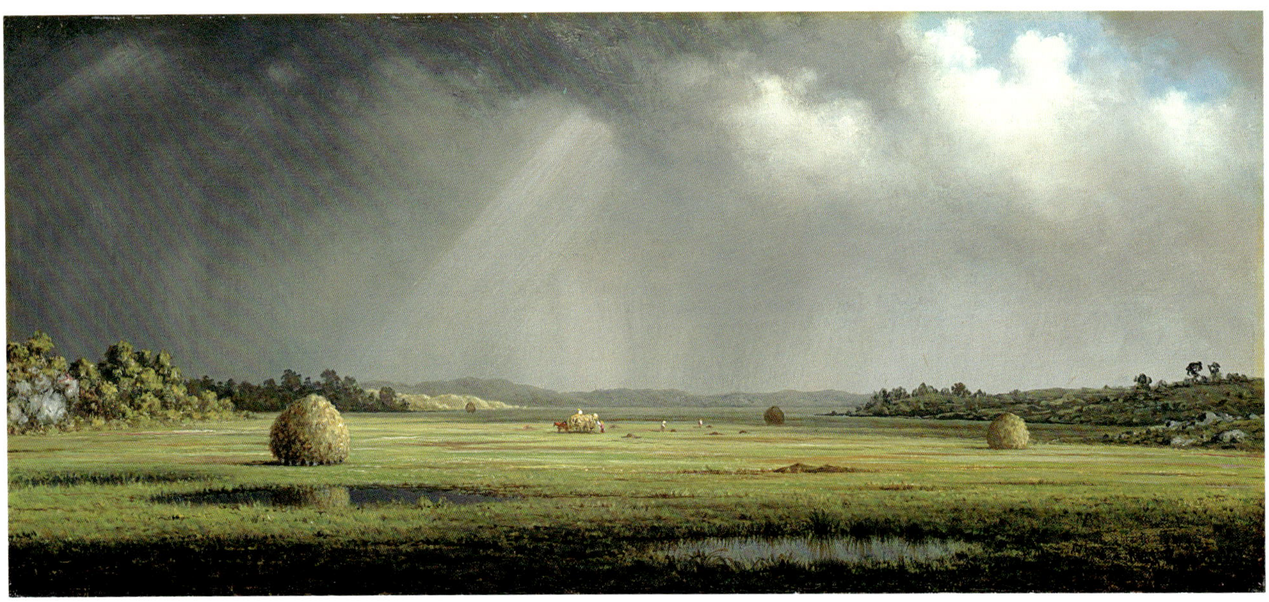

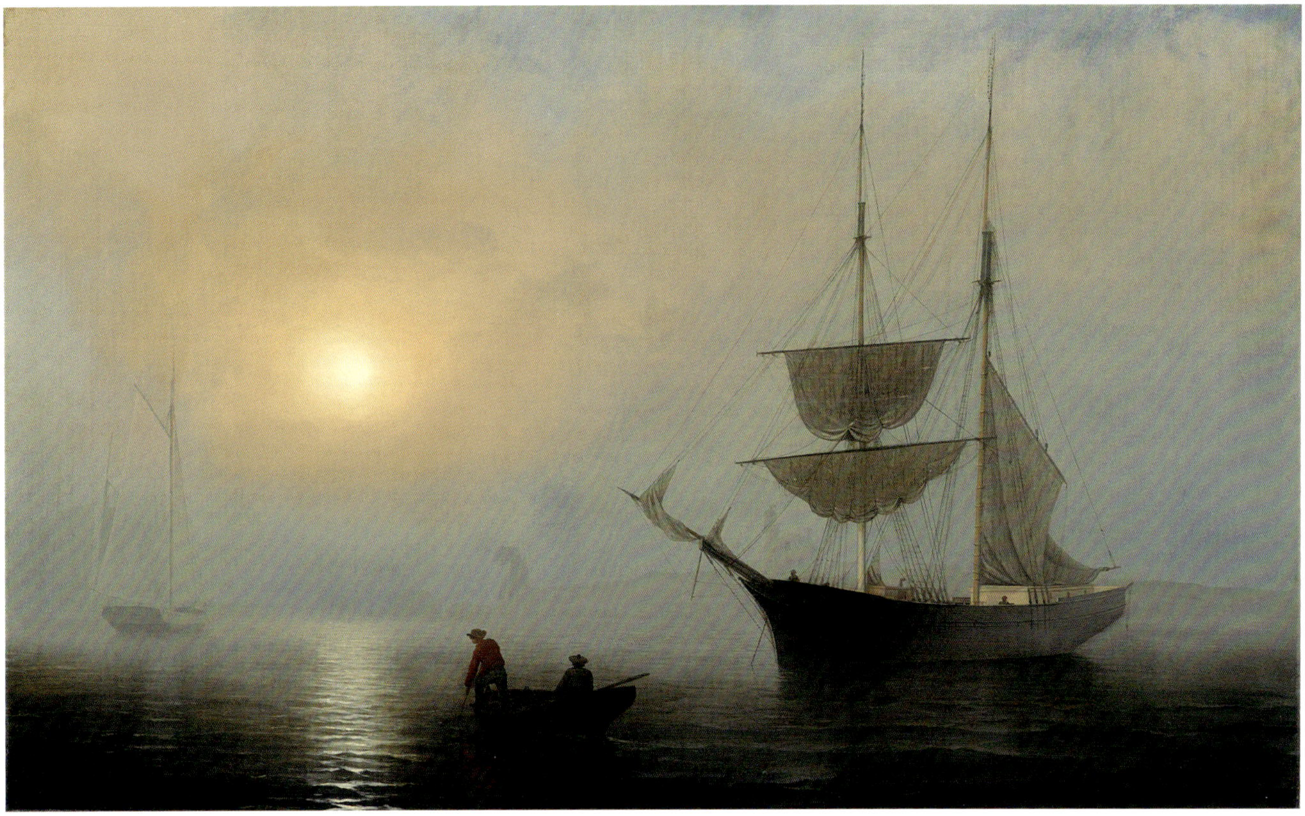

FIGURE 29 Fitz Henry Lane (1804–1865; born and died Gloucester, MA), *Ship in Fog, Gloucester Harbor*, ca. 1860. Oil on canvas, 61 × 99.1 cm. Princeton University Art Museum. Museum purchase made possible by the Fowler McCormick, Class of 1921, Fund; the Kathleen C. Sherrerd Program Fund for American Art; and Celia A. Felsher, Class of 1976, and John L. Cecil, Class of 1976 (2017-10)

of air—that collectively constitute it. In its radical relationality and sense of interdependent flux and change, Lane's portrait of fog expresses, differently, but just as effectively, the fundamentally ecological character of Luminist perception, even as the prosaic details of the scene assert the worth of all nature to be thoughtfully regarded.[50]

Luminism's peculiarly pellucid quality would seem to have little to do with the scumbled, opaque, suggestive, and subjective late paintings of George Inness, but the two share an essential allover focus that accords equal significance to everything within the frame, reflecting a common interest in the various parts of nature and their mutual interaction. Considered the greatest American landscape painter during the last years of the nineteenth century, Inness offered a personalized, self-consciously artistic, ostensively modern alternative to the formal detachment of the Hudson River School. *The Home of the Heron* (fig. 30) is a seminal expression of his fully developed mature style, an evolution that began with the artist's move away from classically descriptive compositions nearly forty years earlier, in midcentury canvases whose limited scope, ambiguous space, and blurred outlines anticipate the brooding, enigmatic intensity fully realized in works completed during the last fifteen years of his life. Inness's work was expressly informed by the eighteenth-century Swedish scientist-theologian Emanuel Swedenborg, who believed all things were spiritually charged and that the earthly, material world was continuous with another heavenly, mystical realm. The artist sought to combine the two in a visual approximation of the "correspondence" Swedenborg posited between them. *Home of the Heron* epitomizes the hazy, twilight ambience—painstakingly achieved through successive glazing and reworking of the paint surface—Inness employed to achieve this end, in which

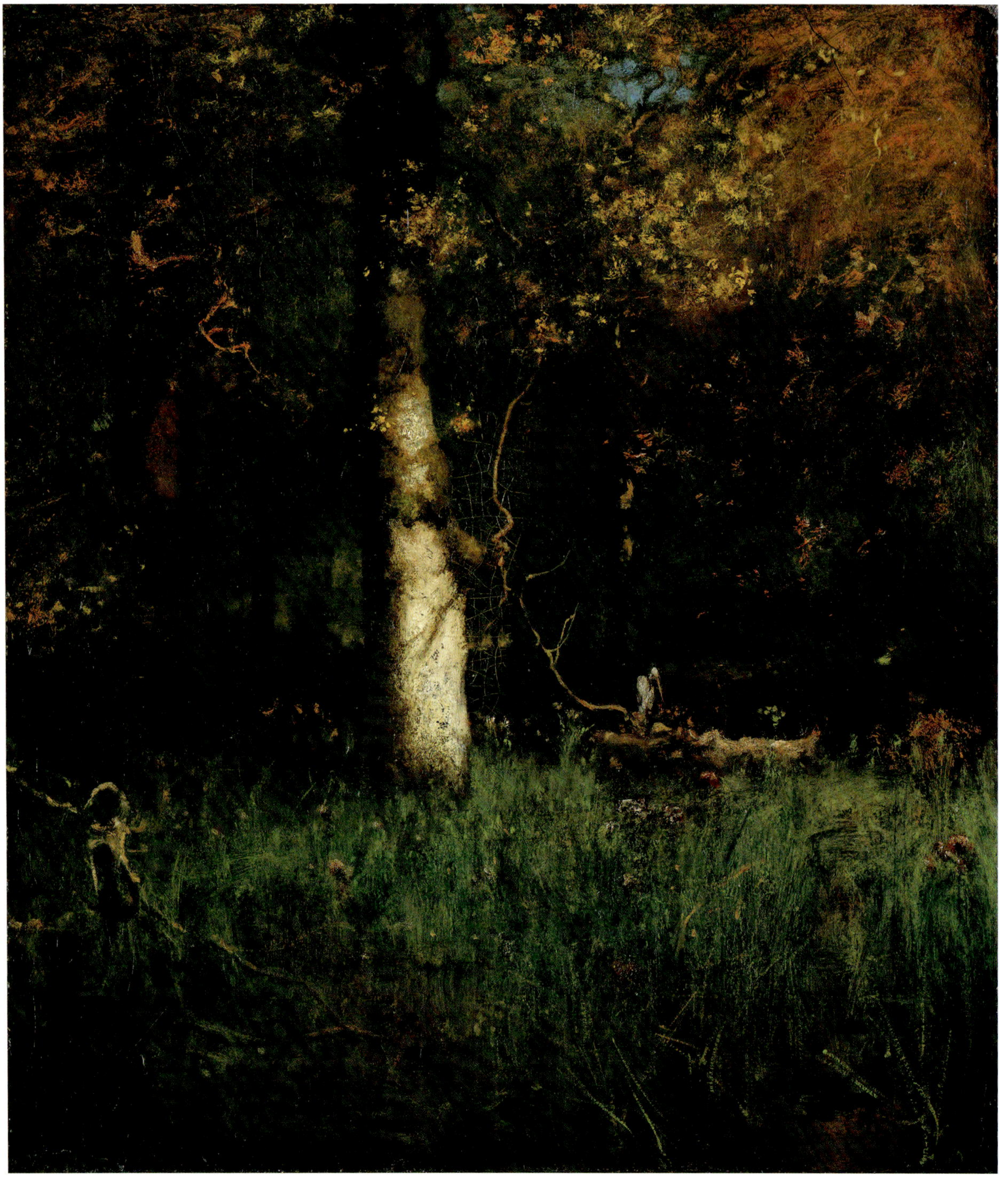

FIGURE 30 George Inness (1825–1894; born Newburgh, NY; died Bridge of Allan, United Kingdom), *The Home of the Heron*, 1891. Oil on canvas, 107 × 94 cm. Princeton University Art Museum. Gift of Victor Stephen Harris, Class of 1940, and David Harris, Class of 1944, in memory of their father, Victor Harris (y1943-93)

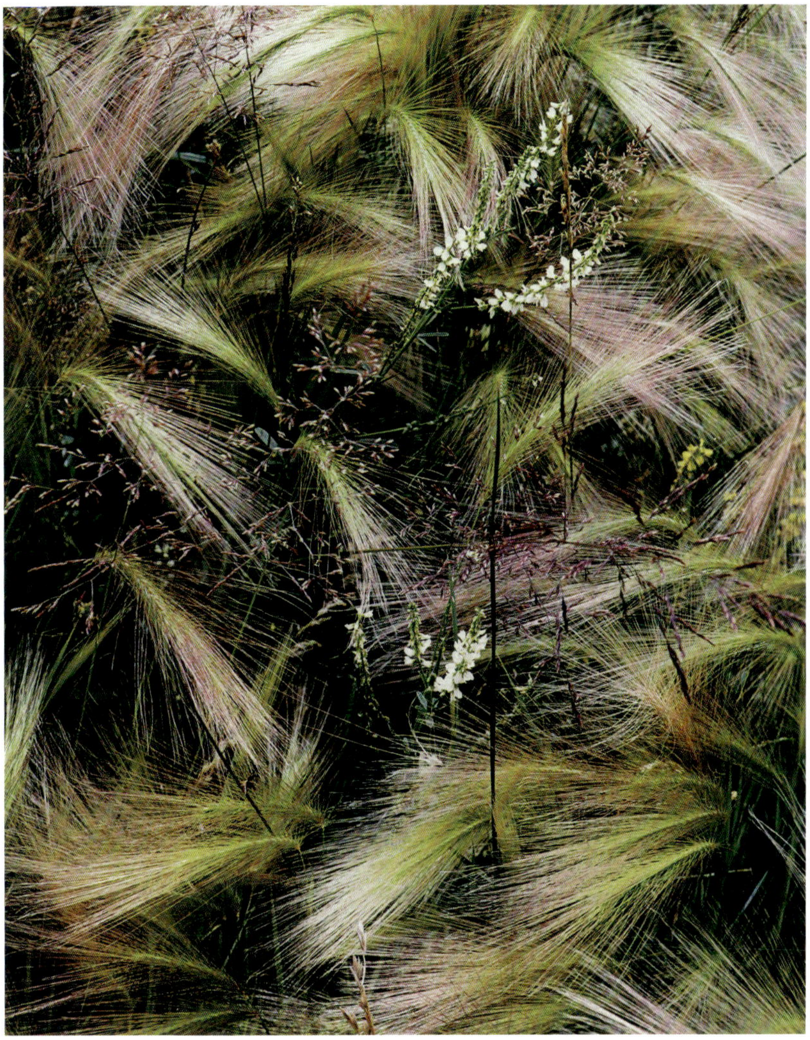

FIGURE 31 Eliot Furness Porter (1901–1990; born Winnetka, IL; died Santa Fe, NM), *Foxtail Grass, Colorado*, 1957, printed 1964. Dye transfer print, 26.7 × 21.2 cm. Princeton University Art Museum. Gift of David H. McAlpin, Class of 1920 (x1971-287 e)

matter and atmosphere seem melded together in a scene at once palpable and intangible, and representation itself becomes a demonstration of life's essential entanglement.[51]

Some six decades after Inness's death, a comment made by another painter speaks to the abiding relevance of his egalitarian, ecologically minded approach. Describing the photography of his brother Eliot, the artist and critic Fairfield Porter (1907–1975) observed, "There is no subject and background, every corner is alive." He meant that Eliot's compositions consistently avoid privileging different parts of nature in a classically hierarchical way; rather, one piece is as important as another, and all exist together as components of a co-dependent system, not construed as if on a laddered scale, with human perspective and interests predominant. *Foxtail Grass, Colorado* (fig. 31) eschews particularized focus on any individual element, advancing instead an aesthetic that prioritizes the closely cropped, richly enmeshed whole—literally a slice of life, unexceptional except for the photographer's determination to see in it what is in fact remarkable about it.[52]

Wordsworth's "Ode" expressed at the beginning of the nineteenth century a growing recognition of the human separation from nature in Western culture—a remove foreordained by Christianity's insistence on our distinction from the rest of life, and fostered by capitalism's rapacious appetite for growth at nature's expense. Much of the art produced since then seems to grapple with that reality. In a Euro-American context, the effort began with an exaltation of nature's grandeur that in the end only abetted alienation and promoted its expropriation through ongoing development. With the gradual acceptance of ecology's central insight—that everything is connected—a countervailing sensibility has emerged to articulate and champion this essential truth. The paintings of the Luminists and of Inness, the photographs of Eliot Porter, and a host of other creative efforts and imaginings increasingly insist on the world's fundamental, existential mutuality. This is the promise of *Mitákuye Oyás'in*, or "we are all related." As our understanding of American art expands through enhanced collections, voices, and perspectives, we can come also to the promise of a broader, more sustainable understanding of what it means to be human.

NOTES

Thanks to Nicola Knipe, Julie Dweck, Caroline Harris, and two anonymous readers for helpful comments and suggestions.

1. Even earlier, Cole had produced on the same paper sheet a pair of highly schematic pencil sketches of the envisioned work (*Two Chiaroscuro Studies for the Savage State, the Course of Empire*, ca. 1833, Detroit Institute of Arts, 39.155.A), and his *Layout for the Course of Empire*, a ruled drawing showing the cycle's anticipated plan of installation in patron Luman Reed's New York City home, includes the roughed in outlines of the composition (Detroit Institute of Arts, 39.351). Princeton's study was acquired by Museum Director Frank Jewett Mather from Florence H. Cole Vincent, the artist's granddaughter. Cooper quoted in Louis Legrand Noble, *The Life and Works of Thomas Cole, N.A.*, 3rd ed. (New York: Sheldon, Blakeman, 1856), 225–26. *The Course of Empire* is elaborately discussed and debated throughout the scholarship on Cole, most recently in Elizabeth Mankin Kornhauser and Tim Barringer, eds., *Thomas Cole's Journey: Atlantic Crossings* (New York: Metropolitan Museum of Art, 2018); and notably in William H. Truettner and Alan Wallach, eds., *Thomas Cole: Landscape into History* (New Haven, CT: Yale University Press, 1994); also see Angela Miller, *The Empire of the Eye: Landscape Representation and American Cultural Politics, 1825–1875* (Ithaca, NY: Cornell University Press, 1993), 23–39; Ellwood C. Parry III, *The Art of Thomas Cole: Ambition and Imagination* (Newark: University of Delaware Press, 1988), 131–87; and Alan P. Wallach, "Cole, Byron, and *The Course of Empire*," *Art Bulletin* 50, no. 4 (December 1968): 375–79. An exhaustive (if not entirely up to date) bibliography on the series is available at New-York Historical Society, https://www.nyhistory.org/exhibit/course-empire-savage-state-0.

2. On early American landscape representation and its implications see Edward J. Nygren, ed., *Views and Visions: American Landscape before 1830* (Washington, DC: Corcoran Gallery of Art, 1986); and Karl Kusserow, "Ordering the Land," in *Nature's Nation: American Art and Environment*, ed. Karl Kusserow and Alan C. Braddock (New Haven, CT: Yale University Press, 2018), 70–101. Also see William H. Gerdts, "American Landscape Painting: Critical Judgments, 1730–1845," *American Art Journal* 17, no. 1 (Winter 1985): 28–59.

3. Indo-European eyes are used to orienting words, and less consciously images, from left to right. Text arranged in the opposite direction, as in numerous Asian systems of writing, is recognized as different to someone accustomed to a Germanic language like English. A similar reversal in the visual language of Western painting is also impactful, though more subtly, and often not readily apprehended for the deviation it represents. Still, on some level images composed in such a way read as organized against the grain, all the more so when it makes conceptual sense. Cole's stolid study for the second *Pastoral* scene (ca. 1834, Collection of Richard Sharp), when compared to Princeton's vibrant one for the

first, reaffirms his wish to project fixedness in the series' middle pictures, just as the replacement in another preparatory work of an immobile lion statue for the striding headless gladiator in *Desolation* underscores his desire for (backward) movement in that picture. (*The Course of Empire* also includes a fifth scene, *Desolation*, a coda in which the ruins of the destroyed city are shown beneath a moonlit sky.)

4. Thomas Cole to Luman Reed, September 18, 1833, in Noble, *Thomas Cole*, 176.

5. See Alan C. Braddock, "Directionality in Thomas Cole's *The Oxbow*: Ecocritical Art History and Visual Communication," in *Routledge Handbook of Ecocriticism and Environmental Communication*, ed. Scott Slovic, Swarnalatha Rangarajan, and Vidya Sarveswaran (New York: Routledge, 2019), 155–66. That it was over a preliminary drawing for *Consummation*, in particular, that Cole painted *The Oxbow* seems telling, as thus *The Course of Empire*'s most complete expression of human ascendancy became the artist's accommodating articulation of the process whereby such a transformation occurred. Many see Cole as an environmentalist avant la lettre. Certainly he was wary of unbridled development, having seen its effects his whole life, first in industrializing North West England, where he grew up, and later in his beloved Catskill Mountains, where he eventually established his studio. Yet although his writings evince a romantic's turmoil over the price of "progress" in Jacksonian America, his paintings are ambivalent with regard to the human-nature nexus, at first decrying the depredations of development, but ultimately accommodating it as a reality of the age. See Karl Kusserow, "The Trouble with Empire," in Kusserow and Braddock, *Nature's Nation*, 102–39. Also see Angela L. Miller, "The Fate of Wilderness in American Landscape Art: The Dilemmas of 'Nature's Nation,'" in *A Keener Perception: Ecocritical Studies in American Art History*, ed. Alan C. Braddock and Christoph Irmscher (Tuscaloosa: University of Alabama Press, 2009), 85–109; and Stephen Daniels, "Thomas Cole and the Course of Empire," chap. 5 in *Fields of Vision: Landscape Imagery and National Identity in England and the United States* (Princeton, NJ: Princeton University Press, 1993), 146–73. For interpretations of Cole's art as more environmentally minded, see Kornhauser and Barringer, *Thomas Cole's Journey*; and Alan Wallach, "Thomas Cole's *River in the Catskills* as Antipastoral," *Art Bulletin* 84, no. 2 (June 2002): 334–50.

6. See Beth Austin, "1619: Virginia's First Africans," Hampton History Museum, revised December 2019, https://hampton.gov/DocumentCenter/View/24075/1619-Virginias-First-Africans; and Martha McCartney, "Africans, Virginia's First," *Encyclopedia Virginia*, last updated March 22, 2022, https://encyclopediavirginia.org/entries/africans-virginias-first. The Pilgrims' evangelizing is often overlooked, yet they had "a great hope and inward zeal . . . to make some way thereunto for the propagating and advancing of the gospel of the kingdom of Christ in those remote parts of the world." William Bradford, *Of Plymouth Plantation, 1620–1647* (1651), ed. Samuel Eliot Morison (repr., New York: Alfred A. Knopf, 2002), 25. For an important, if controversial, reorienting of America's founding around the events of 1619 instead of those of 1620, see Nikole Hannah-Jones et al., eds., *The 1619 Project: A New Origin Story* (New York: One World, 2021).

7. God and "mammon" (material possessions and wealth) are the subject of the well-known New Testament passage Matthew 6:24: "No man can serve two masters: for either he will hate the one, and love the other; or else he will hold to the one, and despise the other. Ye cannot serve God and mammon" (King James Version). Yet this is precisely what early colonists did, the interests of one justifying pursuit of the other in the vast imperial enterprise.

8. The term for the Marxian paradigm is John Bellamy Foster's; see Foster, "Marx's Theory of Metabolic Rift: Classical Foundations for Environmental Sociology," *American Journal of Sociology* 105, no. 2 (September 1999): 366–405; also see Anita Waters, "Marx on the Metabolic Rift: How Capitalism Cuts Us Off from Nature," Communist Party USA, October 11, 2019, https://www.cpusa.org/article/marx-on-the-metabolic-rift-how-capitalism-cuts-us-off-from-nature/.

9. On Valadés, *Rhetorica Christiana*, and its imagery, see Alan C. Braddock, "Mestizo Mnemonics: Diego de Valadés, *Rhetorica Christiana*, and the Earthly Art of Memory," in *Picture Ecology: Art and Ecocriticism in Planetary Perspective*, ed. Karl Kusserow (Princeton, NJ: Princeton University Press, 2021), 114–31; Lauren Kilroy-Ewbank, "Engravings in Diego de Valadés's *Rhetorica Christiana*," Smarthistory, November 5, 2019, https://smarthistory.org/engravings-in-diego-de-valadess-rhetorica-christiana/; and Amy Galpin, "Re-Thinking *Retórica Cristiana* through Space and Performance: A Sixteenth-Century Case of Image and Text," *Working Papers on Design* 2 (2007). A digital scan of Valadés's original text is available at https://archive.org/details/rhetoricachristioovala/page/n3/mode/2up?ref=ol&view=theater. On early Catholicism in Latin America more generally, see John Frederick Schwaller, *The History of the Catholic Church in Latin America: From Conquest to Revolution and Beyond* (New York: New York University Press, 2011).

10. See Braddock, "Mestizo Mnemonics." The essential text on the Great Chain concept remains Arthur O. Lovejoy, *The Great Chain of Being: A Study of the History of an Idea* (Cambridge, MA: Harvard University Press, 1936). For an early and influential articulation of the environmental implications of Christianity's anthropocentrism, see Lynn White Jr., "The Historical Roots of Our Ecologic Crisis," *Science*, n.s., 155, no. 3767 (March 10, 1967): 1205–7.

11. On Potosí and the Spanish American silver industry, see Nicholas A. Robins, *Mercury, Mining, and Empire: The Human and Ecological Cost of Colonial Silver Mining in the Andes* (Bloomington: Indiana University Press, 2011).

12. Information on the chest and its iconography comes principally from a report on the object in the curatorial files of the Princeton University Art Museum prepared in 2021 by Spanish American silver specialist Cristina Esteras Martín; also see the catalogue entry for the piece by Vivian Velar de Irigoyen in *Discovering Viceregal Latin American Treasures*, ed. Jaime Eguiguen and Ariel Yu Shi (Madrid: Colnaghi and Jaime Eguiguren Art & Antiques, 2021), 324. Farocki quoted in Laura Turner Igoe, "Creative Matter: Tracing the Environmental Context of Materials in American Art," in Kusserow and Braddock, *Nature's Nation*, 148. The film was created for the Haus der Kulturen der Welt exhibition *The Potosí Principle*; see the accompanying catalogue, *The Potosí Principle: How Can We Sing the Song of the Lord in an Alien Land? Colonial Image Production in the Global Economy*, ed. Alice Creischer, Max Jorge Hinderer, and Andreas Siekmann (Cologne: Walther König, 2010).

13. De Bry never actually visited America—his images for Hariot's text are based on the watercolors of another expeditioner, John White (ca. 1540–ca. 1593). The ways in which de Bry subtly altered White's compositions to enhance the effect of exotic abundance leaves no doubt as to the intent of their enterprise. On the White / de Bry corpus, see Michael Gaudio, *Engraving the Savage: The New World and Techniques of Civilization* (Minneapolis: University of Minnesota Press, 2008); for an ecocritical reading, see Timothy Sweet, "Filling the Field: The Roanoke Images of John White and Theodor de Bry," in Braddock and Irmscher, *A Keener Perception*, 23–42. For more on early landscape representations of North America, including this image, see Karl Kusserow, "Ordering the Land," in Kusserow and Braddock, *Nature's Nation*, 70–101, esp. 71–78.

14. See Dennis Reinhartz, *The Cartographer and the Literati: Herman Moll and His Intellectual Circle* (Lewiston, NY: Edward Mellen, 1997); and, more generally, Margaret Beck Pritchard and Henry G. Taliaferro, *Degrees of Latitude: Mapping Colonial America* (New York: Harry N. Abrams, 2002).

15. Pemberton quoted in Alexander Leitch, *A Princeton Companion* (Princeton, NJ: Princeton University Press, 1978), 199–200. Dickinson quoted in David C. Humphrey, "The Struggle for Sectarian Control of Princeton, 1745–1760," *New Jersey History* 91 (1973): 83. For a synopsis of Princeton's founding, see Leitch, *Princeton Companion*, 197–200; and John M. Murrin, "Introduction: Princetonians, 1784–1794," in *Princetonians, 1784–1790: A Biographical Dictionary*, ed. Ruth L. Woodward and Wesley Frank Craven (Princeton, NJ: Princeton University Press, 1991), xvii–lviii. The balance of religious and secular education at Princeton has been extensively discussed; see Francis L. Broderick, "Pulpit, Physics, and Politics: The Curriculum of the College of New Jersey, 1746–1794," *William and Mary Quarterly* 6, no. 1 (January 1949): 42–68; Humphrey, "The Struggle for Sectarian Control"; Alison B. Olson, "The Founding of Princeton University: Religion and Politics in Eighteenth-Century New Jersey," *New Jersey History* 87 (1969): 133–50; and Mark A. Noll, *Princeton and the Republic, 1768–1822: The Search for a Christian Enlightenment in the Era of Samuel Stanhope Smith* (Princeton, NJ: Princeton University Press, 1989).

16. On Jonathan Fisher and his production of the Nassau Hall view, see Janet S. Byrne, "An American Pioneer Amateur," *Princeton University Library Chronicle* 6, no. 4 (June 1945): 153–70. For more on Princeton's early history and the role of images in articulating it, see Karl Kusserow, "Memory and Meaning in the Faculty Room," in *Inner Sanctum: Memory and Meaning in Princeton's Faculty Room at Nassau Hall*, ed. Karl Kusserow (Princeton, NJ: Princeton University Press, 2010), 47–113, from which this discussion draws.

17. On the Brainerd lexicon, see Alfred L. Bush, "Otterskins, Eagle Feathers, and Native American Alumni at Princeton," *Princeton University Library Chronicle* 67, no. 2 (Winter 2006): 420–34. The book's otterskin overwrap is decorated with colored bands characteristic of Lenape geometrical design, whose still vivid orange and black tonality coincidentally accords with the colors adopted by the College of New Jersey a century after its creation. Brainerd's own diary, edited and published by Edwards in 1749 as *An Account of the Life of the Late Reverend Mr. David Brainerd*, inspired countless future missionaries in their proselytizing among Native Americans. For a brief but cogent account of the Lenape in New Jersey, see Gregory Evans Dowd, *The Indians of New Jersey* (Trenton: New Jersey Historical Commission, 1992). Like many Indigenous peoples, the Lenape were active stewards of their environment, regularly conducting controlled burns, for example, to promote regrowth of particular species and reinvigorate the soil; however, their management was informed by what is now called Traditional Ecological Knowledge, which entails a deep understanding of local ecosystems and an appreciation of regional biodiversity (see note 19 below). For the distinction between settler colonial environmental attitudes and those of the Lenape, see, in the first instance, Alan Taylor, "'Wasty Ways': Stories of American Settlement," in *American Environmental History*, ed. Louis S. Warren (Malden, MA: Blackwell Publishing, 2003), 102–18; on the Lenape, see Mike Weilbacher, "The Lenape and the Land," Schuylkill Center for Environmental Education, November 1, 2021, https://www.schuylkillcenter.org/news/the-lenape-and-the-land/; and Eric W. Sanderson, *Mannahatta: A Natural History of New York City* (New York: Abrams, 2009). For the historical meeting of the two sensibilities, see Michael Dean Mackintosh, "Ink and Paper, Clamshells and Leather: Power, Environmental Perception, and Materiality in the Lenape-European Encounter at Philadelphia," in *A Greene Country Towne: Philadelphia's Ecology in the Cultural Imagination*, ed. Alan C. Braddock and Laura Turner Igoe (University Park: Pennsylvania State University Press, 2016), 19–33.

18. See Daniel P. Modaff, "*Mitakuye Oyasin* (We Are All Related): Connecting Communication and Culture of the Lakota," *Great Plains Quarterly* 39, no. 4 (Fall 2019): 341–62. For an analysis of the politics of the phrase and its wide adoption, see Jessica L. Horton, "'All Our Relations' as an Eco-Art Historical Challenge: Lessons from Standing Bear's Muslin," in *Ecologies, Agents, Terrains*, ed. Christopher P. Heuer and Rebecca Zorach (Williamstown, MA: Clark Art Institute, 2018), 73–93. The term "ecology" first appeared in 1866 as *Oecologie* in the book *Generelle Morphologie der Organismen* (*General Morphology of Organisms*) by the Prussian naturalist Ernst Haeckel, a follower of Charles Darwin and a promoter of his theory of evolution. For the history of the discipline, see Robert P. McIntosh, *The Background of Ecology: Concept and Theory* (New York: Cambridge University Press, 1985); Donald Worster, *Nature's Economy: A History of Ecological Ideas*, 2nd ed. (New York: Cambridge University Press, 1994); and Edward J. Kormondy, "A Brief Introduction to the History of Ecology," *American Biology Teacher* 74, no. 7 (September 2012): 441–43. A useful overview of Native American environmental belief and interaction is David Rich Lewis, "American Indian Environmental Relations," in *A Companion to American Environmental History*, ed. Douglas Cazaux Sackman (Chichester, UK: Wiley Blackwell, 2014), 191–213. On Native American perceptions of life's essential interconnectedness and its pervasiveness among Indigenous peoples, generally, see Winona LaDuke, *All Our Relations: Native Struggles for Land and Life* (Cambridge, MA: South End Press, 1999); Marilyn Notah Verney, "On Authenticity," in *American Indian Thought: Philosophical Essays*, ed. Anne Waters (Malden, MA: Blackwell Publishing, 2004), 133–39; and Gerald McMaster, "Ntotemuk: Commonalities among Great Differences," in *18th Biennale of Sydney: All Our Relations*, ed. Catherine de Zegher and Gerald McMaster (Woolloomooloo, NSW: Biennale of Sydney, 2012), 307–31.

19. See Shepard Krech III, *The Ecological Indian: Myth and History* (New York: W. W. Norton, 2000); also see Michael E. Harkin and David Rich Lewis, eds., *Native Americans and the Environment: Perspectives on the Ecological Indian* (Lincoln: University of Nebraska Press, 2007); Joy Porter, *Native American Environmentalism: Land, Spirit, and the Idea of Wilderness* (Lincoln: University of Nebraska Press, 2014); and Lewis, "American Indian Environmental Relations." On the implications of Indigenous belief for contemporary environmental concerns, see Daniel R. Wildcat, *Red Alert!: Saving the Planet with Indigenous Knowledge* (Golden, CO: Fulcrum, 2009). For Native American environmental intervention and its influence on social institutions, see Paul E. Minnis and Wayne J. Elisens, eds., *Biodiversity and Native America* (Norman: University of Oklahoma Press, 2000); and Nancy M. Williams and Graham Baines, eds., *Traditional Ecological Knowledge: Wisdom for Sustainable Development* (Canberra: Centre for Resource and Environmental Studies, Australian National University, 1993). On complementary elements of trans-Indigenous worldviews regarding environmental reciprocity and interconnectedness, see Chadwick Allen, *Trans-Indigenous: Methodologies for Global Native Literary Studies* (Minneapolis: University of Minnesota Press, 2012). Also see Richard White, "Indian Peoples and the Natural World: Asking the Right Questions," in *Rethinking American Indian History*, ed. Donald L. Fixico (Albuquerque: University of New Mexico Press, 1997), 87–100.

20. See Nika Collison, "Everything Depends on Everything Else," in *Raven Travelling: Two Centuries of Haida Art*, ed. Peter Macnair, Daina Augaitis, and Marianne Jones (Seattle: University of Washington Press, 2006), 56–69. The literature on the Haida is extensive and varied; for a compelling account of their oral tradition and the belief underlying it, see Robert Bringhurst, *A Story as Sharp as a Knife: The Classical Haida Mythtellers and Their World*, vol. 1, *Masterworks of the Classical Haida Mythtellers*, 2nd ed. (Vancouver, BC: Douglas & McIntyre, 2011). Haida artist Bill Reid (1920–1998) produced a well-known monumental wooden sculpture, *The Raven and the First Men* (1978–80; Museum of Anthropology at the University of British Columbia, Vancouver), depicting the Haida creation myth. The classic account of shamanism is Mircea Eliade, *Shamanism: Archaic Techniques of Ecstasy* (Princeton, NJ: Princeton University Press, 1964); for the practice in Indigenous North America, see Åke Hultkrantz, *Shamanic Healing and Ritual Drama: Health and Medicine in Native North American Religious Traditions* (New York: Crossroad, 1992); for shamanism among First Nations peoples of the Northwest Coast, see Allen Wardwell, *Tangible Visions: Northwest Coast Indian Shamanism and Its Art* (New York: Monacelli, 1996).

21. Haida carver, painter, printmaker, and jeweler Robert Davidson (b. 1946) observes: "It is said that language is the key to a culture. In the Haida language, as in those of many First Nations here in the Americas, we do not have a word for art. So for lack of a better word, I will borrow the English word 'art.' We Haida were once surrounded by art. Art was one with our culture. We had art that was sacred, brought out only for certain ceremonies. We also had art that was on permanent display, validating our place in the world. Art is our only written language. It documented the histories of our families; it documented our progress as a people. Throughout our history, art has kept our spirit alive." Quoted in Robin K. Wright, *Northern Haida Master Carvers* (Seattle: University of Washington Press, 2001), 5–6. On totem poles, see Aldona Jonaitis and Aaron Glass, *The Totem Pole: An Intercultural History* (Seattle: University of Washington Press, 2010). For objects related to Haida shamanism, see Wardwell, *Tangible Visions*; for Haida visual culture, generally, see Macnair, Augaitis, and Jones, *Raven Travelling*; George F. MacDonald, *Haida Art* (Seattle: University of Washington Press, 1996); and Wright, *Northern Haida Master Carvers*.

22. On Stilthda and his evolving oeuvre, see Bill Holm, "Will the Real Charles Edenshaw Please Stand Up?: The Problem of Attribution in Northwest Coast Art," in *The World Is as Sharp as a Knife: An Anthology in Honour of Wilson Duff*, ed. Donald Abbott (Victoria: British Columbia Provincial Museum, 1981), 175–200; Robin K. Wright, "Two Haida Artists from Yan: Will John Gwaytihl and Simeon Stilthda Please Step Apart?," *American Indian Art* 23, no. 3 (Summer 1998): 42–57, 106–7; and especially Wright, *Northern Haida Master Carvers*, 286–305. The other carvings by Stilthda of deceased shamans are at the American Museum of Natural History, New York (accession no. 16/739); British Museum, London (Am1944,02.131); Etnografiska Museet, Stockholm (1904.19.0079); and Saint Louis Art Museum (132:1976). Both the Princeton and American Museum of Natural History figures (the latter situated in a model grave house) clutch what are perhaps gambling sticks in both hands.

23. On Indigenous trade with Euro-Americans and their missionary initiatives, see Robin Fisher, *Contact and Conflict: Indian-European Relations in British Columbia, 1774–1890*, 2nd ed. (Vancouver: UBC Press, 1992); and Susan Neylan, *The Heavens Are Changing: Nineteenth-Century Protestant Missions and Tsimshian Christianity* (Montreal: McGill-Queen's University Press, 2002). On Jackson, see J. Arthur Lazell, *Alaskan Apostle: The Life Story of Sheldon Jackson* (New York: Harper, 1960); and Norman J. Bender, *Winning the West for Christ: Sheldon Jackson and Presbyterianism on the Rocky Mountain Frontier, 1869–1880* (Albuquerque: University of New Mexico Press, 1996). On the adaptation, commodification, endurance, and revitalization of Haida and Northwest Coast artistic traditions, generally, see Janet C. Berlo and Ruth B. Phillips, *Native North American Art*, 2nd ed. (New York: Oxford University Press, 2015), chap. 6; Wright, *Northern Haida Master Carvers*; Macnair, Augaitis, and Jones, *Raven Travelling*; and MacDonald, *Haida Art*; also see, for contemporary Haida reengagement with historical objects collected by foreigners, Cara Krmpotich and Laura Peers, *This Is Our Life: Haida Material Heritage and Changing Museum Practice* (Vancouver: UBC Press, 2013).

24. Postcommodity, http://postcommodity.com/About.html. For the group's extensive bibliography, see http://postcommodity.com/Vitae.html.

25. See Postcommodity, "Do You Remember When?—2009," http://postcommodity.com/DoYouRememberWhen.html; de Zegher and McMaster, *18th Biennale of Sydney: All Our Relations*, 170, 291 (upper); Kate Morris, *Shifting Grounds: Landscape in Contemporary Native American Art* (Seattle: University of Washington Press, 2019), 81–83, 146–47; and especially Mark Watson, "'Centering the Indigenous': Postcommodity's Trans-Indigenous Relational Art," *Third Text* 29, no. 3 (May 2015): 141–54.

26. Postcommodity, "Repellent Fence / Valla Repelente," http://postcommodity.com/Repellent_Fence.html. Twist discusses the relevance of *Repellent Fence* for the group at 2:28–2:43 in "Postcommodity in 'Borderlands': Extended Segment," the expanded version of episode 3, "Borderlands," season 10 of the series *Art in the Twenty-First Century*, airdate October 20, 2020, Art21, https://art21.org/watch/art-in-the-twenty-first-century/s10/postcommodity-in-borderlands-extended-segment/. The most extensive treatment of the project is *Through the Repellent Fence: A Land Art Film*, directed by Sam Wainwright Douglas, 74 min. (Austin, TX: Big Beard Films, 2017). As the film's subtitle suggests, the documentary somewhat problematically places *Repellent Fence* more in the tradition of land art than relational aesthetics—the latter being what Postcommodity believes the project to have become over its long gestation (see "Implementation" in "Postcommodity: 2012 Grantee," Art Matters, https://www.artmattersfoundation.org/texts/postcommodity). The work's creation as "a social collaborative project . . . that culminate[s] with the establishment of a large-scale temporary monument" (http://postcommodity.com/Repellent_Fence_English.html), in keeping with its generally noninvasive quality, aligns *Repellent Fence* more with contemporary Indigenous aesthetics than the land-based artistic practices of the late twentieth century. On relational aesthetics, described as "a set of artistic practices which take as their theoretical and practical point of departure the whole of human relations and their social context," see Nicolas Bourriaud, *Relational Aesthetics* (Dijon, France: Les Presses du Réel, 2002), quote on 113. In addition to the installation photograph illustrated here, the Princeton University Art Museum earlier acquired the northernmost of *Repellent Fence*'s twenty-six balloons, titled *N13: 31°20'50.88"N; 109°29'47.62"W* (2018-3).

27. See Art Matters Foundation, "Indigenous Semiotics," https://www.artmattersfoundation.org/texts/postcommodity. As a kind of forerunner to *Repellent Fence*, in 2008 Postcommodity created *Repellent Eye Over Phoenix*, featuring a single "scare eye" balloon floated over downtown Phoenix, Arizona, as "an intervention repelling the manifestations of the Western worldview and imagination" and underscoring the shamanistic role of birds as "the spiritual mediators between the physical world and spiritual world for Indigenous peoples"—much as in Haida belief (Postcommodity, "Repellent Eye Over Phoenix—2008," http://postcommodity.com/RepellentEyeOverPhoenix.html).

28. See "Centering: Site-Specific and Land-Based Art Practices," chap. 4 in Morris, *Shifting Grounds*, 81–113. *A Very Long Line* (2017) was created using footage of the same section of the Arizona–Sonora border as traversed in *Repellent Fence*; see Postcommodity, "A Very Long Line—2016," http://postcommodity.com/AVeryLongLine.html.

29. Executive Order No. 12898, *Federal Register* 59, no. 32 (February 11, 1994). The foundational text on environmental justice is Robert D. Bullard, *Dumping in Dixie: Race, Class, and Environmental Quality*, 3rd ed. (1990; New York: Routledge, 2000); also see Brendan Coolsaet, ed.,

Environmental Justice: Key Issues (New York: Routledge, 2020); and Renee Skelton and Vernice Miller, "The Environmental Justice Movement," National Resources Defense Council, March 17, 2016, https://www.nrdc.org/stories/environmental-justice-movement.

30. On Weir, see William H. Gerdts, "Robert Weir: Artist and Teacher of West Point," in Cadet Fine Arts Forum, *Robert Weir: Artist and Teacher of West Point* (West Point, NY: Cadet Fine Arts Forum of the United States Corps of Cadets, 1976), 9–23; and Marian Wardle, ed., *The Weir Family, 1820–1920: Expanding the Traditions of American Art* (Hanover, NH: University Press of New England, 2011). For information on the *Greenwich Boat Club*'s sitters and circumstances of production, see Susan G. Larkin, "'A Delicious Day': Robert Weir's *Greenwich Boat Club*," *American Art Journal* 33, no. 1/2 (2002): 21–33. On the painting's environmental implications, see Alan C. Braddock and Karl Kusserow, "Introduction," in Kusserow and Braddock, *Nature's Nation*, 28–30, from which this discussion is adapted.

31. Charles Dickens, *American Notes* (1842; New York: Charles Scribner's Sons, 1905), 76. Pintard quoted in John Noble Wilford, "How Epidemics Helped Shape the Modern Metropolis," *New York Times*, April 15, 2008, review of *Plague in Gotham! Cholera in Nineteenth-Century New York*, an exhibition at the New-York Historical Society. Also see Charles E. Rosenberg, "The Cholera Epidemic of 1832 in New York City," *Bulletin of the History of Medicine* 33, no. 1 (January–February 1959): 37–49; and Rosenberg, *The Cholera Years: The United States in 1832, 1849, and 1866* (1962; Chicago: University of Chicago Press, 1987), excerpted in Warren, *American Environmental History*, 142–55.

32. Durand's assistant and *New York Post* quoted in Wilford, "How Epidemics Helped Shape the Modern Metropolis."

33. See Alfred W. Crosby, *Ecological Imperialism: The Biological Expansion of Europe, 900–1900*, 2nd ed. (1986; New York: Cambridge University Press, 2004); Alfred W. Crosby Jr., *The Columbian Exchange: Biological and Cultural Consequences of 1492* (1972; Westport, CT: Praeger, 2003); and Nathan Nunn and Nancy Qian, "The Columbian Exchange: A History of Disease, Food, and Ideas," *Journal of Economic Perspectives* 24, no. 2 (Spring 2010): 163–88, "80–95 percent" at 165.

34. On Cuthand, see Jen Budney, ed., *Ruth Cuthand: Back Talk, Works 1983–2009* (Saskatoon, SK: Mendel Art Gallery, 2012); and, for *Extirpate This Execrable Race* in particular, Ruth Cuthand (website), https://www.ruthcuthand.ca/extirpate-this-execrable-race/. Amherst quoted in Jonathan B. Tucker, *Scourge: The Once and Future Threat of Smallpox* (New York: Grove, 2001), 20.

35. "I'm Not the Indian You're Looking For," undated artist statement, Ruth Cuthand (website), https://www.ruthcuthand.ca/.

36. For pioneering studies of the implications of artistic materials, see Jennifer L. Anderson, *Mahogany: The Costs of Luxury in Early America* (Cambridge, MA: Harvard University Press, 2012); and Igoe, "Creative Matter."

37. For the cultural milieu of American women sculptors in Italy, see Melissa Dabakis, *A Sisterhood of Sculptors: American Artists in Nineteenth-Century Rome* (University Park: Pennsylvania State University Press, 2015).

38. "The Culprit Fay" was written in 1816 but first published posthumously through the efforts of Drake's daughter; see Joseph Rodman Drake, *The Culprit Fay and Other Poems* (New York: G. Dearborn, 1836). On Drake's life and work, see Joseph Slater, "The Case of Drake and Halleck," *Early American Literature* 8, no. 3 (Winter 1974): 285–97. Fitz-Greene Halleck was a poet and Drake's closest friend; he is also, coincidentally, among those depicted in Robert Weir's *Greenwich Boat Club*. Drake was close to another of that painting's subjects, James De Kay; indeed, it was De Kay's refusal to grant Drake's deathbed request to destroy his papers—including the manuscript for "The Culprit Fay"—that ultimately enabled the sculpture to be made after it (Slater, "Case of Drake and Halleck," 288–89). Cole's earlier "The Complaint of the Forest" and the later published "The Lament of the Forest" are both in Thomas Cole, *Thomas Cole's Poetry*, ed. Marshall B. Tymn (York, PA: Liberty Cap Books, 1972), 100–112. On the "naturalistic nationalism" championed in *The Knickerbocker* and elsewhere, see Eric Kaufmann, "'Naturalizing the Nation': The Rise of Naturalistic Nationalism in the United States and Canada," *Comparative Studies in Society and History* 40, no. 4 (October 1998): 666–95, esp. 671–73.

39. On Jackson, see John F. McGuigan Jr., "A Maine Sculptor in Florence: John Adams Jackson, 1825–1879," *Imagines: Il Magazine delle Gallerie degli Uffizi* 5 (July 2021): 10–31, 18–21 on *The Culprit Fay*. On Carrara, see Joel Leivick, *Carrara: The Marble Quarries of Tuscany* (Stanford, CA: Stanford University Press, 1999); and Eric Scigliano, *Michelangelo's Mountain: The Quest for Perfection in the Marble Quarries of Carrara* (New York: Free Press, 2005). For the labor and environmental implications of quarrying at Carrara, see Laura Turner Igoe, "'A Gruesome Sight': Randolph Rogers's *Nydia* in a Marble World," in *Ecocriticism and the Anthropocene in Nineteenth-Century Art and Visual Culture*, ed. Maura Coughlin and Emily Gephart (New York: Routledge, 2020), 80–92; and Igoe, "Creative Matter," 157–61. For the contemporary account of the Italian laborers, see "A Stronghold of Anarchists," *New York Times*, January 19, 1894. On labor at Carrara today, see G. Angotzi et al., "World at Work: Marble Quarrying in Tuscany," *Occupational and Environmental Medicine* 62, no. 6 (June 2005): 417–21.

40. Hartley quoted in Townsend Ludington, *Marsden Hartley: The Biography of an American Artist* (Ithaca, NY: Cornell University Press, 1998), 258 ("the painter of Maine"), 260 ("no one else so qualified"); and in Elizabeth Mankin Kornhauser, ed., *Marsden Hartley: American Modernist* (New Haven, CT: Yale University Press, 2002), 185 ("I must get that

mountain"). For the artist's Maine production, see Donna M. Cassidy, Elizabeth Finch, and Randall R. Griffey, *Marsden Hartley's Maine* (New York: Metropolitan Museum of Art, 2017); also see, for the Katahdin paintings, Kornhauser, *Marsden Hartley*, esp. 184–85, 322–23; Gail R. Scott, *Marsden Hartley* (New York: Abbeville, 1988), esp. 130–35; and Jeanne Hokin, *Pinnacles & Pyramids: The Art of Marsden Hartley* (Albuquerque: University of New Mexico Press, 1993), esp. chap. 7, "The Return of the Prodigal." On Hartley, Maine, and the marketing of each, see Donna M. Cassidy, pt. I, "Painting and Marketing Region," in *Marsden Hartley: Race, Region, and Nation* (Lebanon, NH: University Press of New England, 2005), 15–96, also 161–65 for more on the Katahdin paintings.

41. The determination of *Blue Landscape*'s support was made by conservator Alexander Katlan; see correspondence in the painting's curatorial file, Princeton University Art Museum. For Masonite and other MDFs (medium-density fiberboards), see Columbia Forest Products, "The History of MDF: Where It Came From and How It's Made," July 8, 2019, https://www.columbiaforestproducts.com/2019/07/08/history-mdf-came-made/; and, contemporary to Hartley's painting, Hans Rhiger, "The Fiber Board Industry" (bachelor of science thesis, Oregon State Agricultural College, 1937), https://ir.library.oregonstate.edu/downloads/6395wd20g?locale=en.

42. See Norman E. Muller, "Marsden Hartley, *Blue Landscape*," conservation report in the painting's curatorial file, Princeton University Art Museum. On lead white's use among artists and its environmental implications, see Igoe, "Creative Matter," 153–57. For zinc white, see Michael Douma, "Pigments through the Ages," s.v. "History of Zinc white," 2008, http://www.webexhibits.org/pigments/indiv/history/zincwhite.html.

43. On Maria Martinez and Julian Martinez, see Kenneth M. Chapman, *The Pottery of San Ildefonso Pueblo* (Albuquerque: University of New Mexico Press, 1970), esp. 29–35; Alice Marriott, *María: The Potter of San Ildefonso* (Norman: University of Oklahoma Press, 1948); and Arizona State University Art Museum, "Maria Poveka Martinez (1887–1980)," September 2007, https://asuartmuseum.asu.edu/sites/default/files/martinez_maria_biography.pdf.

44. Maria quoted at 1:16–1:27 and 8:06–8:19, Popovi Da quoted at 2:14–2:28, in National Park Service, "Indian Pottery of San Ildefonso: Potters Maria Martinez, Popovi Da," VHS, 1972, https://www.youtube.com/watch?v=SkUGm87DEok&t=1s.

45. "Intimations of Immortality," as it is now commonly abbreviated, is the concluding work of *Poems in Two Volumes* (London: Longman Hurst, Rees, Orme & Brown, 1815), 2: 347–55.

46. See Mark Keay, *William Wordsworth's Golden Age: Theories during the Industrial Revolution in England, 1750–1850* (1996; repr., New York: Palgrave, 2001). For Cole's early exposure to industrialization and its effects, see Tim Barringer, "Thomas Cole's Atlantic Crossings," in Kornhauser and Barringer, *Thomas Cole's Journey*, 19–61.

47. On Church, Bierstadt, and the unanticipated effects of their magisterial canvases, see Kusserow, "Trouble with Empire," esp. 117–30. For a sympathetic, in-depth reading of Church's paintings, see Jennifer Raab, *Frederic Church: The Art and Science of Detail* (New Haven, CT: Yale University Press, 2015).

48. For an influential exploration of the implications of attending just to the awesome in nature, and removing the human from it, see William Cronon, "The Trouble with Wilderness; or, Getting Back to the Wrong Nature," in *Uncommon Ground: Rethinking the Human Place in Nature*, ed. William Cronon (New York: W. W. Norton, 1995), 69–90. Cronon writes, "By teaching us to fetishize sublime places and wild open country, these peculiarly American ways of thinking about wilderness encourage us to adopt too high a standard for what counts as 'natural,'" and "Any way of looking at nature that encourages us to believe we are separate from nature . . . is likely to reinforce environmentally irresponsible behavior" (86–87).

49. Ralph Waldo Emerson, *Nature* (1836), reprinted in *Ralph Waldo Emerson: Essays and Lectures*, ed. Joel Porte (New York: Library of America, 1983), 10. Although art historian John I. H. Baur coined the term "Luminism" in a 1954 article, Barbara Novak was its first major theorizer; see Baur, "American Luminism: A Neglected Aspect of the Realist Movement in Nineteenth-Century American Painting," *Perspectives USA* 9 (Autumn 1954): 90–98; Novak, *Nature and Culture: American Landscape and Painting, 1825–1875* (New York: Oxford University Press, 1980); also her *American Painting of the Nineteenth Century: Realism, Idealism, and the American Experience* (New York: Oxford University Press, 1980), and *Voyages of the Self: Pairs, Parallels and Patterns in American Art and Literature* (New York: Oxford University Press, 2009); see as well John Wilmerding et al., *American Light: The Luminist Movement, 1850–1875; Paintings, Drawings, Photographs* (Washington, DC: National Gallery of Art, 1980). On Luminism and transcendentalism, particularly, see Herbert R. Hartel Jr., "Luminism, Transcendentalism, and Abstraction in the Landscape Paintings of John F. Kensett," *Source: Notes in the History of Art* 21, no. 4 (Summer 2002): 3–10; for an alternative reading situating the Luminist aesthetic outside that philosophical movement, see Miller, *Empire of the Eye*, 243–88. More recently, the validity and implications of the belated construct of Luminism itself have been questioned; see J. Gray Sweeney, "Inventing Luminism: 'Labels Are the Dickens,'" *Oxford Art Journal* 26, no. 2 (2003): 93–120; and Alan Wallach, "Rethinking 'Luminism': Taste, Class, and Aestheticizing Tendencies in Mid-Nineteenth-Century American Landscape Painting," in *The Cultured Canvas: New Perspectives on American Landscape Painting*,

ed. Nancy Siegel (Durham: University of New Hampshire Press, 2011), 115–47.

50. Clarence Cook, "Letters on Art—No. IV," *The Independent*, September 7, 1854. This discussion draws on the broader assessment of Luminism in ecological terms in Kusserow, "Trouble with Empire," 130–35. On Lane, see John Wilmerding, *Fitz Hugh Lane* (New York: Praeger, 1971), and *Paintings by Fitz Hugh Lane* (New York: Abrams, 1988); also see James A. Craig, *Fitz H. Lane: An Artist's Voyage through Nineteenth-Century America* (Charleston, SC: History Press, 2006). For Lane's connections to Emerson, Unitarianism, and transcendentalism, see Craig, *Fitz H. Lane*, 115–21; and Mary Foley, "Fitz Hugh Lane, Ralph Waldo Emerson, and the Gloucester Lyceum," *American Art Journal* 27, no. 1/2 (1995/1996): 99–101. (Lane's middle name, formerly given as Hugh, is now understood to be Henry.) Perhaps part of the Luminist aesthetic derives from the predilection of its adherents for portrayals of the watery, flat Eastern Seaboard. But a number of its major practitioners (Sanford R. Gifford, John F. Kensett, and Worthington Whittredge) traveled and painted extensively in the more spectacular environments of the West—just as Bierstadt painted in the East; these artists' differing representation of their sometimes similar subjects suggests a divergence of approach rooted in more than geography.

51. Inness's choice of subject in *Home of the Heron* was perhaps prompted by ecological concerns. The rapacious use of bird feathers in the millinery trade caused widespread alarm at the time, and herons in particular were cast as vulnerable symbols of heedless, encroaching humans by writers including the poet Celia Thaxter ("The Great Blue Heron: A Warning," 1873) and novelist Sarah Orne Jewett ("The White Heron," 1886); see Leo G. Mazow, "George Inness, Softness, and the Vapor Barrier," in *Like Breath on Glass: Whistler, Inness, and the Art of Painting Softly*, ed. Marc Simpson (New Haven, CT: Yale University Press, 2008), 64–68; Jennifer Price, *Flight Maps: Adventures with Nature in Modern America* (New York: Basic Books, 1999); and Emily Gephart and Michael Rossi, "How to Wear the Feather: Bird Hats and Ecocritical Aesthetics," in Coughlin and Gephart, *Ecocriticism and the Anthropocene*, 192–207. On Inness and environmentalism, see Devin P. Zuber, *A Language of Things: Emanuel Swedenborg and the American Environmental Imagination* (Charlottesville: University of Virginia, 2020), esp. chap. 5, "Homes for Herons: The Eco-Aesthetics of Sarah Orne Jewett and George Inness." For Inness more generally, see Rachael Ziady DeLue, *George Inness and the Science of Landscape* (Chicago: University of Chicago Press, 2004); Adrienne Baxter Bell, *George Inness and the Visionary Landscape* (New York: Braziller, 2003); and the artist's catalogue raisonné, Michael Quick, *George Inness: A Catalogue Raisonné*, 2 vols. (New Brunswick, NJ: Rutgers University Press, 2007), in which *Home of the Heron* appears in vol. 2, cat. no. 1029.

52. The interpretation of Fairfield Porter's statement is Rebecca Solnit's; see Solnit, "'Every Corner Is Alive': Eliot Porter as an Environmentalist and Artist," in Braddock and Irmscher, *A Keener Perception*, 225. Also see Alan C. Braddock, "Vital Forms: Modernist Biocentrism," in Kusserow and Braddock, *Nature's Nation*, 322–55, esp. 34–53.

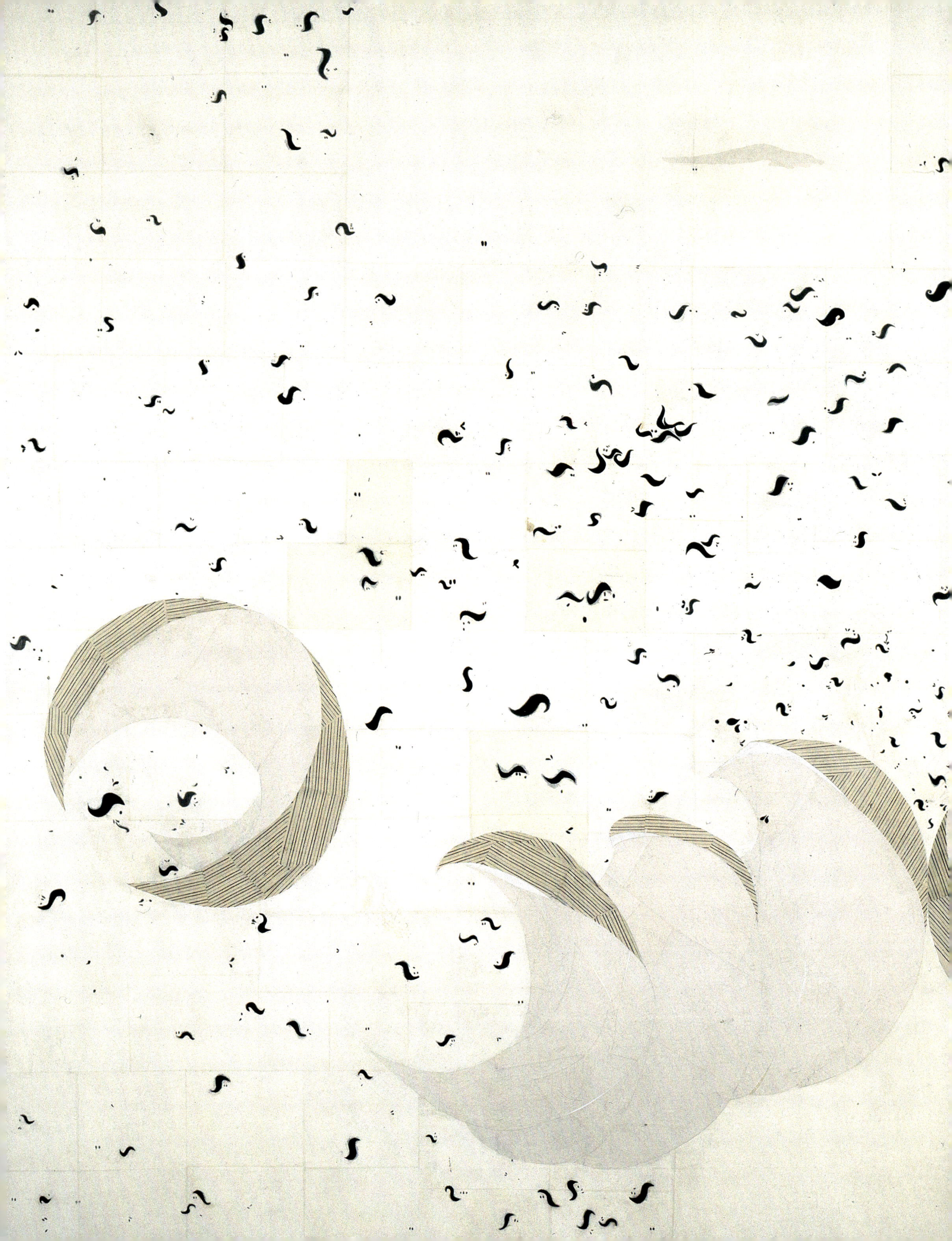

Rebecca Zorach

Material Echoes, Traumatic Histories, and Liquid Transformations: The Romance of the Sea in American Art

If you have spent much time in collections of nineteenth-century American art, undoubtedly you have seen maritime paintings: some that emphasize dramatic weather, the tumult of sea and sky; others that focus on human interest, documenting specific historical events or imagined narratives. Often all but unnoticed in out-of-the-way rooms and narrow corridors are countless paintings that fall into the category of the "ship portrait," a genre that comes close to anthropomorphizing its subjects, identifying vessels by name and type, codifying masts, sails, and rigging. It is hard to find a present-day analogy for what it would have meant in the nineteenth century to own one or more of these portraits—perhaps we could liken it to having a picture of one's car, or even someone else's car, as a personal banner image on a social media site.

The genre developed over the course of the early modern period in Europe, in tandem with European colonialism, so it is no surprise ship portraits were particularly abundant in the Netherlands and England. To modern tastes they may seem stodgy and repetitive. Nonetheless, this genre is a crucial element within a full account of American art, which must contend with the central importance of the sea to both visual culture

Detail, figure 11

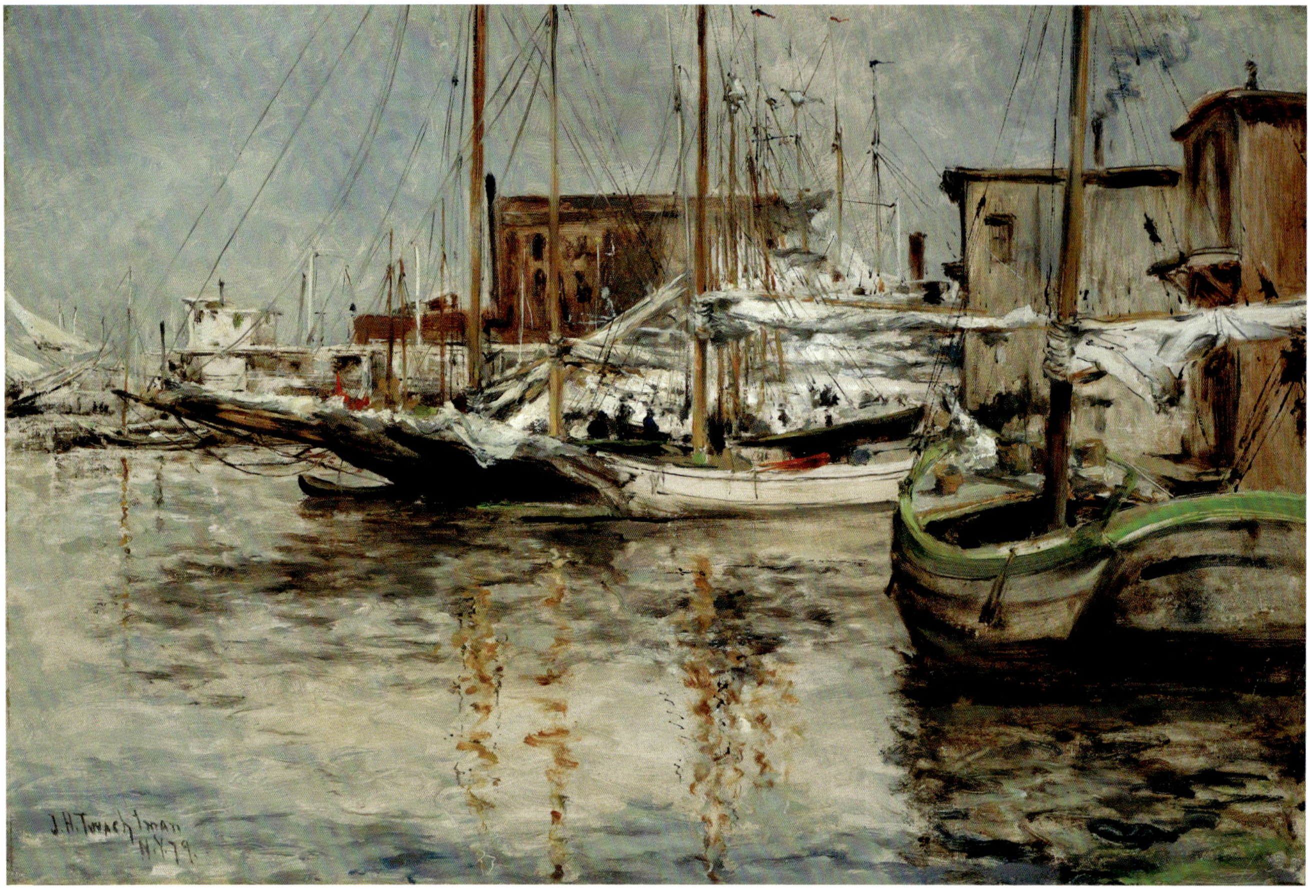

FIGURE 1 John Henry Twachtman (1853–1902; born Cincinnati, OH; died Gloucester, MA), *Oyster Boats, North River*, 1879. Oil on canvas, 41.9 × 61 cm. Princeton University Art Museum. Bequest of Gilbert S. McClintock, Class of 1908 (y1959-69)

and mythmaking. In the early years of the United States, images of ships reinforced the symbolic importance of ocean-based commerce and travel to the nascent republic. Developed around a core of British maritime colonies, with settler and enslaved populations brought—in their very different ways—by the sea, the new nation called the United States of America had already spent decades building its identity around marine activities by the mid-nineteenth century. While maritime painting sometimes depicted the violence of nature, it largely failed to document the relationship of ships and the sea to the human acts of violence that were central to the formation of the new republic: in particular, the violence committed against Indigenous people of the Americas and of Africa. Visual representation has been slow to depict these traumas directly. But if we consider the materiality of ships and their depictions, we might notice more challenging aspects of American history rippling through the surface. We need to look, therefore, at what is obscured in maritime painting and not only what is depicted.

As we might expect, many artworks in *Object Lessons* remind us of the fascination the sea and its shore have held for American painters. In his *Oyster Boats, North River* (fig. 1) of 1879, John Henry Twachtman heaps up a working waterfront as a glorious mess of materiality with broad brushstrokes and a color palette that itself invokes an oyster shell. In this way he also demonstrated his knowledge of the latest European painting styles, just five years after Claude Monet gave a name to the Impressionist movement with *Impression, Sunrise*—itself a port scene. The American modernist painter Arthur Dove found essential lines in the sun and sea; his puffy, colorful abstractions of houses and hills, the golden sun and sky, give a buoyant view eastward across

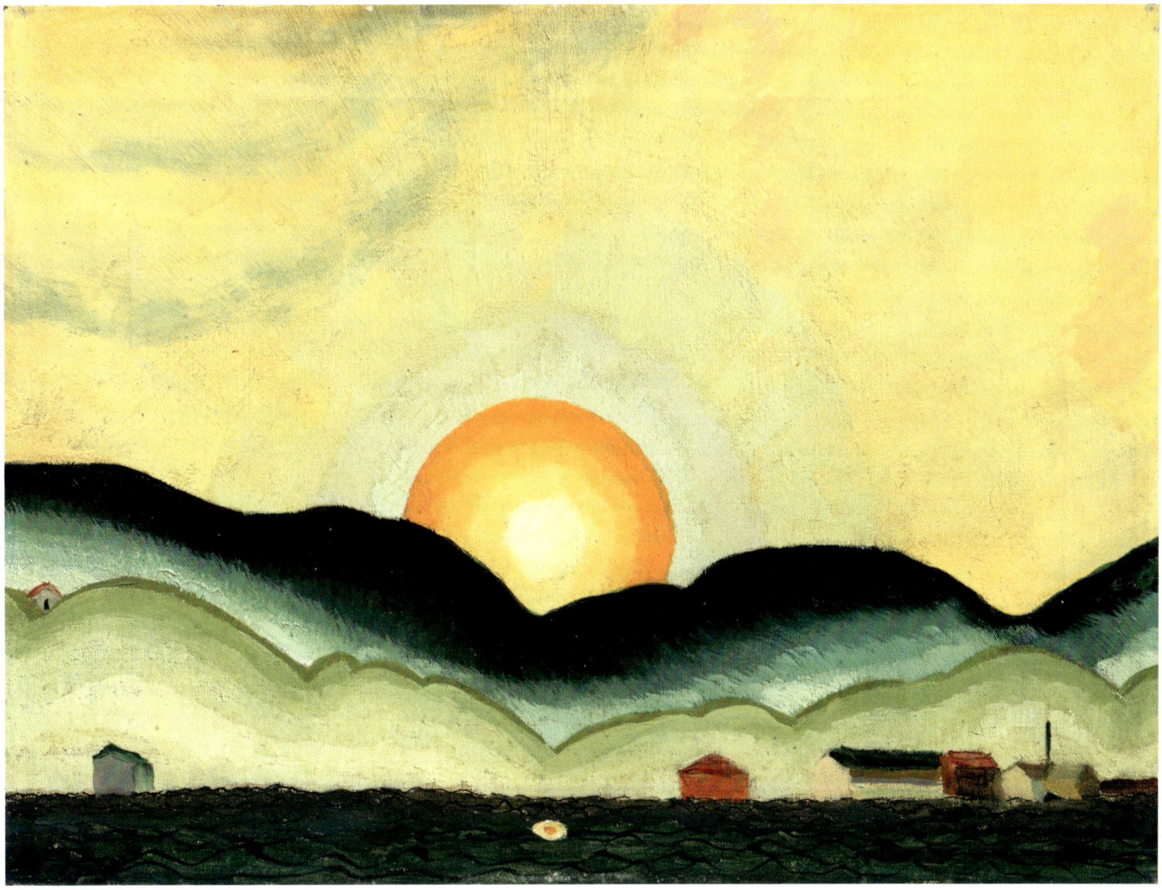

FIGURE 2 Arthur Garfield Dove (1880–1946; born Canandaigua, NY; died Huntington, NY), *Sunrise, Northport Harbor*, 1929. Oil on canvas, 38 × 51 cm. Princeton University Art Museum. Gift of John S. McGovern, Class of 1926 (y1962-44)

a bay on Long Island in *Sunrise, Northport Harbor* (fig. 2). And Milton Avery's *Red Umbrella* (fig. 3) pares a beach view down to strips of color with casual squiggles for waves. While the beach umbrella punctuates the sand and sea with its deep red, the two human figures, like an afterthought, appear almost impossibly small and insignificant.

In these works, the seascape might appear as a mere pretext for the forms and colors that hold the painter's interest—it could be that, for the modern painter, another subject could readily substitute for the sea. In earlier decades, the depiction of ships and sea had other roles to play. In this essay, I follow some of the threads of what is not visible in maritime painting as well as what is, thinking about the artworks and their subject matter in their materiality as well as their meaning. I look to two works in particular—James Buttersworth's *Clipper Ship "Staghound"* of 1851 and Fitz Henry Lane's *Ship in Fog, Gloucester Harbor* of about 1860—as instances of the ship portrait genre. As we have seen, the sea as subject matter continued in a more general sense into the twentieth—and indeed twenty-first—century. The continuing centrality of the sea might also reflect affinities between the materiality of the sea and seafaring and the medium of painting itself, even beyond the basic fact that artistic media often depend on the solidification of materials that must exist in a liquid state in order to be used. But other works complicate the view we receive from the traditional maritime works. Works by Indigenous artists and Black artists in particular can offer counterpoints and resistant narratives that reframe how we understand the romance—and the trauma—of the sea.

Buttersworth's painting of the *Stag Hound* (fig. 4) provides an example of a traditional ship portrait by a practiced ship painter. This general composition is reproduced—with variations—in numerous Currier & Ives prints.[1] Details allow us to identify not just the ship but the specific moment Buttersworth depicts. It is 1851, and the *Stag Hound* is arriving in New York, the residence of its new owner, before setting off on its voyage half-way around the globe. The ship is riding high in the water because it has not yet taken on its cargo bound for San Francisco, its first major stop. It is meeting up with the approaching pilot boat, a small schooner with a "#3" on its sail. In 1851, the official New York harbor pilot boat numbered "3" was also named the *New York*, a clever device the painter found to identify the location. The boat is delivering a local pilot who knows all the peculiarities of this harbor, who will come aboard and steer the ship safely in to dock.[2]

These details would have been more legible to viewers in 1851 than they are to us. As we do the historical work of identifying them, we must remember that what we are seeing is not a documentary image that neutrally and straightforwardly presents a real 1851 view. Perhaps it is too obvious to state, but it would be impossible to produce such precise documentation of sails and rigging of a ship in motion through choppy waves, or even if it were moving at a serene pace through calm seas. The composition was a standard one, basic to the genre. The careful attention to detail probably came about by studying plans, perhaps observing the ship in the harbor. It is a constructed image—meaning that, like most images, it is susceptible to ideology. The admiring portrait of the vessel encodes values—those of its commercial function and its context—and amnesias, as well.

Buttersworth gives us a tranquil vision of the *Stag Hound*, one that gives little evidence of the lashing wind and waves ahead. It appears as a stolid, crafted object, something it shares with the painting that proudly portrayed it. Although we do not often think of them together in this way, ships and paintings in the nineteenth century were constructed from many of the same materials, whose resonances hint at broader ecologies. Wood, for a start. Paintings' stretcher bars or

FIGURE 3 Milton Avery (1885–1965; born Altmar, NY; died New York, NY), *Red Umbrella*, 1945. Oil on canvas, 63.5 × 106.7 cm. Princeton University Art Museum. Gift of Annalee Newman (1995-333)

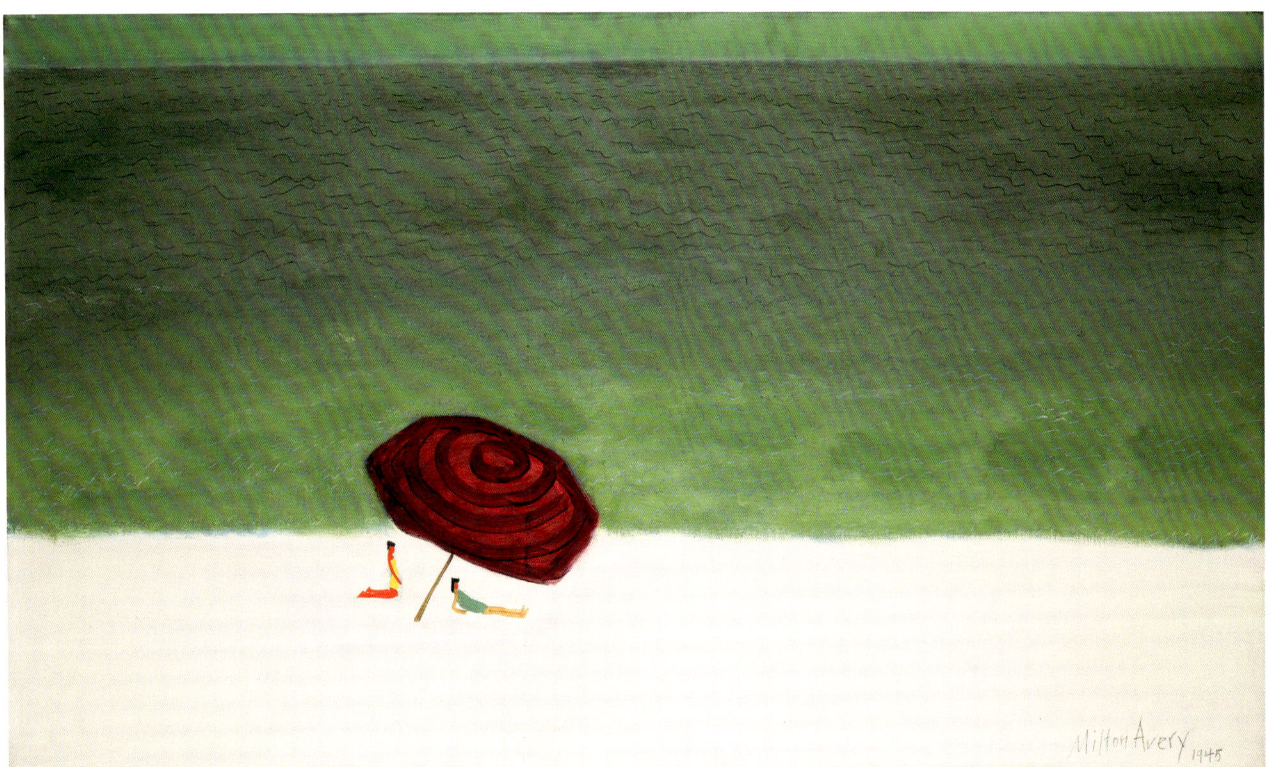

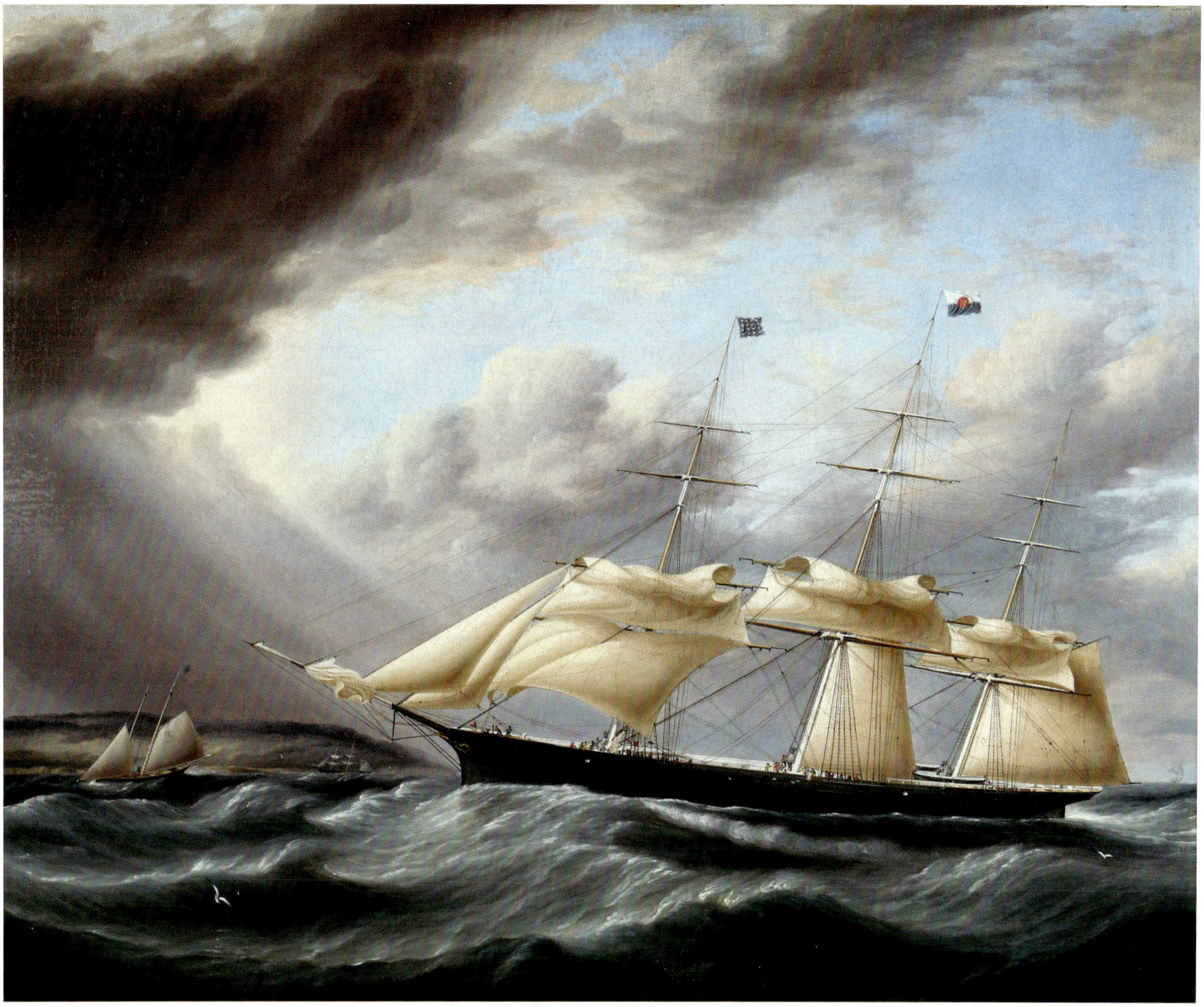

FIGURE 4 James Edward Buttersworth (1817–1894; born Isle of Wight, VA; died Hoboken, NJ), *Clipper Ship "Staghound,"* ca. 1851. Oil on canvas mounted on pressed wood panel, 73.4 × 91.3 cm. Princeton University Art Museum. Gift of Winthrop Page Hersey, Class of 1928, and Audrey Musser Hersey (y1991-67)

wooden panel supports echo the wooden architecture of ships. Trees also supplied other key ingredients. When Henry David Thoreau bemoaned the deforestation of his native village of Concord—caused in no small part by shipbuilding—he noted that "we no longer produce tar and turpentine."[3] Tar and turpentine both derived from pine resin, which, until the twentieth century, was harvested using a method that did not kill the tree but only wounded it, causing the tree to produce resin to heal the cut area. Tar sealed the hulls of boats, and turpentine was used as a solvent for paint that covered them, providing an additional protective layer. (When the deforested northern states could no longer keep up with the demand for these "naval stores," production moved south, where enslaved African workers harvested the resin; this is how the state of North Carolina got its "tar heel" nickname.) Ships were also painted for seaworthiness, using linseed oil pressed from the seeds of the flax plant as the medium with which pigments were mixed. Linseed oil and turpentine were also at the base of the fine art painter's craft. Heavy linen or cotton cloth served as painter's canvas and ship's sails alike.

With his *Stag Hound* portrait, the painter fixes a moment, stills the waves and the sails for an instant, quiets the sounds of the elements and of human activity. He domesticates the ship and the weather, for they also harbored dangers. We could certainly think of a painting like Buttersworth's as a pleasing portrait of a beautiful vessel, a complaisant air of English aristocracy hanging about its name. But what strands of the growing economic power of the new nation are braided into the story of this ship? The *Stag Hound* was what is known as an "extreme clipper," a type of ship built to circle the globe with unprecedented swiftness. After gold was discovered at Sutter's Mill in 1848, extreme clippers brought commodities and travelers from the East Coast to fuel the California gold rush. Built by Donald McKay of Boston, the *Stag Hound*, at 215 feet and 1,535 tons, was the largest merchant ship in the world when it launched in 1851. On its first voyage, the ship traveled from Boston to San Francisco, around Cape Horn—the tip of South America—in what seemed at the time an impossible one hundred twelve days, a pace that would, however, soon be exceeded by other extreme clippers. The crew members necessarily had no experience handling a ship at this scale, with sails that could catch so much wind, and on the first voyage the main topmast and all the topgallant masts—at the top of the ship—broke off. In this portrait Buttersworth represents the ship's sails lowered, clearly displaying the very masts that failed on the ship's first voyage. Despite such mishaps, the Cape Horn route was fast and safe compared to the illnesses and delays that plagued would-be miners toiling along the overland routes. Too expensive for most travelers, shipping by clipper was, however, an attractive solution for delivering supplies.

Journeying onward from San Francisco, the *Stag Hound* and other clippers also plied what was known as the "China trade," a vigorous trade in commodities and travelers between the United States and ports in China and elsewhere in Asia. The very form of the ship—the curve of the bow that helped make it so fast—likely derived from an Asian model.[4] So it is no surprise that after unloading in San Francisco, the *Stag Hound* continued on to Guangdong for a shipment of tea. American consumers desired tea, porcelain, and other commodities from China, while merchants saw China as a source of the hard currency needed to lubricate trade. Merchants traveled to China with ginseng, furs, and—though I have found no evidence the *Stag Hound* carried it—opium. Traders gained access to ginseng from Cherokee foresters in Appalachia. They maintained an exclusive trade in Turkish opium that allowed them to supply the drug to China. And they acquired furs, especially sea otter pelts, from Indigenous hunters of the Pacific Northwest, who may have hunted for them in a boat like the one represented (in walrus ivory) in the exhibition's Iñupiaq umiak (fig. 5). Clipper ships also brought Chinese workers back and forth across the Pacific to work in American gold mines and railroads.[5] The *Stag Hound*, unscathed and jaunty in Buttersworth's rendering, would in its career be no stranger to controversy and conflict. In 1855, members of the ship's crew were prosecuted by American authorities for piracy against Chinese boats.[6] In 1860, the crew mutinied; the ship's captain had not put down a rebellion of four hundred Chinese laborers with enough vigor. The captain had brought the laborers on board under false pretenses, essentially as captives, as was often the case for Chinese men shipped to jobs in American industry.[7]

A small detail of this ship's story hints at another entanglement of economy and ecology. Before arriving in New York, the *Stag Hound* was launched in East Boston to great fanfare; a crowd of fifteen thousand people watched. It was so cold outside that the tallow intended to grease the launch froze, and boiling whale oil had to be poured on the slipway.[8] This story reminds us, too, of how central whaling was to the US economy. One of the biggest maritime industries, supplying oil for soap, machine lubrication, and above all illumination, it literally greased the machinery of emerging American capitalism. It was a global industry: as Jimmy Packham has put it, "America got to know the world . . . through its whaling fleet."[9] In Herman Melville's classic novel *Moby-Dick*, published in the same year the *Stag Hound* was launched, a kind of alchemy operates the liquid transformation of whale oil into gold and—as investment in further shipping ventures—back again. In the novel capitalism serves as a thin veneer of rationality and calculation over wild mania. Investors' desire for profit is only the excuse by which the captain prosecutes his mad pursuit of vengeance against the great white whale. Race and sexuality are at the heart of the story, with the whale's whiteness playing a central role. Whiteness as represented in *Moby-Dick*, epitomized in a haunting, reflective chapter, "The Whiteness of the Whale," oscillates between its cachet as the glorious, shining hue of art and monuments, of European cultural supremacy, and its horrific pallor as a ghostly absence of color.[10]

A few years later, there is no visible trace of such drama in Fitz Henry Lane's *Ship in Fog, Gloucester Harbor* (see p. 149, fig. 29). Painted in 1860, it seems to move us perceptibly in the direction of the modernist works with which I began. The scene is calm, quiet, and reflective, representing a medium-sized ship (a "half-brig") in the foreground, surrounded by quiet boats and misty landscape. The identity of the ship matters less than the

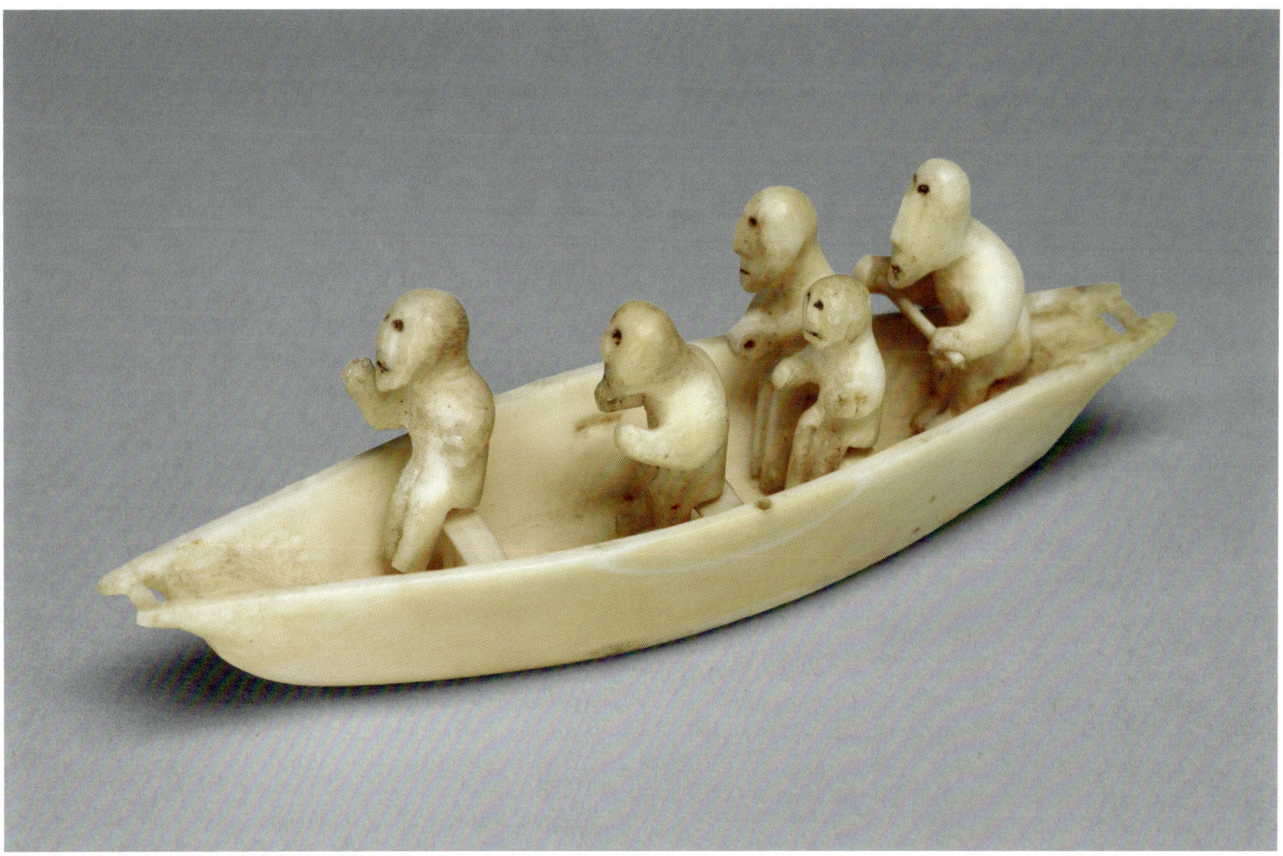

FIGURE 5 Iñupiaq, Umiak with men, after 1800. Walrus ivory, 3 × 9.5 × 1.9 cm. Princeton University Art Museum. The Lloyd E. Cotsen, Class of 1950, Eskimo Bone and Ivory Carving Collection (1997-274)

painter's light effects. Just as knowledgeable about sailing ships as Buttersworth, Lane treats the sails and rigging with muted precision, creating a scene and not primarily a portrait. The fog softens and lightly obscures the vista as glowing puffs of clouds surround the sun, with reflections dappling the gentle waves, the qualities that associate him with the Luminist school.

But what else does Lane soften here? Could the move away from portraying a specific ship be, itself, a kind of dodge? In the middle of the nineteenth century, Gloucester and its larger region of Cape Ann were the largest fishing port in the entire United States.[11] Gloucester's ships—and the town's prominent families—were in 1860 still deeply connected to the legacy of enslavement in the Americas. Not only were many Cape Ann sailing families clandestinely involved in the slave trade, but also quantities of fish caught in Gloucester fed enslaved workers on Dutch plantations in Suriname, traveling on ships like the *Cadet*, which Lane painted in the 1840s (Cape Ann Museum).[12] And then there was cotton—grown in the South and milled in the North—for sails and for canvas. Before the nineteenth century, flax was also commonly used for sail making. But the sails, rigging, and caulking cloth on the ships Lane depicted were just as likely to have been made of cotton. Imported linen sailcloth became scarce during periods of tension and open war with Great Britain. And in 1793, Eli Whitney created his first cotton gin, which facilitated the growth of the cotton industry, with which the new American economy, North as well as South, doubled down on the use of enslaved workers. Indeed, northern companies began to manufacture sailcloth using southern cotton in the first decade of the nineteenth century.[13]

The US Congress made American ships' participation in the transatlantic slave trade illegal as of 1808—not before the introduction of the cotton gin produced a major increase in the numbers of captive Africans trafficked into the American South. At the time of US independence, northern states set timelines for emancipation, but these stretched well into the nineteenth century, and their economic investments carried on their entanglement with slavery. Gloucester was no different. Cotton mills were established in Gloucester and surrounding towns in the 1840s. Another Lane painting, *Burning of the Packet Ship "Boston"* (1830, Cape Ann Museum), depicts a ship that succumbed in 1830 to a fire that spread rapidly through the cargo of cotton it had picked up in Charleston, South Carolina. The painting style suggests Lane may have seen Japanese prints. But how, in 1830? They would have been hard to come by in New England in the first half of the nineteenth century, because Japan was closed to most outsiders until 1853, when (through the efforts of Commodore Matthew Perry) the US government established direct diplomatic relations with the Tokugawa Shogunate. However, the Dutch did conduct trade with Japan. Japanese prints might have traveled through Suriname, where Gloucester ships sold fish to Dutch slave plantations.[14]

For the African captives torn from home and delivered to Suriname—or South Carolina, or Massachusetts—the voyage across the ocean was the hopeless, terrifying Middle Passage. It represented not only the potential violence contained within nature's elemental power, but also the actual violence carried out by human beings on human beings. Among nineteenth-century images of ships, few acknowledge slave ships and their human cargo. There are a few exceptions, such as the oft-reproduced image—a very different type of "ship portrait"—of the obscenely crowded hold of the British slave ship *Brookes* (fig. 6). The image, published in 1788 by the Plymouth chapter of the Society for Effecting the Abolition of the Slave Trade, circulated widely, becoming a visible rallying point for abolitionist activists.[15] Antislavery societies produced other types of images; perhaps more typical was the Sèvres porcelain antislavery medallion (fig. 7), which closely followed Josiah Wedgwood's English version in its presentation of a chained African figure derived from the seal of the Committee for the Abolition of the Slave Trade. This image focuses on the enslaved person as captive and supplicant. Contemporary images that squarely represent the horrific trauma of the Middle Passage itself are few and far between. Even the *Brookes* image, in ordered emphasis on the numerical obscenity, abstracts from the horror of the experience, its relationship to the ocean voyage, and the agency of the African captives.

The Middle Passage marked not only American history in a more general sense but also, in particular, the American maritime experience. Mindful of this history, African American artists have long created images that

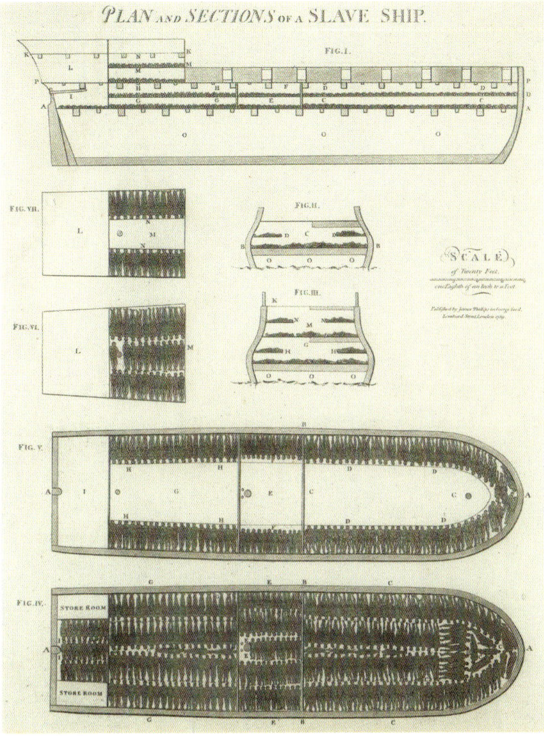

FIGURE 6 *Description of a Slave Ship* (detail), 1789. Printed by James Phillips, London. Broadside. Princeton University Library, Department of Special Collections. Rare Books Division

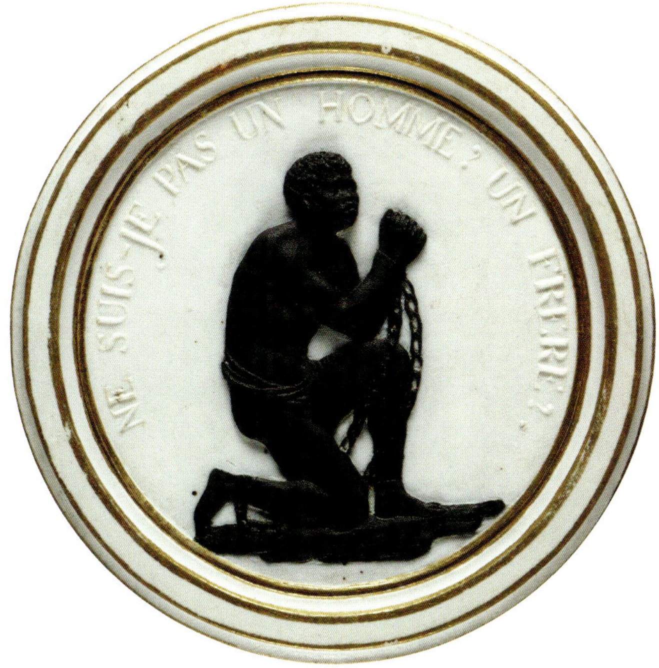

FIGURE 7 Sèvres Porcelain Manufactory (established 1756, France), Antislavery medallion, 1789. Porcelain, diam. 8.6 cm, th. 0.6 cm. Princeton University Art Museum. Trumbull-Prime Collection (y931)

suggest spiritual or surreal transcendence of the material traumas of the sea voyage. Several works in Princeton's collections give a sense of the diversity of these responses. Henry Ossawa Tanner's *The Disciples See Christ Walking on the Water* (fig. 8) of about 1907 depicts sailors in a storm becoming aware of the ghostly figure of Christ in the distance. In Tanner's hands, this biblical story of miraculous deliverance from a storm at sea gains resonance with historical trauma. The Harlem Renaissance painter Ellis Wilson returned repeatedly to scenes of the shore, and particularly of the work of fishing communities in the South and the Caribbean. He displays a sense of the ocean's bounty in his *Fisherwoman* (fig. 9). Viewed as a source of sustenance, the sea seems to hold potential to connect rather than tear asunder, even if in other works, such as his *Figure on Beach* (1947, Bates College Museum of Art), we see a more melancholic view of fishing labor, with an exhausted figure stretched out next to his day's catch and the skeletal hull of a wrecked boat in the background near the water.

Margaret Burroughs's *Black Venus* (fig. 10) presents a commanding figure riding a shell chariot harnessed to a pair of fish. Burroughs reworks the European iconography of the goddess Venus, born—according to legend—of the seafoam created by the severed testicles of the sky god Saturn. Risham Majeed has recently pointed out that the fish drawing Venus's chariot are African mudfish, an important symbol of amphibious power and prosperity in the visual arts of Benin. Burroughs's work thus explicitly and creatively hybridizes African and European iconographies.[16]

Burroughs made this daring print in 1957 soon after returning to Chicago from Mexico, where she studied printmaking at the Taller de Gráfica Popular while on sabbatical from her teaching job at the height of McCarthyism. Her Venus is a triumphant figure of Black love riding above the waves. Ellen Gallagher's

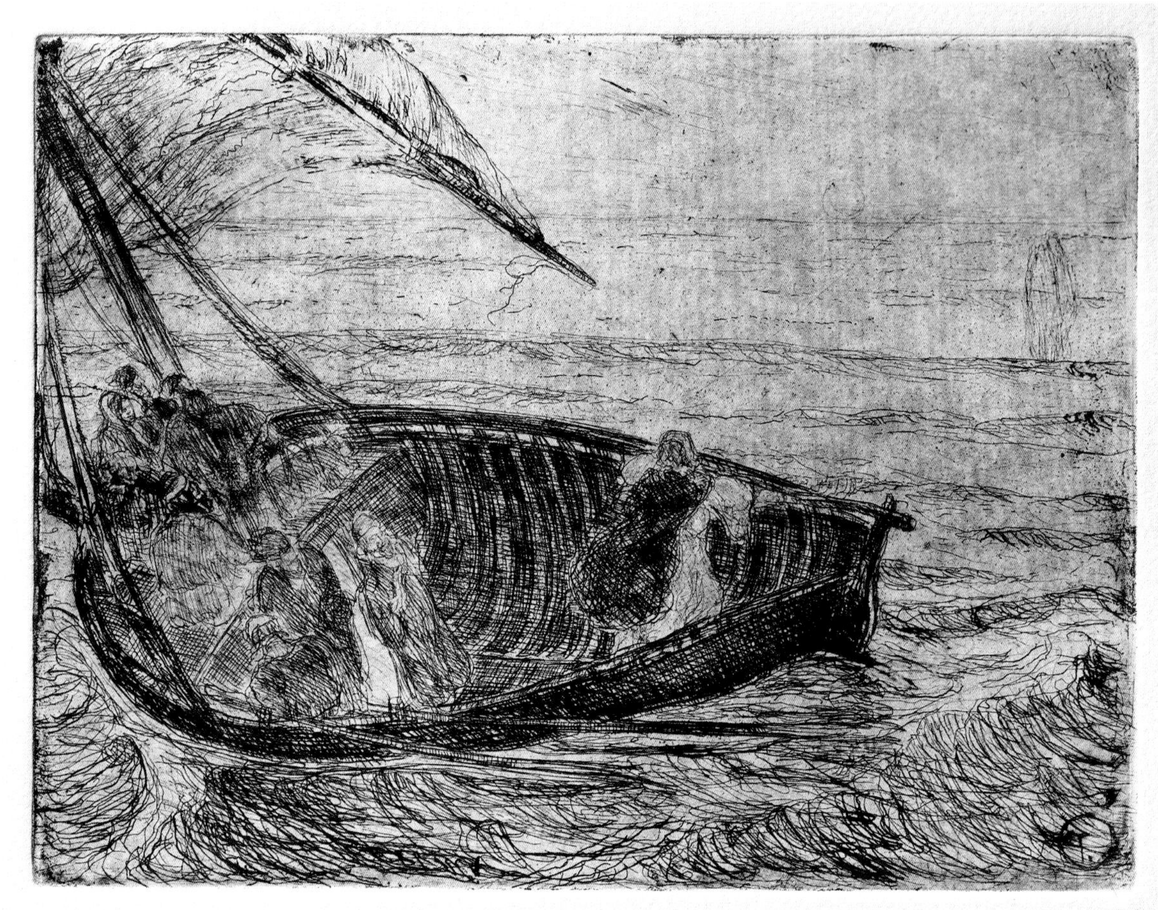

FIGURE 8 Henry Ossawa Tanner (1859–1937; born Pittsburgh, PA; died Paris, France), *The Disciples See Christ Walking on the Water*, ca. 1907. Etching, 18.5 × 24.3 cm. Princeton University Art Museum. Museum purchase, Kathleen Compton Sherrerd Fund for Acquisitions in American Art (2003-30)

FIGURE 9 Ellis Wilson (1900–1977; born Mayfield, KY; died New York, NY), *Fisherwoman*, 1946–48. Oil on Masonite board, 101.6 × 76.2 cm. Princeton University Art Museum. Museum purchase, Hugh Leander Adams, Mary Trumbull Adams, and Hugh Trumbull Adams Princeton Art Fund (2021-177)

subtle, suggestively rich *Blubber* (fig. 11) directly links the Middle Passage with whaling. Blubber refers to the fatty portion of the whale's body from which oil was extracted. Gallagher's technique of carving into her thick watercolor paper is inspired by the nineteenth-century mariners' pastime of scrimshaw, in which they carved designs into whale and walrus ivory. On closer inspection, the almost decorative black dots, drips, and tendrils scattered across the paper's surface represent tiny abstractions of caricatured Black faces—reflecting racist imagery but also suggestive of the elaborate aqua-utopian mythology that Gallagher draws on in her work. The Drexciya—a mythos created by the Detroit house band of the same time—are the survivors of captive African women and children thrown overboard during the Middle Passage.[17] With her soothing, muted palette, Gallagher asks viewers to sit with trauma, death, and survival without offering any simple narrative of redemption.

In Melville's *Moby-Dick*, the harpooners are all Indigenous men of color from different parts of the globe, each one assigned to one of the white mates (first, second, and third), representing the contribution of Indigenous labor to these European and US ventures. The Iñupiaq umiak seen above represents a type of boat used for hunting sea mammals, including sea otters, walrus, and whales. As Evguenia Anichtchenko puts it in an

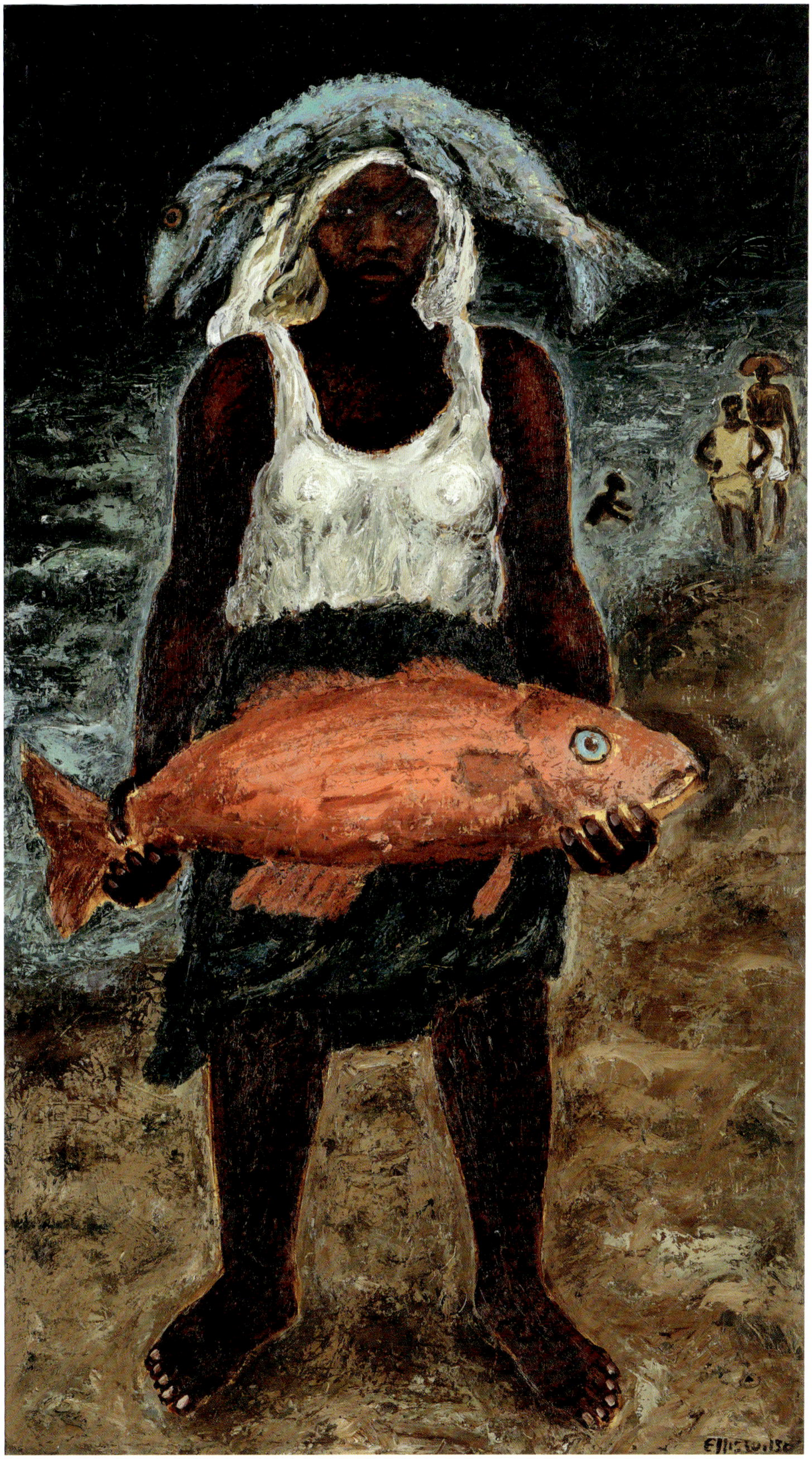

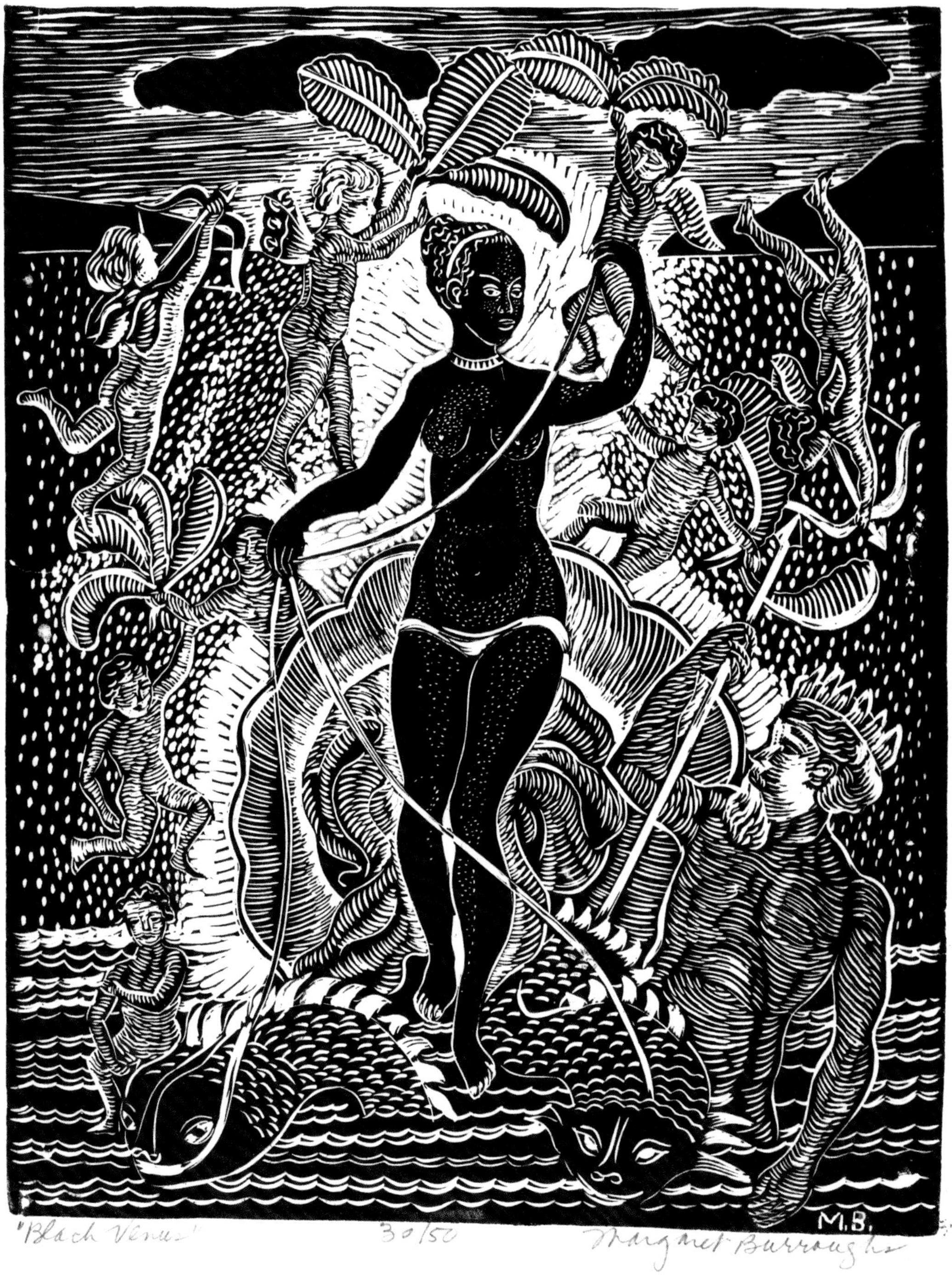

FIGURE 10 Margaret Taylor Burroughs (1915–2010; born Saint Rose, LA; died Chicago, IL), *Black Venus*, 1957. Linocut on white imitation Japanese paper, 35.6 × 28 cm. Princeton University Art Museum. Museum purchase, Felton Gibbons Fund (2009-28)

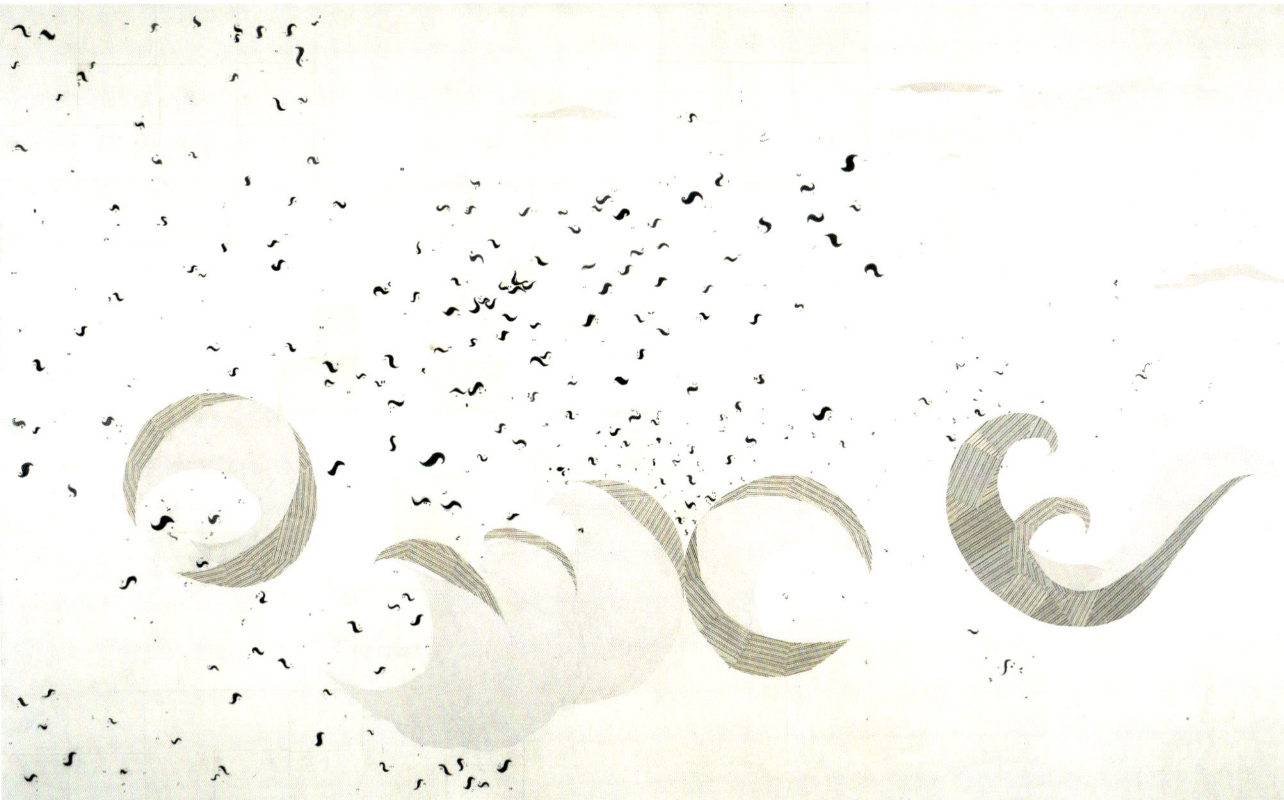

FIGURE 11 Ellen Gallagher (born 1965, Providence, RI; active Rotterdam, Netherlands, and New York, NY), *Blubber*, 2000. Ink, pencil, and paper on linen, 305 × 488 cm. Princeton University Art Museum. Museum purchase and gift of the Class of 1952 in honor of their 50th reunion: Bruce Atwater, Roger S. Berlind, William Polk Carey, George B. E. Hambleton, Craig Lewis, Anne and Constantine Sidamon-Eristoff, James E. Simpson, Gough W. Thompson Jr., Burton J. Weiss and Nan S. Weiss, and Lucius Wilmerding III (2002-294)

article on the umiak, "it is hard to find an item more symbolic of the very identity of Indigenous maritime cultures than boats."[18] The importance of whaling to the economy and spiritual life of Inuit people also manifests in whale-tail ornaments, which, as Feng Qu has noted, grew in popularity in the Punuk (pre-Inuit) period, reflecting increased emphasis on whaling.[19] Carved of walrus ivory, these objects speak of the sea in both their materials and their subject matter (fig. 12). It has been speculated that the whale-tail comb (fig. 13) could have functioned as a hairpiece for the wife of an Iñupiaq whaling captain. Although in many Inuit communities women accompanied men on hunting trips—a possibility suggested by the fact that one of the five figures in the umiak is smaller than the others—a captain's wife who stayed at home typically had to observe behavioral restrictions during a voyage. She took on the role of symbolically representing the whale and had to conduct herself in particular ways, slowing her movements, resting, and abstaining from bathing, in order to ensure a successful hunt.[20] Qu also notes the existence of many ivory figurines representing female hybrids of human and animal.[21] I suggest here that the comb might also reflect stories of Sedna, also known as Nuliajuk, an undersea spirit who sometimes retained sea creatures—the hunters' prey—in her tangled seaweed locks. According to the story, Sedna was once a human woman who, because she refused to marry, was thrown into the sea by her family. Her father cut off her fingers when she tried to return, and her fingers became the creatures of the sea. But because she had lost her hands, she could not run them through her hair, and shamans are sometimes required to comb it ceremonially to release the animals the human community needs for food.[22]

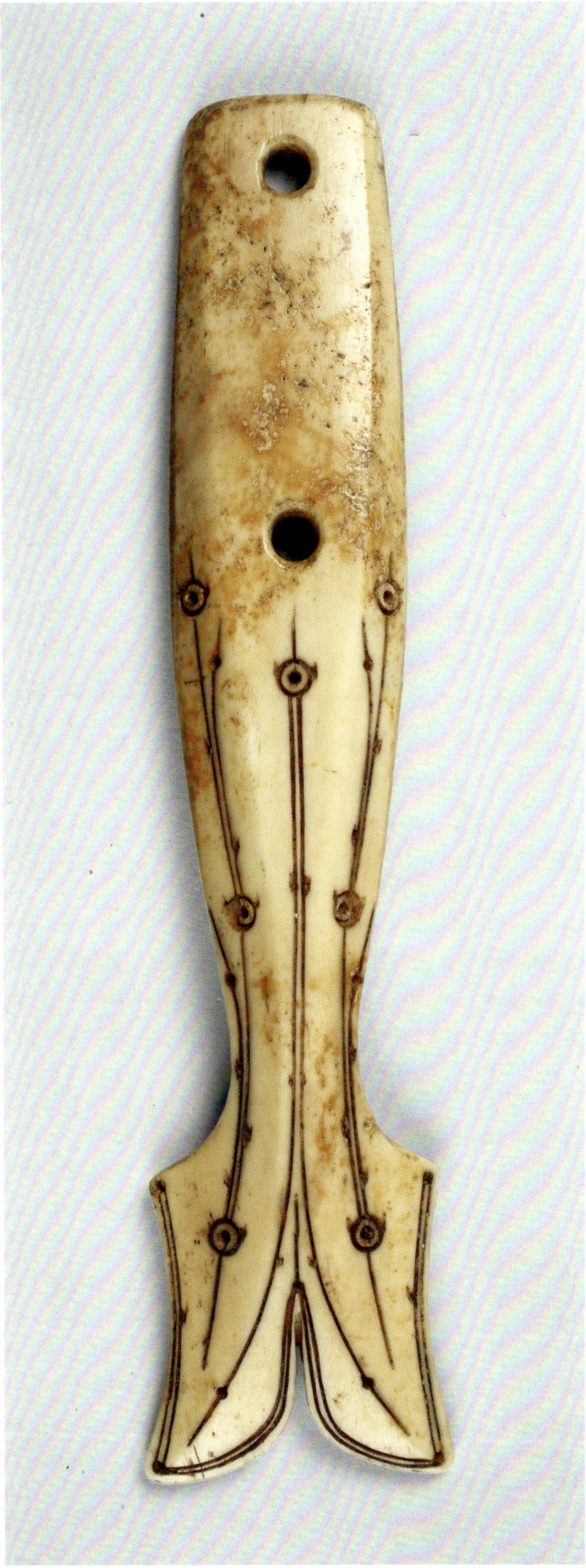

With *What have we become? Gold* (fig. 14), Nicholas Galanin, who is Tlingit and Unangax̂, stages an intervention—a gold-leaf face in profile—into the pages of Frederica de Laguna's work of anthropological scholarship, *Under Mount Saint Elias: The History and Culture of the Yakutat Tlingit* (1972). De Laguna drew on the work of George T. Emmons, whose own story begins around the time of Buttersworth's painting of the *Stag Hound*. Emmons served as a naval officer in Alaska, taking part in the colonial administration of the territory in the 1880s—it had been purchased from Russia by the United States in 1867—and throughout the territory's first gold rushes of the 1890s. The "salvage" ethnography of Emmons and others of his era involved mass dispossession of important Indigenous artifacts, taken from their communities for "safekeeping" in white-led museums. Galanin's work points to the ways in which ethnography and colonialism abet one another in transforming human beings and their relations into "gold" by commodifying knowledge and objects. The liquid mutability of gold serves as a figure for the transformations wrought by commodification.

On the one hand, the word "liquid" in my title alludes to the liquid materiality that bound objects like ships and paintings together, lubricated their movements, and made symbolic meaning and economic value possible. In liquid materialities the economic and the ecological come together—concepts that both harbor the Greek root *oikos*, or "household," even if the sea carries travelers far from home. On the other hand, liquid could also damage, wear away, and overwhelm. As an economic concept, "liquidity" refers to ease of monetary exchange, the ability to transmute one type of matter into another as commodity value—and also to dematerialize and dehumanize, to "liquidate." Water and oil, blood and gold, in their liquid transmutations, drag countless stories into their vortex; what might it mean to dive in to bring them back?

Natural and social ecologies enmesh the works I have surveyed here in complicating myths and histories

FIGURE 12 Punuk, Whale-tail ornament, 800–1200 CE. Walrus ivory, 16.6 × 3.9 × 0.1 cm. Princeton University Art Museum. The Lloyd E. Cotsen, Class of 1950, Eskimo Bone and Ivory Carving Collection (1997-207)

that often hide "beneath" the visible surface. Even if we try to imagine it outside the realm of politics and history, the sea is not simple. Both beauty and peril surge through the American romance with the sea. The shoreline has always proffered restorative encounters with nature—beaches give us the original "found objects," shells and sea urchins, odd stones, twisted driftwood. But elemental nature makes itself felt in both its creative and its destructive capacities. Alive to the startling effects of the sun across water, to the ways wind and water sculpt the shore in the tides' unmaking and remaking of rippled and scalloped patterns in the sand, artists have often noticed parallels with their own liquid materials, which dry and solidify into forms. But while nature can appear to be at peace in a ship painting or seascape, it is ever an uneasy truce where human ambitions are concerned. In 1839, Margaret Fuller, the wide-ranging journalist, author, and women's rights activist, wrote of the restorative effects of the shore to her friend, Elizabeth Hoar, who had fallen ill. "Take me, kind fairies," she writes, "carry me in my sleep to where the tall rock casts its grotesque shadow on the yellow sand. There let the plash of the waves and the fanning of the sea-breeze awake me. That breeze is healing and cheer, mild and earnest it cools my brow, it soothes my brain, and new strings every sense." Fuller advises her friend to observe nature's maternal proximity: "You would feel so too, I think. And there how happy you will be when first embraced by the very arms of nature, your ear and mind filled, needing no thought but of the solemn harmonies of sky and sea, you will feel as if the mighty Mother had always before kept you like a little child studying the hornbook at her knee and that never till now had you been near enough to feel the beating of her heart."[23] As she wrote about the healing power of the shore, Margaret Fuller could not know that she herself would perish in a shipwreck eleven years later.

In admiring the artworks before us we also need to see what isn't visibly presented—whether it's the stories that lie behind the works, or the economic systems and political ideologies that underpinned their making.

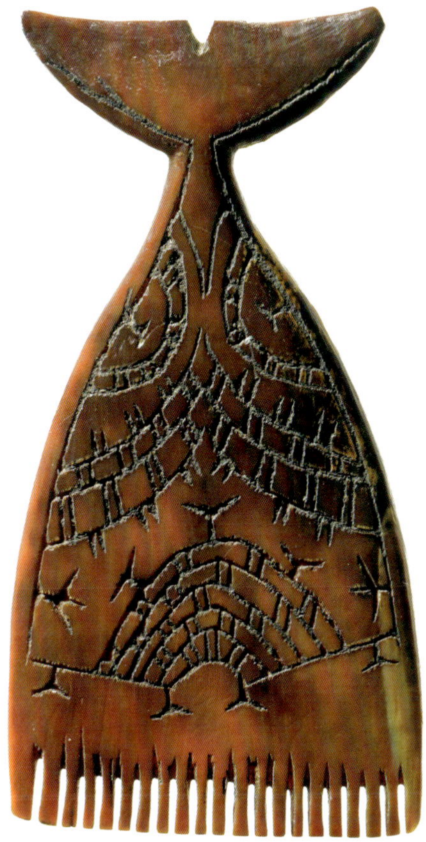

FIGURE 13 Punuk or Western Thule, Whale-tail comb, 800–1850 CE. Walrus ivory, 5.3 × 2.8 × 0.2 cm. Princeton University Art Museum. The Lloyd E. Cotsen, Class of 1950, Eskimo Bone and Ivory Carving Collection (1997-206)

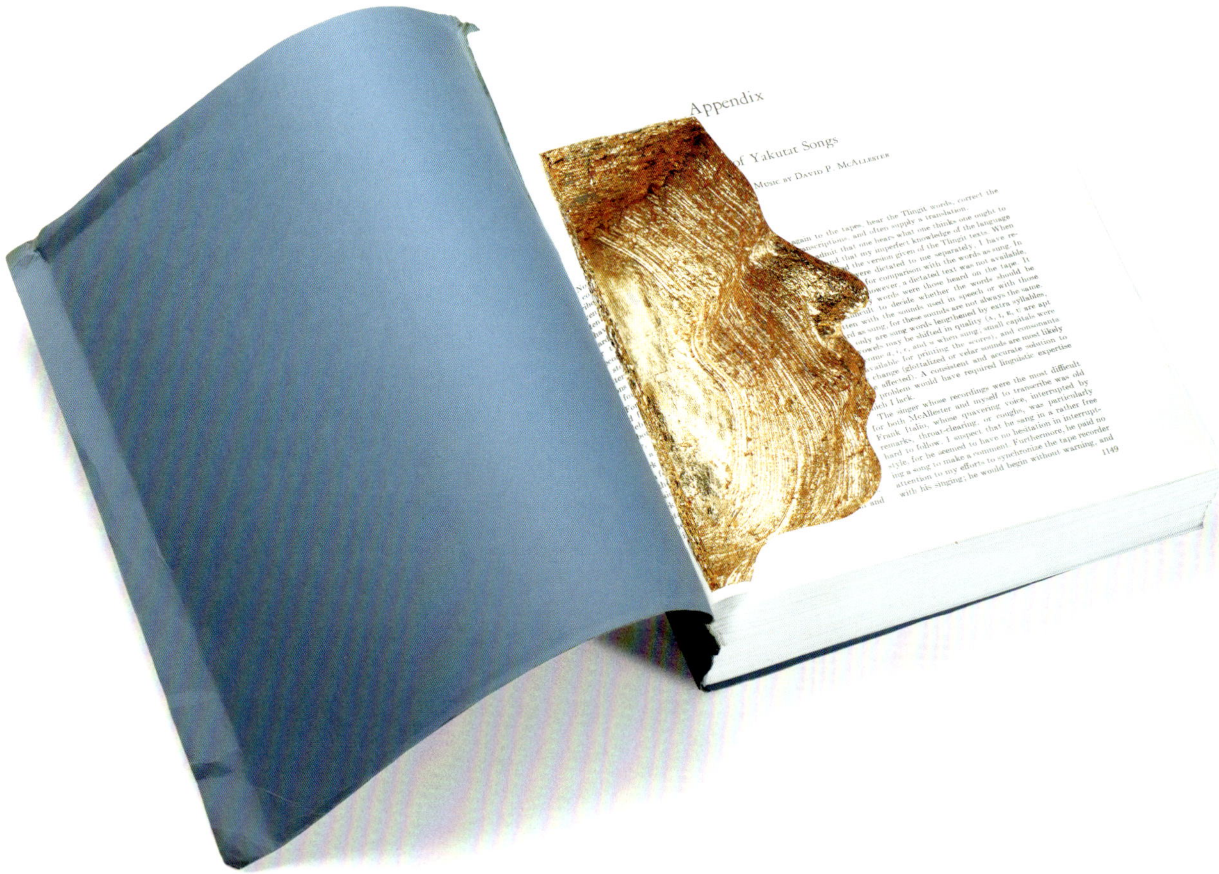

FIGURE 14 Nicholas Galanin (Tlingit/Unangax̂, born 1979, Sitka, AK; active Sitka), *What have we become? Gold*, 2018. Book with gold leaf, 29.4 × 23.6 × 6.5 cm. Princeton University Art Museum. Museum purchase, Fowler McCormick, Class of 1921, Fund (2019-24)

To look for what lies behind the visible surface is not to accuse, but to seek understanding that can help us make sense of the aftereffects of these histories today. To see what, as May Sarton put it in a poem about a different kind of painting that resists disclosure of its maritime undercurrents, "the . . . painter does not tell":

> *The wild skies overhead, dissolving, breaking,*
> *And how that broken light is never still,*
> *And how the roar of waves is always near,*
> *What bitter tumult, treacherous and cold,*
> *Attacks the solemn charm year after year.*[24]

NOTES

1. For more on Buttersworth and Currier & Ives, consult John Wilmerding, *American Marine Painting* (New York: Harry N. Abrams, 1987), 146.
2. "List of New York Pilot Boats," *New York Daily Herald*, January 22, 1840.
3. Henry David Thoreau, *Excursions* (Boston: Ticknor and Fields, 1863), 182–83. Originally published as "Walking," *Atlantic Monthly*, June 1962, 657–74.
4. For many insights and stimulating conversation on what is going on in Buttersworth's painting of the *Stag Hound*, I thank the members of the Facebook group Historic Ship Geek, and in particular Charlie Ipcar, who alerted me to the group and made other contributions to my inquiries. It has been argued that in creating the streamlined curve of the *Stag Hound*'s bow, McKay took inspiration from a Malaysian or Singaporean vessel, a sampan panjang, a model of which was brought from Asia around 1841 by a ship's captain, Robert B. Waterman. The half-hull model, known as the Singapore fast boat, is now in the MIT Museum, Cambridge, MA (CC-X-A2-100[04]). See Charles E. Park, "The Development of the Clipper Ship," *American Antiquarian Society* 39, part 1 (April 1929): 51; and Sydney Greenbie and Marjorie Latta

Barstow Greenbie, *Gold of Ophir; Or, The Lure that Made America* (Garden City, NY: Doubleday, Page, 1925), 228.

5. A news report in California's *Pioneer* magazine, for example, records that 120 Chinese people returned to China on the *Stag Hound* on August 25, 1854. "Monthly Summary of Events," *The Pioneer: Or, California Monthly Magazine* 2, issue 4 (October 1854), 234–238, 236.

6. Adelaide Rosalia Hasse, ed., *Index to United States Documents Relating to Foreign Affairs, 1828–1861*, Issue 185, Part 1 (Washington, DC: Carnegie Institution of Washington, 1914), 350.

7. "The Mutineers of the Stag-Hound; Arrival of the Clipper-Ship Hussar, having on Board the Mutineers and the Murderer of the Second Officer of the Stag-Hound," *New York Times*, December 31, 1860. Also see Renee C. Redman, "From Importation of Slaves to Migration of Laborers: The Struggle to Outlaw American Participation in the Chinese Coolie Trade and the Seeds of United States Immigration Law," *Albany Government Law Review* 3, no. 1 (January 2010): 1–55, esp. 42–48.

8. "When she was launched, the *Stag Hound* was the largest merchant ship ever built, being 215 feet long, and having a register of 1,535 tons. No less than 15,000 people gathered to see her launched despite the cold, and, as the tallow froze, boiling whale oil was poured upon the ways." State Street Trust Company, *Some Ships of the Clipper Ship Era, Their Builders, Owners, and Captains* (Boston: State Street Trust, 1913), 16. In 1860, the ship won a prize as the first ship to reach London with a copy of Abraham Lincoln's inaugural address. On the ship's return, loaded with coal for San Francisco, the cargo caught fire, destroying the ship. Much of the crew escaped, saving only (so the story goes) an American flag. See Helen La Grange, *Clipper Ships of America and Great Britain, 1833–1869* (New York: G. P. Putnam's Sons, 1936), 83–84.

9. Jimmy Packham, "The Maritime Self on the American Whaleship," in *Shipboard Literary Cultures: Reading, Writing, and Performing at Sea*, ed. Susann Liebich and Laurence Publicover (Cham, Switzerland: Palgrave, 2021), 131–56, 136.

10. For Melville, whiteness is an "intensifying agent in things the most appalling to mankind." Herman Melville, *Moby-Dick* (1851), chap. 42.

11. George Brown Goode, *The Fisheries and Fishery Industries of the United States: A Geographical Review of the Fisheries Industries and Fishing Communities for the Year 1880*, 4 (1884), 115–280, esp. 116–17, 137–40.

12. See "Gloucester's Ties to the Surinam Trade as Evidenced in the Work of Fitz Henry Lane," Cape Ann Museum, https://www.capeannmuseum.org/surinam-trade/.

13. See import tables in N. B. Harte, "The British Linen Trade with the United States in the Eighteenth and Nineteenth Centuries," *Textiles in Trade: Proceedings of the Textile Society of America Biennial Symposium*, September 14–16, 1990, Washington, DC, 15–23, and State of Massachusetts, "Statistics of Manufactures," *Public Documents of Massachusetts, Being the Annual Reports of Various Public Officers and Institutions, For the Year 1898* (Boston: Wright & Potter, 1899), vol. 11, doc. 36, 220–21.

14. John Wilmerding suggested that Lane's watercolor *Burning of the Packet Ship Boston* is reminiscent of Chinese painting and Japanese prints. Wilmerding, *Fitz Henry Lane* (1971; repr., Gloucester, MA: Cape Ann Historical Association, 2005), 19. Regarding Japanese prints and the Dutch connection, I have benefited greatly from exchanges with Chelsea Foxwell.

15. It was published as a broadsheet in 1788 and then included in Thomas Clarkson's *History of the Rise, Progress, and Accomplishment of the Abolition of the African Slave-Trade by the British Parliament* (London: R. Taylor, 1808). For a review of scholarship on the *Brookes*, including scholarship on contemporary artists who have used the image as the basis for their work, see Nicholas Radburn and David Eltis, "Visualizing the Middle Passage: The *Brookes* and the Reality of Ship Crowding in the Transatlantic Slave Trade," *Journal of Interdisciplinary History* 49, no. 4 (Spring 2019): 533–65.

16. Risham Majeed, "Dormant Yet Deadly: Metaphors for Regeneration in African Art," lecture, Art Meets Science Symposium, Mount Desert Island Biological Laboratory, Bar Harbor, Maine, August 2022.

17. For more on Gallagher, see Suzanna Chan, "'Alive . . . again.' Unmoored in the Aquafuture of Ellen Gallagher's *Watery Ecstatic*," *Women's Studies Quarterly* 45, no. 1/2 (Spring/Summer 2017): 246–63.

18. Evguenia Anichtchenko, "Open Skin Boats of the Aleutians, Kodiak Island, and Prince William Sound," *Études Inuit Studies* 36, no. 1 (2012): 157–81, 158.

19. Feng Qu, *An Exploration of Prehistoric Ontologies in the Bering Strait Region: Boundaries and Structures* (Newcastle upon Tyne, UK: Cambridge Scholars Publishing, 2021), 136.

20. Barbara Bodenhorn, "'I'm Not the Great Hunter, My Wife Is': Iñupiat and Anthropological Models of Gender," *Études Inuit Studies* 14, no. 1/2 (1990): 55–74.

21. Qu, *Exploration*, 136–38.

22. There are many references to Sedna's story and many versions of it. One example is found in Joseph Epes Brown, *Teaching Spirits: Understanding Native American Religious Traditions* (Oxford: Oxford University Press, 2001), 104.

23. Margaret Fuller to Elizabeth Hoar, Jamaica Plain, August 17, 1839, in *The Letters of Margaret Fuller, 1839–1841*, ed. Robert Hudspeth (Ithaca, NY: Cornell University Press, 2018), 83–84.

24. May Sarton, "Dutch Interior," in *Selected Poems of May Sarton*, ed. Serena Sue Hilsinger and Lois Brynes (New York: W. W. Norton, 1978), 20.

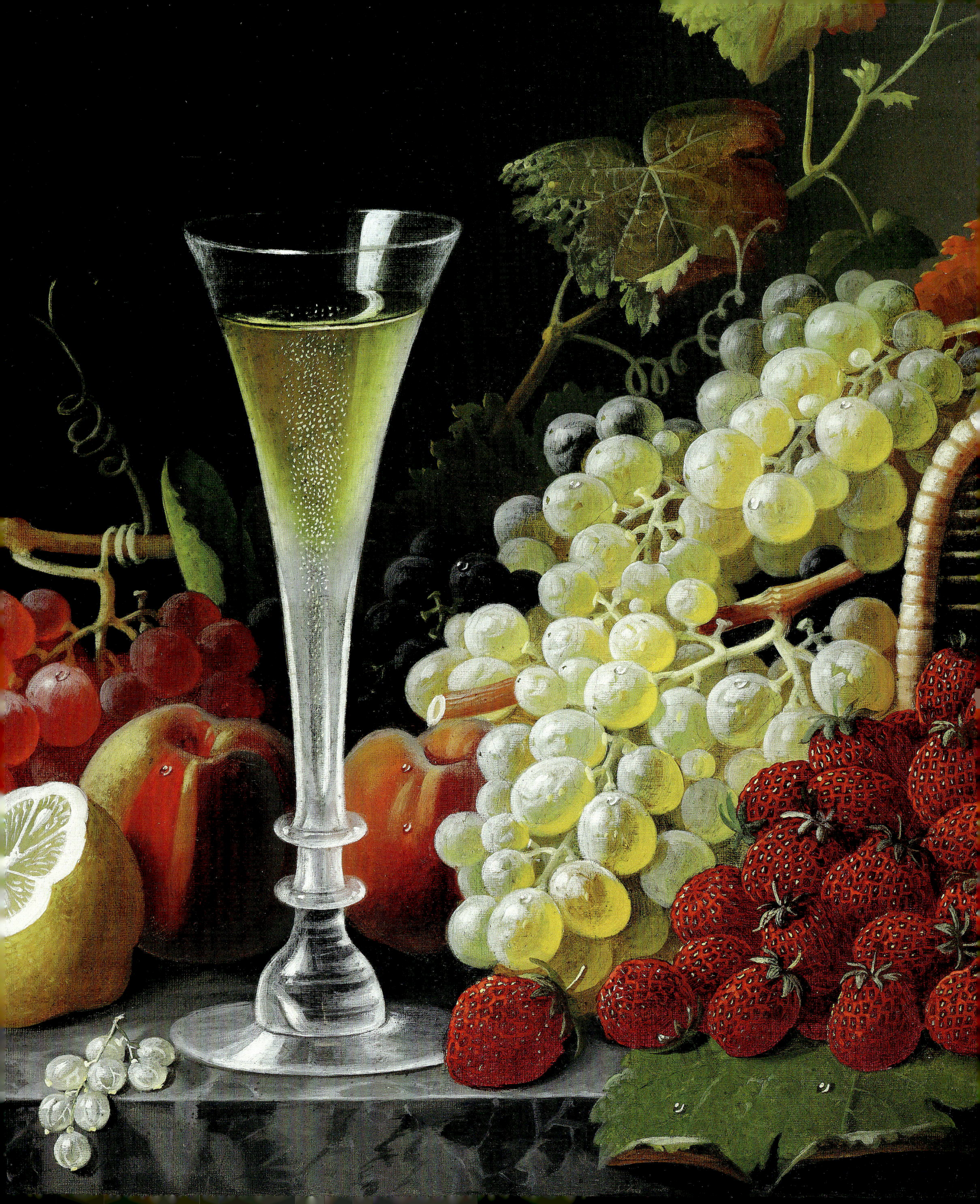

Jeffrey Richmond-Moll

Learning from Object Lessons: Toward a Curatorial Pedagogy of Unfixing and Defamiliarizing the Past

At Princeton, American art and object-based education have long been interwoven. When the college formed a department for art history and archaeology in 1883—the first of its kind in the country—an accompanying proposal advocated for establishing a new art museum on campus. "The foundation of any system of education in Historic Art must obviously be in object teaching," the authors asserted.[1] By 1922, under the leadership of Frank Jewett Mather Jr., the Princeton University Art Museum solidified this entwined commitment to art collecting and art education. To this day, object-based teaching remains pivotal to art historical instruction at the University.

This essay extends the model of the object lesson into the realm of curatorial practice and argues for its elegance and conceptual power for the twenty-first-century museum. In tandem with other approaches, such as community mobilization, gallery activations using new media, or decolonizing approaches to acquisitions, object lessons offer a mutable methodology, which curators can carry across collections and geographies, and which can expand perspectives and transform American art as a historical category. For both art historians in training and practicing curators, object lessons are a

Detail, figure 5

lifelong endeavor, especially as institutions, collecting practices, and the moral imperatives of curatorial work change. This essay is inspired by my own object lessons from the Museum's collections, from my time as an undergraduate through the beginnings of my curatorial career. It also demonstrates how such lessons can continually shape one's work as a museum professional in new institutional contexts, including in my case as a curator at the Georgia Museum of Art.

Sarah Anne Carter observes that, beginning in the early 1860s, "object lessons shaped the ways Americans reasoned from the material world and have impacted how scholars have worked to find meaning in the world ever since." Through exercises in close looking and critical thinking, such instruction helped bridge the gap between the material world and the realm of language and concept. Object lessons unfolded in an iterative process over the course of many years, slowly teaching children "to derive meaning from the material world and to reason both critically and morally based on this knowledge."[2] By forming a gallery for both fine art and natural history in Nassau Hall's present-day Faculty Room in the 1870s, Princeton extended the linguistic, logical, and moral value of the object lesson into the realm of college-level education.[3]

I, too, am the product of object lessons. During my first week on campus as a Princeton freshman, Professor William Childs gathered students in his ancient Greek and Roman art course around a long table in the bowels of the old Art Museum, handing us a red-figure kylix or a marble figurine, one after another. Grasp them, turn them over, and feel their weight, he told us. Two years later, during the last gasps of the carousel slide lecture, the rickety clicks and humming fans of John Wilmerding's dual projectors breathed life into a Thomas Eakins portrait or a Claes Oldenburg soft sculpture. Here, too, was the objecthood of art history—a pre-PowerPoint era when reproductions of art objects still played on the fuller human sensorium, and where no technological sleight-of-hand could wholly manipulate the visual wonders held within a small 35-millimeter transparency. Standing in the galleries with American art historian Rachael Z. DeLue, we trained our eyes together, learning to articulate the images and objects before us. In those discussions, any of us could unearth an important observation or make a critical intervention. Discovery was not solely the purview of the professoriate.

In this sense, the term "object lesson" has two meanings, which are intertwined: the teaching function of the material work of art, in the form of hands-on instruction and object-based research; and also the step that precedes the experience of in-gallery education, which is the object lesson as a form of curatorial pedagogy. The didactic conceit of the object lesson for a curator entails instructive juxtaposition, experimental contextualization, and open-ended conversations often liberated from the constraints of geography, chronology, or materiality. Rather than a heavy-handed curatorial intervention, such lessons also depend on the viewer to unpack objects' interrelationships or, in certain cases, to confront the silences within the material, textual, and visual record that these juxtapositions lay bare—in the case of this project, around issues of race, gender, and the environment.

At their core, object lessons unsettle entrenched understandings about American history and American art, particularly those that reinforce traditional hierarchies, alleviate the complicity of individuals and institutions from systems of oppression and exploitation, and heroize the achievements of white male artists. The history of American art is instead marked by rifts between the nation's beliefs in equality and the realities of inequality. Prevailing understandings of American art and culture have often exempted northerners from the evils of genocide, resource extraction, and Black trauma. Yet, as critic Jasmine Amussen trenchantly observes, the South may be "the place where the nation expresses all of its sins" and "where the nastiest parts of American history are closer to the surface," but the North cannot pretend that any of that foulness "isn't clogged in their pipes either."[4]

One recent acquisition to Princeton's collections, a stoneware storage jar from the 1850s by the enslaved potter David Drake (see p. 34, fig. 2), shatters any illusion that the bucolic northern campus of the College of New Jersey was detached from the landscape of chattel slavery. Inscribed down the shoulder in Drake's singular hand are five words: "Princeton / College in / New Jersey." The University's enrollment archives suggest several candidates for the Princeton student who may have prompted Dave's inscription. Perhaps it was one of the roughly half-dozen students from the Edgefield district of South Carolina enrolled at Princeton in the 1850s, or even an alumnus, Thomas J. Davies, whose own pottery was located only ten miles from the Miles pottery where Drake was enslaved. Davies may even have rented the labor of Drake and other potters from Lewis Miles in those years. As Drake's jar demonstrates, Princeton was entangled with slavery not only because the first nine presidents of Princeton at some point were enslavers, or because Princeton professors enslaved people of African descent as late as the 1840s, or because its institutional wealth today derives from its founding generations who were enriched by that system.[5] The economy of slavery also coursed through the institution in vernacular objects, like the stoneware pottery its students brought to campus, fashioned by the very enslaved men and women the college's alumni bought, rented, or sold.

In 2019, I relocated from Princeton—the landscape of mythic battles where George Washington turned the tide of the American Revolution—to become a curator at the University of Georgia, a southern terrain marked by military skirmishes and geopolitical fault lines of a different kind. In 1786, amid ongoing warfare, the lands that now make up part of my university's campus were seized from the Creek Confederacy through the Shoulder-Bone Treaty, one in a series of controversial treaties with the Creek people. One year prior, the state legislature had chartered a public university. But it would take over two decades for the University of Georgia to hold its first classes. After all, in those years, much of Georgia, including its current campus, was a frontier battleground. When we recently rehung a portrait of John Habersham by the renowned southern portraitist Jeremiah Theus (fig. 1), we came face to face with this history—a history otherwise absent from previous wall labels and curatorial files. One of the charter members of the university's board of trustees, Habersham was the son of a plantation owner and was appointed an Indian agent under George Washington. Habersham was also one of eight state commissioners present to negotiate with Creek representatives at Shoulder-Bone, although Creek chief Alexander McGillivray refused to attend, protesting the coercion of other recent treaties. The treaty would cede to the United States all lands east of the Oconee River—which runs through the east side of our campus, a stone's throw from the museum—with one additional condition, as Habersham later recounted in a letter to the governor: the Creek had to give up five of their people as hostages.[6]

Now, in an object lesson of its own, Habersham's portrait hangs beside ambitious portraits of post-Revolutionary politicians from Georgia who actively sought to preserve the economy of slavery on local and national levels.[7] Together these portraits evoke the entwined projects of settler colonialism and chattel slavery in the early United States. By raising these sorts of counternarratives, museums can provide, in the words of Stephanie E. Smallwood, "an account of the entanglements of dispossession and slavery as colonialism's twin tools of domination."[8]

Dispossession and slavery also converged at Princeton in the same years, when John Witherspoon aggressively recruited students from southern planter families and expanded the school's westward reach to the Mississippi River, as settlers continued to remove Indigenous peoples from their homelands.[9] By placing vernacular forms like Drake's storage jar alongside elite objects like Henry Benbridge's portrait of the female generations of another enslaving household, the Hartley family (fig. 2), object lessons help dismantle dichotomies between the elite and the vernacular, the dominant and the disenfranchised.

Just as object lessons destabilize racial and economic hierarchies, they also upset the historical hierarchies within museum collections regarding artistic genres and media. This is not purely an arcane art-historical intervention. The categorization—and the conventional segregation—of artistic media in museum galleries ("fine art" here, but "decorative art" over there) reifies social, racial, and cultural hierarchies and silences historical voices outside the dominant culture. This is especially true for those without access to wealthy patrons, costly materials, and elite institutions of artistic education. As a result, we ought to ask ourselves: How do the forms that museums have traditionally privileged also obscure other histories? And, given the historical disparities around artistic media, how does the past sometimes require remaking? To place David Drake's jar on equal footing with a portrait by Benbridge—showing the same sort of South Carolina family that claimed ownership of Drake—is the kind of moral statement that object lessons powerfully perform. Similarly, in Georgia, a vignette of objects featuring nineteenth-century African American artists—a small landscape by Edward Mitchell Bannister, a storage jar turned by enslaved men and glazed by enslaved women, and a chest of drawers by the Virginia "free man of color" Thomas Day—appears alongside canonized Hudson River School paintings by Albert Bierstadt, Homer Dodge Martin, and Sanford Gifford (fig. 3).

Object lessons undercut hierarchies across and *within* artistic categories. This includes the often undersung critical poignance of still-life painting, the lowest of genres in the traditional academic system. When interrogating the ecocritical aspects of American still lifes, we might begin with their greatest early proponents, the Peale family.[10] Rubens Peale's *Still Life with Watermelon* (fig. 4), for instance, must be interpreted in light of his deep knowledge of natural systems, particularly the Linnaean taxonomies and hierarchies of nature that structured the Peale Museum. Due to his poor eyesight, Rubens was enlisted to manage the natural history and art displays of the museum under the direction of his father, Charles Willson Peale. (He would not learn to paint until age seventy-one.) Even as late as 1865 Rubens envisioned ecology through the same European classical ideas about harmony, order, and bounty that informed the museum's elaborately painted and decorated dioramas, showing animal specimens in their natural habitats stacked up the wall in an enlivened version of Carolus Linnaeus's *System of Nature*.[11]

Peale's counterpart in Princeton's collections, Severin Roesen, produced still-life paintings at the very same midcentury moment yet was embedded in other environmental attitudes. *Still Life with Fruit and Champagne* (fig. 5) shares certain features with Peale: the crystalline clarity of the scene, the illusionistic positioning of a floating tabletop, even the mounded clusters of grapes. Roesen's painting, however, pictures a natural world of unlimited resources. The upturned berry basket overflows like a cornucopia, the grapes dangle over the marble surface in overabundance, and the snipped branches and vines miraculously crawl and climb. Across his large body of work, including in still lifes with such titles as *Abundance of Nature*, Roesen was transparent in his efforts to reinforce nature's limitless bounty amid rapid industrialization. The artist painted scores of these paintings for industrialists in central Pennsylvania who made their fortunes in the timber trade. Descended within a Williamsport, Pennsylvania, family, Princeton's still life reflects this system of patronage. By hanging Roesen's paintings in their opulent homes, these patrons must have sought out visions of the natural world that reassured them that the vast deforestation by their nineteenth-century lumber industry posed no threat to nature's perpetual abundance. The fluted glass of

FIGURE 1 Jeremiah Theus (1716–1774; born Chur, Switzerland; died Charleston, SC), *Portrait of John Habersham*, 1772. Oil on canvas, 76.2 × 63.5 cm. Georgia Museum of Art, University of Georgia, Athens. Museum purchase with funds provided by the W. Newton Morris Charitable Foundation (2012.202)

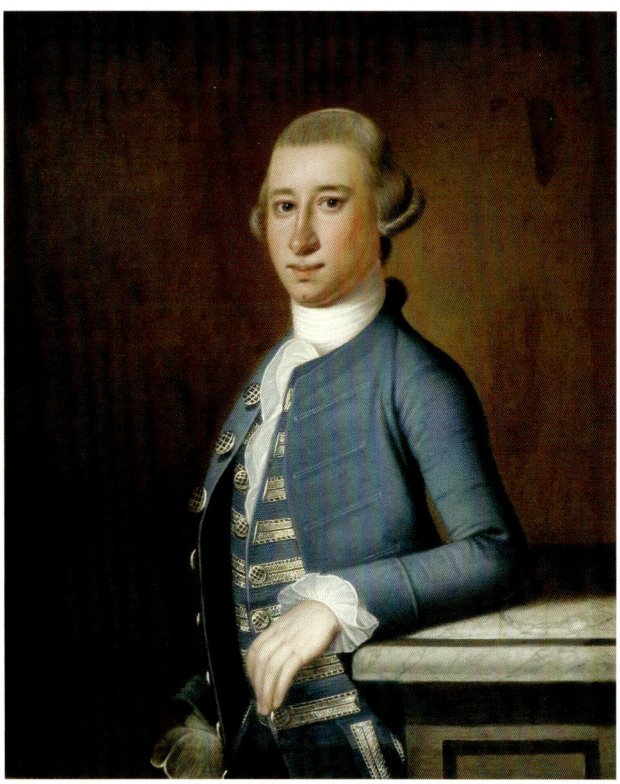

FIGURE 2 Henry Benbridge (1743–1812; born and died Philadelphia, PA; active Charleston, SC), *The Hartley Family*, ca. 1787. Oil on canvas, 194 × 151 cm. Princeton University Art Museum. Gift of Maitland A. Edey, Class of 1932 (y1986-84)

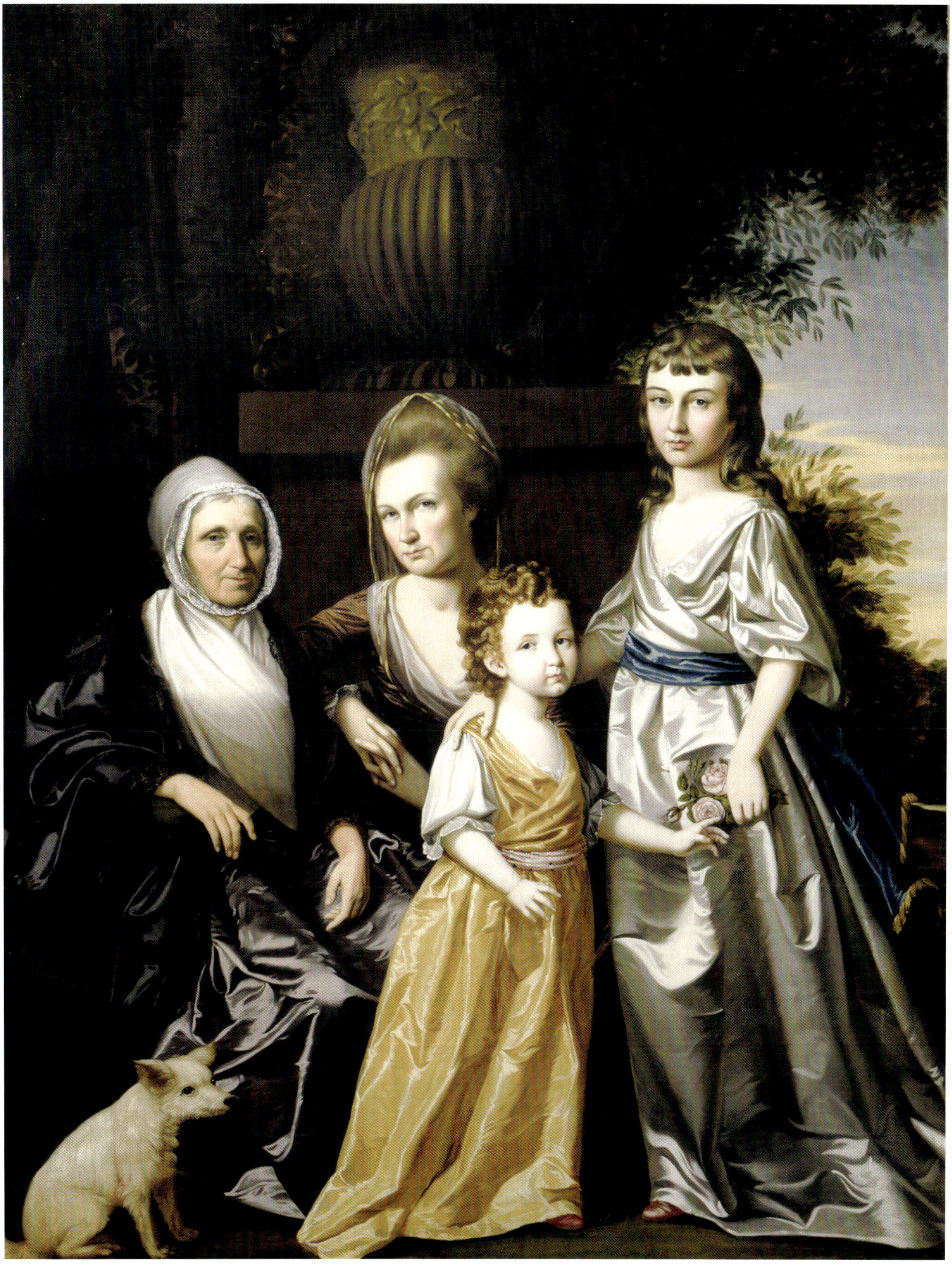

champagne is another transubstantiation of raw natural materials (in this case, of the piled green grapes beside the glass). In naturalizing the transformation of nature into commodified form, Roesen's painting assures viewers that such commodification in no way imperils the bounteous resources on which these industries, and the personal wealth of their proprietors, depended.

One might add to this group the berry paintings of African American artist Charles Ethan Porter (fig. 6). Depicted in front of a lush backdrop of berry bushes, Porter's strawberries present a bountiful harvest, though a mass-produced one, in which wooden fruit baskets provide a standardized form of packaging that ensures a uniformity of weight across each unit of fruit. In this way, Porter pictures the incursion of a highly regulated marketplace into this seemingly natural setting. The number of Porter's berry paintings themselves is also plentiful. His replication of subject and composition across countless strawberry pictures reveals the parallels between an industrializing marketplace for foodstuffs and the expectations of a quasi-industrial repetition among his audiences, who desired to see and own standardized images of the natural world. Perhaps unintentionally, Porter's prolific berry series reifies the commodification of nature at the close of the nineteenth century.

If these are the kind of art historical categories and aesthetic hierarchies that tradition has given us, how do object lessons allow us to activate and mobilize the past to different ends? When Van Wyck Brooks famously coined the notion of a "usable past" in 1918, he not only

FIGURE 4 Rubens Peale (1784–1865; born and died Philadelphia, PA), *Still Life with Watermelon*, 1865. Oil on canvas, 48.3 × 69.9 cm. Princeton University Art Museum. Gift in honor of Professor John Wilmerding from his friends and former students and the Kathleen C. Sherrerd Fund for Acquisitions in American Art (2007-20)

FIGURE 5 Severin Roesen (1816–ca. 1872; born Boppard, Germany; active Williamsport, PA), *Still Life with Fruit and Champagne*, ca. 1863–72. Oil on canvas, 51.4 × 78.1 cm. Princeton University Art Museum. Museum purchase, Kathleen Compton Sherrerd Fund for Acquisitions in American Art (2019-107)

FIGURE 3 Installation view of the American art galleries, Georgia Museum of Art, University of Georgia, 2022

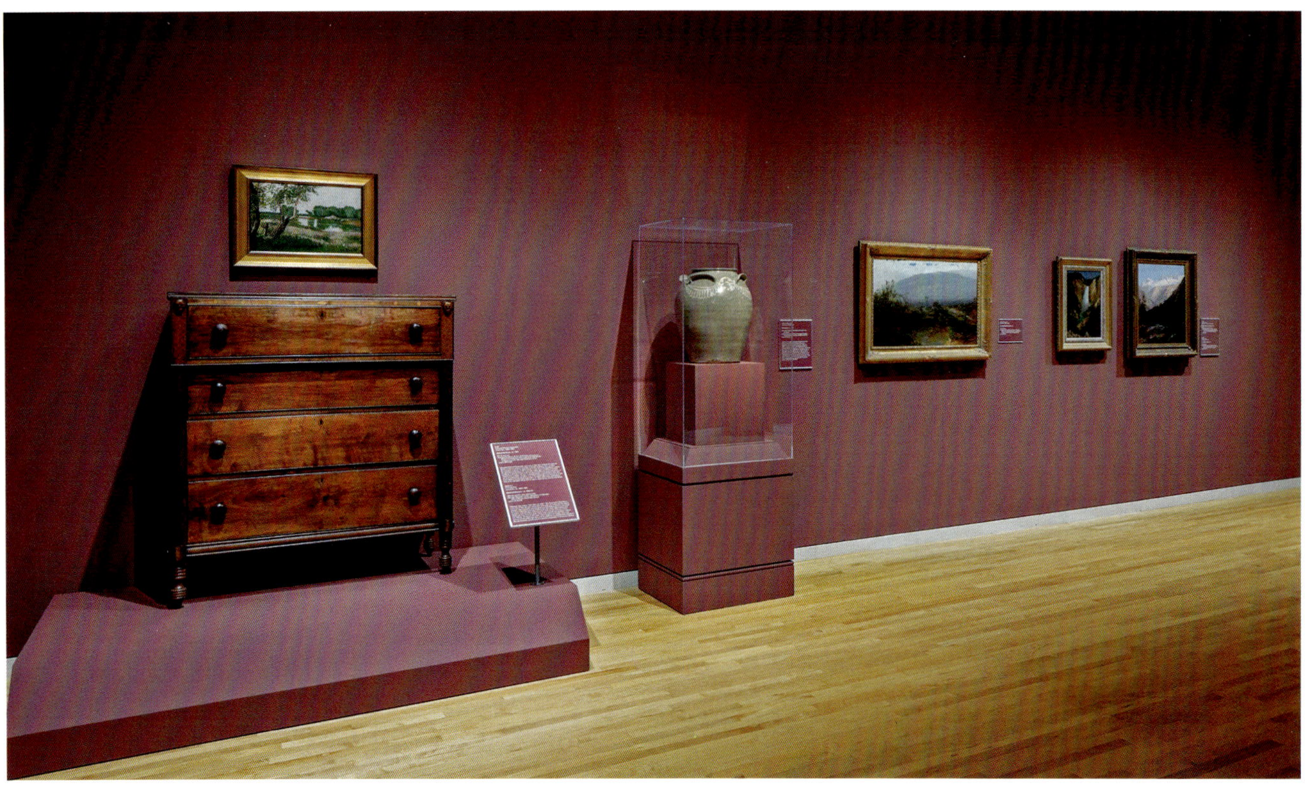

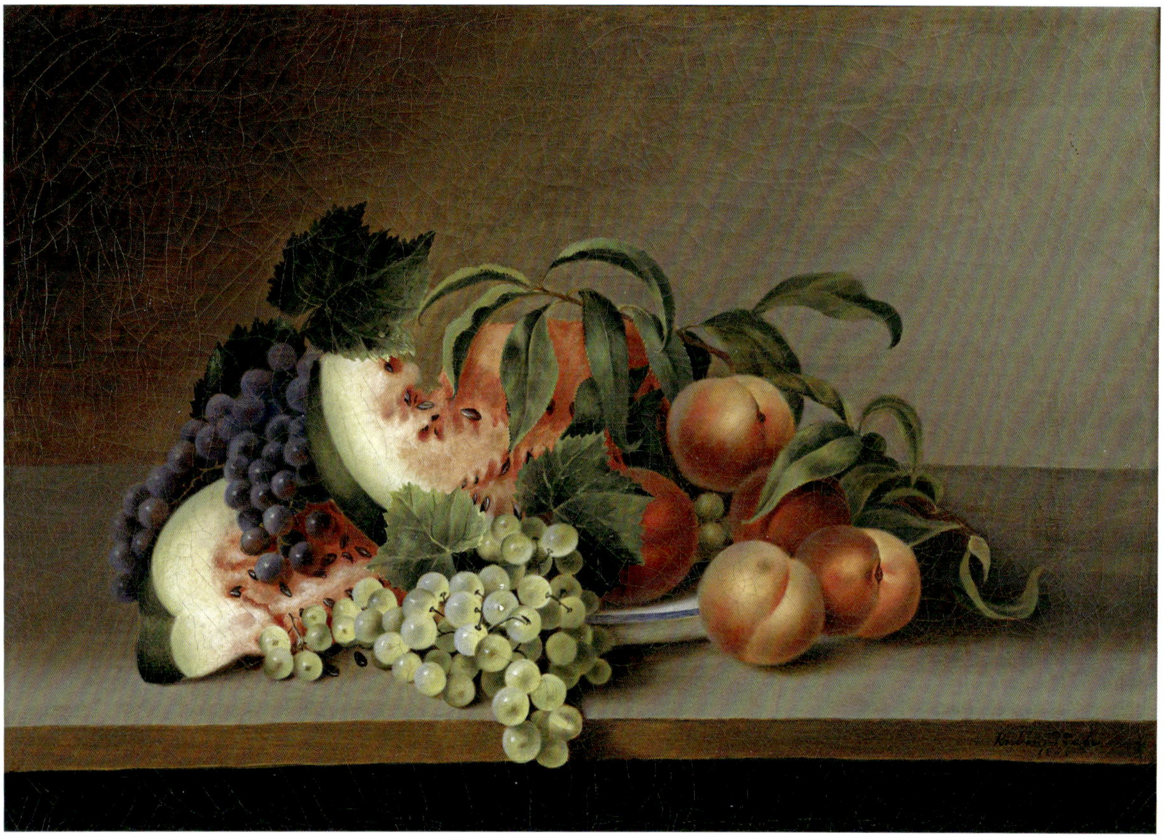

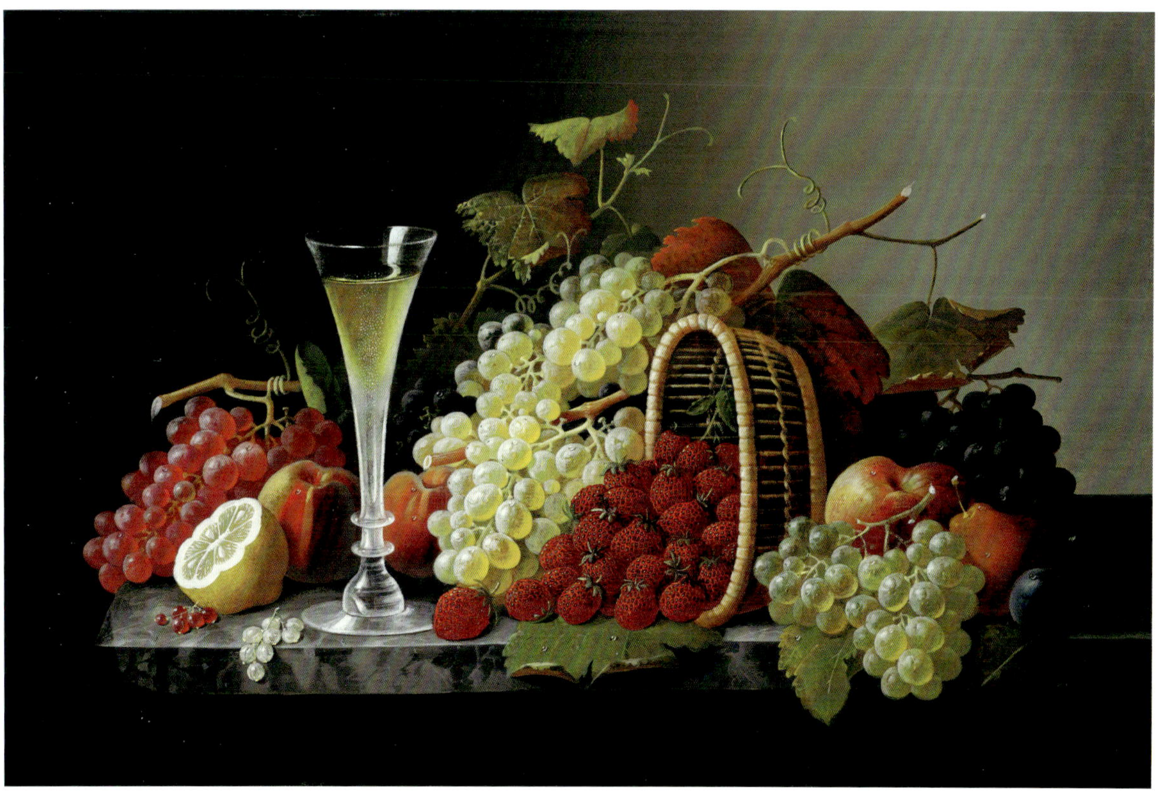

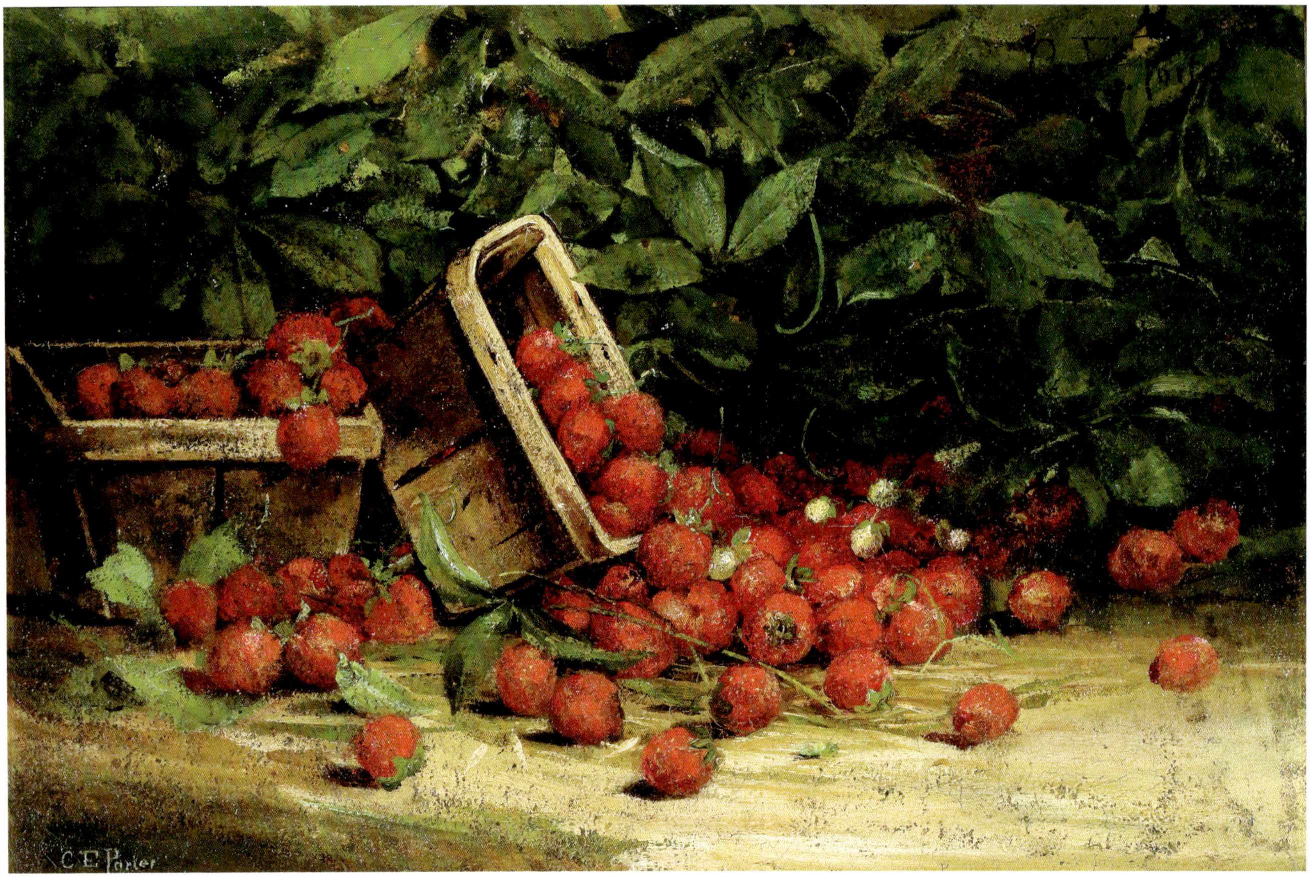
C.E. Porter

encouraged critics and artists to search the past for a living value that could help American culture to progress. He also suggested that sometimes culture-makers need to remember the past selectively, even inventively: "If we need another past so badly, is it inconceivable that we might discover one, that we might even invent one? Discover, invent a usable past we certainly can, and that is what a vital criticism always does."[12] Object lessons can be similarly inventive for the ways that they question the inevitability of US history and ask how the past might have been otherwise. Here we discover the potential for a reimagined, reusable past of the kind Renee Cox offers in her extravagant restaging of the signing of the Constitution (see pp. 16–17, fig. 4).

The curatorial pedagogy of the object lesson pressures the boundaries of what counts as "American" art. Objects that address waterways—like British-born painter James E. Buttersworth's *Clipper Ship "Staghound"* (see p. 165, fig. 4), American Impressionist John Henry Twachtman's *Oyster Boats, North River* (see p. 162, fig. 1), and an Iñupiaq carved walrus ivory depicting an umiak with men (see p. 167, fig. 5)—help emphasize American art's fluid contours. We might also consider the work of Ellis Wilson, who immersed himself in the African diasporic cultures of the sea islands off the Carolinas through the support of a Guggenheim Fellowship in 1944. As a departure from his more rigorously documentary approach in earlier works, Wilson's coastal paintings embrace fantasy through pulsating brushstrokes and vibrant colors. His figures, like *Fisherwoman* (see p. 171, fig. 9), stand as icons of "the simple poise and dignity" that characterized these communities and that, Wilson believed, were in danger of disappearing.[13] Wilson's exploration of diasporic cultures in the American South underscores the stories that are often absent—erased, ignored, or otherwise—in conventional "object lessons" on American art, which too often perpetuate Joseph Downs's offhand remark in 1949 that "little of artistic merit was made south of Baltimore."[14] By extension, the diasporic lifeways of the sea islands and the Caribbean elements of Wilson's work stretch the contours of "American" art as the field often defines it to encompass broader geographies and cultural histories.

FIGURE 6 Charles Ethan Porter (1847–1923; born Hartford, CT; died Rockville, CT), *Still Life: Two Baskets of Strawberries*, ca. 1900. Oil on canvas, 34.9 × 53.3 cm. Georgia Museum of Art, University of Georgia, Athens. The Larry D. and Brenda A. Thompson Collection of African American Art (2012.145)

Object lessons from the American South push the boundaries of American art in other ways, particularly when considering Indigenous-settler relations in the region—relations that were transnational by definition. At the Georgia Museum, two portraits by Henry Inman hang above a mantelpiece as a material acknowledgment of the ancestral homelands our university occupies (fig. 7).[15] One portrait shows Timpoochee Barnard, a chief and acting dignitary for the Yuchi tribe, who served on the Creek National Council and supported efforts to maintain Creek borders.[16] Beside Barnard's portrait hangs a painting of an unidentified Seminole. His likeness reveals how Indigenous leaders fashioned their appearance as a strategy for government negotiations: by balancing Indigenous and settler clothing, the viewer understands his diplomatic duties to the land and his people on one hand, and his role as a mediator between nations on the other.

Below Inman's two portraits stands a mantelpiece from the Cherokee-built home of John Martin, the treasurer of the Cherokee Nation and a justice of its supreme court, who lived in present-day Murray County, Georgia. From the early 1800s, Moravian missionaries from Salem, North Carolina, were active among the Cherokee people and trained many craftsmen in joinery. The molded tracery and arched opening suggest this Moravian influence. Its craftsmanship attests to the impact of other cultures on the Cherokee people even as they maintained their fundamental cultural identity. With this grouping, which highlights three of the so-called Five Civilized Tribes of the American Southeast, the museum cedes the focal point of its earliest American gallery to the Native peoples whom wealthy, white colonizers sought to assimilate into settler culture before eventually pushing for their removal from the South.

For curators, object lessons present a kind of paradox. In museums, the works of art that cohere into object lessons in our galleries are the product of deep archival and object-based research, critical recoveries of silenced and absented voices, and highly intentional juxtapositions of sometimes incongruous materials. Yet the conceptual

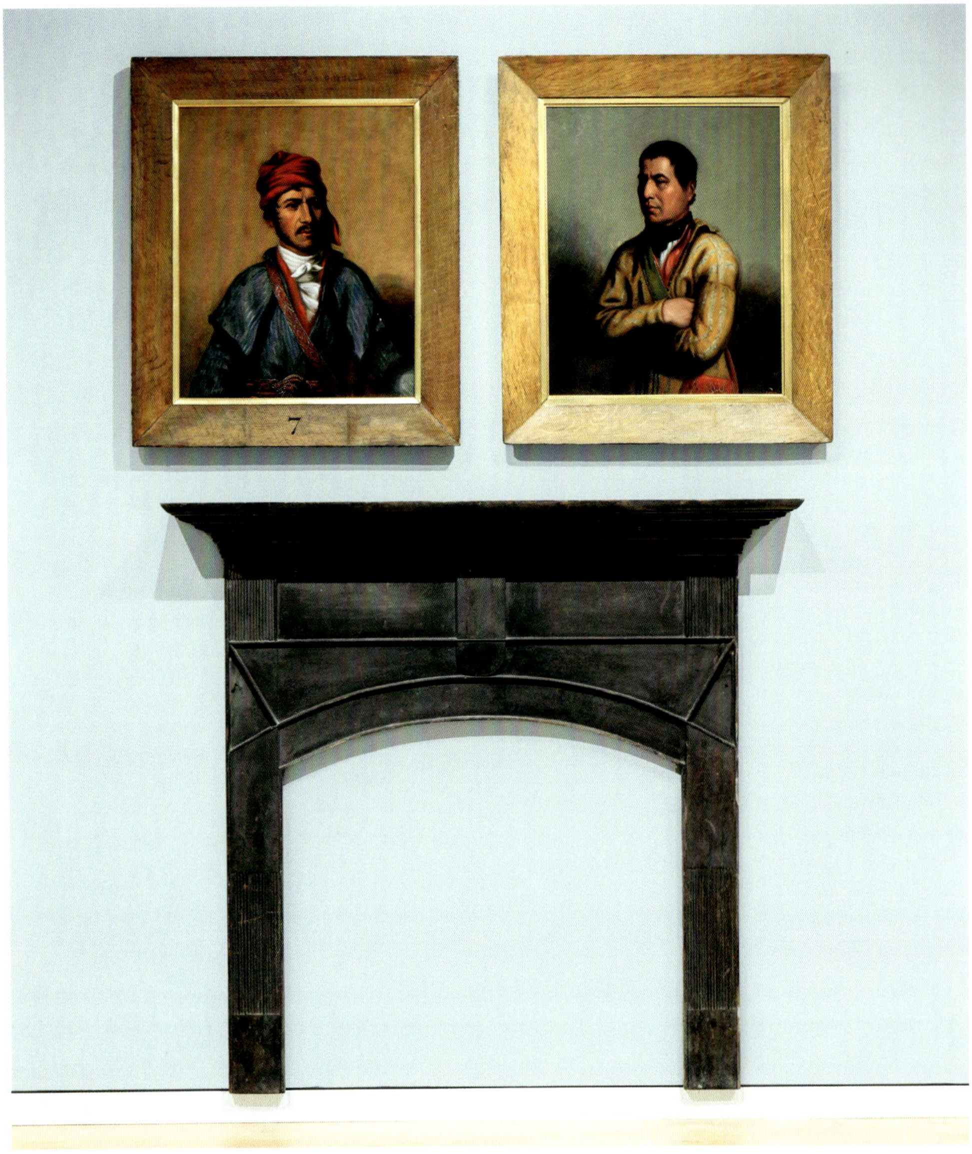

FIGURE 7 Installation view, top: Henry Inman (1801–1846; born Utica, NY; died New York, NY), *Timpoochee Barnard*, ca. 1831–34. Oil on canvas, 76.8 × 64.1 cm; and *Unidentified Seminole*, 1831–34. Oil on canvas, 76.8 × 64.1 cm. High Museum of Art, Atlanta. Gift of Ann and Tom Cousins (2017.122 and 2017.123); bottom: Unidentified maker, active in Cherokee Territory (present-day Georgia), Mantel, ca. 1800–30. Yellow pine with paint, 165.1 × 149.9 × 20.3 cm. Georgia Museum of Art, University of Georgia. Gift of Mrs. Nancy Carter Bland (2013.108)

beauty and edifying power of this curatorial pedagogy lies in the fact that—just like the carefully crafted curricula of object lessons in the nineteenth-century classroom—these lessons, once set in motion, seem to cede authority to the objects and their makers, as if speaking directly to the viewer on their own behalf. In other words, perhaps the most elegant and subversive kind of object lesson is one that works to downplay the institutional voice of the curator, guiding viewers through an initial shock of incongruity, through certain discomforting realities, into a new form of self-understanding. In destabilizing hierarchies, unfixing categories, and defamiliarizing entrenched narratives of national identity, object lessons can decolonize American art in the twenty-first-century museum, offering new ways of understanding our collective past.

NOTES

1. William C. Prime and George B. McClellan, *Suggestions on the Establishment of a Department of Art Instruction in the College of New Jersey* (Trenton, NJ: W. S. Sharp, 1882).

2. Sarah Anne Carter, *Object Lessons: How Nineteenth-Century Americans Learned to Make Sense of the Material World* (New York: Oxford University Press, 2018), 1–3.

3. For more on this history, see Karl Kusserow, ed., *Inner Sanctum: Memory and Meaning in Princeton's Faculty Room at Nassau Hall* (Princeton, NJ: Princeton University Press, 2010).

4. Jasmine Amussen, "Our Mascots, Ourselves," Burnaway, May 16, 2022, https://burnaway.org/magazine/our-mascots-ourselves/.

5. Martha A. Sandweiss and Craig Hollander, "Princeton and Slavery: Holding the Center," The Princeton & Slavery Project, https://slavery.princeton.edu/stories/princeton-and-slavery-holding-the-center.

6. John Habersham to Edward Telfair, Governor of Georgia, October 25, 1786. Hargrett Rare Book and Manuscript Library, The University of Georgia Libraries, Telamon Cuyler Collection, box 77, folder 22, document 1.

7. See, for example, a portrait of the family of Archibald Bulloch, the first governor of the Revolutionary state of Georgia, painted by Henry Benbridge. Jeffrey Richmond-Moll, "A Note on a Colonial Portrait of the Bullochs," in *Georgia Matters: Celebrating Two Decades of Scholarship; The Tenth Henry D. Green Symposium of the Decorative Arts*, ed. Dale L. Couch (Athens: Georgia Museum of Art, University of Georgia, 2022), 140–54.

8. Stephanie E. Smallwood, "Reflections on Settler Colonialism, the Hemispheric Americas, and Chattel Slavery," *William and Mary Quarterly* 76, no. 3 (July 2019): 414. This story is complicated by the fact that, upon its founding in 1735, Georgia was the only British colony that instituted a parliamentary ban on slavery. Only after great public, political, and economic pressure did the British House of Commons lift that ban in 1751.

9. As the Princeton & Slavery Project demonstrates, one finds a one-to-one correlation between the cotton boom in Mississippi and the enrollment of students from Mississippi in those same years. See Trip Henningson, "Princeton and Mississippi," The Princeton & Slavery Project, https://slavery.princeton.edu/stories/princeton-and-mississippi.

10. Jeffrey Richmond-Moll, "A Knot of Species: Raphaelle Peale's *Still Life with Steak* and the Ecology of Food," in *Nature's Nation: American Art and Environment*, ed. Karl Kusserow and Alan C. Braddock (New Haven, CT: Yale University Press, 2018), 170–77.

11. Alan C. Braddock, "The Order of Things," in Kusserow and Braddock, *Nature's Nation*, 43–69, esp. 48–54.

12. Van Wyck Brooks, "On Creating a Usable Past," *The Dial*, April 11, 1918, 339.

13. Quoted in Justus Bier, "Ellis Wilson, Kentucky Negro Artist," *Courier-Journal Magazine* (Louisville, KY), April 30, 1950, 39.

14. Quoted in Maurie D. McInnis, "Little of Artistic Merit?: The Problem and Promise of Southern Art History," *American Art* 19, no. 2 (Summer 2005): 11.

15. In 1831, Superintendent of Indian Affairs Thomas L. McKenney hired Inman to copy the hundred-some portraits of Indigenous leaders by Charles Bird King for a series of portfolios entitled *History of the Indian Tribes of North America* (1832–43). For more on the many southern patrons of these portfolios and the "visual statecraft" of treaty portraits in the early nineteenth century that helped advance federal policies of Indigenous dispossession from the Southeast, see Julia Anne Grummitt, "'The Great National Work': James Otto Lewis, Thomas McKenney, Henry Rowe Schoolcraft and the Visual Politics of American Empire, 1789–1871" (PhD diss., Princeton University, 2022).

16. The Yuchi lived in Georgia at this time as allies and neighbors of the Creek people.

Contributors

Karl Kusserow is the John Wilmerding Curator of American Art at the Princeton University Art Museum. He is author and editor of six books, most recently *Nature's Nation: American Art and Environment* (2018), with Alan C. Braddock, and *Picture Ecology: Art and Ecocriticism in Planetary Perspective* (2021). He is currently writing an ecocritical study of representations of the moon, the subject of the 2022 Franklin D. Murphy Lectures at the University of Kansas.

Horace D. Ballard is the Theodore E. Stebbins Associate Curator of American Art at the Harvard Art Museums. He received his PhD in American studies and American visual culture from Brown University.

Kirsten Pai Buick is professor of art history and chair of Africana Studies at the University of New Mexico. Her areas of research and teaching include the material and visual culture of the first British Empire, US art, African American art and material culture, women as patrons and collectors of art, and landscape representation. Her book *In Authenticity: "Kara Walker" and the Eidetics of Racism* is in progress.

Ellery E. Foutch is associate professor in the American Studies Program at Middlebury College, where she teaches classes on the art and material culture of the United States. After earning her PhD in the History of Art from the University of Pennsylvania, she held postdoctoral teaching fellowships at the University of Wisconsin–Madison and the Courtauld Institute of Art, London.

Jeffrey Richmond-Moll is curator of American art at the Georgia Museum of Art. A graduate of Princeton University and the University of Delaware, he has published essays on American still-life painting, neoclassical sculpture, modernism in the Southwest, and wartime material culture. He is editor and lead author of *Extra Ordinary: Magic, Mystery, and Imagination in American Realism* (2021) and *Reckonings and Reconstructions: Southern Photography from the Do Good Fund* (2022).

Rebecca Zorach is the Mary Jane Crowe Professor in Art and Art History at Northwestern University. She writes on European and North American art, visual culture, and politics. Her books include *Blood, Milk, Ink, Gold: Abundance and Excess in the French Renaissance* (2005), *The Passionate Triangle* (2011), and *Art for People's Sake: Artists and Community in Black Chicago, 1965–1975* (2019).

Index

Note: Page numbers in italic type indicate illustrations.

Photography Credits

Introduction, figs. 1, 5–7: Photo by Bruce M. White; fig. 2: © The Trustees of the British Museum; fig. 3: Courtesy Architect of the Capitol; fig. 4: © Renee Cox; fig. 8: Photo by Jeffrey Evans; fig. 9: Courtesy Princeton University Library; fig. 10: © 2022 Romare Bearden Foundation / Licensed by VAGA at Artists Rights Society (ARS), New York. Photo by Jeffrey Evans; figs. 11, 12: Photo by Jeffrey Evans; fig. 13: © Guerrilla Girls. Courtesy guerrillagirls.com. Photo by Adam Boggs; fig. 14: Photo by Bruce M. White

Buick, fig. 1: Photo by Emile Askey; figs. 2, 4, 10, 11, 14: Photo by Jeffrey Evans; figs. 3, 8: Photo by Bruce M. White; fig. 6: © Courtesy Fine Arts Museums of San Francisco. Photo by Randy Dodson; fig 9: © Virginia Museum of Fine Arts. Photo by Travis Fullerton; fig. 12: © Postcommodity. Courtesy Postcommodity and Bockley Gallery, Minneapolis. Photo by Michael Lundgren; fig. 13: Ann Ronan Pictures / Print Collector / Getty Images; fig. 15: © Titus Kaphar. Photo by Emile Askey

Foutch, figs. 1, 9, 11, 15: Courtesy Princeton University Library. © Trustees of Princeton University (fig. 9); figs. 2, 5, 6, 12, 14: Photo by Jeffrey Evans; figs. 3, 4: © The Metropolitan Museum of Art / Art Resource, NY; fig. 8: Photo by Emile Askey; fig. 10: © Historical Society of Princeton, NJ; figs. 13, 16, 18, 23: Photo by Bruce M. White; fig. 20: Courtesy the Buffalo Bill Center of the West, Cody, Wyoming; fig. 22: © Harriet Whitney Frishmuth. Photo by Emile Askey; fig. 25: © 2022 Estate of Henrietta Pettway / Artists Rights Society (ARS), New York. Photo by Emile Askey

Ballard, fig. 1: Photo by Bruce M. White; fig. 2: Photo by Jeffrey Evans

Kusserow, figs. 1, 9, 19, 23, 24, 29, 30: Photo by Jeffrey Evans; fig. 2: Photo by Mitro Hood; figs. 3–6, 20, 21: Courtesy New-York Historical Society; figs. 10, 13, 14: Courtesy Princeton University Library; figs. 12, 16, 27: Photo by Bruce M. White; fig. 15: Courtesy the Canadian Museum of History (VII-C-2149, CD1994-0633-028); figs. 17, 18: © Postcommodity. Courtesy Postcommodity and Bockley Gallery, Minneapolis. Photo by Jason Grubb (fig. 17). Photo by Emile Askey (fig. 18); fig. 22: © Ruth Cuthand. Photo by Emile Askey; fig. 25: © Maria Montoya Martinez. Photo by Jeffrey Evans; fig. 31: © 1990 Amon Carter Museum of American Art. Photo by Jeffrey Evans

Zorach, figs. 1, 5, 7, 12: Photo by Jeffrey Evans; figs. 2, 8, 13: Photo by Bruce M. White; fig. 3: © 2022 The Milton Avery Trust / Artists Rights Society (ARS), New York. Photo by Jeffrey Evans; fig. 4: Photo by Jacqueline Fletcher; fig. 9: © Ellis Wilson. Photo by Emile Askey; fig. 10: © Margaret Taylor Goss Burroughs. Photo by Jeffrey Evans; fig. 11: © Ellen Gallagher. Photo by Bruce M. White; fig. 14: © Nicholas Galanin. Photo by Emile Askey

Richmond-Moll, figs. 1, 3, 6, 7: Courtesy the Georgia Museum of Art, University of Georgia. Photo by Alvaro Santistevan (figs. 3, 7); figs. 2, 4: Photo by Bruce M. White; fig. 5: Photo by Jeffrey Evans

This book is published on the occasion of the exhibition *Object Lessons in American Art: Selections from the Princeton University Art Museum*.

Georgia Museum of Art, University of Georgia
Athens, Georgia
February 4–May 14, 2023

Florence Griswold Museum
Old Lyme, Connecticut
June 3–September 10, 2023

Speed Art Museum
Louisville, Kentucky
September 29, 2023–January 7, 2024

Object Lessons in American Art is organized by the Princeton University Art Museum. The exhibition was made possible by the leadership support of the Terra Foundation for American Art. The accompanying publication is made possible by the generous support of Annette Merle-Smith; and by additional support from the Barr Ferree Foundation Fund for Publications, Department of Art and Archaeology, Princeton University.

TERRA
FOUNDATION FOR AMERICAN ART

Published by the Princeton University Art Museum
Princeton, NJ 08544-1018
artmuseum.princeton.edu

Distributed by Princeton University Press
41 William Street, Princeton, NJ 08540-5237
99 Banbury Road, Oxford OX2 6JX
press.princeton.edu

Produced by Marquand Books, Seattle
marquandbooks.com

Copyedited by Tanya Heinrich
Designed by Ryan Polich
Typeset in Electra, Freight, and Metro Nova by Brynn Warriner
Proofread by Ted Gilley
Indexed by Dave Luljak

Prepress and printing by Meridian Printing, East Greenwich, RI
Printed on Opus Matte 100 lb.

ISBN: 978-0-691-97885-7
Ebook ISBN: 978-0-691-97887-1

Library of Congress Control Number: 2022921273
British Library Cataloging-in-Publication Data is available

Printed and bound in the United States
10 9 8 7 6 5 4 3 2 1

Front cover and flap: Renee Cox, *The Signing* (detail), 2018. © Renee Cox (fig. 4, p. 16)

Back cover: Robert Walter Weir, *The Greenwich Boat Club* (detail), 1833. Photo by Jeffrey Evans (fig. 19, p. 136)

Frontispiece: Artist unidentified, Viceroyalty of Peru (probably Lima), Chest (detail), ca. 1780. Photo by Jeffrey Evans (fig. 9, p. 124)

Pages 4–5: Arthur Garfield Dove, *Sunrise, Northport Harbor* (detail), 1929. Photo by Mitro Hood (fig. 2, p. 163)